DELTA'S Key to the Next Generation TOEFL® Test

Six Practice Tests for the iBT

by

Nancy Gallagher

NEW AGE INTERNATIONAL PUBLISHERS

First Indian Sub-Continent Edition: 2007
by New Age International (P) Ltd., Publishers

BRANCHES

- **Bangalore** 37/10, 8th Cross (Near Hanuman Temple), Azad Nagar, Chamarajpet, Bangalore-560 018
  Tel.: (080) 26756823, Telefax: 26756820, E-mail: bangalore@newagepublishers.com
- **Chennai** 26, Damodaran Street, T. Nagar, Chennai-600 017
  Tel.: (044) 24353401, Telefax: 24351463, E-mail: chennai@newagepublishers.com
- **Cochin** CC-39/1016, Carrier Station Road, Ernakulam South, Cochin-682 016
  Tel.: (0484) 2377004, Telefax: 4051303, E-mail: cochin@newagepublishers.com
- **Guwahati** Hemsen Complex, Mohd. Shah Road, Paltan Bazar, Near Starline Hotel, Guwahati-781 008
  Tel.: (0361) 2513881, Telefax: 2543669, E-mail: guwahati@newagepublishers.com
- **Hyderabad** 105, 1st Floor, Madhiray Kaveri Tower, 3-2-19, Azam Jahi Road, Nimboliadda, Hyderabad-500 027
  Tel.: (040) 24652456, Telefax: 24652457, E-mail: hyderabad@newagepublishers.com
- **Kolkata** RDB Chambers (Formerly Lotus Cinema) 106A, 1st Floor, S.N. Banerjee Road, Kolkata-700 014
  Tel.: (033) 22273773, Telefax: 22275247, E-mail: kolkata@newagepublishers.com
- **Lucknow** 16-A, Jopling Road, Lucknow-226 001
  Tel.: (0522) 2209578, 4045297, Telefax: 2204098, E-mail: lucknow@newagepublishers.com
- **Mumbai** 142C, Victor House, Ground Floor, N.M. Joshi Marg, Lower Parel, Mumbai-400 013
  Tel.: (022) 24927869, Telefax: 24915415, E-mail: mumbai@newagepublishers.com
- **New Delhi** 22, Golden House, Daryaganj, New Delhi-110 002
  Tel.: (011) 23262368, 23262370, Telefax: 43551305, E-mail: sales@newagepublishers.com

---

ISBN : 978-81-224-2071-5

₹ 495.00

C-13-8-7106

Printed in India at Ajit Printers, Delhi.

PUBLISHING FOR ONE WORLD
NEW AGE INTERNATIONAL (P) LIMITED, PUBLISHERS
7/30 A, Daryaganj, New Delhi-110002
Visit us at **www.newagepublishers.com**

CONTENTS

ABOUT THE TEST 1

The TOEFL® IBT 1

The TOEFL® ITP 2

How to Use this Book 3

To the Student 4

Reading 5

Listening 9

Speaking 18

Writing 24

TEST 1 29

TEST 2 73

TEST 3 117

TEST 4 161

TEST 5 203

TEST 6 247

ANSWER KEY 291

AUDIO SCRIPTS 329

HOW TO SCORE SPEAKING 375

HOW TO SCORE WRITING 377

PROGRESS CHARTS 379

SCORE CONVERSION TABLES 384

ABOUT THE TEST

The Test of English as a Foreign Language® (TOEFL®) is a standardized test that measures the English proficiency of students who wish to enter college and university programs in the United States and Canada. The TOEFL is produced by Educational Testing Service (ETS), a professional test development organization in Princeton, New Jersey, USA.

THE TOEFL® iBT

The Internet–based TOEFL (iBT) was administered for the first time in 2005. This new version of the TOEFL replaces the earlier computer–based test (CBT) and the paper–based test (PBT). The TOEFL iBT has four sections, which assess the language skills of reading, listening, speaking, and writing. The test is approximately four hours long, with one 10–minute break after the Listening section.

TOEFL® iBT				
Section	**Content**	**Approximate Time**	**Number of Questions**	**Section Score**
Reading	3–5 passages	60–100 minutes	36–70	0–30
Listening	2–3 conversations 4–6 lectures	60–90 minutes	34–51	0–30
Break		10 minutes		
Speaking	2 independent tasks 4 integrated–skills tasks	20 minutes	6	0–30
Writing	1 integrated–skills task 1 independent task	60 minutes	2	0–30
			Total Test Score	0–120

The content of the TOEFL iBT reflects the language that is used in real academic settings. The content is based on a collection of spoken and written language that Educational Testing Service obtained from college and university lectures, class discussions, office hours, service interactions, study groups, textbooks, and various course materials.

The most important differences between the TOEFL iBT and earlier versions of the test are:

- note taking is permitted throughout the test
- speaking skills are assessed
- some questions involve integrated skills, such as reading–listening–speaking
- knowledge of grammar is not tested separately but is tested indirectly in all sections of the test

The Speaking and Writing sections of the test include some tasks that integrate, or combine, language skills. For example, a student might read a passage, listen to a lecture, and then write or speak in response. The integrated–skills tasks reflect how people use language in real life; thus, they give academic programs a more realistic measure of how well prospective students will be able to communicate in an English–speaking environment.

In each section of the test, the number of points earned is converted to a scaled section score of 0 to 30. The four section scores are combined to obtain the total test score, which is on a scale of 0 to 120. The TOEFL iBT score report will show:

- a separate score of 0 to 30 for each of the four language skills
- a total test score of 0 to 120

The admissions office of an educational institution will look at a student's TOEFL score to determine if the student's English skills are adequate for enrollment in a specific program of study. There is no single passing score for all institutions; rather, each institution or program sets its own standards for admission. Generally, graduate programs require a higher score than do undergraduate programs.

The scoring scale of the TOEFL iBT is different from the scoring scale for the computer–based TOEFL (CBT) or the paper–based TOEFL (PBT). The table below shows a general comparison of the three different scales.

TOTAL SCORE COMPARISON		
TOEFL® iBT	TOEFL® CBT	TOEFL® PBT
120	300	677
110	270	637
100	250	600
90	233	577
80	213	550
70	193	523
60	170	497
50	143	463
40	120	433

For the most current information about the TOEFL iBT, including the schedule of test dates, the location of test centers, and information on how to register to take the test, visit the official TOEFL Web site at: **www.ets.org/toefl**.

THE TOEFL® ITP

The TOEFL Institutional Testing Program (ITP) is a paper–based form of the test that academic institutions administer for their own internal use. Scores from the TOEFL ITP may be used only within the college, university, or language school that administers the test. Scores may not be sent to outside institutions.

Like all other forms of the TOEFL, the institutional TOEFL evaluates the English proficiency of students who are pursuing academic studies. Institutions may require the TOEFL ITP for various reasons, such as placement in a program, assessment of progress, requirement for graduation, or practice for the TOEFL iBT.

Beginning in 2007, the TOEFL ITP will have two sections, Reading and Listening, which will consist of questions from previously administered forms of the TOEFL iBT. The new TOEFL ITP will be approximately two hours long.

TOEFL® ITP				
Section	**Content**	**Approximate Time**	**Number of Questions**	**Section Score**
Reading	3 passages	60 minutes	36–42	0–30
Listening	2 conversations 4 lectures	60 minutes	34	0–30
			Total Test Score	0–60

For more information about the TOEFL ITP, contact the program director or academic adviser at your school.

HOW TO USE THIS BOOK

Delta's Key to the Next Generation TOEFL® Test: Six Practice Tests for the iBT is a book/audio program that can be used in a number of ways:

- as the primary or secondary text in a TOEFL preparation course
- as a companion to *Delta's Key to the Next Generation TOEFL® Test: Advanced Skill Practice for the iBT*
- as a supplemental text in reading, listening, speaking, or writing courses
- as a resource for independent study or laboratory

Test 1—Test 6

The six full–length practice tests contain questions that are similar in form and content to the questions on the TOEFL iBT and TOEFL ITP. The tests can be used to evaluate English proficiency, practice essential skills and strategies, and assess readiness to take the real TOEFL.

Answer Key

The Answer Key provides the correct answer for each question, along with a brief explanation and a reference to the relevant unit in *Delta's Key to the Next Generation TOEFL® Test: Advanced Skill Practice for the iBT*. The Answer Key can easily be removed from the book.

Audio Scripts

The Audio Scripts include complete transcripts for all listening material in the book. The scripts can be used for checking answers, for reading and pronunciation practice, and for learning vocabulary in context. The scripts can easily be removed from the book.

How to Score Speaking and *How to Score Writing*

These charts provide criteria for evaluating responses in the Speaking and Writing sections, with a description for each score level in the independent and integrated–skills tasks.

Progress Charts and *Score Conversion Tables*

The Progress Charts are for recording test scores and monitoring achievement. The Score Conversion Tables convert points earned in each test section to an approximate TOEFL iBT score. All charts can easily be removed from the book.

Audio CDs

The companion set of six compact disks contains all of the audio texts for the Listening, Speaking, and Writing sections of the tests. The recordings can be used for practice in note taking, summarizing, pronunciation, and learning vocabulary in context.

ALSO IN THE SERIES: *ADVANCED SKILL PRACTICE FOR THE iBT*

Delta's Key to the Next Generation TOEFL® Test: Advanced Skill Practice for the iBT is a comprehensive test preparation course for high intermediate and advanced students. The book/audio program contains 36 skill units, four practice tests, and a companion set of 10 compact disks.

TO THE STUDENT

Six Practice Tests for the iBT will help you prepare for either the TOEFL iBT or the new TOEFL ITP.

TOEFL® iBT

If you are going to take the TOEFL iBT as a requirement for admission to a college or university program, use this book to become familiar with all four sections of the test.

- Read the information about Reading, Listening, Speaking, and Writing on pages 5–28. Become familiar with the different types of questions and how to answer them.
- Complete all sections of Test 1 through Test 6. Use a timer to simulate actual test conditions.
- Listen to the companion Audio CDs for all audio portions.
- Record your Speaking responses on a cassette, or record as computer files.
- Type your Writing responses on a computer, and print or save as computer files.
- Use the Answer Key and Audio Scripts to check your answers. For Speaking, also use How to Score Speaking. For Writing, also use How to Score Writing.
- Record your section scores on the Progress Charts. Use the Score Conversion Tables to find your approximate TOEFL scores.

TOEFL® ITP

If your current English program requires you to take the new institutional TOEFL, use this book to become familiar with the Reading and Listening sections of the test.

- Read the information about Reading and Listening on pages 5–17. Become familiar with the different types of questions and how to answer them.
- Complete the Reading and Listening sections of Test 1 through Test 6. Use a timer to simulate actual test conditions.
- Listen to the companion Audio CDs for all audio portions.
- Use the Answer Key and Audio Scripts to check your answers.
- Record your section scores on the Progress Charts. Use the Score Conversion Tables to find your approximate TOEFL scores.

READING

The Reading section of the TOEFL measures your ability to read and understand passages in English. You will be tested on your comprehension of major ideas, important information, vocabulary, and relationships among ideas in the passages. You will be required to:

- identify major ideas and distinguish them from minor ideas
- verify what information is true and what information is not true or not included in the passage
- define words and phrases as they are used the passage
- make inferences about information that is not directly stated
- identify the author's purpose
- connect ideas within sentences and among sentences
- summarize and organize important ideas from across the passage

The passages are about subjects that students usually study in their first two years of university, such as natural sciences, social sciences, business, and the arts. All of the questions are based on the information in the passage. You do not need special knowledge of the topics to answer the questions.

In some forms of the TOEFL iBT, the Reading section will have three passages. In other forms, the Reading section will have five passages. The TOEFL ITP will have three reading passages.

READING SECTION					
Form of Test	**Reading Texts**	**Time Allowed per Passage**	**Words per Passage**	**Questions per Passage**	**Total Number of Questions**
Short	3 passages	20 minutes	600–700	12–14	36–42
Long	5 passages	20 minutes	600–700	12–14	60–70

The time allowed includes the time that you spend reading the passages and answering the questions. You may take notes and you may use your notes to help you answer the questions. However, at the end of the test, you must give all of your notes to the test supervisor. Your notes will not be scored.

A few words in the passages, especially technical terms, may be defined in a glossary that is available to you during the test. If a word is highlighted in bold type, you may click on the word to read a definition of it.

The computer will give you one question at a time. You will be able to see the passage while you are answering the questions. You may skip questions and return to them later by clicking either the **Back** button or the **Review** button at the top of the screen. The **Back** button will take you to the previous question. The **Review** button will take you to a list of all of the Reading questions on the test. From this list, you may return to any previous question to review or change your answer.

There are three types of reading questions. For each type of question, you will use the mouse to click on an answer or to move text. Some questions are worth more than one point. These questions have special directions that indicate how many points you can receive.

Question Type 1 – Click on One Answer

For this type of question, you will choose the best of four possible answers.

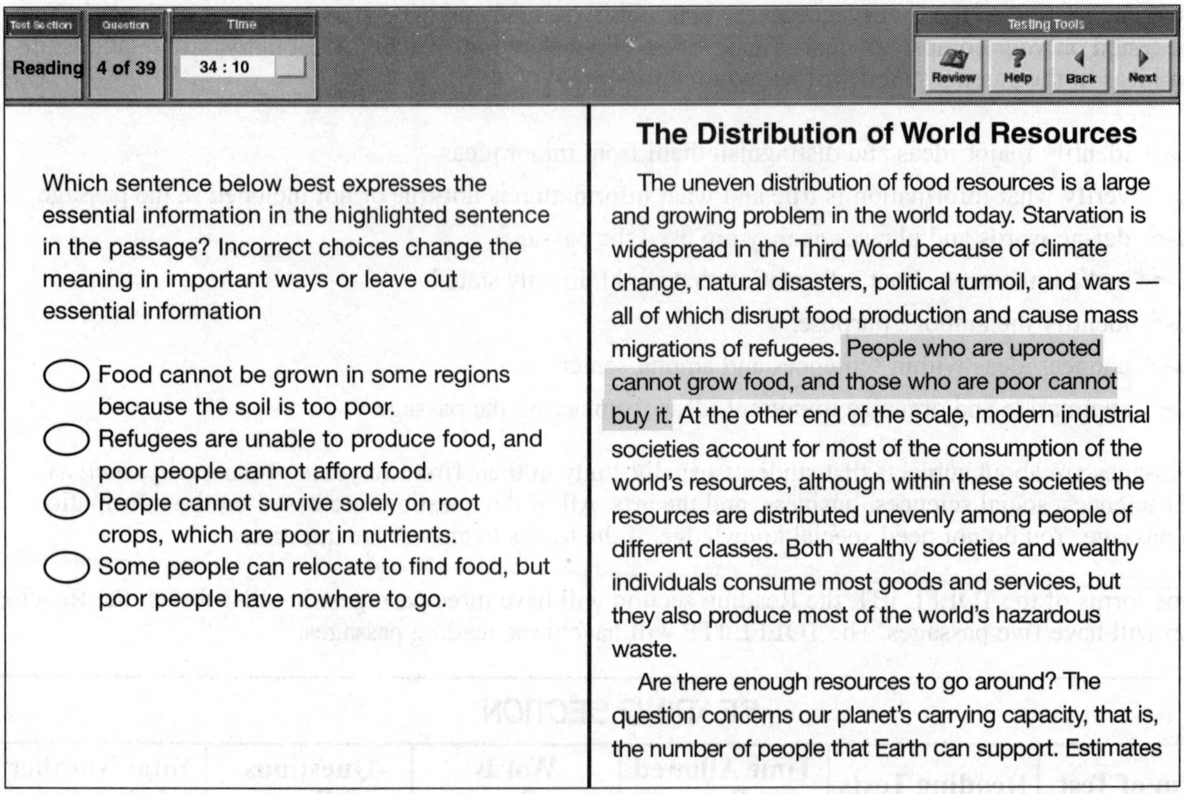

When you click on an oval, the oval will darken. To change your answer, click on a different oval. When you are satisfied that you have chosen the right answer, click on **Next**. The computer will go to the next question.

Question Type 2 – Add a Sentence

For this type of question, you will click on a square to add a sentence to the passage.

Test Section: Reading | Question: 12 of 39 | Time: 29 : 26 | Testing Tools: Review, Help, Back, Next

Look at the four squares [■] that indicate where the following sentence could be added to the passage.

Contingencies are events that might affect what you plan to do, but rarely are out of your control.

Where would the sentence best fit?

Click on a square [■] to add the sentence to the passage.

Even the best plans are rarely carried out without some problems. Good managers learn to deal with problems as they come up. ■ They make decisions as they are needed and adjust plans when necessary. Flexible plans allow for several contingencies. ■ For example, rain is a contingency that might affect the success of an outdoor event. ■ Trying to move indoors at the last minute could be a disaster. ■ Therefore, your plan should include a "rain plan."

You need to reserve some money and time for the unexpected. If you budget your money down to the last penny, you might not be able to take advantage of a bargain that you suddenly hear about. Similarly, if you schedule your time too tightly, you might not be able to deal with those "unexpected events" that always seem to happen.

Adding the sentence at the correct square will keep the paragraph coherent. Adding the sentence at an incorrect square will interrupt the logical flow of ideas from one sentence to the next.

Test Section: Reading | Question: 12 of 39 | Time: 29 : 26 | Testing Tools: Review, Help, Back, Next

Look at the four squares [■] that indicate where the following sentence could be added to the passage.

Contingencies are events that might affect what you plan to do, but rarely are out of your control.

Where would the sentence best fit?

Click on a square [■] to add the sentence to the passage.

Even the best plans are rarely carried out without some problems. Good managers learn to deal with problems as they come up. ■ They make decisions as they are needed and adjust plans when necessary. Flexible plans allow for several contingencies. **Contingencies are events that might affect what you plan to do, but rarely are out of your control.** For example, rain is a contingency that might affect the success of an outdoor event. ■ Trying to move indoors at the last minute could be a disaster. ■ Therefore, your plan should include a "rain plan."

You need to reserve some money and time for the unexpected. If you budget your money down to the last penny, you might not be able to take advantage of a bargain that you suddenly hear about. Similarly, if you schedule your time too tightly, you might not be able to deal with those "unexpected events" that always seem to happen.

When you click on a square, the sentence will appear there. To change your answer, click on a different square.

Question Type 3 – Drag Answer Choices

For this type of question, you will use the mouse to drag text to complete a table. Here are two examples.

Test Section	Question	Time	Current Task	Testing Tools
Reading	13 of 39	12 : 55	View Text / View Question	Review / Help / Back / Next

Directions: Read the first sentence of a summary of the passage. Complete the summary by selecting the THREE answer choices that express the most important ideas in the passage. Some sentences do not belong in the summary because they express ideas that are not presented in the passage or are minor ideas in the passage. ***This question is worth 2 points.***

The history of the piano began in the late seventeenth century.

-
-
-

Answer Choices

The dulcimer, a wooden box with strings, was similar to the piano.

A harpsichord maker invented the pianoforte, which could play both softly and loudly.

Composers preferred the harpsichord and were slow in accepting the piano.

Piano construction improved as the instrument became more popular with composers.

Several smaller types of pianos provided homes with musical entertainment.

The gramophone replaced the upright parlor piano in the twentieth century.

Test Section	Question	Time	Current Task	Testing Tools
Reading	39 of 39	6 : 05	View Text / View Question	Review / Help / Back / Next

Directions: Select the appropriate sentences from the answer choices and match them to the type of substance that they describe. TWO of the answer choices will NOT be used. ***This question is worth 3 points.***

Answer Choices

The solution does not have an electrical charge.

The solution has a pH value greater than that of pure water.

The substance measures 5.0 on the pH meter.

When added to food, it gives the food a sour taste.

The substance has a bitter taste and a slippery feel.

The compound is odorless and tasteless.

It can be added to soil to lower the soil's acidity.

Acid

-
-

Base

-
-
-

To answer, move the cursor to the answer choice that you want to move. Click and hold to drag the sentence to the space where it belongs. The sentence will appear in that space. To change an answer, click on it. Then drag your new choice to the correct space.

LISTENING

The Listening section of the TOEFL measures your ability to understand conversations and lectures in English. You will listen to several conversations and lectures and answer questions about them. You will be tested on your comprehension of the general ideas and supporting details of the conversations and lectures. You will also be asked to identify a speaker's purpose in making a particular statement or to identify a speaker's attitude toward a particular topic.

The conversation topics reflect typical experiences of North American university students. The lecture topics are academic and come from various fields of study in the natural sciences, the social sciences, business, and the arts. All of the questions are based on what the speakers state or imply. You do not need special knowledge of the topics to answer the questions.

In some forms of the TOEFL iBT, the Listening section will have two conversations and four lectures. In other forms, the Listening section will have three conversations and six lectures.

LISTENING SECTION				
Form of Test	**Audio Texts**	**Length of Each Audio Text**	**Questions per Audio Text**	**Total Number of Questions**
Short	2 conversations 4 lectures	2–3 minutes 3–5 minutes	5 6	34
Long	3 conversations 6 lectures	2–3 minutes 3–5 minutes	5 6	51

You will use headphones to listen to the conversations and lectures. You can change the volume of the sound at any time during the test. You may take notes on paper while you are listening. You may use your notes to help you answer the questions. However, at the end of the test, you must give all of your notes to the test supervisor. Your notes will not be scored.

The Listening section takes approximately 60 to 90 minutes to complete. This includes the time that you spend listening to the directions, listening to the conversations and lectures, and answering the questions. A clock at the top of the screen shows how much time is left. The clock counts down only during your response time; it does not count down while you are listening to the conversations, lectures, and questions.

You will hear each conversation and lecture only one time. You will both *hear* and *see* each question. You must answer each question before you can go on to the next question. You can change your answer as many times as you like—until you click on **OK**. When you click on **OK**, the computer will go to the next question. Once you have finished a question, you cannot return to that question or to any other previous question.

There are six types of listening questions. For each type of question, you will use the mouse to click on one or more answers or to move text. Some of the questions have special directions, which will appear in a gray box. Most correct answers will earn one point, but some questions are worth two points.

Here is an example of a lecture, followed by the six types of listening questions.

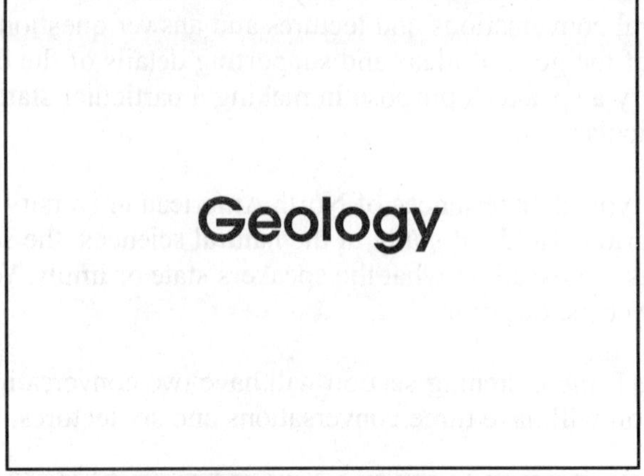

(Narrator) Listen to part of a lecture in a geology class.

While you are listening, you will see a picture of the class.

(Professor) After the water drains from a cave, a new kind of growth may begin. Delicate straws grow from the ceiling. Twisted fingers protrude from the walls and floor. Smooth mounds appear in pools. All of these amazing formations are called speleothems. They sometimes grow in sandstone and lava–tube caves, but most commonly we see them in limestone caves.

Among the most interesting speleothems are stalactites and stalagmites. People always want to know: how do you keep straight… which is a stalactite and which is a stalagmite? There's an easy way to remember. "Stalactite" is spelled with a "c" and it hangs from the ceiling. "Stalagmite" is spelled with a "g" and it grows up from the ground.

Both stalactites and stalagmites begin with a drop of water on a cave ceiling. The ground–water seeping into the cave contains carbon dioxide from the atmosphere or the soil, as well as dissolved limestone that it picked up from the layers of rock above the cave.

As a drop of water hangs from the ceiling, a tiny amount of carbon dioxide escapes—just like bubbles from a can of soda pop. Now the water drop can't carry much dissolved limestone, and a tiny ring of stone called dripstone forms around its outside edges. The drop of water hangs for a moment, then it falls.

Each drop of water adds another layer as it trickles down through the growing ring of dripstone. Eventually, the dripstone forms a slender tube. These slender, hollow tubes are called tubular stalactites, or—because they look like straws—soda–straw stalactites. They're very fragile. As they grow, their own weight may cause them to break off and fall to the floor. Soda straws can grow into conical stalactites as dripstone builds up on the outside. Stalactites don't grow very quickly… on average, only about a half–inch in a hundred years.

The dripping water that hits the floor still contains some dissolved limestone. The impact of the water hitting the floor causes it to break into droplets, releasing the excess carbon dioxide. Then limestone crystals start to grow upward, forming stalagmites… starting with tiny finger–like structures, and eventually forming large, rounded domes up to ten meters tall and ten meters in diameter.

Question Type 1 – Click on One Answer

For this type of question, you will choose the best of four possible answers.

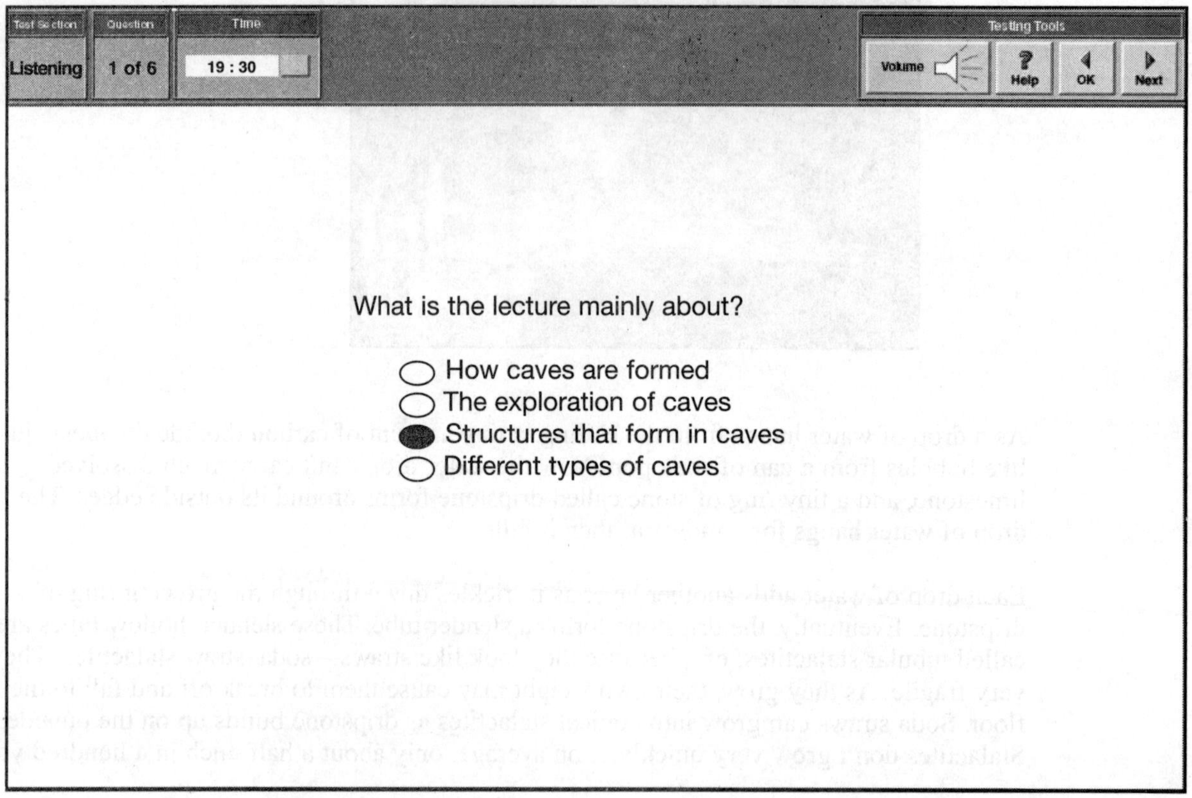

The topic of the lecture is *Structures that form in caves*. Therefore, you should click on the oval next to the third answer.

When you click on an oval, the oval will darken. To change your answer, click on a different oval. When you are satisfied that you have chosen the correct answer, click on **Next**. Then click on **OK**. The computer will go to the next question.

Question Type 2 – Click on Two Answers

For this type of question, you will click on two answers. You will click on boxes instead of ovals.

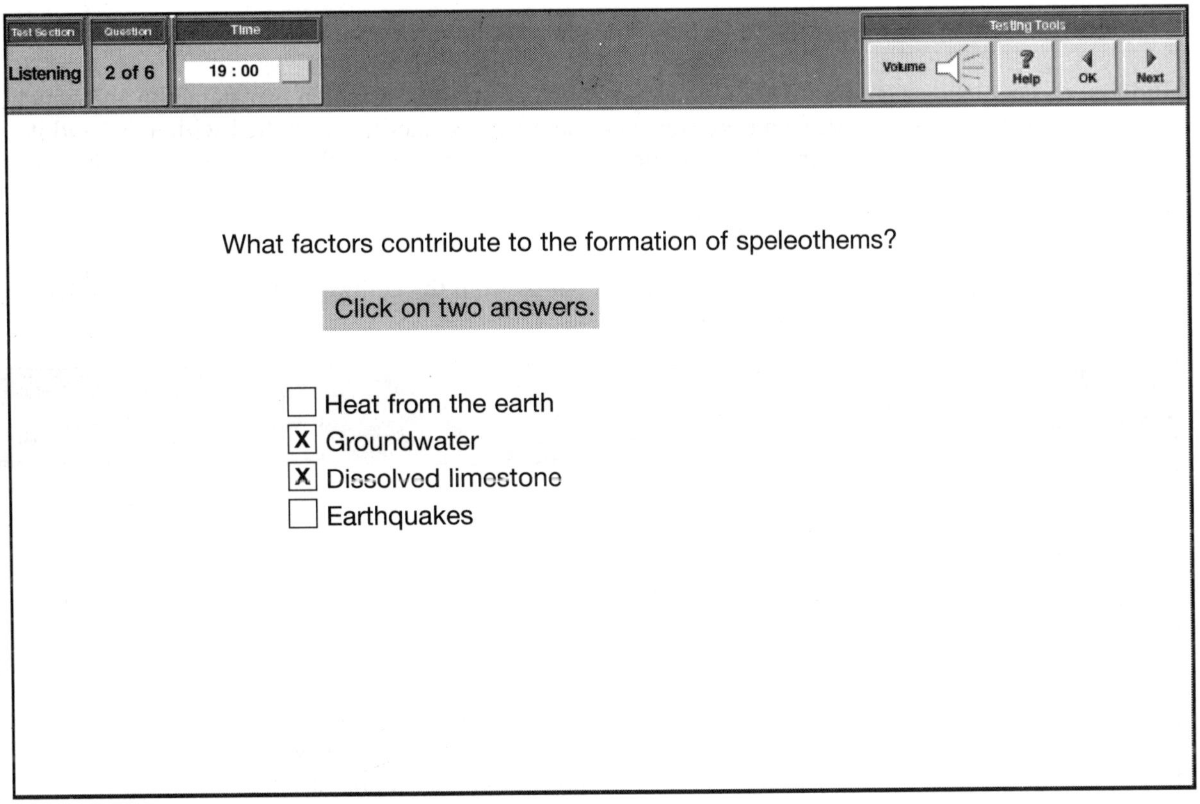

The professor says:

> Both stalactites and stalagmites begin with a drop of water on a cave ceiling. The groundwater seeping into the cave contains carbon dioxide from the atmosphere or the soil, as well as dissolved limestone that it picked up from the layers of rock above the cave.

Therefore, you should click on the boxes next to *Groundwater* and *Dissolved limestone*.

When you click on a box, an **X** will appear in it. To change an answer, click on the **X** to erase it. Then click on a different box.

You must choose both correct answers to earn a point for answering the question correctly.

Question Type 3 – Listen Again to Part of the Text

For this type of question, you will hear part of the audio again.

(Narrator) Listen again to part of the lecture. Then answer the question.

(Professor) People always want to know: how do you keep straight… which is a stalactite and which is a stalagmite? There's an easy way to remember. "Stalactite" is spelled with a "c" and it hangs from the ceiling. "Stalagmite" is spelled with a "g" and it grows up from the ground.

(Narrator) Why does the professor say this:

(Professor) "Stalactite" is spelled with a "c" and it hangs from the ceiling. "Stalagmite" is spelled with a "g" and it grows up from the ground.

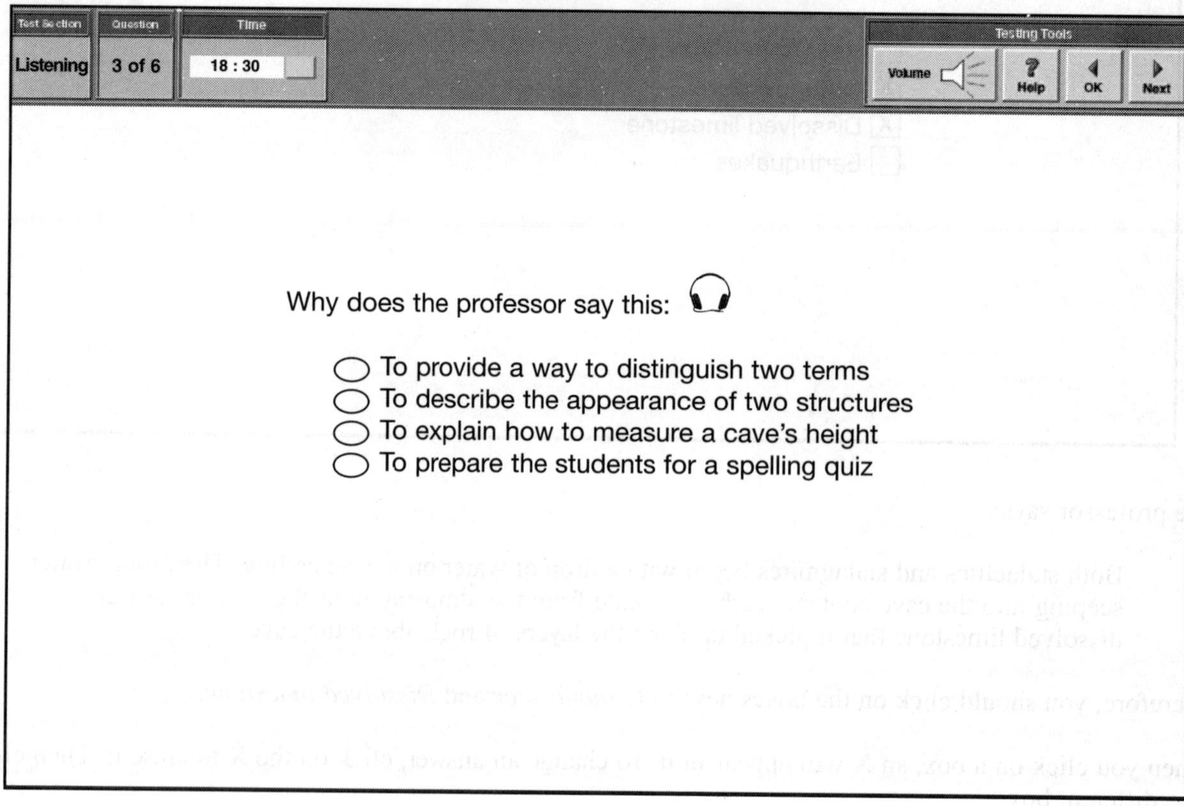

When you see the icon next to a question, it means that part of the question will not appear on the screen. It means that you will hear part of the lecture again, and you must listen carefully in order to answer the question.

The professor says:

> People always want to know: how do you keep straight ... which is a stalactite and which is a stalagmite? There's an easy way to remember.

Then the professor discusses the spelling of stalactite and stalagmite. The correct answer is *To provide a way to distinguish two terms*. Therefore, you should click on the oval next to the first answer.

Question Type 4 – Click on a Picture

For this type of question, you will click on a picture or part of a picture.

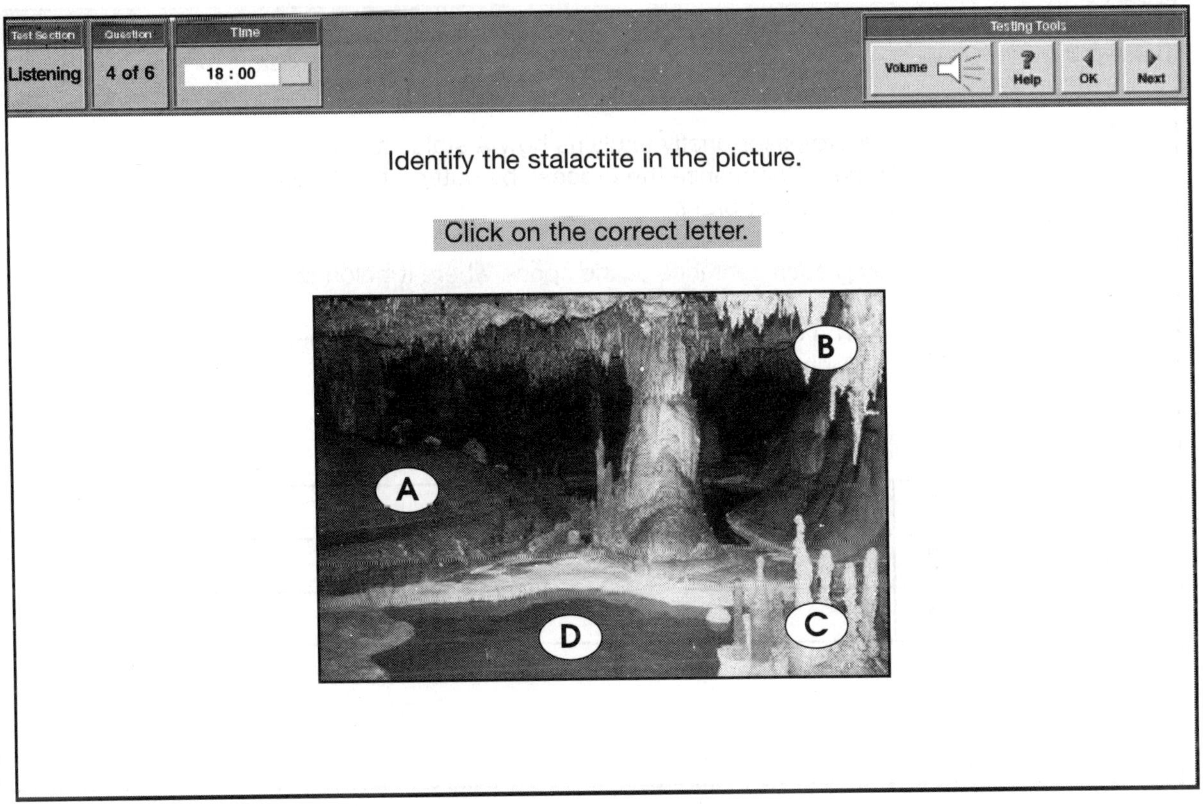

The professor says:

> "Stalactite" is spelled with a "c" and it hangs from the ceiling.

The stalactite is at (B) in the picture. Therefore, you should click on (B).

When you click on a letter, the letter will highlight. To change your answer, click on a different letter.

Question Type 5 – Drag Answer Choices

For this type of question, you will use the mouse to drag text to complete a list, table, or summary.

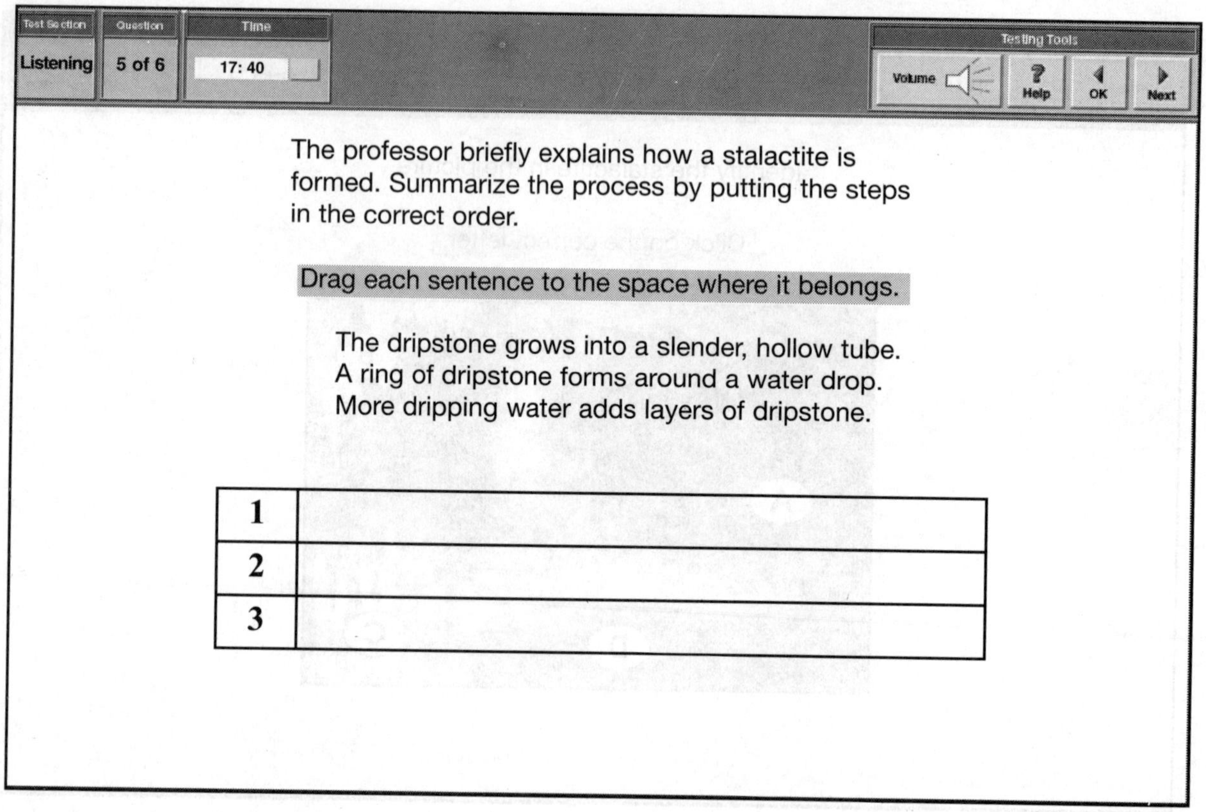

The professor says:

> Now the water drop can't carry much dissolved limestone, and a tiny ring of stone called dripstone forms around its outside edges….
>
> Each drop of water adds another layer as it trickles down through the growing ring of dripstone. Eventually, the dripstone forms a slender tube. These slender, hollow tubes are called tubular stalactites….

Therefore, the correct order is:

1	A ring of dripstone forms around a water drop.
2	More dripping water adds layers of dripstone.
3	The dripstone grows into a slender, hollow tube.

Move the cursor to the answer choice that you want to move. Click and hold to drag the text to the space where it belongs. The text will appear in that space. To change an answer, click on it. Then drag your new answer choice to the space. You must put all of the answer choices in the correct space to receive credit for answering the question correctly.

ABOUT THE TEST

Question Type 6 – Click on a Table

For this type of question, you will click on boxes in a table.

Test Section: Listening | Question: 6 of 6 | Time: 16: 55 | Testing Tools: Volume, Help, OK, Next

Based on the information in the lecture, indicate whether each sentence below describes a stalactite or a stalagmite.

For each sentence, click in the correct box.

	Stalactite	Stalagmite
It grows up from limestone deposits on the cave floor.		
It hangs from the ceiling of a cave.		
It is long and hollow like a soda straw.		
It can grow into a dome ten meters tall.		

The professor says:

> "Stalactite"… hangs from the ceiling. "Stalagmite"… grows up from the ground.
>
> These slender, hollow tubes are called… because they look like straws—soda–straw stalactites.
>
> Then limestone crystals start to grow upward, forming stalagmites… eventually forming large, rounded domes up to ten meters tall….

Therefore, the correct answers are:

	Stalactite	Stalagmite
It grows up from limestone deposits on the cave floor.		✓
It hangs from the ceiling of a cave.	✓	
It is long and hollow like a soda straw.	✓	
It can grow into a dome ten meters tall.		✓

When you click on a box, a ✓ will appear in it. You must click on one box in each row. To change an answer, click on a different box in the same row.

In most questions like this, you must put all of the ✓s in the correct space to earn one point. Some questions like this are worth two points, and you will earn one point if your answer is partly correct.

SPEAKING

The Speaking section of the TOEFL measures your ability to speak in English about a variety of topics. There are six questions in this section. All of the questions are about topics that are appropriate for international students. You do not need special knowledge of any subject to respond to the questions. You will respond to two questions about your own experience and four integrated–skills questions about texts that you listen to or read during the test.

SPEAKING SECTION				
Question	**Reading Time per Task**	**Listening Time per Task**	**Preparation Time per Task**	**Speaking Time per Task**
2 independent tasks	—	—	15 seconds	45 seconds
2 integrated tasks	45 seconds	1 – 2 minutes	30 seconds	60 seconds
2 integrated tasks	—	1 – 2 minutes	20 seconds	60 seconds

The Speaking section takes approximately 20 minutes to complete. This includes the time for reading the directions, reading the passages, listening to the audio texts, and preparing and recording your responses. For the integrated–skills tasks, you will use headphones to listen to the conversations and lectures. You will be able to change the volume of the sound.

You may take notes, and you may use your notes to help you respond to the tasks. However, at the end of the test you must give all of your notes to the test supervisor. Your notes will not be scored; only what you say during the recording time will be scored.

For each speaking task, you will both *hear* and *see* the question. You will have time to prepare your response before you begin speaking. A clock on the screen will show you how much preparation time is left. When the preparation time is over, the response time will begin. You will answer each question by speaking into a microphone. You will have either 45 or 60 seconds to record each response. The clock will show you how much time is left. When the response time is over, the computer will go to the next question.

Two qualified evaluators will listen to each of your responses. They will rate each response on a scale of 1 to 4, with 4 being the highest score possible. You will receive a score of 0 if you do not respond to the given question. Your scores for the six tasks will be combined, and the total number of points you earn will be converted to a Speaking section score of 0 to 30.

INDEPENDENT SPEAKING TASKS

The first two questions are independent speaking tasks in which you will speak from your own personal knowledge and experience. You will have 15 seconds to prepare your response and 45 seconds to speak.

In your responses, you must demonstrate your ability to:

- state and support an opinion
- develop points with appropriate details and explanation
- express ideas coherently
- make yourself understood by speaking clearly and fluently

Here is an example of an independent speaking task.

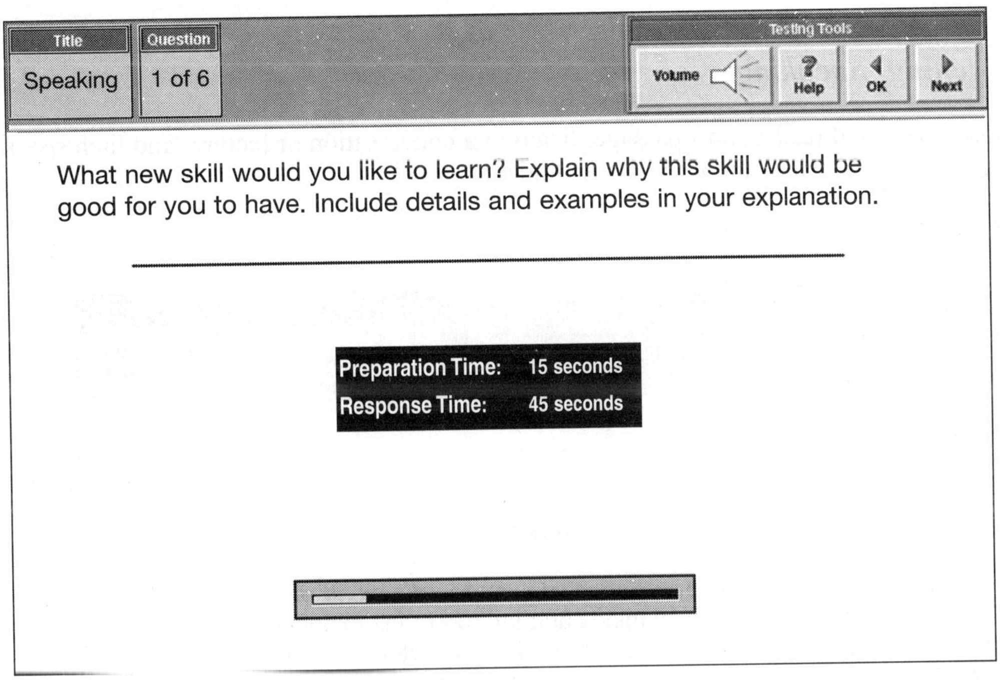

INTEGRATED SPEAKING TASKS

The middle two questions are integrated–skills tasks in which you will read a passage, listen to a conversation or lecture, and then speak in response to a question about what you have read and heard. The last two questions are integrated–skills tasks in which you will listen to a conversation or lecture, and then speak in response to a question about it.

In your responses, you must demonstrate your ability to:

- convey relevant information from one or two sources
- develop points with appropriate details and explanation
- express ideas coherently
- make yourself understood by speaking clearly and fluently

Reading–Listening–Speaking

For these two tasks, you will read a short passage, listen to a conversation or lecture, and then speak in response to a question about what you have read and heard.

First, you have 45 seconds to read a passage.

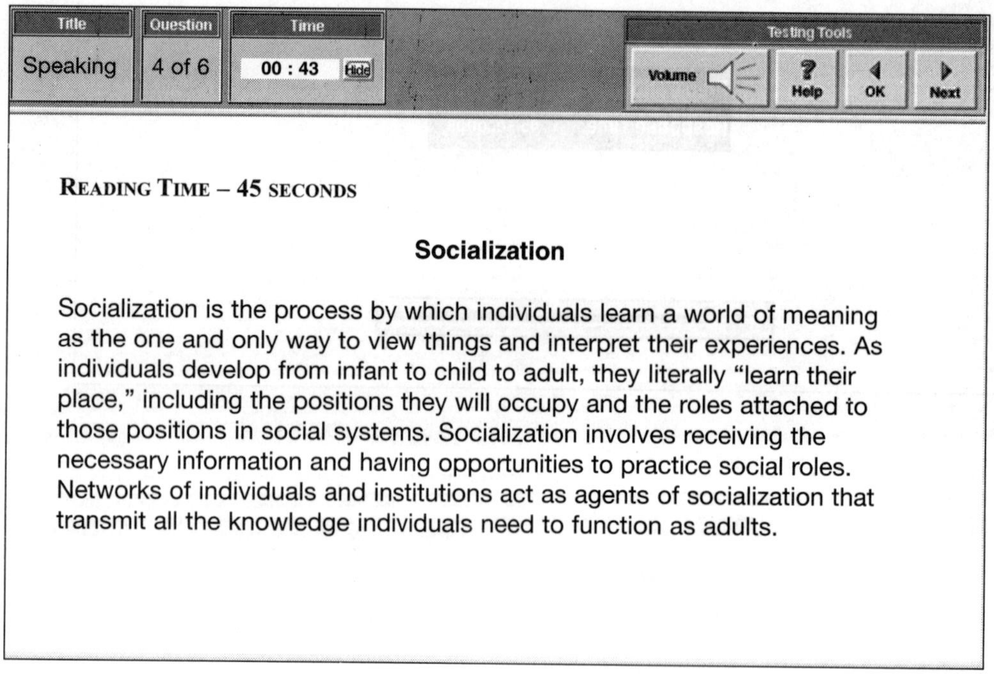

READING TIME – 45 SECONDS

Socialization

Socialization is the process by which individuals learn a world of meaning as the one and only way to view things and interpret their experiences. As individuals develop from infant to child to adult, they literally "learn their place," including the positions they will occupy and the roles attached to those positions in social systems. Socialization involves receiving the necessary information and having opportunities to practice social roles. Networks of individuals and institutions act as agents of socialization that transmit all the knowledge individuals need to function as adults.

Then the passage will disappear from the screen, and you will not see it again. You will listen to a conversation or lecture about the same topic. You will see a picture of the speaker or speakers.

(Narrator) Now listen to part of a talk in a sociology class.

(Professor) Agents of socialization are the people and institutions that teach you about the culture you live in, including its rules. The first agents of socialization are your parents or other adults who take care of you when you're a baby. Your parents give you the first important lessons in how to behave in society.

When you're a teenager, your peers—your friends and classmates—are agents of socialization. Your peers support you and help you grow up and out of your family's nest. Your parents and peers are important in different ways. Your parents give you guidance on long–term goals, like career choice, but your peers are more likely to influence your immediate lifestyle choices, like how you dress and what you do for fun.

And since you spend so many years in school under the guidance of teachers, teachers are also agents of socialization. Teachers give you knowledge and also serve as models for responsible adulthood. Institutions—like clubs and religious organizations—are also agents of socialization. So are the mass media—television, magazines, popular music, and the Internet.

Then you will both *hear* and *see* the speaking question. After the question appears, you will have 30 seconds to prepare your response and 60 seconds to speak.

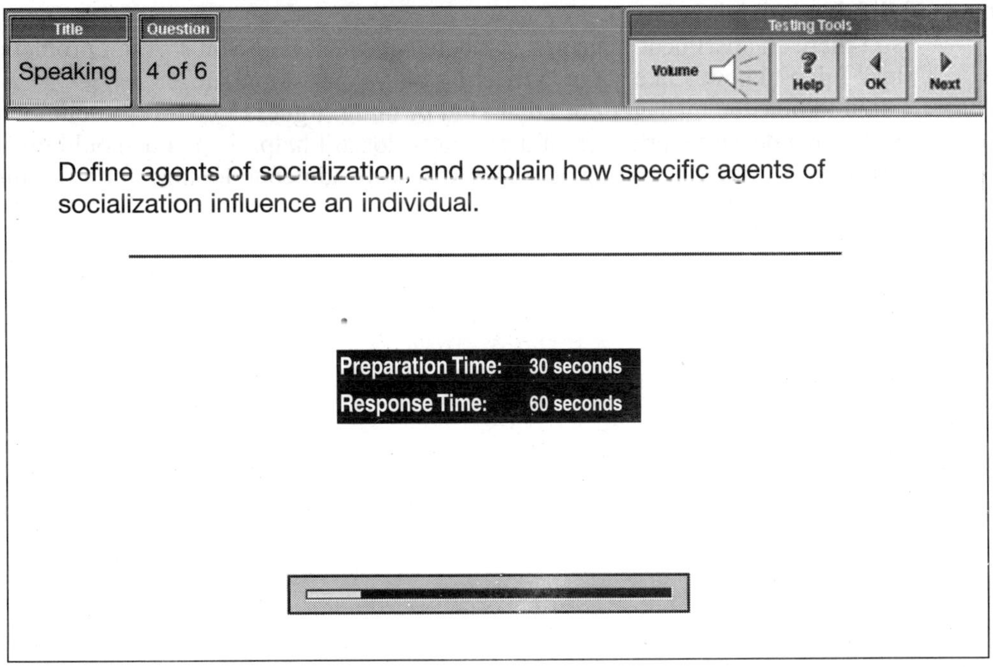

Listening–Speaking

For these two tasks, you will listen to a conversation or lecture and then speak in response to a question about it.

While you are listening, you will see a picture of the speaker or speakers.

(Narrator)	Listen to part of a conversation between two students.
(Man)	How do you like living in the campus apartments?
(Woman)	Well ... it's OK. I mean, I like the apartment, but my roommate is kind of a problem. Sometimes she uses my things without asking—mostly little things, like paper and toothpaste, but once it was my favorite sweater. And she never cleans the bathroom when it's her turn.
(Man)	Have you sat down with her and had a good talk about these things?
(Woman)	Maybe if I saw her more often. The problem is, she's hardly ever home.
(Man)	Try leaving her a note.
(Woman)	I did, but it didn't help.
(Man)	Isn't there an apartment manager, someone who will help you sort out problems like this? I don't know…like set up a meeting with your roommate?
(Woman)	I didn't know the manager does that kind of thing. I guess I could find out.
(Man)	And if that doesn't work ... if talking it over doesn't help, then you should probably just move out, find another place. There's always someone looking for a roommate.

Then you will both *hear* and *see* the speaking question. After the question appears, you will have 20 seconds to prepare your response and 60 seconds to speak.

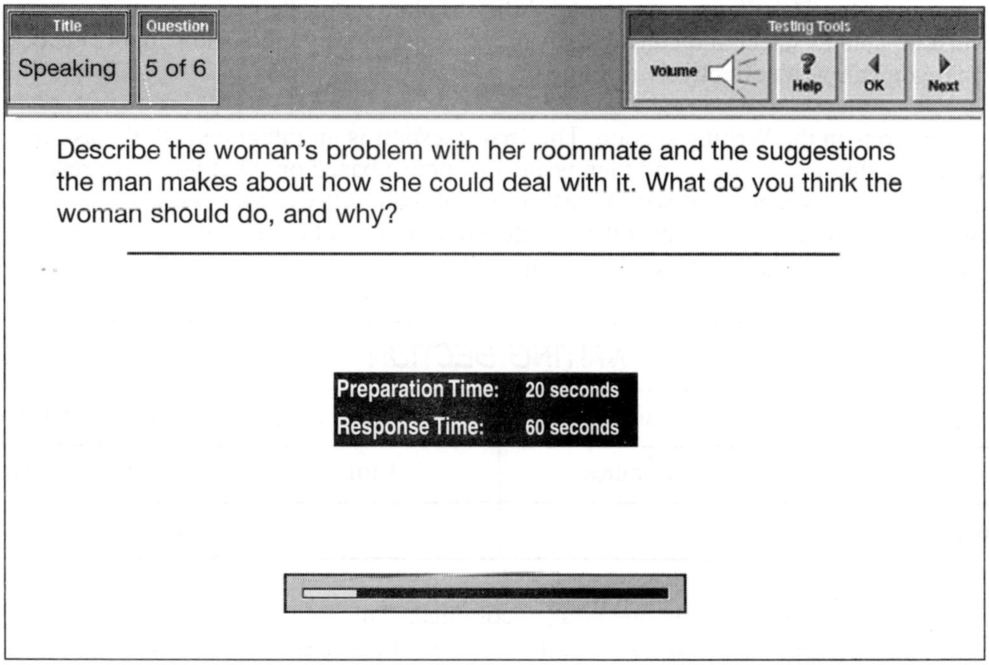

WRITING

The Writing section of the TOEFL measures your ability to plan and write responses to questions in essay format. You must be able to select and convey relevant information, organize and support ideas, and demonstrate that you can write effectively in English.

There are two questions in the Writing section. The first question is an integrated–skills task in which you will read a passage, listen to a lecture, and then write a response based on what you have read and heard. The second question is an independent writing task in which you will write an essay based on your own experience. Both questions are about topics that are appropriate for international students. You do not need special knowledge of any subject to respond to the questions.

WRITING SECTION			
Question	**Reading Time**	**Listening Time**	**Writing Time**
Integrated task	3 minutes	2–3 minutes	20 minutes
Independent task	—	—	30 minutes

The Writing section takes approximately one hour to complete. This includes the time for reading the directions, reading the passage, listening to the lecture, and writing your responses to both questions. A clock at the top of the screen shows how much writing time is left for each question.

For the integrated task, you will use headphones to listen to the lecture. You will be able to change the volume of the sound. The clock does not count down while you are listening to the lecture.

You may take notes during both tasks, and you may use your notes while writing your responses. However, at the end of the test you must give all of your notes to the test supervisor. Your notes will not be scored; only what you type on the computer keyboard will be scored.

You must type your responses to both writing questions. You will not be allowed to write your responses by hand.

Two qualified evaluators will read your responses. They will rate each response on a scale of 1 to 5, with 5 being the highest score possible. You will receive a score of 0 if you do not write a response, do not write about the given question, or do not write in English. Your scores on the two writing tasks will be combined, and the total number of points you earn will be converted to a Writing section score of 0 to 30.

THE INTEGRATED WRITING TASK

The integrated writing task measures your ability to understand key ideas from an academic reading passage and a short lecture, and to write a response to a question about them. You must determine what information in the lecture relates in some way to information in the reading. Then you must organize and compose a response in standard written English.

In your response, you must demonstrate your ability to:

- organize ideas effectively in answering the question
- draw requested connections between the lecture and the reading
- develop ideas with appropriate examples and explanation
- display unity and coherence
- use English words and sentences effectively

First, you will have three minutes to read a passage of 250 to 300 words.

> The discovery of penicillin and other antibiotic drugs is the most dramatic medical development of the twentieth century. These new drugs quickly became known as "wonder drugs" because they saved so many lives that were threatened by major forms of infection. The research that led to their development rested on the belief that chemicals could be found that would destroy specific microorganisms without injuring the human body at the same time. Advances in chemistry and in the knowledge of bacteria quickened the discovery of such chemicals.
>
> In 1933, the first of the sulfa drugs, prontosil, was tested clinically on humans and was found to cure blood infections that would otherwise have been fatal. In 1941, the first successful human tests of penicillin were conducted on cases of streptococcus infections. The discovery of penicillin laid the foundation for even more powerful weapons against specific diseases. Within the next decade, researchers identified some 200 antibiotic substances that were effective against one or another type of bacteria. One of the most important was streptomycin, found to be potent against tuberculosis and other infections that were not affected by penicillin.
>
> Antibiotics gave the medical profession powerful tools that could directly fight a very wide range of specific diseases. They made possible the survival of patients during and after surgery. No longer was it necessary to depend largely on the body's own immune system to fight off major infections; these infections could be attacked directly with drugs. Among the most spectacular effects of antibiotics were reductions in the number of deaths from pneumonia and tuberculosis.

Then the passage will disappear temporarily while you listen to a short lecture on the same topic. The passage will reappear later and be available to you during the writing time.

While you are listening, you will see a picture of the class.

(Narrator) Now listen to part of a lecture in a biology class.

(Professor) As soon as we developed antibiotics, new strains of bacteria appeared that were resistant to some or all of the drugs. Hospitals started using antibiotics regularly in the 1950s, but resistance started appearing within a few years. Today, one–third of the patients in hospitals are on antibiotics, but antibiotic resistance is increasing the danger of hospital infections—to the point where people are almost safer staying home than going to a hospital.

In the forties, penicillin really was a wonder drug. Back then, you could give a patient with bacterial pneumonia ten thousand units of penicillin four times a day and cure the disease. Today, you could give 24 million units of penicillin a day, but the patient might still die. Why? Well, in a way, bacteria are smarter than us. They evolve to counteract any drug we attack them with. A lot of bacteria are now completely resistant to penicillin.

Bacteria can evolve very effective weapons against antibiotics. Some of them develop enzymes to match every antibiotic we throw at them. All these weapons and counter–weapons match one another—just like the weapons in real military warfare. So, no matter what antibiotic we use, the bacteria will come up with a way to make it useless.

How does this happen? Well, if you douse a colony of bacteria with an antibiotic, the colony will be killed—that is, all except for a few cells. A few cells will survive because they carry a resistance gene for that particular antibiotic. The surviving cells quickly multiply, and they pass along this lucky gene to their offspring. And soon you have a new strain of bacteria that's resistant to that drug.

One consequence of antibiotic resistance is the reappearance of tuberculosis as a major illness. Twenty years ago, doctors thought tuberculosis was a defeated disease. Since then, however, new cases of tuberculosis have increased by 20 percent. And several strains of the disease are resistant to any drug we can attack them with.

(Narrator) Summarize the main points made in the lecture, explaining how they differ from points made in the reading.

After the lecture, you will both *hear* and *see* the writing question. You will have 20 minutes to plan, write, and revise your response.

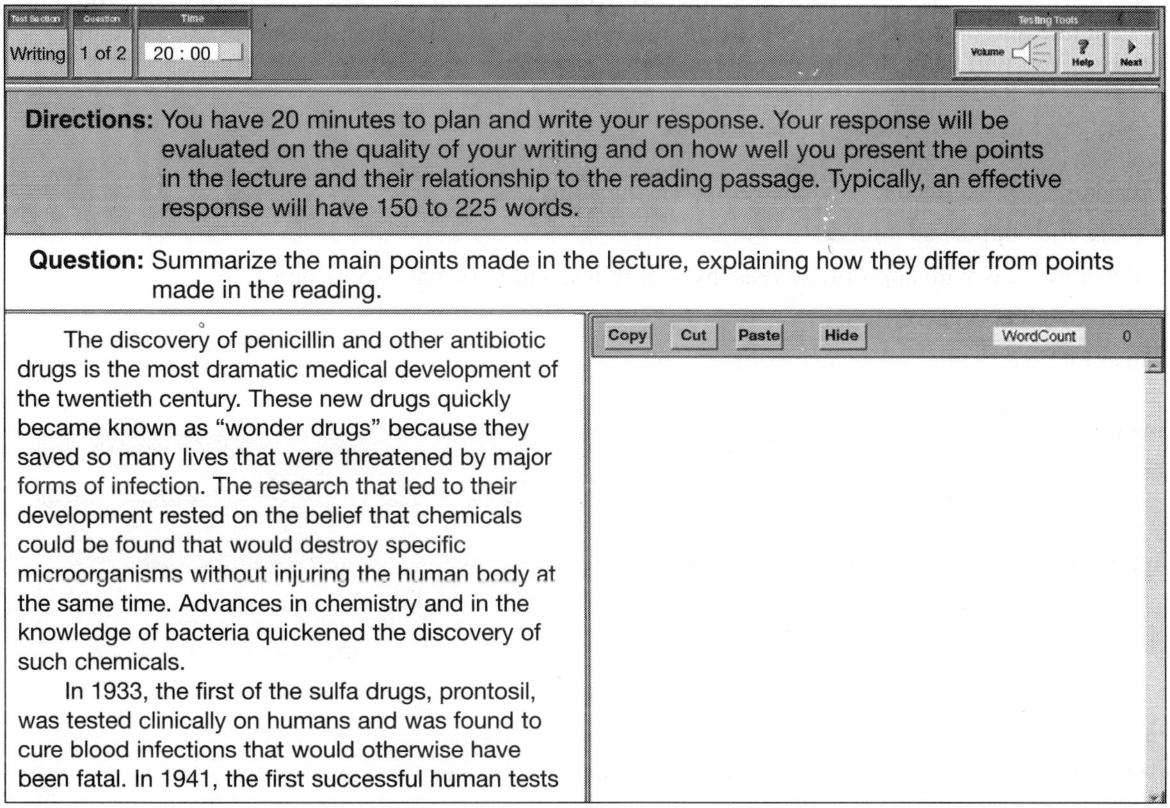

You may use your notes from the lecture to help you write your response. You will be able to see the reading passage. As you type, the computer will show your word count—how many words you have written. An effective response usually has approximately 150 to 225 words.

THE INDEPENDENT WRITING TASK

The independent writing task measures your ability to write an essay in response to a given topic. You must be able to generate and organize ideas, to develop and support these ideas, and to compose in standard written English. You will have 30 minutes to plan, write, and revise your essay.

In your essay, you must demonstrate your ability to:

- organize ideas effectively in answering the question
- state and support an opinion
- develop ideas with appropriate reasons, examples, and personal experience
- display unity and coherence
- use English words and sentences effectively

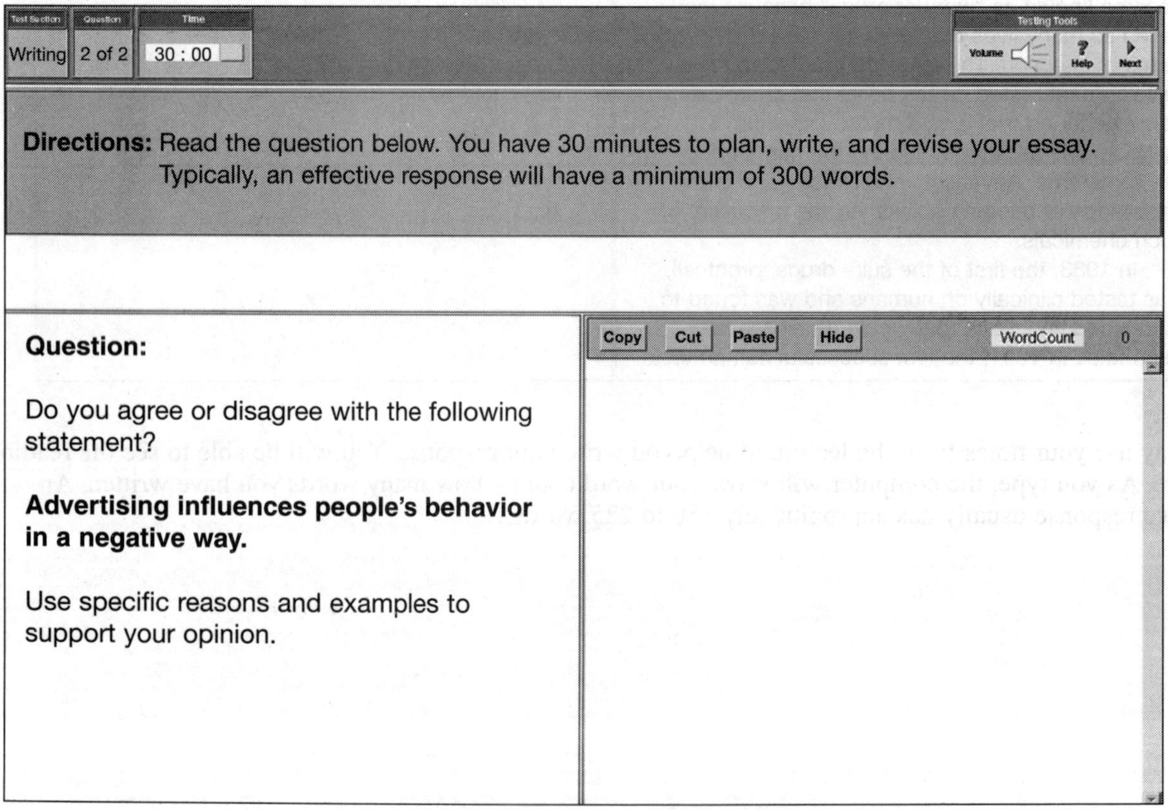

You may make notes on paper to help you plan your response. As you type, the computer will show your word count. An effective response usually has at least 300 words.

TEST 1

READING SECTION DIRECTIONS

The Reading section measures your ability to read and understand passages in English. You will read five passages and answer questions about them. Answer all questions based on what is stated or implied in the passages.

Most questions are worth one point. The last question in each set is worth more than one point. For this question, the directions will indicate how many points you can receive.

Some passages have one or more words in bold type. For these bolded words, you will see a definition in a glossary at the end of the passage.

Allow 20 minutes to read each passage and answer the questions about it. You may now begin the first passage.

Time – 100 minutes

NORTH AMERICAN GRASSLANDS

1 In North America, native grasslands occur primarily in the Great Plains in the middle of the continent. The North American prairie **biome** is one of the most extensive grasslands in the world, extending from the edge of the Rocky Mountains in the west to the deciduous forest in the east, and from northern Mexico in the south to Canada in the north. Average annual rainfall ranges from about 40 cm (16 inches) in the west to 80 cm (31 inches) in the east. Average annual temperatures range between 10 degrees and 20 degrees Celsius (50 to 68 degrees Fahrenheit). In the moist regions of the North American grasslands, especially in the northern Great Plains, rainfall is distinctly seasonal, and temperatures can vary widely from very hot in summer to bitter cold in winter.

2 One hundred years ago, the Great Plains grasslands were one vast, unbroken prairie. Much of the prairie is now farmland, the most productive agricultural region in the world, dominated by **monocultures** of cereal grains. Wheat, barley, soybeans, corn, and sunflowers occupy the land that was once prairie. In areas given over to grazing lands for cattle and sheep, virtually all the major native grasses have been replaced by alien species.

3 An important feature of the northern Great Plains grasslands is the presence of millions of glacial depressions that are now small ponds known as prairie potholes. They were formed during the most recent Ice Age, when streams flowed in tunnels beneath glacially formed sandy ridges. When the Ice Age ended around 12,000 years ago, the retreating glaciers created about 25 million depressions across a 300,000–square–mile landscape—about 83 potholes per square mile. As the ice blocks melted, much of the water was left behind, forming wetlands ranging in size from a tenth of an acre to several acres. The wetlands were soon surrounded by fluttering waves of grasses: shortgrass, mixed grass, and tallgrass.

4 Today these small wetlands still cover the prairies, although much of the landscape—including both native grasses and potholes—has been transformed to cropland and grassland for grazing. What does remain of the wetlands, however, still serves as an important breeding area for more than 300 bird species, including large numbers of migrating shorebirds and waterfowl. The potholes fill up with water during spring rains and usually dry out by late summer. Every spring, birds arrive in great numbers—northern pintails, mallards, coots, and pied–billed grebes—4 to 6 million strong, to mate in the seasonal wetlands that dot portions of Minnesota, Iowa, North and South Dakota, Montana, Alberta, Saskatchewan, and Manitoba. Prairie pothole country produces half of North America's 35 to 40 million ducks and is renowned worldwide as a "duck factory."

5 Recently biologists have discovered that the prairie pothole region is potentially a vast carbon sink: a natural sponge that absorbs carbon dioxide emissions from cars, factories, and power plants. Carbon dioxide is the most common of all the pollutants acting as greenhouse gases that heat up the atmosphere. Fortunately, however, carbon dioxide is captured naturally and stored in trees, soil, and plants. Scientists have termed this "carbon sequestration." They have determined that prairie potholes hold an average of 2.5 tons of carbon per acre per year when not being farmed. This means that if the entire pothole region in the United States and Canada were to stop being farmed, the region would store about 400 million tons of carbon over 10 years—the equivalent of taking almost 4 million cars off the road. Thus, preserving the potholes could be a way to offset greenhouse gas emissions that are warming the planet.

Glossary:

biome: one of the world's major natural communities, classified by predominant vegetation
monoculture: cultivation of large land areas with a single plant variety

1. All of the following statements are true of the northern Great Plains EXCEPT

   (A) Summer temperatures are very hot, while winter temperatures are very cold.
   (B) An unbroken prairie now extends from the western mountains to the eastern forest.
   (C) The original vegetation consisted of shortgrass, mixed grass, and tallgrass.
   (D) A large number of small wetlands are found throughout the region.

2. What has taken place in the Great Plains grasslands during the last century?

   (A) The average annual rainfall has risen and fallen several times.
   (B) Large parts of the prairie have been converted to agricultural use.
   (C) Melting glaciers have formed numerous depressions in the soil.
   (D) Scientists have transformed the region into one large carbon sink.

3. The word alien in paragraph 2 is closest in meaning to

   (A) healthy
   (B) simple
   (C) cheaper
   (D) imported

4. The prairie potholes owe their origins mainly to

   (A) the variation in temperature throughout the year
   (B) the glaciers that melted at the end of the last Ice Age
   (C) the heavy rains that fall in the spring and summer
   (D) the increase in greenhouse gases in the atmosphere

5. Which sentence below best expresses the essential information in the highlighted sentence in paragraph 4? Incorrect choices change the meaning in important ways or leave out essential information.

   (A) The wetlands completely cover the landscape, making it difficult to grow crops and grass for grazing.
   (B) The native grasses that grew in the potholes have been replaced with crops that are more beneficial.
   (C) Except for the potholes region, the entire prairie has been converted to cropland and grazing land.
   (D) Even though a large portion of the prairies is used for crops and grazing, the small ponds remain.

6. The word dot in paragraph 4 is closest in meaning to

   (A) cover
   (B) drain
   (C) warm
   (D) damage

7. Why does the author use the term "duck factory" in paragraph 4?

   (A) To point out that ducks are the region's main product for export
   (B) To emphasize the area's value as a breeding ground for ducks
   (C) To illustrate the tremendous growth of the poultry industry
   (D) To show that the potholes are important to the region's economy

8. What is the function of a carbon sink?

   (A) It regulates carbon emissions from human activities.
   (B) It measures the amount of carbon dioxide in the ecosystem.
   (C) It collects and drains seasonal rainwater from the soil.
   (D) It removes carbon dioxide naturally from the atmosphere.

9. The word this in paragraph 5 refers to

(A) the emission of carbon dioxide from cars, factories, and power plants
(B) the action of carbon dioxide as a greenhouse gas
(C) the capture and storage of carbon dioxide in trees, soil, and plants
(D) the average amount of carbon dioxide in one acre of land

10. What can be inferred from paragraph 5 about carbon sequestration in the prairie pothole region?

(A) It depends on the land not being disturbed by agriculture.
(B) It creates a beneficial habitat for many species of birds.
(C) It is a leading cause of the warming of the atmosphere.
(D) It exceeds the amount of carbon captured anywhere else.

11. The word offset in paragraph 5 is closest in meaning to

(A) preserve
(B) transform
(C) counteract
(D) measure

12. Look at the four squares, **A**, **B**, **C**, and **D**, which indicate where the following sentence could be added to the passage. Where would the sentence best fit?

Today, however, the original grassland associations of plants and animals have been almost completely destroyed by human settlement.

One hundred years ago, the Great Plains grasslands were one vast, unbroken prairie. **A** Much of the prairie is now farmland, the most productive agricultural region in the world, dominated by monocultures of cereal grains. **B** Wheat, barley, soybeans, corn, and sunflowers occupy the land that was once prairie. **C** In areas given over to grazing lands for cattle and sheep, virtually all the major native grasses have been replaced by alien species. **D**

13. Read the first sentence of a summary of the passage. Complete the summary by selecting the THREE answer choices that express the most important ideas in the passage. Some sentences do not belong in the summary because they express ideas that are not presented in the passage or are minor ideas in the passage. ***This question is worth 2 points.***

The grasslands of North America consist mainly of the prairies in the Great Plains.

•
•
•

Answer Choices

(A) Grasslands are found in the intermediate zone between dry desert and moist forest habitats.

(B) Most of the native prairie grasses have been replaced with cereal crops and grasses for grazing.

(C) Millions of glacial potholes that function as seasonal wetlands are an important feature of the region.

(D) Waterfowl such as northern pintails, mallards, coots, and pied–billed grebes live in the northern Great Plains.

(E) The prairie potholes have environmental value as a breeding ground for birds and as a potential carbon sink.

(F) Storing 400 million tons of carbon is the equivalent of removing 4 million cars from the road.

How to Score 2–Point Questions	
Answers Correct	**Points Earned**
3	2
2	1
0–1	0

POLITICAL SYSTEMS OF THE TWENTIETH CENTURY

1 Monarchy is a form of government in which authority is held by a single person, a monarch, whose right to rule is generally hereditary and lifelong. At the start of the twentieth century, monarchs ruled over most of the world, but by the middle of the century, only a handful remained. A series of revolutions in the preceding centuries had weakened the European monarchies, and while monarchs remained symbols of national unity, real power had passed to constitutional assemblies. Monarchy survived as a form in Europe only where the king or queen functioned as the symbolic head of a parliamentary state, as in Britain, the Low Countries, and Scandinavia. It lasted longer in the few small states of Asia and Africa that had never come under direct colonial rule. By the 1960s, **autocratic** monarchy had become an outdated form of government. Throughout most of the world, people were considered citizens, not subjects, and the totality of the people were seen as constituting the state.

2 In most states where monarchical authority was removed, some form of liberal democracy took its place. A liberal democracy is a state where political authority rests in the people acting through elected representatives and where an elected executive is responsible to the will of the people as a whole. The term applies to a broad group of states with a parliamentary or representative political tradition. Liberal democracies differ from the communist states known as people's democracies, in which the Communist party holds the ultimate authority. Generally, liberal democracies follow the parliamentary pattern, with the executive power vested in a cabinet responsible to the parliament and drawn from the majority party or combination of parties. In the United States, an independently elected executive, the president, functions separately from the legislative authority, the congress.

3 The doctrine that all of the people had effective authority, or sovereignty, became the basis for the functioning of democratic states. This doctrine of popular sovereignty became all–inclusive as citizenship rights were extended to classes formerly excluded and to women. The liberal democratic state claimed the right to control every aspect of human life according to the will of the people, except where limits on state control were directly stated in a bill of rights in a democratic constitution and recognized in practice.

4 All democratic states, both parliamentary and presidential, changed in form during the twentieth century. To meet the needs of an urban industrial society, states generally enlarged their scope of activity to control economic power and to provide common services to the people. The expansion of state activity and extension of state services involved a new view of legislation and its role in society. The passing of laws came to be seen as a way to promote the well being of the people. With this new concept of legislation, the number of new laws increased immensely, particularly in the areas of social welfare, education, health and safety, and economic development.

5 The trend toward liberal democracy continued throughout the century, but at various times there was also a tendency toward a revival of **authoritarian** rule. In a number of states, democratic governments could not cope with the crises of the time. In these cases, some form of totalitarian dictatorship emerged, replacing popular sovereignty with the total power of the state. In some instances, monarchy gave way directly to dictatorship. In others, dictatorial regimes took over democratically organized states, notably in Eastern Europe in the years between the two world wars, in new states of Asia and Africa in the 1950s, and sporadically in Central and South America.

6 Authoritarian governments showed three principle characteristics. First, there was a head of state or leader with exceptional powers, with a party to support him. Second, the legislative body was elected by a system that prohibited parties opposed to the regime, and third, there was a bureaucratic administration that was in no way subject to popular control. The most extreme position on these points was taken by Hitler's totalitarian National Socialist State in the 1930s.

Glossary:

autocratic: characterized by unlimited power
authoritarian: characterized by complete obedience to authority, lacking individual freedom

14. What point does the author make about monarchs in the twentieth century?

(A) Monarchs did not allow the people to vote in democratic elections.
(B) Monarchs did not have real power but were symbols of national unity.
(C) The monarch in most countries was a king rather than a queen.
(D) Monarchs were responsible for starting many popular revolutions.

15. The word survived in paragraph 1 is closest in meaning to

(A) remained
(B) developed
(C) changed
(D) returned

16. The phrase The term in paragraph 2 refers to

(A) monarchical authority
(B) liberal democracy
(C) will of the people
(D) communist

17. Why does the author mention people's democracies in paragraph 2?

(A) To contrast two concepts of where political authority rests
(B) To suggest that people's democracies originated in liberal democracies
(C) To explain differences between one–party and two–party systems
(D) To describe the parliamentary system of people's democracies

18. The word pattern in paragraph 2 is closest in meaning to

(A) choice
(B) party
(C) model
(D) purpose

19. According to the passage, which of the following is a limit on state control in a liberal democracy?

(A) A cabinet drawn from the majority party
(B) The existence of only one political party
(C) An independently elected executive
(D) A bill of rights stated in a constitution

20. According to the passage, what is one way in which every democratic state changed during the twentieth century?

(A) An authoritarian regime replaced the democratic institutions.
(B) The executive's power became stronger than that of the parliament.
(C) State–run bureaucracies came under the control of the majority party.
(D) State activity expanded to promote the well being of the people.

21. Which sentence below best expresses the essential information in the highlighted sentence in paragraph 5? Incorrect choices change the meaning in important ways or leave out essential information.

(A) Dictatorships were more popular in countries where the majority of people wanted the state to have total power.
(B) In a totalitarian dictatorship, the government replaced authoritarian rule with popular sovereignty.
(C) Totalitarian dictatorships took over some democracies with the idea that the state, not the people, held all power.
(D) Some dictatorships gave the state total authority to rule, while others maintained the concept of popular sovereignty.

22. According to the passage, all of the following are characteristics of authoritarian governments EXCEPT

(A) the absence of political parties opposed to the regime
(B) the authority of the people through elected representatives
(C) a leader with a great amount of power
(D) an administration that does not answer to the people

23. It can be inferred from the passage that the author most likely believes which of the following statements about political systems in the twentieth century?

(A) There was a general movement away from monarchy toward democracy, with some cases of authoritarian rule.
(B) The ultimate purpose of many dictatorships was the development of effective democracy.
(C) Authoritarian governments are more likely to emerge in countries that had previously been ruled by a monarch.
(D) There are more similarities than differences between liberal democracies and people's democracies.

24. Look at the four squares, [A], [B], [C], and [D], which indicate where the following sentence could be added to the passage. Where would the sentence best fit?

The British Parliament, for example, passed more laws in the first half of the twentieth century than in all its previous history.

[A] All democratic states, both parliamentary and presidential, changed in form during the twentieth century. [B] To meet the needs of an urban industrial society, states generally enlarged their scope of activity to control economic power and to provide common services to the people. The expansion of state activity and extension of state services involved a new view of legislation and its role in society. The passing of laws came to be seen as a way to promote the well being of the people. [C] With this new concept of legislation, the number of new laws increased immensely, particularly in the areas of social welfare, education, health and safety, and economic development. [D]

25. Select the appropriate sentences from the answer choices and match them to the type of government that they describe. TWO of the answer choices will NOT be used. ***This question is worth 3 points.***

Answer Choices

(A) The leader's authority to rule is usually hereditary and lifelong.
(B) An elected executive is responsible to the will of the people as a whole.
(C) Every political unit is subject to the control of the unit just above it.
(D) A powerful leader and party have total control of the government.
(E) In some places, the ruler is the symbolic head of a parliamentary state.
(F) Government is based on a belief in popular sovereignty.
(G) Private corporations make up the bureaucratic administration.

Monarchy

-
-

Liberal Democracy

-
-

Dictatorship

-

How to Score 3–Point Questions	
Answers Correct	**Points Earned**
5	3
4	2
3	1
0–2	0

THE SENSE OF SMELL

1 Smell is the most direct of all the senses. It is thought to be the oldest sense in terms of human evolution, which may explain why smell is hard–wired into the brain. The olfactory nerve, which manages the perception of smells, is essentially an extension of the brain. The olfactory nerve provides a direct link from receptors at the top of the nose to the portion of the brain that controls memory, emotion, and behavior.

2 The olfactory system detects certain airborne chemicals that enter the nose and then transmits this chemical information to the limbic system in the brain. The olfactory region at the upper end of each nostril is yellow, moist, and full of fatty substances. The shade of yellow indicates the strength of the sense of smell: the deeper the shade, the keener and more acute it is. Animals have a very strong sense of smell, so their olfactory regions are dark yellow to reddish brown, while those of humans are light yellow.

3 When an odorous substance enters the nose, it binds to olfactory receptor cells, the neurons lining the yellow upper portion of the nasal cavity. Olfactory receptor cells contain microscopic hairs called cilia that extend into the layer of mucus coating the inside of the nose. Odor molecules diffuse into this region and are absorbed by the cilia of the olfactory receptor cells. What this means is that when we hold a rose to our nose and inhale, odor molecules float up into the nasal cavity, where they are absorbed by five million olfactory receptor cells. The receptor cells alert the olfactory nerve, which sends impulses to the brain's olfactory bulb, or smell center. Thus, olfactory information about the rose enters the brain's limbic system, where, in most of us, it stimulates a feeling of pleasure.

4 The limbic system of the brain integrates memory, emotion, and behavior. The system is composed of a group of related nervous system structures that are the functional center of emotions such as anger, fear, pleasure, and sadness. The components of the limbic system are linked to the cerebral cortex, the part of the brain involved in complex learning, reasoning, and personality. The cerebral cortex makes decisions about the emotional content of these unique human qualities after "consulting" the limbic system and other brain centers in processing and retrieving memories. It may, in turn, use memories to modify behavior.

5 Scent may be the strongest trigger of memory and emotions. When we inhale a scent, receptors in the brain's limbic center compare the odor entering our nose to odors stored in our memory. Along the way, memories associated with those odors are stimulated. A smell can be overwhelmingly **nostalgic** because it triggers powerful images and emotions. The waxy fragrance of crayons can instantly transport us to our second–grade classroom, or the scent of freshly mown grass can flood us with the joy of summer freedom. What we see and hear may fade quickly in short–term memory, but what we smell is sent directly to long–term memory.

6 Smells can increase alertness and stimulate learning and **retention**. In one study, children memorized a word list, which was presented both with and without accompanying scents. The children recalled words on the list more easily and with higher accuracy when the list was given with scents than without, showing the link between smell and the ability to retain information. In another study, researchers examined how various smells can increase alertness and decrease stress. They found that the scent of lavender could wake up the metabolism and make people more alert. They also found that the smell of spiced apples could reduce blood pressure and avert a panic attack in people under stress.

Glossary:

nostalgic: causing a desire for things, persons, or situations of the past; causing homesickness
retention: the act of retaining; keeping, holding, or maintaining

26. Why does the author use the term hard–wired in describing the sense of smell and the brain?

(A) To describe the texture and feel of the olfactory nerve
(B) To emphasize the close connection between smell and the brain
(C) To compare the power of smell with that of other senses
(D) To explain how the sense of smell evolved in early humans

27. The word detects in paragraph 2 is closest in meaning to

(A) notices
(B) destroys
(C) fights
(D) compares

28. Of what significance is the color of the olfactory region at the upper end of each nostril?

(A) The color changes with different airborne chemicals.
(B) The significance of the color is little understood.
(C) The color becomes darker when an odor is present.
(D) The color shows the strength of the ability to smell.

29. The word diffuse in paragraph 3 is closest in meaning to

(A) drop
(B) flow
(C) cut
(D) bend

30. What happens when the cilia of the olfactory receptor cells absorb odor molecules?

(A) The tiny hairs inside the nose become darker in color.
(B) The nervous system activates the digestive system.
(C) The olfactory nerve sends impulses to the brain.
(D) Some receptor cells die and are replaced by new cells.

31. The word integrates in paragraph 4 is closest in meaning to

(A) predicts
(B) connects
(C) damages
(D) slows

32. When a scent is inhaled, all of the following occur in the limbic system EXCEPT

(A) The scent is compared to other scents stored in memory.
(B) The scent is transmitted to the other sensory organs.
(C) The brain stimulates memories associated with the scents.
(D) The person may feel an emotion related to a memory.

33. Why does the author mention crayons and freshly mown grass in paragraph 5?

(A) To give examples of smells that can trigger memories and emotions
(B) To compare typical responses to two common smells
(C) To explain why smells are likely to affect a person's behavior
(D) To identify smells that can increase alertness and work efficiency

34. Which sentence below best expresses the essential information in the highlighted sentence in paragraph 5? Incorrect choices change the meaning in important ways or leave out essential information.

(A) We can accurately remember things that we see and hear, but we eventually forget things that we smell.
(B) Short–term memory contains unimportant information, and long–term memory contains sensory information.
(C) Smells go straight to long–term memory, while sights and sounds may be held only briefly.
(D) It is difficult for us to use short–term memory, but we remember things in long–term memory.

35. The word which in paragraph 6 refers to

(A) learning
(B) study
(C) list
(D) smell

36. What can be inferred from paragraph 6 about learning?

(A) Learning cannot take place unless all of the senses are stimulated.
(B) Scents can strengthen the ability to hold new information in the memory.
(C) It is easier to recall previous learning than it is to retain new information.
(D) Children will not learn much if they are distracted by offensive odors.

37. Look at the four squares, [A], [B], [C], and [D], which indicate where the following sentence could be added to the passage. Where would the sentence best fit?

One of these structures is a kind of central processing unit that connects memory with physical functions.

The limbic system of the brain integrates memory, emotion, and behavior. The system is composed of a group of related nervous system structures that are the functional center of emotions such as anger, fear, pleasure, and sadness. [A] The components of the limbic system are linked to the cerebral cortex, the part of the brain involved in complex learning, reasoning, and personality. [B] The cerebral cortex makes decisions about the emotional content of these unique human qualities after "consulting" the limbic system and other brain centers in processing and retrieving memories. [C] It may, in turn, use memories to modify behavior. [D]

38. Read the first sentence of a summary of the passage. Complete the summary by selecting the THREE answer choices that express the most important ideas in the passage. Some sentences do not belong in the summary because they express ideas that are not presented in the passage or are minor ideas in the passage. ***This question is worth 2 points.***

Smell, the oldest and most direct of all the senses, is connected with memory and emotions.

•
•
•

Answer Choices

(A) Every time we inhale, airborne chemicals enter the olfactory regions of our nose.

(B) The olfactory nerve links the nose to the part of the brain that integrates memory, emotion, and behavior.

(C) The brain's limbic center stimulates memories and emotions associated with a particular scent.

(D) The sense of smell is stronger in animals than it is in humans.

(E) Olfactory receptor cells contain microscopic hairs called cilia that absorb odor molecules.

(F) Smells can trigger emotions, increase alertness, and impr e the ability to learn.

How to Score 2–Point Questions	
Answers Correct	**Points Earned**
3	2
2	1
0–1	0

THE TRICKSTER FIGURE IN MYTHOLOGY

1 In the study of mythology, the character known as the trickster is a god, spirit, human, or animal who breaks the rules of the gods or nature, sometimes maliciously but usually with results that are positive. The rule breaking often takes the form of **mischief** or **thievery**. The trickster is usually male but occasionally disguises himself in female form. He can be cunning or foolish, or both, and often very humorous. His curiosity leads him into trouble, but he rescues himself with his sly wit. When he plays tricks, he performs important cultural tasks that benefit humans, and for this reason the trickster is a significant figure in world mythology.

2 In different cultures, the trickster and the hero are combined in various ways. In Greek mythology, Prometheus steals fire from the gods and gives it to humans, a feat making him more of a hero than a trickster, and he is usually portrayed as an intellectual. In many Native American stories, Coyote also steals fire from the gods, but Coyote is usually more of a jokester or a prankster than an intellectual.

3 The trickster is both creator and destroyer, giver and taker, one who tricks others and is tricked in return. The pranks of the trickster are compulsive and uncontrollable. He does not act consciously; he acts out of passion and impulse. He knows neither good nor evil, yet he is responsible for both. He possesses no morals, yet through his behavior morality comes into being. According to psychologist Carl Jung, the trickster is "a primitive cosmic being of divine–animal nature, on the one hand superior to man because of his superhuman qualities, and on the other hand inferior to him because of his unreason and unconsciousness."

4 In Native American mythology, the majority of trickster myths concern the creation or transformation of the earth. Such stories have a trickster who is always wandering, who is always hungry, who is not guided by normal ideas of good and evil, and who possesses some magical powers. In some stories he is a deity, and in others he is an animal or human subject to death. Several of these myths feature Raven or Coyote as the trickster–hero.

5 In many creation myths of the Pacific Northwest, Raven illustrates the transformational nature of tricksters. Raven is the greatest shapeshifter of all and can change into anything to get what he wants. In one story, there is darkness at the beginning of the world, so Raven decides he will find light. He flies far from the earth, searching in the darkness, until he spots a glimmer of light coming from a window in the house of the gods. Raven knows the gods are protective of their possessions, so he devises a trick. He perches on a pine branch next to the house and watches each day as the chief god's daughter draws water from a nearby lake. He magically transforms himself into a **pinyon seed** and falls into the girl's drinking cup. The girl swallows the seed, which grows within her body, and she eventually gives birth to a boy. The child delights his grandparents, and his laughter tricks the elder gods into revealing where they hide a shining ball of light. The gods give the child the ball to play with, and then Raven transforms back to a bird and flies off carrying the ball of light in his beak. He hangs the ball—the sun—in the sky, bringing light to the world.

6 Coyote's character is similar to that of Raven's, and both appear in stories carrying out similar roles. In several stories from the American Southwest, Coyote steals fire from a group of "fire beings" and gives it to humans. In some tales Coyote wants to make human life more interesting, so he introduces sickness, sorrow, and death. He often teaches through negative example by employing the human vices of lying, cheating, and stealing. His tricks often bring about destructive natural phenomena, such as a great flood that destroys the earth. However, by causing the flood, Coyote leads the human race to a new and better world. Coyote shows us that at the heart of the trickster is a savior whose great gift to humans is showing them new ways of knowing and doing.

Glossary:

mischief: tendency to play tricks or cause minor trouble
thievery: the act of theft; stealing
pinyon seed: the seed of a pine tree; pine nut

39. The word maliciously in paragraph 1 is closest in meaning to

(A) destructively
(B) falsely
(C) bravely
(D) mistakenly

40. Which sentence below best expresses the essential information in the highlighted sentence in paragraph 1? Incorrect choices change the meaning in important ways or leave out essential information.

(A) In world mythology, every important aspect of human culture is the result of the trickster's behavior.
(B) The trickster develops human culture by tricking people into performing dangerous cultural tasks.
(C) When the trickster wants to be helpful, he devises a trick that will teach people what is important.
(D) The trickster is an important mythological character because his tricks contribute positively to human culture.

41. The author discusses Prometheus and Coyote in paragraph 2 in order to

(A) illustrate two different views of the trickster–hero
(B) explain how humans received the gift of fire
(C) argue that the trickster is an intellectual hero
(D) encourage readers to study world mythology

42. The word pranks in paragraph 3 is closest in meaning to

(A) funny stories
(B) complex plans
(C) mischievous acts
(D) divine traits

43. The word both in paragraph 3 refers to

(A) creator and destroyer
(B) passion and impulse
(C) good and evil
(D) morals and morality

44. All of the following are traits of the trickster EXCEPT

(A) a desire to break the rules
(B) the ability to disguise himself
(C) superhuman powers
(D) awareness of good and evil

45. Native American stories with a trickster–hero are usually about

(A) the victory of good over evil
(B) the creation or transformation of the world
(C) the struggle to control one's nature
(D) the punishment of humans by the gods

46. The author tells a story about Raven in which the trickster

(A) gives humans the gift of fire
(B) changes into a young girl
(C) steals the sun from the gods
(D) causes a destructive flood

47. The word savior in paragraph 6 is closest in meaning to

(A) one who wants total power
(B) one who rescues others from harm
(C) one who causes terrible suffering
(D) one who cares about only himself

48. It can be inferred from the passage that the author most likely believes which statement about the trickster?

(A) The trickster is responsible for many serious problems in the world today.
(B) The trickster shows us that there is no difference between good and evil.
(C) The trickster serves as an explanation for creation, change and renewal.
(D) The trickster teaches children that lying and stealing are acceptable behavior.

49. Look at the four squares, [A], [B], [C], and [D], which indicate where the following sentence could be added to the passage. Where would the sentence best fit?

Like Raven, Coyote is a master transformer whose mischievous power is responsible for events that benefit humanity.

Coyote's character is similar to that of Raven's, and both appear in stories carrying out similar roles. [A] In several stories from the American Southwest, Coyote steals fire from a group of "fire beings" and gives it to humans. In some tales Coyote wants to make human life more interesting, so he introduces sickness, sorrow, and death. [B] He often teaches through negative example by employing the human vices of lying, cheating, and stealing. [C] His tricks often bring about destructive natural phenomena, such as a great flood that destroys the earth. However, by causing the flood, Coyote leads the human race to a new and better world. [D] Coyote shows us that at the heart of the trickster is a savior whose great gift to humans is showing them new ways of knowing and doing.

50. Select the appropriate phrases from the answer choices and match them to the trickster that they describe. TWO of the answer choices will NOT be used. ***This question is worth 3 points.***

Answer Choices

(A) Introduces sickness, sorrow, and death to make life more interesting
(B) Transforms into various shapes to achieve his purposes
(C) Appears as an intellectual hero in stories of good and evil
(D) Creates a ball of silver light that becomes the moon
(E) Changes into a seed to gain entrance to the house of the gods
(F) Causes a great flood and then leads humans to a better world
(G) Brings light to the world by playing a trick on the gods

Raven
•
•
•

Coyote
•
•

How to Score 3–Point Questions	
Answers Correct	**Points Earned**
5	3
4	2
3	1
0–2	0

THE DOMESTICATION OF ANIMALS

1 The domestication of wild species led directly to denser human populations by yielding more food than the hunter–gatherer lifestyle could provide. In societies that possessed domestic animals, livestock helped to feed more people by providing meat, milk, and fertilizer, and by pulling plows. Large domestic animals became the societies' main source of animal protein, replacing wild game, and they also furnished wool, leather, and land transport. Humans have domesticated only a few species of large animals, with "large" defined as those weighing over 100 pounds (45 kilograms). Fourteen such species were domesticated before the twentieth century, all of them **terrestrial** mammals and **herbivores**. The five most important of these are sheep, goats, pigs, horses, and cattle or oxen.

2 Small animals such as ducks, geese, rabbits, dogs, cats, mink, bees, and silkworms have also been domesticated. Many of these small animals provided food, clothing, or warmth. However, none of them pulled plows or wagons, none carried riders, and none except dogs pulled sleds. Furthermore, no small domestic animals have been as important for food as have large domestic animals.

3 Early herding societies quickly domesticated all large mammal species that were suitable for domestication. There is archaeological evidence that these species were domesticated between 10,000 and 4,500 years ago, within the first few thousand years of the origins of farming–herding societies after the last Ice Age. The continent of Eurasia has been the primary site of large mammal domestication. Having the most species of wild mammals to begin with, and losing the fewest to extinction in the last 40,000 years, Eurasia has generated the most candidates for domestication.

4 Domestication involves transforming wild animals into something more useful to humans. Truly domesticated animals differ in many ways from their wild ancestors. These differences result from two processes: human selection of individual animals that are more useful to humans than other individuals of the same species, and evolutionary responses of animals to the forces of natural selection operating in human environments rather than in wild environments.

5 To be domesticated, a wild species must possess several characteristics. A candidate for domestication must be primarily a herbivore because it takes less plant biomass to feed a plant eater than it does to feed a carnivore that consumes plant eaters. No carnivorous mammal has ever been domesticated for food simply because it would be too costly. A candidate must not only weigh an average of over 100 pounds but also grow quickly. That eliminates gorillas and elephants, even though they are herbivores. Moreover, candidates for domestication must be able to breed successfully in captivity.

6 Since almost any sufficiently large mammal species is capable of killing a human, certain qualities disqualify a wild animal for domestication. The animal cannot have a disposition that is nasty, dangerous, or unpredictable—characteristics that eliminate bears, African buffaloes, and some species of wild horses. The animal cannot be so nervous that it panics around humans. Large herbivorous mammal species react to danger from predators or humans in different ways. Some species are nervous, fast, and programmed for instant flight when they perceive danger. Others are less nervous, seek protection in herds, and do not run until necessary. Most species of deer and antelope are of the former type, while sheep and goats are of the latter.

7 Almost all domesticated large mammals are species whose wild ancestors share three social characteristics: living in a herd, maintaining a dominance hierarchy in the herd, and having herds that occupy overlapping home ranges instead of mutually exclusive territories. Humans have taken advantage of these characteristics in keeping domestic animals together with others of their species and in close proximity to other species of domestic animals.

Glossary:

terrestrial: living on land rather than in water
herbivores: animals that feed mainly on plants

51. The word furnished in paragraph 1 is closest in meaning to

(A) demanded
(B) invented
(C) provided
(D) changed

52. According to the passage, what benefit of large domestic animals is not also provided by small animals?

(A) A source of food
(B) A source of clothing
(C) The ability to pull a plow
(D) The ability to be ridden

53. Which of the following can be inferred about large mammal species?

(A) Relatively few species have the necessary characteristics for domestication.
(B) More species of large mammals are domesticated as pets than for food.
(C) Only a few large terrestrial mammal species are primarily herbivores.
(D) All large mammals can be classified into one of five important groups.

54. According to the passage, when did early humans domesticate all suitable large mammal species?

(A) After humans had populated every continent
(B) Before the Ice Age caused many animals to become extinct
(C) At the same time they domesticated small animals
(D) Within a few thousand years after farming and herding began

55. According to the passage, what is one reason that domesticated animals differ from their wild ancestors?

(A) Wild animals find food easily, but domesticated animals must work for food.
(B) Domesticated animals live near humans, so they forget their wild ancestors.
(C) Animals' evolutionary responses in captivity differ from those in the wild.
(D) More animals survive in human environments than in wild environments.

56. Which sentence below best expresses the essential information in the highlighted sentence in paragraph 5? Incorrect choices change the meaning in important ways or leave out essential information.

(A) Plant food is less expensive than meat, which explains why plant–eating animals are perfect candidates for domestication.
(B) Herbivorous animals are likely to be domesticated because they eat less plant matter than what carnivores consume indirectly.
(C) Domesticated animals are primarily plant eaters, but most wild animals are carnivores that feed on other animals.
(D) It is more difficult and costly to domesticate carnivores than to domesticate herbivores because carnivores are more dangerous.

57. Why does the author mention gorillas and elephants in paragraph 5?

(A) To suggest that some overlooked animals could be domesticated
(B) To illustrate the wide variety among large herbivores
(C) To identify animals intelligent enough to avoid domestication
(D) To give examples of animals that grow too slowly for domestication

58. The word disqualify in paragraph 6 is closest in meaning to

(A) identify
(B) display
(C) reject
(D) punish

59. The word panics in paragraph 6 is closest in meaning to

(A) feels terror
(B) refuses to eat
(C) attacks others
(D) becomes ill

60. What can be inferred from paragraph 6 about deer and antelope?

(A) They run away from humans only if threatened.
(B) They do not supply meat of a consistent quality.
(C) They are as dangerous as certain wild horses.
(D) They have not successfully been domesticated.

61. All of the following are characteristics favorable to domestication EXCEPT

(A) weighing over 100 pounds
(B) unpredictable behavior
(C) ability to breed in captivity
(D) living in a herd with a hierarchy

62. Look at the four squares, [A], [B], [C], and [D], which indicate where the following sentence could be added to the passage. Where would the sentence best fit?

Eurasia is a huge, ecologically diverse landmass, and therefore has a great many large mammal species.

Early herding societies quickly domesticated all large mammal species that were suitable for domestication. [A] There is archaeological evidence that these species were domesticated between 10,000 and 4,500 years ago, within the first few thousand years of the origins of farming–herding societies after the last Ice Age. [B] The continent of Eurasia has been the primary site of large mammal domestication. [C] Having the most species of wild mammals to begin with, and losing the fewest to extinction in the last 40,000 years, Eurasia has generated the most candidates for domestication. [D]

63. Read the first sentence of a summary of the passage. Complete the summary by selecting the THREE answer choices that express the most important ideas in the passage. Some sentences do not belong in the summary because they express ideas that are not presented in the passage or are minor ideas in the passage. ***This question is worth 2 points.***

The domestication of animals provided humans with food, clothing, and other benefits.

•
•
•

Answer Choices

(A) The most important domestic animals are large herbivorous mammals that live in herds.

(B) Ducks, geese, rabbits, dogs, cats, and many other small animals have been domesticated.

(C) Although herbivores eat mainly plant matter, some species occasionally eat small animals.

(D) Humans quickly domesticated all large mammal species that were suitable for domestication.

(E) Animals must have several essential characteristics in order to be domesticated successfully.

(F) Large herbivorous mammals respond in various ways when threatened by predators.

How to Score 2–Point Questions	
Answers Correct	**Points Earned**
3	2
2	1
0–1	0

Answers are on page 291.

Record your Reading section score on page 380.

Disk 1, Track 1

LISTENING SECTION DIRECTIONS

The Listening section measures your ability to understand conversations and lectures in English. You will hear each conversation and lecture only one time. After each conversation or lecture, you will hear some questions about it. Answer the questions based on what the speakers state or imply.

You may take notes while you listen. You may use your notes to help you answer the questions.

In some questions, you will see this icon: . This means that you will hear, but not see, part of the question.

Some questions have special directions, which appear in a gray box. Most questions are worth one point. If a question is worth more than one point, the directions will indicate how many points you can receive.

You will now begin the first part of the Listening section.

Time – maximum of 60 minutes

Disk 1, Track 2

QUESTIONS 1–5

Conversation

1. What problem does the man have?

   (A) He does not know where to register for classes.
   (B) His dog was poisoned by something it ate.
   (C) He does not know what type of transcript to order.
   (D) He needs to replace his identification card.

2. Why does the man talk about his dog?

   (A) His dog enjoys visiting the campus.
   (B) He needs to buy special food for his dog.
   (C) His dog destroyed his student ID card.
   (D) He is worried about his dog's health.

3. Listen again to part of the conversation. Then answer the question.

   What can be inferred about riding the bus?

   (A) Dogs are not allowed to ride the bus.
   (B) There is no bus fare if you have a student ID.
   (C) All students are required to ride the bus.
   (D) The man does not like riding the bus.

4. What is one difference between an unofficial transcript and an official transcript?

   (A) An unofficial transcript can be obtained free of charge.
   (B) An unofficial transcript includes less information.
   (C) An unofficial transcript takes five days to receive.
   (D) An unofficial transcript can be used for a scholarship.

5. What will the man probably do?

   Click on two answers.

   [A] Have his picture taken in the photo shop
   [B] Take his dog to the animal hospital
   [C] Print an unofficial copy of his transcript
   [D] Request an official copy of his transcript

Disk 1, Track 3

QUESTIONS 6–11

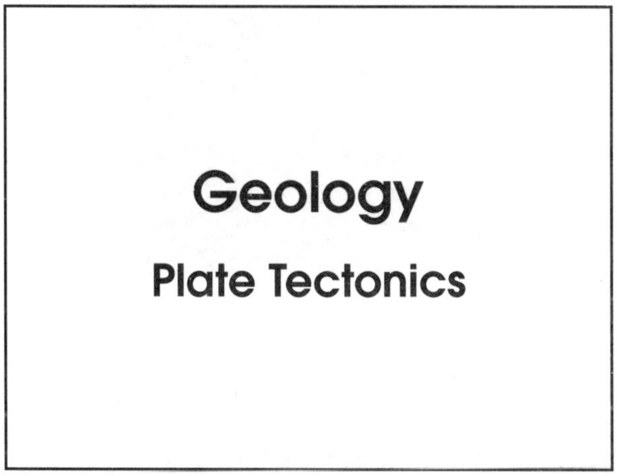

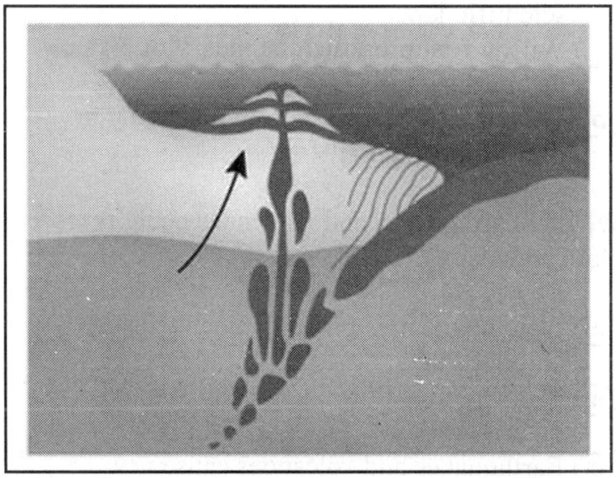

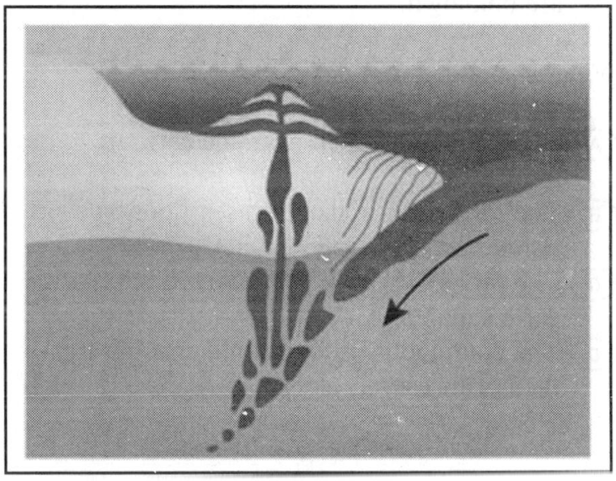

6. Why does the professor talk about Tuzo Wilson?

(A) Wilson developed a warning system for earthquakes.
(B) Wilson wrote an article that contradicted scientific law.
(C) Wilson first proposed the theory of plate tectonics.
(D) Wilson discovered sea floor spreading in the North Atlantic.

7. Why do earthquakes and volcanoes occur at plate boundaries?

(A) Plate boundaries undergo much tension and friction.
(B) Temperatures fluctuate greatly at plate boundaries.
(C) Earthquakes and volcanoes cause new plates to form.
(D) The causes of earthquakes and volcanoes are unknown.

8. What is subduction?

(A) The eruption of rock from the earth in molten form
(B) The formation of the deep sea floor by rising lava
(C) The process of rock being forced into the earth's mantle
(D) The continuous drift of continents toward the northwest

9. Identify the area in the diagram where subduction occurs.

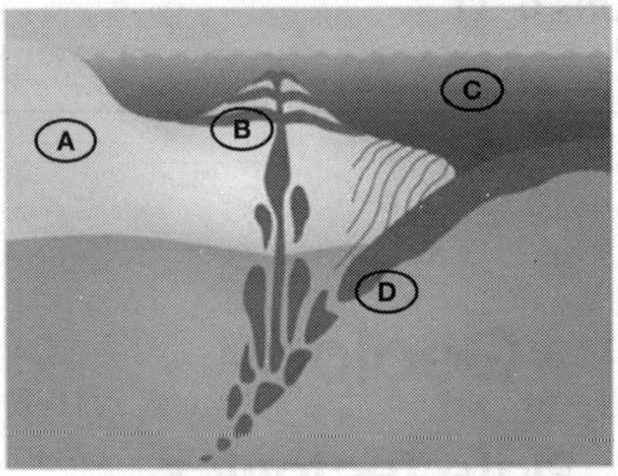

10. Listen again to part of the lecture. Then answer the question.

Why does the professor ask this:

(A) To test the students' understanding of plate tectonics
(B) To describe an event that confuses many scientists
(C) To point out a theory that has never been confirmed
(D) To introduce a phenomenon that he intends to explain

11. Which of the following are associated with subduction zones?

Click on two answers.

[A] The pollution of the sea floor
[B] Chains of volcanic islands
[C] The sliding of one plate under another
[D] Frequent thunderstorms and tornadoes

Disk 1, Track 4

QUESTIONS 12–17

12. What is the main purpose of the talk?

(A) To explain why anthropologists study the home
(B) To describe how early people built shelters
(C) To trace the evolution of home design
(D) To evaluate various home–building materials

13. The professor briefly describes developments in home building. Put the developments in the order in which they occurred.

Drag each answer to the space where it belongs.

(A) Round structure built of stone
(B) Building with multiple living units
(C) Round hut made of branches and leaves
(D) Box–shaped structure with four walls

1	
2	
3	
4	

14. According to the professor, why was the box shape a major development in home building?

(A) It was easier to build than the round shape.
(B) It led to the invention of the window.
(C) It could be built in a shorter length of time.
(D) It allowed rooms to be joined to one another.

15. According to the professor, what ancient features still exist in the homes of today?

Click on two answers.

[A] Hallway
[B] Outer boundary
[C] Garden
[D] Round window

16. Why does the professor say this: 🎧

(A) To illustrate the social importance of the hallway
(B) To explain how walls determine who may enter a room
(C) To point out that homes are larger than in the past
(D) To describe the flow of traffic in the typical home

17. What does the professor imply about the rooms inside the homes of today?

(A) They have the same functions as those in ancient homes.
(B) They are more often round than box–shaped.
(C) They are arranged to progress from public to private.
(D) They are forbidden to any person outside the family.

Disk 1, Track 5

QUESTIONS 18–22

Conversation

Oral Report

18. What are the students mainly discussing?

(A) Statistics about major diseases
(B) Symptoms of influenza infection
(C) A major epidemic of influenza
(D) Different strains of the flu virus

19. Why does the woman mention her great–grandfather?

(A) Her great–grandfather died during a major epidemic.
(B) Her great–grandfather worked in the field of public health.
(C) Her great–grandfather was affected by the 1918 epidemic.
(D) Her great–grandfather was a soldier in World War I.

20. According to the man, what group first reported large numbers of influenza cases?

(A) Business owners
(B) The army
(C) Public health officials
(D) Public schools

21. What information will the students probably include in their report?

Click on two answers.

[A] Statistics on other major disease epidemics
[B] Effects of war on the general population
[C] Arguments for developing a better public health system
[D] The connection between World War I and influenza

22. What do the students agree to do?

(A) Ask their professor for advice
(B) Meet again to discuss their research
(C) Interview people who survived the flu
(D) Change the topic of their oral report

Disk 1, Track 6

QUESTIONS 23–28

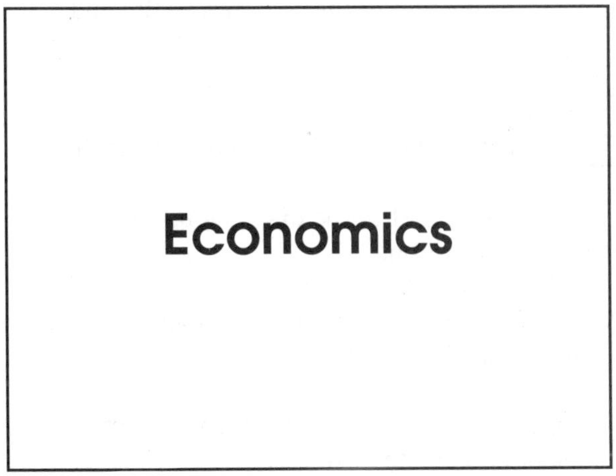

23. What is the discussion mainly about?

(A) The history of large corporations
(B) The regulation of business by government
(C) Why corporations have so much power
(D) Ways that governments spend money

24. Why do the students say this: 🎧

(A) To recommend against buying stock in a corporation
(B) To explain why consumers need to be very cautious
(C) To give reasons why governments regulate corporations
(D) To complain about negative trends in advertising

25. According to the discussion, governments influence economic activity through which methods?

Click on two answers.

[A] Taxation
[B] Elections
[C] Spending
[D] Diplomacy

26. Listen again to part of the discussion. Then answer the question.

Why does the professor say this: 🎧

(A) To state his opinion about the role of government
(B) To describe a controversial government policy
(C) To show that corporations have political power
(D) To explain the origins of government regulation

27. According to the professor, what is the function of social regulation?

(A) The control of social activities in a corporation
(B) The protection of the society's health and safety
(C) The restriction of competition among businesses
(D) The establishment of the school curriculum

28. Listen again to part of the discussion. Then answer the question.

What can be inferred about government regulation of business?

(A) Many people agree that the government should regulate business.
(B) Capitalism does not succeed if there is government regulation.
(C) Attitudes about regulation have changed very little in a century.
(D) The government has no right to control how businesses operate.

Disk 1, Track 7

QUESTIONS 29–34

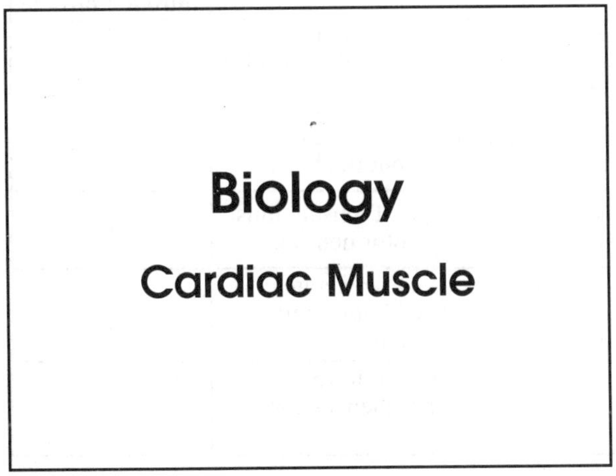

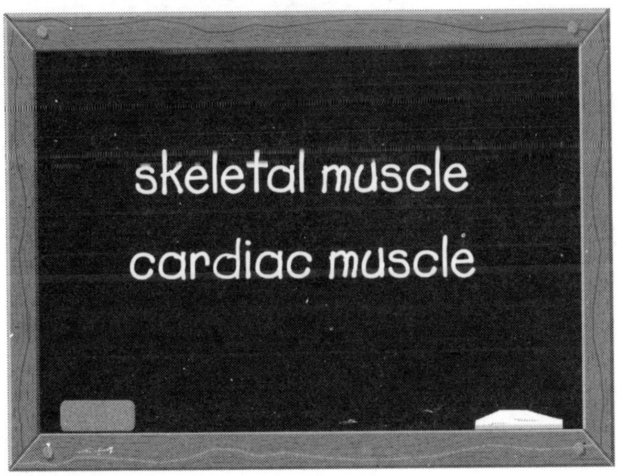

29. How does the professor develop the topic of cardiac muscle?

    (A) By describing evolutionary changes in cardiac muscle
    (B) By classifying the types of muscle in the body
    (C) By explaining what happens if the heart stops beating
    (D) By comparing cardiac muscle and skeletal muscle

30. Why does the professor say this:

    (A) To introduce the topic of cardiac muscle
    (B) To find out how much the students already know
    (C) To tell the students what will be on the next test
    (D) To point out a question that has no clear answer

31. Why does the professor say this:

    (A) To correct one of her previous statements
    (B) To make sure the students are paying attention
    (C) To review material the class has already studied
    (D) To give the students time to write down what she says

32. Based on the information in the lecture, indicate whether each sentence below describes skeletal muscle or cardiac muscle.

    For each sentence, click in the correct box.

	Skeletal muscle	**Cardiac muscle**
These muscles are connected to the bones, which move when the muscles contract.		
When this type of muscle contracts, blood moves throughout the body.		
To contract, this type of muscle must be stimulated by a motor neuron.		
These muscle cells can generate electrical impulses without input from the nervous system.		
This muscle cannot stop to rest without serious consequences for the body.		

33. What happens when an electrical impulse generated in one part of the heart spreads to all the cardiac muscle cells?

    (A) The impulse spreads to the bones.
    (B) The cardiac muscles extend.
    (C) The heart beats faster.
    (D) The whole heart contracts.

34. Listen again to part of the lecture. Then answer the question.

    What can be inferred about the contraction of cardiac muscle?

    (A) Cardiac muscle contracts automatically because it contains motor neurons.
    (B) The contraction depends on the action of sodium, calcium, and potassium.
    (C) The nervous system tells cardiac muscle cells when to contract.
    (D) Cardiac muscle cells will live for several weeks in a laboratory dish.

Stop

Answers are on page 295.

Record your Listening section score on page 381.

Disk 1, Track 8

SPEAKING SECTION DIRECTIONS

The Speaking section measures your ability to speak in English about a variety of topics. There are six questions in this section.

Questions 1 and 2 are independent tasks in which you will speak about familiar topics. Your responses will be scored on your ability to speak clearly and coherently about the topics.

Questions 3 and 4 are integrated speaking tasks. You will read a passage, listen to a conversation or lecture, and then speak in response to a question about what you have read and heard. You will need to combine relevant information from the two sources to answer the question completely. Your responses will be scored on your ability to speak clearly and coherently and on your ability to accurately convey information about what you read and heard.

Questions 5 and 6 are integrated speaking tasks. You will listen to part of a conversation or lecture, and then speak in response to a question about what you have heard. Your responses will be scored on your ability to speak clearly and coherently and on your ability to accurately convey information about what you heard.

You will hear each conversation and lecture only one time. You may take notes while you listen. You may use your notes to help you answer the questions.

Stop

QUESTION 1

In this question, you will be asked to talk about a familiar topic. After you hear the question, you will have 15 seconds to prepare your response and 45 seconds to speak.

Disk 1, Track 9

Describe the qualities of a good teacher and explain why these qualities are effective. Include details and examples to support your explanation.

Stop

Preparation Time – 15 seconds
Response Time – 45 seconds

QUESTION 2

In this question, you will be asked to give your opinion about a familiar topic. After you hear the question, you will have 15 seconds to prepare your response and 45 seconds to speak.

Disk 1, Track 10

Some people like to cook their own meals at home. Others prefer to eat in a restaurant or a cafeteria. Which do you prefer and why? Include details and examples in your explanation.

Stop

Preparation Time – 15 seconds
Response Time – 45 seconds

QUESTION 3

In this question, you will read a short passage about a campus situation, listen to a conversation, and then speak in response to a question about what you have read and heard. After you hear the question, you have 30 seconds to prepare your response and 60 seconds to speak.

Reading Time – 45 seconds

PARKING ON CAMPUS

A permit is required for all students who park a vehicle on the main campus during the day or evening, Monday through Friday. Parking permits can be purchased from the Cashier's Office and picked up at the Security Office on the first floor of Building 21. Students must park in the new parking lot near the east entrance.

Quarterly parking permits cost $50 for full–time students and $40 for part–time students. Annual permits are $120 and are sold Fall Quarter only. Owners of vehicles without a valid parking permit may purchase a daily parking permit for $3 at the pay station located at the east entrance.

Now cover the passage and listen to the recording. When you hear the question, begin preparing your response.

Disk 1, Track 11

The man expresses his opinion about parking on campus. State his opinion and explain the reasons he gives for holding that opinion.

Stop

Preparation Time – 30 seconds
Response Time – 60 seconds

QUESTION 4

In this question, you will read a short passage on an academic subject, listen to a lecture on the same topic, and then speak in response to a question about what you have read and heard. After you hear the question, you have 30 seconds to prepare your response and 60 seconds to speak.

Reading Time – 45 seconds

BEHAVIORISM

Behaviorism is a school of psychology that explains behavior entirely in terms of observable responses to environmental conditions. Behaviorists think that the human traits of personality and character are not determined inside a person. Rather, these traits are the result of behavior patterns developed through environmental conditioning, a central idea in behaviorism. Behaviorists believe that if we understand specific behaviors and the environmental stimuli that cause them, we can learn how behavior occurs. Behaviorists believe that it is possible to determine the laws of behavior and to exercise control over behavior.

Now cover the passage and listen to the recording. When you hear the question, begin preparing your response.

Disk 1, Track 12

Describe Pavlov's experiments with dogs, and explain how these experiments contributed to the psychology of behaviorism.

Stop

Preparation Time – 30 seconds
Response Time – 60 seconds

QUESTION 5

In this question, you will listen to a conversation. You will then be asked to talk about the information in the conversation and to give your opinion about the ideas presented. After you hear the question, you have 20 seconds to prepare your response and 60 seconds to speak.

Disk 1, Track 13

Describe the woman's problem and the two suggestions the man makes about how to solve it. Then state which of the two solutions you prefer and explain why.

Stop

Preparation Time – 20 seconds
Response Time – 60 seconds

QUESTION 6

In this question, you will listen to part of a lecture. You will then be asked to summarize important information from the lecture. After you hear the question, you have 20 seconds to prepare your response and 60 seconds to speak.

Disk 1, Track 14

Using examples and details from the lecture, describe the causes and effects of problems that threaten the world's oceans.

Stop

Preparation Time – 20 seconds
Response Time – 60 seconds

Key points for the Speaking responses are on page 297.

Each response earns a score of 1, 2, 3 or 4.

Record your total Speaking score on page 382.

Disk 1, Track 15

WRITING SECTION DIRECTIONS

The Writing section measures your ability to use writing to communicate in an academic environment. There are two writing questions.

Question 1 is an integrated writing task. You will read a passage, listen to a lecture, and then answer a question based on what you have read and heard. You have 20 minutes to plan and write your response.

Question 2 is an independent writing task. You will answer a question based on your own knowledge and experience. You have 30 minutes to plan and write your response.

Stop

QUESTION 1

For this task, you will write a response to a question about a reading passage and a lecture. You may take notes, and you may use your notes to help you write your response. Your response will be scored on the quality of your writing and on how well you connect the points in the lecture with points in the reading. Typically, an effective response will have 150 to 225 words.

Reading Time – 3 minutes

Some foods are endowed with super powers that give you more energy and greater protection against disease. Eating a diet rich in blueberries, tomatoes, broccoli, and garlic will change your life for the better. By making these superpower foods part of your regular eating habits, you can actually change the course of your biochemistry and stop the gradual changes in your body that lead to diseases such as Alzheimer's, cancer, high cholesterol, obesity, and diabetes.

The concept of superpower foods is supported by research. Studies on blueberries show that they have a positive effect on brain function and motor movement in aging rats. Blueberries also appear to prevent mental decline in mice genetically engineered to develop Alzheimer's disease. Eating one cup of blueberries every day will reduce aging–related damage in our brain. Blueberries are an excellent source of antioxidants, nutrients in fruits and vegetables that neutralize the products of our metabolism before they can harm brain cells. Researchers believe that blueberries protect our brain through their antioxidant and anti–inflammatory action. Blueberries also seem to influence the way brain cells communicate with each other.

Tomatoes and tomato–based products are the major source of many carotenoids including lycopene. Research shows that lycopene, the red pigment in tomatoes, helps lower cholesterol and reduces the risk of prostate cancer. Studies show that the antioxidants in broccoli and cabbage help prevent colon cancer. Other studies show that garlic is the natural enemy of high cholesterol and the common cold. Eating foods with garlic or taking garlic supplements will produce a drop in LDL blood cholesterol.

Now listen to the recording. When you hear the question, begin your response. You may look at the passage during the writing time.

Disk 1, Track 16

Summarize the points made in the lecture you just heard, explaining how they cast doubt on points made in the reading.

Stop

Writing Time – 20 minutes

QUESTION 2

For this task, you will write an essay in response to a question that asks you to state and support your opinion on a topic. Your essay will be scored on the quality of your writing, including how well you organize and develop your ideas and how well you use language to express your ideas. Typically, an effective essay will have a minimum of 300 words.

Read the question below and make any notes that will help you plan your response. Then begin writing your essay.

> Do you agree or disagree with the following statement?
>
> **The government should require all young adults to perform some kind of national service, such as military service or social work.**
>
> Use specific reasons and details to support your answer.

Writing Time – 30 minutes

Key points for the Writing section are on page 297.

Each response earns a score of 1, 2, 3, 4 or 5.

Record your total Writing score on page 382.

TEST 2

Reading Section Directions

The Reading section measures your ability to read and understand passages in English. You will read three passages and answer questions about them. Answer all questions based on what is stated or implied in the passages.

Most questions are worth one point. The last question in each set is worth more than one point. For this question, the directions will indicate how many points you can receive.

Some passages have one or more words in bold type. For these bolded words, you will see a definition in a glossary at the end of the passage.

Allow 20 minutes to read each passage and answer the questions about it. You may now begin the first passage.

Time – 60 minutes

DADA AND POP ART

1 Dada was a subversive movement in the arts that flourished mainly in France, Switzerland, and Germany from 1916 to 1923. Dada was based on the principles of deliberate irrationality and **anarchy**. It rejected laws of beauty and social organization and attempted to discover authentic reality through the destruction of traditional culture and **aesthetic** forms. The movement's founders included the French artist Jean Arp and the writers Tristan Tzara and Hugo Ball. At a meeting of young artists in 1916 in Zurich, one of them inserted a paper knife into a French–German dictionary. The knife pointed to the word *dada*, a French baby–talk word for a hobby–horse, which the group saw as an appropriate term for their anti–art.

2 Dada emerged from despair over the First World War and disgust for the conservative values of society. Dada was the first expression of protest against the war. Dadaists used absurdity to create artworks that mocked society yet defied intellectual analysis, such as the use of "found" objects in sculptures and installations. The forerunner of the Dadaists, and ultimately their leading member, was Marcel Duchamp, who in 1913 created his first "ready–made," the *Bicycle Wheel*, consisting of a wheel mounted on the seat of a stool. In his effort to discourage aesthetics, Duchamp shocked the art establishment with these ready–mades—manufactured objects that he selected and exhibited—including a bottle rack and a comb. The Dada movement extended to literature and music and became international after the war. In the United States the movement was centered in New York City. Dadaists on both sides of the Atlantic had one goal in common: to demolish current aesthetic standards.

3 Fifty years after the Dadaists, another generation of artists reacted to the standards and values of society. However, instead of rejecting ordinary things, the young artists of the Pop movement of the 1960s embraced them. Pop artists were curious about the commercial media of ads, billboards, newsprint, television, and all aspects of popular culture. Thus, the barrier between "high" and "low" art collapsed, which the Dadaists had aimed for and the Pop artists attained with an energy not seen before.

4 Pop art received its name from critic Lawrence Alloway, who considered Pop to be the culture of the mass media, photographs, and posters—a style that must be popular, transitory, and witty. The subject matter of Pop art was derivative, depicting something that had already been published or produced, such as comic strips, soft–drink bottles, and photographs of movie stars. Pop art caught on quickly; it was art about mass consumption that was eagerly consumed by the masses.

5 The most popular of the Pop artists was the painter Roy Lichtenstein. Lichtenstein painted enlarged copies of the least "arty" things he could find: romance and adventure comic strips. He was the first American artist to react to comic strips, finding beauty in these crude designs, along with a distinct sense of style. Lichtenstein also painted other pictorial styles, including blowups of other artists' brushstrokes and parodies of Cubism and Art Deco.

6 Andy Warhol, more than any other Pop artist, took on the mind–numbing overload of American mass culture. Warhol began his career as a commercial illustrator, and in 1962 he had his first exhibition in an art gallery, where he showed his *32 Campbell's Soup Cans*. The thirty–two soup cans are about sameness: same brand, same size, same paint surface, and same fame. They mimic the condition of mass advertising. All of Warhol's work flowed from one central insight: mass culture is filled with images that become meaningless by being repeated again and again, and in this glut of information is a role for art. Warhol felt this and embodied it. He conveyed a collective state of mind in which celebrity—a famous brand name or the image of a famous person—had completely replaced sacredness in art.

Glossary:

anarchy: absence of any form of authority; disorder; confusion
aesthetic: relating to beauty; artistic

1. According to the passage, the main goal of the Dada movement was to

(A) stimulate public interest in art
(B) change the goals of art education
(C) destroy traditional standards of art
(D) make mass media the subject of art

2. The author mentions a hobby–horse in paragraph 1 in order to

(A) explain the origin of the name "Dada"
(B) illustrate how Dadaists created art
(C) compare art to a children's game
(D) give an example of a "ready–made"

3. According to the passage, one way in which the Dadaists mocked society was by

(A) refusing to fight in the First World War
(B) writing plays about social class
(C) using "found" objects in works of art
(D) criticizing the commercial media

4. The word forerunner in paragraph 2 is closest in meaning to

(A) leading writer
(B) earliest artist
(C) main critic
(D) fastest runner

5. The passage gives all of the following as examples of "ready–mades" EXCEPT

(A) a bicycle wheel
(B) a bottle rack
(C) a soup can
(D) a comb

6. The word them in paragraph 3 refers to

(A) the Dadaists
(B) standards and values
(C) ordinary things
(D) the young artists

7. It can be inferred from paragraph 3 that the Pop artists

(A) reacted against the Dada movement
(B) were more popular than the Dadaists
(C) criticized art for being too commercial
(D) succeeded in changing ideas about art

8. Which sentence below best expresses the essential information in the highlighted sentence in paragraph 4? Incorrect choices change the meaning in important ways or leave out essential information.

(A) Pop art could be produced and consumed more quickly than any other mass media.
(B) The public enthusiastically accepted Pop art, which portrayed commercial culture.
(C) The mass media quickly reached large audiences, thus influencing attitudes about art.
(D) Large numbers of people bought Pop art, even though they could not understand it.

9. Which artist created works based on other styles and the work of other artists?

(A) Marcel Duchamp
(B) Lawrence Alloway
(C) Roy Lichtenstein
(D) Andy Warhol

10. The phrase took on in paragraph 6 is closest in meaning to

(A) hated
(B) was afraid of
(C) invented
(D) responded to

11. The word glut in paragraph 6 is closest in meaning to

(A) excess
(B) definition
(C) fear
(D) absence

TEST 2

12. Look at the four squares, **A**, **B**, **C**, and **D**, which indicate where the following sentence could be added to the passage. Where would the sentence best fit?

Whereas the visual arts had previously ignored current events, Dadaists reacted to the crisis and accused society of allowing it to happen.

Dada emerged from despair over the First World War and disgust for the conservative values of society. Dada was the first expression of protest against the war. **A** Dadaists used absurdity to create artworks that mocked society yet defied intellectual analysis, such as the use of "found" objects in sculptures and installations. **B** The forerunner of the Dadaists, and ultimately their leading member, was Marcel Duchamp, who in 1913 created his first "ready–made," the *Bicycle Wheel*, consisting of a wheel mounted on the seat of a stool. In his effort to discourage aesthetics, Duchamp shocked the art establishment with these ready–mades—manufactured objects that he selected and exhibited—including a bottle rack and a comb. **C** The Dada movement extended to literature and music and became international after the war. **D** In the United States the movement was centered in New York City. Dadaists on both sides of the Atlantic had one goal in common: to demolish current aesthetic standards.

13. Select the appropriate phrases from the answer choices and match them to the art movement that they describe. TWO of the answer choices will NOT be used. ***This question is worth 4 points.***

Answer Choices

(A) Reflected the mass media of advertising, newsprint, and television
(B) Was an anti–art movement in the visual arts, literature and music
(C) Focused on transitory impressions and the changing effects of light
(D) Depicted things that had already been produced in other media
(E) Originated as a protest against the First World War
(F) Found beauty in comic strips and other images from popular culture
(G) Emphasized the act of creating art over the finished work of art
(H) Used "found" objects and "ready–mades" in works of art
(I) Created art out of famous brand names and images of famous people

Dada

Dada
•
•
•

Pop Art

Pop Art
•
•
•
•

How to Score 4–Point Questions	
Answers Correct	**Points Earned**
7	4
6	3
5	2
4	1
0–3	0

DEFORESTATION IN NORTH AMERICA

1 The land area of the United States and Canada is just over 4.8 billion acres. When large numbers of Europeans began to arrive in the eighteenth century, almost one–third of that area was covered with old–growth forests. In the eastern half of the continent, nearly 90 percent of the land was thick with forests of elm, ash, beech, maple, oak, and hickory. By the end of the nineteenth century, after several decades of intensive deforestation, only half of the original forests remained.

2 During the first two centuries of European colonization, settlement was concentrated along the East Coast, having almost no effect on the vast forests covering the continent. Then, in the first half of the nineteenth century, agriculture expanded and settlers began to move westward in search of land for new farms. Land for agriculture came almost exclusively from clearing forests. The demand for farmland and timber continued to soar, and by 1850, more than 100 million acres of old–growth forest had been cut or burned off in the Northeast, the Southeast, the Great Lakes region, and along the St. Lawrence River.

3 Along with agriculture, industrialization was a major cause of deforestation. The Industrial Revolution was fueled by North America's abundance of wood, as iron makers relied on charcoal, or charred wood, to fire their furnaces. Hardwoods such as oak produced the best charcoal, which charcoal burners made by slowly burning logs in kilns until they were reduced to concentrated carbon. It took eight tons of wood to make two tons of charcoal to smelt one ton of iron. Thus, the toll on the forests was high, as countless acres were cut to feed the furnaces of the iron industry.

4 The transportation technology of the Industrial Revolution contributed greatly to deforestation. The river steamboats that came into operation after 1830 had a voracious appetite for wood. To keep their wheels turning, steamboats typically took on fuel twice a day. The wood was supplied by thousands of "wood hawks" along the banks of the Ohio and Mississippi with stacks of cut firewood. Annual consumption of wood on riverboats continued to increase until 1865. Consequently, river valleys that had the heaviest traffic were stripped of their forests.

5 After 1860, immigration and westward expansion surged, and railroads swept over the continent. Clean–burning hardwood was the preferred fuel of the "iron horses," which required the cutting of 215,000 acres of woodland to stay in operation for one year. Not only did wood fuel the steam engines, but enormous amounts of oak and locust also went into the manufacture of railcars, ties, fencing, bridges, and telegraph poles. Railroads in the United States and Canada stretched from coast to coast by 1885, and each additional mile of railroad meant at least two more miles of fencing and 2,500 ties.

6 Other major consumers of forest products included ordinary homeowners. More than four out of five of the houses constructed in the early nineteenth century—from log cabins to clapboard cottages—were built mainly of wood and roofed with wooden shingles. All were filled with wooden furniture. Two–thirds of all households in North America were heated by open, wood–burning fireplaces, and it took between 10 and 20 acres of forest to keep a single fireplace burning for one year.

7 Throughout the century, the timber industry continued to supply the single most valuable raw material for a rapidly expanding population. Between 1840 and 1860, the annual production of lumber rose from 1.6 million to 8 billion board feet. This increase was made possible by the widespread application of steam power. Wood–fueled steam engines powered the sawmills, moved and barked the logs, and finished the boards. Railroad lines were now built right into the forests so that felled logs could be shipped directly to market. These innovations had their greatest impact in the Great Lakes region. By 1890 the technology of the timber industry had triumphed over the natural abundance of the forests, and woodlands that had once seemed endless were now depleted.

14. What point does the author make about deforestation in North America?

(A) It occurred mostly within a single century.
(B) It changed how people thought about trees.
(C) It provided jobs in several related industries.
(D) It caused an economic crisis in two countries.

15. According to the passage, all of the following contributed to deforestation EXCEPT

(A) the expansion of agriculture
(B) an increase in forest fires
(C) the use of charcoal as a fuel
(D) steamboat transportation

16. The word they in paragraph 3 refers to

(A) furnaces
(B) logs
(C) kilns
(D) forests

17. Why does the author use the word toll in discussing the iron industry in paragraph 3?

(A) To show that the process of smelting iron was expensive
(B) To illustrate the impact of forest fires on the iron industry
(C) To point out that the iron industry had to pay high taxes
(D) To emphasize that large areas of woodland were eliminated

18. The word voracious in paragraph 4 is closest in meaning to

(A) varying
(B) greedy
(C) strange
(D) moderate

19. The phrase "wood hawks" in paragraph 4 describes

(A) a type of riverboat
(B) a species of tree
(C) people who sold wood
(D) large woodland birds

20. The word surged in paragraph 5 is closest in meaning to

(A) stopped
(B) competed
(C) fluctuated
(D) increased

21. It can be inferred from paragraph 5 that "iron horses" were

(A) machines that made ties and fencing
(B) railroad company executives
(C) steam engines that moved trains
(D) animals that helped build railroads

22. Which sentence below best expresses the essential information in the highlighted sentence in paragraph 6? Incorrect choices change the meaning in important ways or leave out essential information.

(A) Most of the houses in the nineteenth century were log cabins or clapboard cottages with simple roofs.
(B) There were four or five main house styles in the early nineteenth century, and all were built of wood.
(C) In the nineteenth century, wood construction was popular because wood could be used in a number of ways.
(D) Wood was the primary construction material of the vast majority of houses built in the early nineteenth century.

TEST 2

23. It can be inferred from paragraph 6 that in the early nineteenth century

(A) wooden houses were more popular than they are today
(B) the construction industry dominated the economy
(C) more people owned homes than they do today
(D) home heating was a major reason for cutting trees

24. According to paragraph 7, the tremendous increase in the production of lumber was primarily due to

(A) the availability of land
(B) an increase in the labor supply
(C) innovations in technology
(D) timber industry leadership

25. Look at the four squares, [A], [B], [C], and [D], which indicate where the following sentence could be added to the passage. Where would the sentence best fit?

No other industry or consumer of wood could match the timber industry itself for the exploitation of North America's forests.

[A] Throughout the century, the timber industry continued to supply the single most valuable raw material for a rapidly expanding population. Between 1840 and 1860, the annual production of lumber rose from 1.6 million to 8 billion board feet. [B] This increase was made possible by the widespread application of steam power. Wood–fueled steam engines powered the sawmills, moved and barked the logs, and finished the boards. Railroad lines were now built right into the forests so that felled logs could be shipped directly to market. [C] These innovations had their greatest impact in the Great Lakes region. [D] By 1890 the technology of the timber industry had triumphed over the natural abundance of the forests, and woodlands that had once seemed endless were now depleted.

26. Read the first sentence of a summary of the passage. Complete the summary by selecting the THREE answer choices that express the most important ideas in the passage. Some sentences do not belong in the summary because they express ideas that are not presented in the passage or are minor ideas in the passage. ***This question is worth 2 points.***

Many factors contributed to the deforestation of North America in the nineteenth century.

•
•
•

Answer Choices

(A) Dense forests of elm, ash, beech, maple, oak, and hickory covered most of the eastern half of the continent.

(B) Several million acres of forest were cut to meet the growing population's demand for farmland and wood.

(C) The iron, steamboat, railroad, and construction industries required huge amounts of wood.

(D) Each mile of railroad required two miles of fencing and 2,500 ties, which were made of oak and locust.

(E) After 1890, the timber industry moved into the West and South, cutting another 125 million acres of forest.

(F) Innovations in the timber industry greatly increased wood production but led to the depletion of forests.

How to Score 2–Point Questions	
Answers Correct	**Points Earned**
3	2
2	1
0–1	0

THE EFFECTS OF SLEEP DEPRIVATION

1 Sleep restores the body and the mind and helps prevent disease by strengthening the immune system. However, many adults do not get the recommended eight hours of sleep each night. The average adult today gets only 6.4 hours of sleep, nearly an hour and a half less than what the average person received a century ago. Only in recent years have health professionals begun to realize the prevalence and severity of sleep deprivation in the working population. A significant number of people work at night, work long shifts, or suffer from **insomnia** or **jet lag**. Others are deprived of sleep because they work too hard, stay out too late, or try to do too many things in a day. Adults who regularly sleep six hours or less might think they accomplish more by staying up late, but they pay for it the next day when they feel sleepy or irritable or are unable to concentrate, remember things, or be very effective at their work.

2 Studies show that the brain is adversely affected by sleep deprivation because certain patterns of electrical and chemical activity that occur during sleep are interrupted and the brain cannot function normally. In one study, thirteen healthy adult subjects who usually had normal sleep patterns were kept awake and carefully monitored in a hospital sleep laboratory during a period of 35 hours. During the experiment, the subjects were asked to perform several **cognitive** tasks, such as arithmetic and word problems, while undergoing magnetic resonance scans of their brain activity. The scans recorded each subject's brain activity from a rested state through various stages of sleep deprivation over the 35–hour period. The scans produced images showing increased activity in some regions of the brain and decreased activity in others. The researchers found that the temporal lobe of the brain, the region involved in language processing, was activated during verbal tasks in rested subjects but not in sleep–deprived subjects. When subjects were fully rested, their magnetic resonance scans showed that the temporal lobe was very active. However, after several hours without sleep, there was no activity within this region. The effects of the inactivity included slurred speech in the subjects who had gone for prolonged periods with no sleep.

3 Several studies show that getting fewer than six hours of sleep a night can impair short–term memory, coordination, reaction time, and judgment—thus posing a serious risk of accident or injury. In one study of drivers, researchers reported that sleep deprivation had some of the same hazardous effects as being drunk. They found that people who drove after being awake for 17 to 19 hours performed worse than those with a blood alcohol level of .05 percent, the legal limit for drunk driving in most western European countries. The study also found that 16 to 60 percent of road accidents involved sleep deprivation. The researchers concluded that countries with drunk driving laws should consider similar restrictions against sleep–deprived driving.

4 There are other problems associated with sleep deprivation beyond impaired motor skills and judgment. Drivers who get too little sleep may have higher levels of stress, anxiety and depression, may take unnecessary risks, or may express rage toward other drivers. These dangers affect not only drivers but also people who work long shifts or night shifts, such as medical personnel and other emergency workers. The dangers of sleep deprivation go far beyond the obvious risks and can, in fact, undermine all areas of an individual's physical and mental health.

5 Sleep deprivation weakens the immune system, making an individual more prone to diseases such as the common cold and diabetes. Without sleep, the number of disease–fighting white blood cells within the body decreases, as does the activity of the remaining white blood cells. Sleep deprivation has been linked to a decrease in the body's production of hormones such as insulin. Results of a recent study suggested that healthy young adults who regularly got under 6.5 hours of sleep a night had greater insulin resistance than people who got 7.5 to 8.5 hours of sleep. Insulin resistance is a silent condition in which the pancreas does not make enough insulin or the body is unable to use the insulin that is present. Thus, the muscle and liver cells cannot metabolize the sugar called glucose. As a result, glucose builds up in the bloodstream, setting the stage for diabetes and heart disease.

Glossary:
insomnia: the inability to fall asleep or remain asleep
jet lag: the disruption of bodily rhythms caused by high–speed travel across time zones
cognitive: relating to mental processes

27. Which sentence below best expresses the essential information in the highlighted sentence in paragraph 1? Incorrect choices change the meaning in important ways or leave out essential information.

    (A) A century ago, health professionals did not experience sleep deprivation; however, now it is a part of their jobs.
    (B) It is difficult to understand why health professionals have not studied the consequences of sleep deprivation.
    (C) Sleep deprivation used to affect only certain professions, but now it occurs in all sectors of the working population.
    (D) Health professionals have just started to understand that sleep deprivation in workers is a serious problem.

28. The passage mentions all of the following as causes of sleep deprivation EXCEPT

    (A) jet lag
    (B) long work hours
    (C) boring work
    (D) working at night

29. The phrase deprived of in paragraph 1 is closest in meaning to

    (A) disgusted by
    (B) capable of
    (C) kept from
    (D) worried about

30. The word adversely in paragraph 2 is closest in meaning to

    (A) barely
    (B) negatively
    (C) permanently
    (D) slowly

31. The purpose of the study described in paragraph 2 was to determine

    (A) how many hours people can survive without sleep
    (B) how people react when their sleep is interrupted
    (C) the changes in brain activity that occur during sleep
    (D) the effects of sleep deprivation on brain activity

32. The word others in paragraph 2 refers to

    (A) magnetic resonance scans
    (B) stages of sleep deprivation
    (C) regions of the brain
    (D) rested subjects

33. According to paragraph 2, what did researchers learn about subjects who had gone several hours without sleep?

    (A) The subjects were unable to complete simple word problems.
    (B) The subjects had no activity in part of the brain during verbal tasks.
    (C) The subjects could solve some cognitive tasks better than others.
    (D) The subjects felt irritable and expressed anger in their speech.

34. Why does the author mention blood alcohol level in paragraph 3?

    (A) To show how sleep deprivation reduces the blood alcohol level
    (B) To compare the effects of sleep deprivation and alcohol
    (C) To suggest that sleep–deprived drivers are also likely to drink
    (D) To argue against raising the legal limit for drunk driving

35. It can be inferred from paragraph 4 that medical personnel and other emergency workers

(A) are at risk for experiencing anxiety and depression
(B) are more likely than drivers to be deprived of sleep
(C) are not aware that they may suffer from sleep deprivation
(D) are rarely able to find jobs with daytime hours

36. According to the passage, sleep deprivation can affect the body's immune system by

(A) increasing the number of white blood cells
(B) decreasing the body's resistance to insulin
(C) reducing the body's ability to make or use insulin
(D) raising the heart rate and blood pressure

37. The phrase setting the stage in paragraph 5 is closest in meaning to

(A) lowering the risk
(B) changing the treatments
(C) eliminating the cure
(D) providing the conditions

38. Look at the four squares, [A], [B], [C], and [D], which indicate where the following sentence could be added to the passage. Where would the sentence best fit?

Drivers are especially at risk, and fatigue caused by sleep deprivation causes thousands of traffic accidents every year.

[A] Several studies show that getting less than six hours of sleep a night can impair short–term memory, coordination, reaction time, and judgment—thus posing a serious risk of accident or injury. [B] In one study of drivers, researchers reported that sleep deprivation had some of the same hazardous effects as being drunk. [C] They found that people who drove after being awake for 17 to 19 hours performed worse than those with a blood alcohol level of .05 percent, the legal limit for drunk driving in most western European countries. The study also found that 16 to 60 percent of road accidents involved sleep deprivation. The researchers concluded that countries with drunk driving laws should consider similar restrictions against sleep–deprived driving. [D]

39. Read the first sentence of a summary of the passage. Complete the summary by selecting the THREE answer choices that express the most important ideas in the passage. Some sentences do not belong in the summary because they express ideas that are not presented in the passage or are minor ideas in the passage. ***This question is worth 2 points.***

Sleep deprivation affects the human body in numerous ways.

•
•
•

Answer Choices

(A) The average adult gets only 6.4 hours of sleep a night, which is less than the recommended eight hours.

(B) Illness, depression, pain and discomfort at night, and significant life stress are common causes of insomnia.

(C) Lack of sleep disrupts normal activity in parts of the brain, affecting one's ability to perform certain tasks.

(D) Subjects in one study were deprived of sleep for 35 hours, and their brain activity was scanned by magnetic resonance.

(E) Sleep deprivation can have effects similar to being drunk, such as impairment of motor skills and judgment.

(F) Not getting enough sleep can weaken the immune system and harm a person's physical and mental health.

How to Score 2–Point Questions	
Answers Correct	**Points Earned**
3	2
2	1
0–1	0

Answers are on page 298.

Record your Reading section score on page 380.

Disk 2, Track 1

LISTENING SECTION DIRECTIONS

The Listening section measures your ability to understand conversations and lectures in English. You will hear each conversation and lecture only one time. After each conversation or lecture, you will hear some questions about it. Answer the questions based on what the speakers state or imply.

You may take notes while you listen. You may use your notes to help you answer the questions.

In some questions, you will see this icon: . This means that you will hear, but not see, part of the question.

Some questions have special directions, which appear in a gray box. Most questions are worth one point. If a question is worth more than one point, the directions will indicate how many points you can receive.

You will now begin the first part of the Listening section.

Time – maximum of 90 minutes

Disk 2, Track 2

QUESTIONS 1–5

Conversation

1. What are the students mainly discussing?

   (A) The man's favorite style of music
   (B) The woman's love of sculpture
   (C) The man's upcoming art show
   (D) The woman's recent photographs

2. How does the man probably feel when he says this: 🎧

   (A) "I hope that a lot of people come to the opening reception."
   (B) "I am concerned that your friends will not understand my work."
   (C) "I am surprised that my sculpture is getting so much attention."
   (D) "I feel nervous about meeting the Friends of the Gallery."

3. Which features are included in the man's sculpture?

   Click on two answers.

   [A] Various types of metal
   [B] Boxes of different colors
   [C] Several white objects
   [D] Different styles of music

4. How did the man get the idea for his sculpture?

   (A) He listened to the same music on different CD players.
   (B) He looked at photographs of different types of boxes.
   (C) He read an article about how people see music as colors.
   (D) He studied the philosophy of the Friends of the Gallery.

5. Why does the woman say this: 🎧

   (A) To persuade the man to look at the catalog
   (B) To explain a possible use of her photograph
   (C) To describe her favorite place to study on campus
   (D) To imply that the dean will like the man's sculpture

Disk 2, Track 3

QUESTIONS 6–11

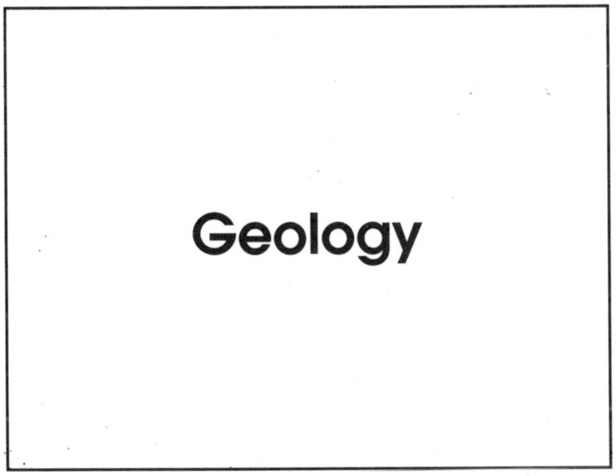

6. What is the lecture mainly about?

   Click on two answers.

   A The world's largest glaciers
   B How glaciers are created
   C The movement of glaciers
   D Why glaciers are melting

7. What point does the professor make about the snow that forms a glacier?

   (A) It is conserved.
   (B) It is light and fluffy.
   (C) It is denser than ice.
   (D) It is very dirty.

8. Listen again to part of the lecture. Then answer the question.

   Why does the professor say this:

   (A) To explain why it snows frequently in the mountains
   (B) To show why mountain scenery attracts many visitors
   (C) To describe conditions that lead to glacier formation
   (D) To compare mountain glaciers with Arctic ice sheets

9. The professor briefly explains a process that occurs in mountain valleys. Indicate whether each sentence below is a stage in the process.

   For each sentence, click in the correct box.

	Yes	No
Precipitation falls as freezing rain or ice pellets.		
Snow accumulates and gradually turns into ice.		
Minerals in the meltwater change the texture of snowflakes.		
Snow crystals become rounded and coarse, like grains of sugar.		
Weight and movement compress the air out of ice crystals.		

10. Why are some glaciers called surging glaciers?

   (A) They move much faster than other glaciers.
   (B) They form during one winter–summer cycle.
   (C) They continuously change form as they move.
   (D) They add a lot of silt to mountain rivers.

11. Listen again to part of the lecture. Then answer the question.

   What can be inferred about glaciers in warmer climates?

   (A) They are drier than glaciers in very cold climates.
   (B) They can change the shape of a mountain valley.
   (C) They are found on only one side of a mountain.
   (D) They move more quickly during the winter.

Disk 2, Track 4

QUESTIONS 12–17

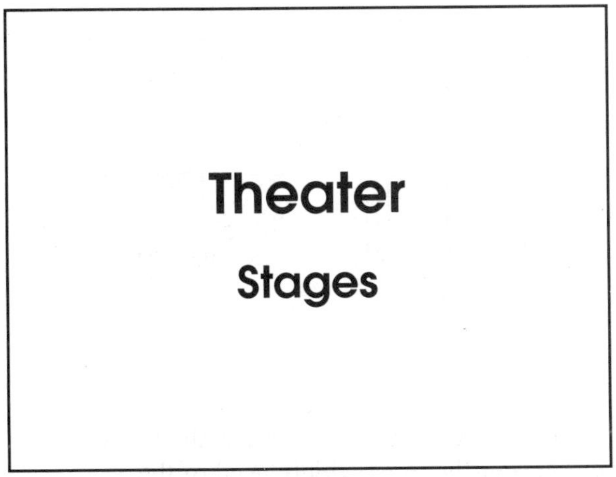

12. What does the professor imply about the various types of stages?

   (A) Each design gives the audience a different experience.
   (B) All three types were created at the same time in history.
   (C) The proscenium theater accommodates the largest audience.
   (D) Theater schools usually focus on one of the three types.

13. Which of the following is a disadvantage of the proscenium stage?

   (A) The proscenium stage does not allow for scenery or scene changes.
   (B) The people sitting in the back rows cannot hear what the actors say.
   (C) The proscenium creates a barrier between the actors and the audience.
   (D) Ticket prices are higher for plays produced in proscenium theaters.

14. Which type of performance would probably best be produced on an arena stage?

   (A) A story requiring several scene changes
   (B) An intimate drama about everyday life
   (C) A play in which distance is an advantage
   (D) An opera with elaborate sets and costumes

15. Why does the professor say this:

   (A) To explain why he likes the circle stage
   (B) To show that dance is important in theater
   (C) To describe the origins of the arena stage
   (D) To promote the study of traditional drama

16. Which diagram represents the thrust stage theater?

   (A) 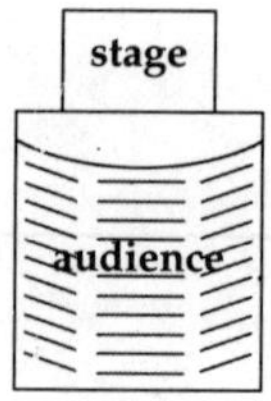

   (C) 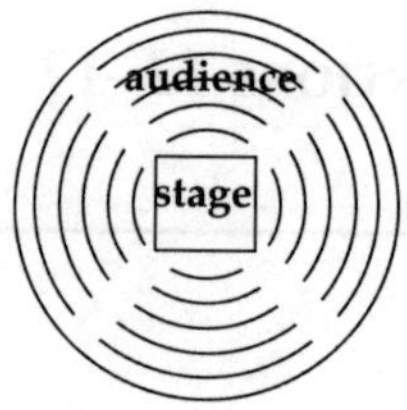

   (B) 

   (D) 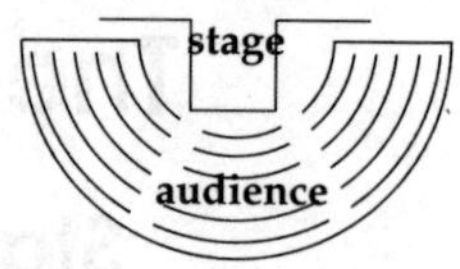

17. According to the professor, why is the thrust stage theater the most widely used of the three designs?

   Click on two answers.

   [A] It combines the advantages of the other two styles.
   [B] The other two designs are more expensive to build.
   [C] It is the stage that most actors and directors prefer.
   [D] Many great plays were written for the thrust stage.

Disk 2, Track 5

QUESTIONS 18–22

18. Why does the student go to see her professor?

    (A) She is thinking of changing her field of study.
    (B) She needs advice about a problem with geese.
    (C) She wants to discuss the topic of her research.
    (D) She will not be able to complete her research.

19. Listen again to part of the conversation. Then answer the question.

    Why does the student say this: 🎧

    (A) To ask for advice about a problem that she has with geese
    (B) To explain why she wants to change the focus of her research
    (C) To express her opinion about geese in urban areas
    (D) To tell a story about an accident that she experienced

20. What does the professor mean when he says this: 🎧

    (A) Results are tragic when airplanes strike birds.
    (B) Sightings of birds from aircraft are unusual.
    (C) Airplanes do not frighten away most birds.
    (D) There is little similarity between birds and jets.

21. According to the conversation, which statements about peregrine falcons are true?

    Click on two answers.

    [A] They naturally prey on geese and ducks.
    [B] They are the largest of all predatory birds.
    [C] They are more intelligent than geese.
    [D] They can fly faster than any other bird.

22. What is the student's opinion of the falcon program?

    (A) It is not as effective as shooting problem birds.
    (B) It should be discontinued because it is too expensive.
    (C) It is a good opportunity to promote peregrine falcons as pets.
    (D) It is interesting because it uses biology to solve a problem.

Disk 2, Track 6

QUESTIONS 23–28

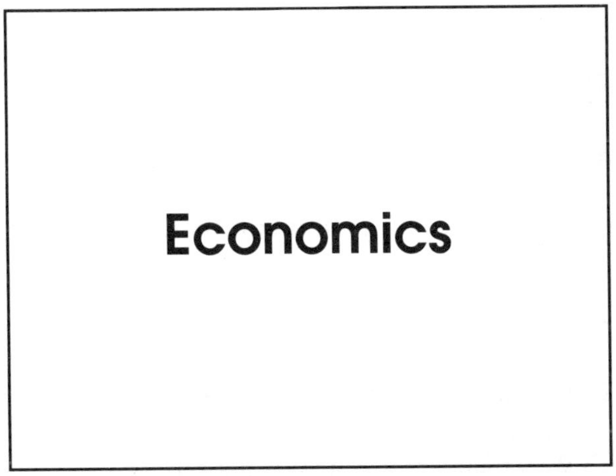

23. What is the lecture mainly about?

(A) Basic problems in every society
(B) How a market economy works
(C) The power of consumers
(D) Economics as a career choice

24. Listen again to part of the lecture. Then answer the question.

Why does the professor say this: 🎧

(A) To complain about government's power over business
(B) To give examples of economic organizations
(C) To criticize the unfairness of the capitalist system
(D) To contrast a pure market economy with a mixed economy

25. What does the professor mean when she says this: 🎧

(A) Consumers prefer buying goods that are well made.
(B) Consumers have the right to vote to elect their leaders.
(C) Consumers use their money like votes when they buy goods.
(D) Consumers and voters are both manipulated by advertising.

26. According to the professor, why does the demand for a good increase when the price decreases?

(A) Decreasing the price will improve the quality of the good.
(B) More people are able to buy the good at the lower price.
(C) Suppliers have higher production costs and higher profits.
(D) Consumers will have access to a greater variety of goods.

27. Listen again to part of the lecture. Then answer the question.

What does the professor imply about the supply of a good?

(A) The supply of a good can increase, but never decrease.
(B) An economist determines how much of a good to supply.
(C) Producers have little control over the supply of a good.
(D) The supply of a good is directly related to its price.

28. What will the next lecture probably be about?

(A) Examples of how supply and demand affect prices
(B) Why the market system is not fair to consumers
(C) How the factory system developed in the real world
(D) Market economics in communist and tribal societies

Disk 2, Track 7

QUESTIONS 29–34

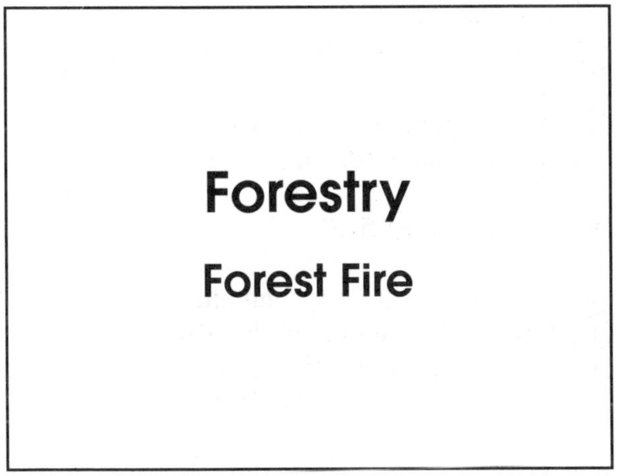

29. What is the main idea of the talk?

(A) Forest management agencies have eliminated forest fire.
(B) Fire contributes to the beauty and mystery of the forest.
(C) Fire revitalizes the forest and promotes a diversity of life.
(D) Forest fire limits the amount of habitat taken by humans.

30. Listen again to part of the talk. Then answer the question.

What does the instructor mean by this statement: 🎧

(A) Fire prevention has actually damaged the forest ecosystem.
(B) Every tree in the forest passes through its own life cycle.
(C) Protecting one species will benefit every other species.
(D) Foresters will never fully understand the laws of nature.

31. According to the instructor, why is periodic fire necessary to forest ecosystems?

Click on two answers.

[A] Fire releases nutrients into the soil.
[B] Fire creates employment for firefighters.
[C] Fire controls insect pests that harm trees.
[D] Fire reduces water and air pollution.

32. According to the instructor, how does the elimination of fire endanger the forest?

(A) Insect populations die without the heat provided by fire.
(B) Dead wood and litter accumulate as fuel for large fires.
(C) Too many people move into the forest, destroying wildlife habitat.
(D) Animal populations grow too fast for the forest to support them.

33. What is prescribed fire?

(A) Fire that is caused by lightning
(B) Fire that humans carefully manage
(C) Fire that inspires artists and writers
(D) Fire in areas where people live

34. Why does the instructor say this: 🎧

(A) To explain why good firefighters are needed
(B) To tell about his own observation of a large fire
(C) To find out if students have ever seen a fire
(D) To give examples of the negative effects of fire

Disk 2, Track 8

QUESTIONS 35–39

Conversation
Learning Resource Center

35. Why does the man go to the learning resource center?

(A) He wants to know where to register to take a test.
(B) He is looking for a quiet place to study.
(C) He needs help in improving his study skills.
(D) He would like to find a tutor to help him study.

36. What does the woman suggest the man do?

(A) Attend one of the special workshops
(B) Register for a class that she teaches
(C) Read an article about time management
(D) Look at the list of available tutors

37. When do most of the special workshops take place?

(A) In the morning
(B) In the evening
(C) On Wednesday
(D) On Saturday

38. Listen again to part of the conversation. Then answer the question.

Why does the man say this:

(A) To show disappointment that the classes are full
(B) To express hope that the workshop will help him
(C) To state that the classes sound interesting
(D) To express pleasure that the workshops are free

39. What will the man probably do next?

(A) Search for information on the computer
(B) Look at the workshops that are available
(C) Pay the fee for an evening workshop
(D) Ask the woman about finding a tutor

Disk 2, Track 9

QUESTIONS 40–45

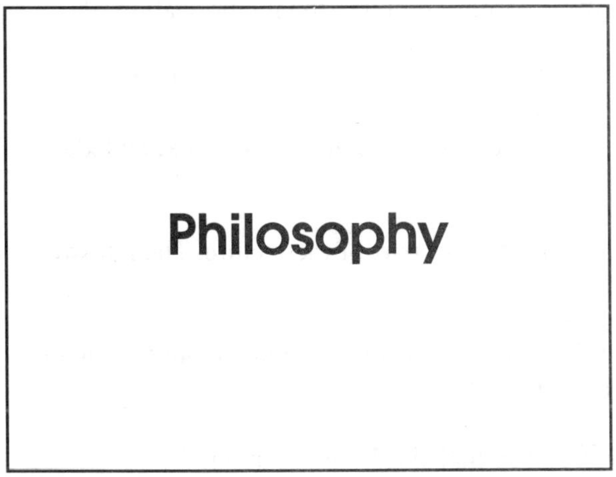

40. Which of the following best describes the organization of the lecture?

(A) A history of educational philosophy
(B) A comparison of two philosophers
(C) A classification of educational practices
(D) A description of the learning process

41. Listen again to part of the lecture. Then answer the question.

Why does the professor quote Confucius?

(A) To illustrate Confucius's respect for tradition
(B) To explain why Confucius was a successful statesman
(C) To portray Confucius as a radical philosopher
(D) To compare Confucianism with another philosophy

42. According to the professor, in what way was Confucius a revolutionary?

(A) He emphasized the ancient wisdom of the classical texts.
(B) He believed that education was more a science than an art.
(C) He wrote critically about the Six Classics of Chinese literature.
(D) He thought that children of all social classes should be educated.

43. With which philosophy is John Dewey associated?

(A) Confucianism
(B) Idealism
(C) Pragmatism
(D) Socialism

44. Which ideas are important in the philosophy of both Confucius and Dewey?

Click on two answers.

[A] Great books are the only true source of knowledge.
[B] Learning requires the memorization of information.
[C] The education of the individual will benefit society.
[D] Education is a combination of knowledge and experience.

45. Listen again to part of the lecture. Then answer the question.

What does the professor imply about Confucius and Dewey?

(A) They had similar ideas about the continuous nature of learning.
(B) Their teachings combined ideas from several different philosophies.
(C) They rejected many traditional beliefs of their own societies.
(D) Their ideas are less influential today than they were in the past.

Disk 2, Track 10

QUESTIONS 46–51

Zoology

Animal Defenses

46. What topics does the professor mainly discuss?

Click on two answers.

[A] How predators find, catch, and eat prey
[B] Behaviors that help prey avoid predators
[C] Changes in predator and prey populations
[D] Defensive coloration in prey animals

47. Why does the professor say this: 🎧

(A) To explain why prey animals must be fast runners
(B) To compare the amount of energy used by predators and prey
(C) To illustrate a disadvantage of an active anti–predator response
(D) To give an example of an adaptation that benefits predators

48. What takes place during a mobbing event?

(A) A prey animal runs away from a predator.
(B) Prey species chase, scold, and attack a predator.
(C) Predators join together in a group to hunt prey.
(D) The population of a prey species increases rapidly.

49. Listen again to part of the lecture. Then answer the question.

Why does the professor say this: 🎧

(A) To explain why camouflage is not a perfect defense
(B) To imply that birds and moths evolved at the same time
(C) To describe how birds use their eyesight to find food
(D) To compare the survival strategies of birds and moths

50. What does the professor mean when she says this: 🎧

(A) Some birds have discovered that brightly–colored insects taste good.
(B) Some birds have chemical defenses similar to those of insects.
(C) Some birds appear able to manage the poison of bees and wasps.
(D) Some birds may have forgotten the meaning of bright coloration.

51. Based on the information in the lecture, indicate whether each situation below involves camouflage, chemical weapons, or warning coloration.

For each sentence, click in the correct box. This question is worth 2 points.

	Camouflage	Chemical weapons	Warning coloration
A toad squirts a nerve poison from glands on its back.			
A fish cannot be seen against rocks of the same color.			
A bird avoids eating a black and yellow striped wasp.			
An insect disguises itself to look like a leaf.			

Stop

How to Score 2–Point Questions	
Answers Correct	**Points Earned**
4	2
3	1
0–2	0

Answers are on page 300.

Record your Listening section score on page 381.

Disk 2, Track 11

SPEAKING SECTION DIRECTIONS

The Speaking section measures your ability to speak in English about a variety of topics. There are six questions in this section.

Questions 1 and 2 are independent tasks in which you will speak about familiar topics. Your responses will be scored on your ability to speak clearly and coherently about the topics.

Questions 3 and 4 are integrated speaking tasks. You will read a passage, listen to a conversation or lecture, and then speak in response to a question about what you have read and heard. You will need to combine relevant information from the two sources to answer the question completely. Your responses will be scored on your ability to speak clearly and coherently and on your ability to accurately convey information about what you read and heard.

Questions 5 and 6 are integrated speaking tasks. You will listen to part of a conversation or lecture, and then speak in response to a question about what you have heard. Your responses will be scored on your ability to speak clearly and coherently and on your ability to accurately convey information about what you heard.

You will hear each conversation and lecture only one time. You may take notes while you listen. You may use your notes to help you answer the questions.

Stop

QUESTION 1

In this question, you will be asked to talk about a familiar topic. After you hear the question, you will have 15 seconds to prepare your response and 45 seconds to speak.

Disk 2, Track 12

> What is your favorite style of dress? Describe this clothing style and explain why it appeals to you. Include details and examples in your explanation.

Stop

Preparation Time – 15 seconds
Response Time – 45 seconds

QUESTION 2

In this question, you will be asked to give your opinion about a familiar topic. After you hear the question, you will have 15 seconds to prepare your response and 45 seconds to speak.

Disk 2, Track 13

> Some students learn better by reading. Others learn more from listening to a teacher. Which way of learning is better for you, and why? Include details and examples to support your explanation.

Stop

Preparation Time – 15 seconds
Response Time – 45 seconds

QUESTION 3

In this question, you will read a short passage about a campus situation, listen to a conversation, and then speak in response to a question about what you have read and heard. After you hear the question, you have 30 seconds to prepare your response and 60 seconds to speak.

Reading Time – 45 seconds

PROJECT REPORTS

Your group's project report will inform the class about the objectives and scope of your project. Generally, a project report includes a description of the project's purpose, activities, results, and conclusions. Each group must submit a formal written report following the guidelines in your textbook. In addition, your group must also present your project to the class. The format of your presentation—the way that you communicate information to your audience—can be handled in a number of ways. Possible formats include an oral report, a media presentation, a product exhibit, a display board, or a Web page.

Now cover the passage and listen to the recording. When you hear the question, begin preparing your response.

Disk 2, Track 14

The man expresses his preference for the format they should use for their project report. State his preference and explain the reasons he gives for his choice.

Stop

Preparation Time – 30 seconds
Response Time – 60 seconds

QUESTION 4

In this question, you will read a short passage on an academic subject, listen to a lecture on the same topic, and then speak in response to a question about what you have read and heard. After you hear the question, you have 30 seconds to prepare your response and 60 seconds to speak.

Reading Time – 45 seconds

WORK AND FAMILY ROLES

Family roles clearly have different effects on men's and women's work roles, and there is a difference in the way men and women experience conflicts between the two roles. For women, there is less of a boundary between family and work, as family roles spill over more into their work life. For men, work and family are more separated; however, emotional strain from family interactions often has a negative effect on a man's performance at work. For both women and men, problems or long hours at work have an impact on family life, and negative emotions from the workplace are likely to be expressed at home that evening.

Now cover the passage and listen to the recording. When you hear the question, begin preparing your response.

Disk 2, Track 15

Explain how women and men experience conflict between their work and family roles.

Stop

Preparation Time – 30 seconds
Response Time – 60 seconds

QUESTION 5

In this question, you will listen to a conversation. You will then be asked to talk about the information in the conversation and to give your opinion about the ideas presented. After you hear the question, you have 20 seconds to prepare your response and 60 seconds to speak.

Disk 2, Track 16

Describe the man's problem and the suggestions the woman makes about what he should do. What do you think the man should do, and why?

Stop

Preparation Time – 20 seconds
Response Time – 60 seconds

QUESTION 6

In this question, you will listen to part of a lecture. You will then be asked to summarize important information from the lecture. After you hear the question, you have 20 seconds to prepare your response and 60 seconds to speak.

Disk 2, Track 17

Using points and examples from the lecture, explain why the human hand is a valuable possession.

Stop

Preparation Time – 20 seconds
Response Time – 60 seconds

Key points for the Speaking responses are on page 303.

Each response earns a score of 1, 2, 3 or 4.

Record your total Speaking score on page 382.

Disk 2, Track 18

WRITING SECTION DIRECTIONS

The Writing section measures your ability to use writing to communicate in an academic environment. There are two writing questions.

Question 1 is an integrated writing task. You will read a passage, listen to a lecture, and then answer a question based on what you have read and heard. You have 20 minutes to plan and write your response.

Question 2 is an independent writing task. You will answer a question based on your own knowledge and experience. You have 30 minutes to plan and write your response.

Stop

QUESTION 1

For this task, you will write a response to a question about a reading passage and a lecture. You may take notes, and you may use your notes to help you write your response. Your response will be scored on the quality of your writing and on how well you connect the points in the lecture with points in the reading. Typically, an effective response will have 150 to 225 words.

Reading Time – 3 minutes

A hydropower facility consists of a plant for electricity production and a water reservoir formed by a dam in a river. The dam has gates that can open or close depending on how much water is needed to produce a certain amount of electricity. The electricity is transported through transmission lines to an electric utility company.

Hydropower is very convenient because it can respond quickly to fluctuations in demand. The production of hydroelectricity is increased on hot summer afternoons when power is needed for air conditioners and decreased at night when people use less energy. The reservoir of water behind the dam is stored energy that can support fisheries and provide various forms of water–based recreation for local residents and tourists. Thus, hydropower reservoirs contribute to the local economy and quality of life.

Hydroelectricity is "clean and green." Once the system has been installed, the burning of fossil fuels is not required to produce the electricity. Hydropower is good for the environment because it does not release greenhouse gases into the atmosphere nor produce waste that requires special containment, as do other forms of energy production. After the water powers the turbines, it simply returns unchanged to the water cycle.

Hydroelectric power is also very efficient and relatively inexpensive. The earth's water cycle naturally replenishes the supply of "fuel" water. Wherever enough rain falls, there will be rivers. If a particular section of river has the right terrain to form a reservoir, it may be suitable for dam construction. Modern hydroelectric turbines can convert as much as 90 percent of the available energy into electricity. In contrast, the best fossil–fuel plants are only about 50 percent efficient.

Now listen to the recording. When you hear the question, begin your response. You may look at the passage during the writing time.

Disk 2, Track 19

Summarize the points made in the lecture you just heard, explaining how they contrast with points made in the reading.

Stop

Writing Time – 20 minutes

QUESTION 2

For this task, you will write an essay in response to a question that asks you to state and support your opinion on a topic. Your essay will be scored on the quality of your writing, including how well you organize and develop your ideas and how well you use language to express your ideas. Typically, an effective essay will have a minimum of 300 words.

Read the question below and make any notes that will help you plan your response. Then begin writing your essay.

> Do you agree or disagree with the following statement?
>
> **It is better to have one or two close friends than to have a large number of casual acquaintances.**
>
> Use specific reasons and examples to support your answer.

Writing Time – 30 minutes

Key points for the Writing section are on page 303.

Each response earns a score of 1, 2, 3, 4 or 5.

Record your total Writing score on page 382.

TEST 3

Reading Section Directions

The Reading section measures your ability to read and understand passages in English. You will read five passages and answer questions about them. Answer all questions based on what is stated or implied in the passages.

Most questions are worth one point. The last question in each set is worth more than one point. For this question, the directions will indicate how many points you can receive.

Some passages have one or more words in bold type. For these bolded words, you will see a definition in a glossary at the end of the passage.

Allow 20 minutes to read each passage and answer the questions about it. You may now begin the first passage.

Time – 100 minutes

DEVELOPMENTS IN THE CONSTRUCTION OF TALL BUILDINGS

1 Until the nineteenth century, most tall buildings were constructed of load–bearing masonry walls. Masonry walls had to be thick, particularly at the base, to support a building's great weight. Stoneworkers built these walls by placing stone upon stone or brick upon brick, adding strength and stability by placing layers of mortar or cement between the stones. Floors and roofs had to be supported by wooden beams, but the major vertical force of buildings was supported by thick masonry walls. This imposed serious limitations on the number and size of windows.

2 In the 1850s, an alternative was emerging that would eliminate the need for exterior weight–bearing walls: a three–dimensional grid of metal beams and columns. The introduction of metal construction made it possible to build larger interior spaces with fewer columns than before. The new construction was capable of supporting all the loads to which a building might be subjected, including the vertical forces caused by the weight of the floors and the horizontal forces caused by the wind or earthquakes.

3 The first buildings to depart from the load–bearing wall tradition were iron–framed. Wrought iron, shaped by hammering the heated metal or rolling it under extreme pressure, contains almost no carbon, and when used as floor beams, it can support a great deal of weight. An interior wrought iron skeleton supported all of the building's weight. Exterior walls of reinforced concrete acted mainly as weatherproofing. As masonry yielded to concrete, walls that once bore weight evolved into thin curtain walls that would allow more windows. These modifications produced sturdier, lighter, and taller buildings that quickly became known as skyscrapers. Skyscrapers satisfied the growing need for office space, warehouses, and department stores. Buildings of eight or more stories quickly transformed the city skyline and dominated the central business districts of American cities such as New York, Chicago, and St. Louis.

4 Skyscrapers differed from previous tall structures with their use of technical innovations such as cast iron and the elevator. The development of cast iron technology, in which molten iron is poured into a mold, made modern plumbing possible. Cast iron pipes, fittings, and valves could deliver pressurized water to the many floors of tall buildings and drain wastewater out. The invention of the mechanical elevator made it possible to construct even taller buildings. Before the elevator, office buildings were rarely more than four or five stories high. In 1857, the first passenger elevator equipped with safety brakes prevented the elevator from falling to the basement when a cable broke. The elevator made the upper floors as rentable as the first floor, liberating architecture from dependence on stairways and human muscle.

5 Not only did these innovations have important uses in the engineering of tall buildings, but they also erased the traditional architectural distinctions separating the bottom, middle, and top of a building. Architects designed towers that reached to the heavens in a continuous vertical grid. Iron construction established the principle of repetitive rhythms as a natural expression of construction, as well as the idea that buildings could be made of new materials on a vast scale.

6 Construction techniques were refined and extended over the next several decades to produce what architectural historians have called "true skyscrapers," buildings over twenty stories high. The invention of steel was particularly significant, as steel T–beams and I–beams replaced iron in these new structures. Steel weighs less than half as much as masonry and exceeds both masonry and iron in tension and compression strength as well as resistance to fatigue. Steel rivets replaced iron bolts and were in turn replaced by electric arc welding in the 1920s. The skyscraper's steel skeleton could meet all of the structural requirements while occupying very little interior space. Exterior curtain walls could be quite thin, since their only function now was to let in light and keep the weather out.

1. Which of the following was a typical characteristic of tall buildings before the nineteenth century?

   (A) Stone floors and roofs
   (B) Thick walls of stone or brick
   (C) A large number of tall windows
   (D) An interior frame of metal

2. The word force in paragraph 1 is closest in meaning to

   (A) appearance
   (B) shape
   (C) load
   (D) movement

3. All of the following are given as benefits of iron–frame construction EXCEPT

   (A) sturdy walls made of stone or brick
   (B) large interior spaces with few columns
   (C) a skeleton that supported heavy loads
   (D) exterior walls with many windows

4. Which sentence below best expresses the essential information in the highlighted sentence in paragraph 3? Incorrect choices change the meaning in important ways or leave out essential information.

   (A) Although masonry walls could bear heavier loads, architects preferred concrete walls because they were easier to build.
   (B) Walls used to be made of load–bearing masonry; now they were thin and made of concrete, so more windows were possible.
   (C) Because tall buildings had such thin exterior walls, the windows needed curtains to prevent heat loss through the concrete.
   (D) Masonry replaced concrete as the material for outside walls, and this allowed skyscrapers to have a lot of windows.

5. According to the passage, which of the following statements is true of the earliest skyscrapers?

   (A) They required the labor of stoneworkers.
   (B) They were eight or more stories high.
   (C) They had very thick exterior walls.
   (D) They were constructed with steel beams.

6. Why does the author discuss the elevator in paragraph 4?

   (A) To illustrate an important use of cast iron technology
   (B) To compare the elevator with the office building
   (C) To explain why early elevators were dangerous
   (D) To show how an innovation contributed to architecture

7. The word rentable in paragraph 4 is closest in meaning to

   (A) strong
   (B) beautiful
   (C) large
   (D) desirable

8. The word they in paragraph 5 refers to

   (A) innovations
   (B) uses
   (C) buildings
   (D) architects

9. The word refined in paragraph 6 is closest in meaning to

   (A) reviewed
   (B) copied
   (C) made cheaper
   (D) improved

10. According to the passage, why did steel replace iron in the construction of skyscrapers?

    (A) Steel is stronger than iron and resists fatigue better.
    (B) Steel allows architects more freedom of expression.
    (C) Steel is more available and less expensive than iron.
    (D) Steel does not rust, so it lasts longer than iron does.

TEST 3

11. It can be inferred from the passage that the author most likely believes which of the following about the skyscraper?

(A) The skyscraper is most beautiful when constructed of traditional materials.
(B) Cast iron technology and the elevator made the skyscraper possible.
(C) Most technology used in the skyscraper existed before the nineteenth century.
(D) The definition of "true skyscraper" will probably change in the future.

12. Look at the four squares, **A**, **B**, **C**, and **D**, which indicate where the following sentence could be added to the passage. Where would the sentence best fit?

Sophisticated plumbing was needed to service bathrooms and also to heat buildings with either steam or hot water.

A Skyscrapers differed from previous tall structures with their use of technical innovations such as cast iron and the elevator. The development of cast iron technology, in which molten iron is poured into a mold, made modern plumbing possible. **B** Cast iron pipes, fittings, and valves could deliver pressurized water to the many floors of tall buildings and drain wastewater out. The invention of the mechanical elevator made it possible to construct even taller buildings. **C** Before the elevator, office buildings were rarely more than four or five stories high. In 1857, the first passenger elevator equipped with safety brakes prevented the elevator from falling to the basement when a cable broke. The elevator made the upper floors as rentable as the first floor, liberating architecture from dependence on stairways and human muscle. **D**

13. Read the first sentence of a summary of the passage. Complete the summary by selecting the THREE answer choices that express the most important ideas in the passage. Some sentences do not belong in the summary because they express ideas that are not presented in the passage or are minor ideas in the passage. ***This question is worth 2 points.***

In the nineteenth century, there were several important developments in the construction of tall buildings.

•
•
•

Answer Choices

Ⓐ Masonry walls were built very thick at the base to support the building's mass.

Ⓑ The development of metal–frame construction eliminated the need for load–bearing walls.

Ⓒ Heating iron or subjecting it to pressure enabled ironworkers to create new shapes.

Ⓓ An iron or steel skeleton supported the building's weight, and concrete walls kept the weather out.

Ⓔ A growing need for office buildings and department stores led to the invention of the skyscraper.

Ⓕ Inventions such as the elevator and steel beams allowed taller buildings than ever before.

How to Score 2–Point Questions	
Answers Correct	**Points Earned**
3	2
2	1
0–1	0

GENERAL SYSTEMS THEORY

1 The Greek word "systema" means union, and scientists use the word "system" to describe a collection of several components that are linked to one another by functional relationships. Everything outside the system is known as the surroundings. Most scientific literature is a description of the components of a system, their relationships with one another, and their relationships with other systems. Although each science has its own systems with their own subject matter and networks of relationships, the formal characteristics of systems are similar for all sciences. The scientific discipline called general systems theory formulates principles that are valid for systems in general, no matter the elements involved and the relations or forces among them.

2 Systems can be divided into two types: closed systems and open systems. A closed system receives no supply of energy from outside and transfers no energy outwards. An open system receives energy from its surroundings and transfers it out again.

3 A closed system is isolated from its surroundings. The energy supply of a closed system is limited and is progressively used up by the processes operating within the system. The ability of the system to function decreases as the available energy is exhausted. Without any additional energy supplied from the outside, the system's processes stop altogether and no further change is possible in the system. A mill wheel supplied with water from a non–refillable container is a closed system. Once the container of water is empty, the wheel no longer turns because there is no water to turn it. In a truly closed system, the water would have to be collected below the mill wheel in a second container to ensure that the system did not supply any energy to the outside.

4 Some scientists argue that there are few truly closed systems in nature, and many define closed systems more broadly as those allowing energy but not mass to cross the system boundary. By this definition, the Earth system as a whole is a closed system. The boundary of the Earth system is the outer edge of the atmosphere, and except for the occasional meteorite, virtually no mass is exchanged between the Earth system and the rest of the universe. However, energy in the form of solar radiation passes from the sun, through the atmosphere to the Earth's surface, which in turn radiates energy back out to space across the system boundary. Hence, energy passes across the Earth's system boundary, but mass does not, making it a closed system.

5 In an open system, energy and mass can be transferred between the system and its surroundings. Living organisms are open systems. They absorb light energy or chemical energy in the form of organic molecules and release heat and metabolic waste products, such as carbon dioxide, to the surroundings. Generally, relationships exist between the components of a system and its surroundings, that is, other systems. Each open system is part of a larger system that receives and gives off energy. In an open system, the energy is continually resupplied from sources outside the system. In the example of the mill wheel, if the non–refillable water container is replaced by a reservoir fed continuously by a stream, it becomes an open system because the energy supply is renewed from the outside.

6 The natural environment is made up of open systems. These can behave as closed systems temporarily if the energy supply is halted for a period. If, for example, the stream to the reservoir supplying the mill dries up for a long period, the energy consumption of the mill wheel cannot be balanced by new energy supply. The water in the reservoir is used up, and if the dry period is long enough, the mill wheel stops turning. Eventually, the stream may flow again, filling the reservoir and turning the mill wheel again. This occurs because the stream–reservoir–mill system is itself a part of the Earth's much larger systems of water circulation and water budget, which include condensation, precipitation, run–off, and evaporation. The water systems receive their energy supply from the Earth's heat budget, which in turn receives its energy supply from the sun's radiation.

14. According to the passage, the concept of systems involves all of the following EXCEPT

(A) the components of a collection
(B) the functional relationships among parts
(C) the links between different systems
(D) the origin of the scientific method

15. Which sentence below best expresses the essential information in the highlighted sentence in paragraph 1? Incorrect choices change the meaning in important ways or leave out essential information.

(A) Every science has a unique set of systems with characteristics and relationships that do not exist in any other science.
(B) The subject matter of systems is the same for all sciences, but the structure of system relationships can vary.
(C) System components and relationships differ for each science, yet systems in all sciences share similar properties.
(D) It is difficult to distinguish one system from another because all systems in all sciences have similar characteristics.

16. The word them in paragraph 1 refers to

(A) sciences
(B) principles
(C) elements
(D) forces

17. The word exhausted in paragraph 3 is closest in meaning to

(A) increased
(B) used
(C) resupplied
(D) wasted

18. In paragraph 3, the author discusses the example of a mill wheel to illustrate what point about closed systems?

(A) The energy supply of a closed system is limited.
(B) Closed systems are rare in the natural environment.
(C) The Earth system as a whole is a closed system.
(D) Closed systems get energy from their surroundings.

19. According to paragraph 4, the Earth system as a whole is a closed system because

(A) the Earth receives no energy from outside the system boundary
(B) the boundary of the Earth system is clearly defined
(C) no mass crosses the system boundary, but some energy does
(D) the Earth system uses energy from solar radiation to support life

20. It can be inferred from paragraph 5 that living organisms

(A) are part of a larger system that receives and gives off energy
(B) can transfer energy but not mass across the system boundary
(C) do not have functional relationships with their surroundings
(D) can survive in a closed system only if there is a water supply

21. The phrase dries up in paragraph 6 is closest in meaning to

(A) slowly rises
(B) becomes warmer
(C) is polluted
(D) stops flowing

22. Which of the following statements can be inferred from paragraph 6?

(A) If a mill wheel stops turning, it will not start again until the following year.
(B) The mill wheel is temporarily a closed system during long dry periods.
(C) Condensation, precipitation, run–off, and evaporation act as closed systems.
(D) The Earth's heat budget is a closed system because its energy supply is limited.

23. Why does the author mention water circulation and water budget in paragraph 6?

Ⓐ To give examples of open systems that behave as closed systems
Ⓑ To illustrate the point that open systems are part of larger systems
Ⓒ To emphasize the importance of water in the Earth system
Ⓓ To introduce a discussion of threats to the Earth's energy supply

24. Look at the four squares, **A**, **B**, **C**, and **D**, which indicate where the following sentence could be added to the passage. Where would the sentence best fit?

For example, the hot tea in a vacuum bottle does not interact with the environment outside the bottle.

A closed system is isolated from its surroundings. **A** The energy supply of a closed system is limited and is progressively used up by the processes operating within the system. **B** The ability of the system to function decreases as the available energy is exhausted. Without any additional energy supplied from the outside, the system's processes cease altogether and no further change is possible in the system. **C** A mill wheel supplied with water from a non–refillable container is a closed system. Once the container of water is empty, the wheel no longer turns because there is no water to turn it. In a truly closed system, the water would have to be collected below the mill wheel in a second container to ensure that the system did not supply any energy to the outside. **D**

25. Select the appropriate sentences from the answer choices and match them to the type of system that they describe. TWO of the answer choices will NOT be used. ***This question is worth 3 points.***

Answer Choices

(A) It is a collection of things that have no relationship to one another.
(B) Its processes eventually use up all of its limited energy supply.
(C) Both energy and mass can pass across the system boundary.
(D) It is part of a larger system with which it interacts and exchanges energy.
(E) No exchanges of mass occur between the system and its surroundings.
(F) It is a large mass of a single element that cannot be changed in any way.
(G) The energy supply is continually renewed from the surroundings.

Closed System

•
•

Open System

•
•
•

How to Score 3–Point Questions	
Answers Correct	**Points Earned**
5	3
4	2
3	1
0–2	0

LIFE SUCCESS AND SATISFACTION

1 Life satisfaction, which can be defined as general happiness or well being, is related to several **demographic** and personal qualities. The factor of age is important because the elements that make up life satisfaction may differ from one age to the next. Income is more likely to predict life satisfaction among middle–aged and older adults than among young adults. Health is a more significant predictor of happiness among older adults than among the young or the middle–aged. However, average levels of life satisfaction do not change significantly with age. Generally speaking, older adults are as satisfied with their lives as are younger or middle–aged adults.

2 There is no single element that guarantees high life satisfaction for everyone who possesses it. Happiness seems to consist of many things that each person weighs differently, such as income, education, work, and relationships. However, certain factors are reliable predictors of life satisfaction. One such predictor is health, especially one's perception of one's own health rather than a doctor's objective health assessment. Another predictor of life satisfaction is a feeling of being in charge of one's own life and a sense of authority over one's own decisions. Adults who feel that they have some choices and options are generally happier than those who feel that their lives are controlled by others or by fate or chance. For example, older adults who experience financial strain feel less life satisfaction mainly because the problem signals a loss of control over their lives.

3 The largest predictor of life satisfaction appears to be the adequacy of social relationships, especially marriage and family relationships. The perceived quality rather than the quantity of social interactions is most strongly related to happiness. Satisfaction with one's close personal relationships is more closely linked to overall life satisfaction than either demographic factors or satisfaction with other key aspects of adult life such as occupation. This is true even among highly educated men, who typically have a very high commitment to their work. The quality of social support available in one's key relationships affects the ability to handle stress and life changes as well as one's ongoing level of life satisfaction.

4 Studies suggest that family background and early–adulthood resources are predictors of psychological health or success at midlife. People who age well are those who start out well. One study showed that the happiest and most successful middle–aged adults had grown up in warm, supportive, intellectually stimulating families. Well–adjusted or successful middle–aged adults began adulthood with more personal resources, including better psychological and physical health at college age. They also had been practical and well organized in college and had shown greater intellectual competence.

5 However, no measure of early family environment or early–adult competence remained a significant predictor of psychological well being at the end of middle age. One study of men revealed that at the age of 65, there were no childhood or early–adulthood characteristics that distinguished between men who had turned out well and those who had not. However, what did predict success and well being at age 65 was the men's health and adjustment at midlife. These results suggest that a successful adult life is not something preordained from childhood or early adulthood but rather something created out of the opportunities available over the course of one's life. Late–life success is related more directly to midlife qualities or experiences. People who start out with certain advantages have a greater chance of experiencing further advantages; however, it is what one does with the experiences—both positive and negative—that determines long–term life satisfaction. The choices that people make in early adulthood help shape who they are at midlife, and those midlife qualities in turn influence who they become later in life.

Glossary:
demographic: relating to demography, the study of human populations

26. What point does the author make about the relationship of age to life satisfaction?

(A) Age is the primary factor in determining life satisfaction.
(B) The factors that determine life satisfaction are the same at every age.
(C) Average levels of life satisfaction are similar for every age group.
(D) Young adults are more satisfied with their lives than older adults are.

27. According to the passage, all of the following are predictors of life satisfaction EXCEPT

(A) health
(B) age
(C) control of own life
(D) family relationships

28. The phrase in charge of in paragraph 2 is closest in meaning to

(A) worried about
(B) responsible for
(C) lucky in
(D) controlled by

29. The word problem in paragraph 2 refers to

(A) authority
(B) fate or chance
(C) financial strain
(D) less life satisfaction

30. The word adequacy in paragraph 3 is closest in meaning to

(A) knowledge
(B) appearance
(C) memory
(D) quality

31. What can be inferred from paragraph 3 about social relationships?

(A) Close social relationships are likely to influence long–term health and happiness.
(B) People with good family relationships also have good social relationships at work.
(C) Highly educated people usually have many different kinds of social relationships.
(D) The number of social relationships is more important than the type of relationship.

32. What does the author say about people who are well adjusted and successful at midlife?

(A) They are more satisfied with their lives than young adults are.
(B) They perceive themselves as successful even when it is not true.
(C) They are generally better adjusted than their parents were.
(D) They probably had positive personal qualities as young adults.

33. Which sentence below best expresses the essential information in the highlighted sentence in paragraph 5? Incorrect choices change the meaning in important ways or leave out essential information.

(A) The most important predictors of psychological health do not change between early adulthood and midlife.
(B) Neither family background nor qualities of early adulthood can predict life satisfaction beyond middle age.
(C) Middle–aged people are likely to be well adjusted if their experiences as young adults were mostly positive.
(D) There is no reliable way to measure the influence of family relationships on the mental health of older adults.

34. Why does the author discuss a study of men in paragraph 5?

(A) To illustrate a point about satisfaction late in life
(B) To explain differences among men of different ages
(C) To emphasize the importance of family relationships
(D) To argue for more psychological studies about men

35. The word preordained in paragraph 5 is closest in meaning to

(A) appreciated
(B) forgotten
(C) determined
(D) organized

36. It can be inferred from paragraph 5 that the author most likely believes which of the following about long–term life satisfaction?

(A) It is affected by the decisions made throughout adulthood.
(B) It is measured differently for men and for women.
(C) It is directly related to having advantages during childhood.
(D) It is purely the result of chance and cannot be predicted.

37. Look at the four squares, **A**, **B**, **C**, and **D**, which indicate where the following sentence could be added to the passage. Where would the sentence best fit?

Men who had had good relationships with both of their parents in childhood were better adjusted at midlife than were other men in the study.

Studies suggest that family background and early–adulthood resources are predictors of psychological health or success at midlife. People who age well are those who start out well. **A** One study showed that the happiest and most successful middle–aged adults had grown up in warm, supportive, intellectually stimulating families. **B** Well–adjusted or successful middle–aged adults began adulthood with more personal resources, including better psychological and physical health at college age. **C** They also had been practical and well organized in college and had shown greater intellectual competence. **D**

38. Read the first sentence of a summary of the passage. Complete the summary by selecting the THREE answer choices that express the most important ideas in the passage. Some sentences do not belong in the summary because they express ideas that are not presented in the passage or are minor ideas in the passage. ***This question is worth 2 points.***

Several factors influence the life success and satisfaction of adults.

•
•
•

Answer Choices

(A) Health is very important to the happiness of older adults but less significant for the young and middle–aged.

(B) Health and a sense of personal control are important elements of a person's happiness and well being.

(C) The perceived quality of one's social relationships is the most reliable predictor of life satisfaction.

(D) Young adults experience both positive and negative feelings more strongly than older adults do.

(E) Health and adjustment during midlife have a direct effect on the life satisfaction of men at age 65.

(F) Experiences and choices at each stage of life influence one's success and satisfaction at the next stage.

How to Score 2–Point Questions	
Answers Correct	**Points Earned**
3	2
2	1
0–1	0

THE ILLUSION OF FILM

1 Film is an illusion because the moving pictures seen on the screen are not moving at all. A film is actually a series of tiny still pictures, or frames. They appear to be moving because the retina of the human eye retains the impression of an object for a split second after that object has actually disappeared. This principle is known as the persistence of vision. When we look at a single frame of film, the image persists in the brain's visual center for a fraction of a second. Then, the next frame comes along and the brain has to catch up with the new image. Thus, our eyes and brain trick us into thinking that we see a smoothly moving image rather than a series of still ones.

2 Another illusion of film is known collectively as special effects, the tricks and techniques that filmmakers use when makeup, costume, and stunts are still not enough to make a scene convincing. Special–effects artists apply science to filmmaking, showing us things that no plain camera could ever photograph. Even since the introduction of computer graphics in recent decades, the films of today still rely on some special effects that have existed since the early years of cinema.

3 One category of special effects is called optical or visual effects, tricks made with the camera. One of the pioneers of optical effects was the French filmmaker Georges Méliès, who invented a technique called stop–motion photography. With this technique, a scene is filmed, the camera is stopped, the scene is changed in some way, and then the camera rolls again. Stop–motion photography can create the illusion of an actor disappearing on screen. In one short film, an actor's clothes keep returning to his body as he tries to get undressed. Méliès also invented a technique known as split screen. By putting a card over the camera lens, he prevented half of the frame of film from being exposed. He filmed a scene on the uncovered half of the frame and then backed up the same strip of film in his camera. For the second shot, he covered the exposed half and took another series of pictures on the half that had been covered the first time. With the technique of split screen, it is possible to achieve illusions such as having the same actor play twins.

4 Mechanical effects are another category of special effects. Mechanical effects are objects or devices used during the filming to create an illusion, such as feathers or plastic chips to simulate snow, and wires to create the illusion that people are flying. Many sound effects are mechanical effects. Wood blocks create a horse's hoofbeats, and a vibrating sheet of metal sounds like thunder. During the silent film era, the music machine called the Kinematophone was popular because it could produce the sounds of sirens, sleigh bells, gunfire, baby cries, and kisses—all at the press of a key.

5 Other mechanical effects are puppets, robots of all sizes, and tiny copies of buildings or cities. To reduce the cost of studio sets or location photography, special–effects technicians create painted or projected backgrounds, which replace the set or add to it. For example, in a long shot of a town, the set might be only a few feet high, and the remainder of the town is painted onto a sheet of glass positioned in front of the camera during filming. In a 1916 silent film called *The Flying Torpedo*, mechanical effects created the appearance of an enemy invasion of the California seacoast. Technicians threw small contact–rigged explosives into toy cities, scattering the tiny buildings into the air. An artist painted a row of battleships on a board that was only six feet long. Carpenters drilled small holes in the ships, which were filled with small charges of flash powder to simulate guns. An electrician wired the charges so they could be fired on cue from a small battery. For audiences of the time, the effect was of a real fleet of ships firing on the California coast.

6 Sometimes optical and mechanical effects are used together. For the original 1933 version of *King Kong*, the filmmakers wanted to show the giant ape climbing the Empire State Building in New York City. To show Kong's climb, the special–effects technicians built a

tiny movable model of the ape and a proportionately small model of the Empire State Building. Then, stop–motion photography was used to create the illusion that Kong was moving up the building.

39. Why does the author discuss the principle of persistence of vision in paragraph 1?

(A) To introduce a discussion of human vision
(B) To explain how we remember images
(C) To support the idea that film is an illusion
(D) To compare two types of special effects

40. The phrase catch up with in paragraph 1 is closest in meaning to

(A) hurry to process
(B) put aside
(C) search for
(D) obtain from memory

41. The author primarily defines special effects as

(A) phenomena that cannot be explained logically
(B) techniques and devices to create illusions in film
(C) sounds and images that cause an emotional response
(D) methods used by filmmakers of the silent film era

42. The word rolls in paragraph 3 is closest in meaning to

(A) changes
(B) operates
(C) breaks
(D) reverses

43. The word simulate in paragraph 4 is closest in meaning to

(A) make it easier to film
(B) put on top of
(C) improve the texture of
(D) create the appearance of

44. It can be inferred from paragraph 4 that silent films

(A) were projected by a machine called the Kinematophone
(B) relied more on special effects than on acting ability
(C) used sound effects to make scenes more convincing
(D) are still very popular with movie audiences today

45. All of the following would necessarily involve mechanical effects EXCEPT

(A) using wires to make objects fly
(B) filming each half of a frame separately
(C) hitting a sheet of metal to create thunder
(D) building a small model of a town

46. Which sentence below best expresses the essential information in the highlighted sentence in paragraph 5? Incorrect choices change the meaning in important ways or leave out essential information.

(A) The most effective way to lower the cost of a film is to replace location photography with studio sets or backgrounds.
(B) Special effects technicians build painted or projected backgrounds that appear more realistic than location photography.
(C) One way to reduce costs is to repaint old studio sets and use them again; this also adds to the number of available sets.
(D) Painted and projected backgrounds are special effects that improve or replace sets, thus making filming less expensive.

47. The word which in paragraph 5 refers to

(A) carpenters
(B) holes
(C) ships
(D) guns

TEST 3

48. What point does the author make in paragraph 6 about the 1933 film *King Kong*?

Ⓐ The film combined two different types of special effects.
Ⓑ The filmmakers trained a giant ape to climb up a building.
Ⓒ Stop–motion photography was invented during the filming.
Ⓓ *King Kong* remains very popular with audiences today.

49. Look at the four squares, **A**, **B**, **C**, and **D**, which indicate where the following sentence could be added to the passage. Where would the sentence best fit?

In another example, an actor appears to take off his head and place it on a table.

One category of special effects is called optical or visual effects, tricks made with the camera. One of the pioneers of optical effects was the French filmmaker Georges Méliès, who invented a technique called stop–motion photography. With this technique, a scene is filmed, the camera is stopped, the scene is changed in some way, and then the camera rolls again. **A** Stop–motion photography can create the illusion of an actor disappearing on screen. In one short film, an actor's clothes keep returning to his body as he tries to get undressed. **B** Méliès also invented a technique known as split screen. **C** By putting a card over the camera lens, he prevented half of the frame of film from being exposed. He filmed a scene on the uncovered half of the frame and then backed up the same strip of film in his camera. For the second shot, he covered the exposed half and took another series of pictures on the half that had been covered the first time. With the technique of split screen, it is possible to achieve illusions such as having the same actor play twins. **D**

50. Select the appropriate sentences from the answer choices and match them to the category of special effects that they describe. TWO of the answer choices will NOT be used. ***This question is worth 3 points.***

Answer Choices

(A) Objects and devices are used during filming to create an illusion.
(B) The eye retains the image of an object after the object has actually disappeared.
(C) Tricks of the camera produce images of things that are not real.
(D) Puppets, robots, explosives, and small models are examples of these effects.
(E) Stop–motion photography makes an actor disappear on screen.
(F) A computer program makes one object appear to change into another.
(G) They created the illusion of ships attacking a town in a 1916 silent film.

Optical Effects
•
•

Mechanical Effects
•
•
•

How to Score 3–Point Questions	
Answers Correct	**Points Earned**
5	3
4	2
3	1
0–2	0

WATER AND LIFE ON MARS

1 The presence or absence of water has a direct bearing on the possibility of life on other planets. In the nineteenth century, it was commonly accepted that life, perhaps even intelligent life, was widespread in the solar system, and Mars was an obvious target in the search for life. New photographic technology offered a way for astronomers to learn more about the red planet. In 1888, Italian astronomer Giovanni Schiaparelli produced images that showed a network of long, thin, dark lines crossing the surface of Mars. He called these features *canali* in Italian, which became "canals" or "channels" in English. The strange appearance of the canals suggested to some scientists that they had been formed artificially rather than naturally. The mystery deepened when Schiaparelli observed that many of the canals in the photographs were actually double.

2 Other photographic images of Mars revealed its seasonally changing polar ice caps and features that appeared to be ancient islands located in what was now a dry streambed. When the islands were first discovered, some scientists speculated that a thick water–laden atmosphere capable of generating heavy rains had once existed on Mars. However, others remained unconvinced of the presence of water. Then, in 1963, a team of astronomers obtained a good photographic plate of the near–infrared spectrum of Mars. The photograph showed that, faintly but definitely, water vapor lines could be seen. This photograph established that there really was water on Mars, though the amount was very small. Today, the presence of water vapor in the Martian atmosphere is generally accepted, as is the belief that the atmosphere was once much denser than it is now, with a much greater abundance of water vapor.

3 The surface of Mars is dry today, but it does contain significant amounts of ice and signs that liquid water once flowed over the planet. All of the locations where evidence of water has been found are ancient, probably formed very early in Martian history. Data transmitted from spacecraft on Mars in 2004 have revealed that water was once common across a vast region of the planet, possibly as shallow lakes or seas that dried out and then filled up again. There are signs that the wind blew debris around during dry stages. These seas and lakes extended across hundreds of thousands of square miles, creating habitable conditions during long stretches of time billions of years ago.

4 Evidence of water includes the presence of various minerals known as evaporates, deposits left behind when liquid water turns to vapor. Small areas of mineral deposits have been found in Valles Marineris, a huge hole on Mars that is larger than the Grand Canyon on Earth. The minerals there contain water, so they had to be formed in the presence of water. Geologic research has also turned up clay and gypsum deposits that were formed by water in the soil. Rocks that clearly formed in water extend throughout 300 meters of layered materials in several locations across the Martian plains. The layers were built up over time, which means water was present, at least temporarily, for extended periods on ancient Mars.

5 Besides the ice packs at Mars's poles, astronomers have discovered a frozen sea near its equator. This frozen sea is the size of the North Sea on Earth and appears similar to the ice packs on Antarctica. Scientists have also detected evidence of lava flows 20 million years ago as well as signs that some volcanoes may still be active. Several recently formed volcanic cones near Mars's North Pole indicate that the planet's core may interact with the surface, meaning there was both warmth and moisture in the recent past—circumstances that might have supported life.

6 Liquid water is the key ingredient for life as we know it. Of all the other planets in the solar system, Mars is most like Earth. The fact that water existed on ancient Mars does not necessarily mean life ever emerged there; however, all of the available evidence does suggest that Mars meets all the requirements that are needed for life to exist.

51. According to the passage, what has been a major focus of research about Mars?

(A) How Mars compares to other planets in the solar system
(B) Who built the network of canals on the surface of Mars
(C) Whether signs of water indicate that life has existed on Mars
(D) How soon astronauts from Earth will be able to go to Mars

52. Astronomers of the nineteenth and twentieth centuries studied Mars mainly through

(A) ancient writings
(B) photographic images
(C) Martian soil samples
(D) data sent by spacecraft

53. It can be inferred from paragraph 1 that Schiaparelli's observation of canals on Mars led to

(A) direct proof that life has existed on Mars
(B) the rejection of Schiaparelli's ideas by other scientists
(C) the search for canals on other planets in the solar system
(D) new questions about intelligent life on Mars

54. What discovery led some scientists to think that the Martian atmosphere had produced heavy rains in the past?

(A) A network of canals on the surface
(B) Ancient islands in a dry streambed
(C) Water vapor lines on a photographic plate
(D) Volcanic cones near the planet's North Pole

55. Which sentence below best expresses the essential information in the highlighted sentence in paragraph 2? Incorrect choices change the meaning in important ways or leave out essential information.

(A) Most scientists believe there is water vapor in the Martian atmosphere, which is now less dense than it was in the past.
(B) The amount of water vapor in the Martian atmosphere has changed many times in the past, and scientists generally accept this.
(C) The atmosphere of Mars used to contain only water vapor, but now scientists know that several other gases are also present.
(D) Scientists used to believe that Mars had no atmosphere, but now most think it has a very dense atmosphere of water vapor.

56. The phrase filled up in paragraph 3 is closest in meaning to

(A) got smaller
(B) were frozen
(C) became wet
(D) turned to rock

57. The word habitable in paragraph 3 is closest in meaning to

(A) dangerous
(B) suitable for life
(C) mysterious
(D) capable of changing

58. Layers of rock in several places on the Martian plains are evidence that

(A) Mars was formed at the same time as Earth
(B) both wind and water erosion occurred there
(C) water was present there for a long time
(D) liquid water is no longer present on Mars

59. All of the following indicate the presence of water on Mars EXCEPT

(A) images of polar ice caps
(B) a 1963 photograph
(C) clay and gypsum deposits
(D) evidence of lava flows

TEST 3

60. The word ingredient in paragraph 6 is closest in meaning to

(A) factor
(B) definition
(C) image
(D) result

61. Why does the author compare Mars to Earth in paragraph 6?

(A) To emphasize that there is more water on Earth than on Mars
(B) To point out that Mars has the conditions for life to exist
(C) To state that there are no differences between Mars and Earth
(D) To explain why life emerged on Earth but not on Mars

62. Look at the four squares, [A], [B], [C], and [D], which indicate where the following sentence could be added to the passage. Where would the sentence best fit?

Astronomers already knew that Mars had some kind of atmosphere because of the occasional presence of bright features that looked like clouds.

The presence or absence of water has a direct bearing on the possibility of life on other planets. [A] In the nineteenth century, it was commonly accepted that life, perhaps even intelligent life, was widespread in the solar system, and Mars was an obvious target in the search for life. [B] New photographic technology offered a way for astronomers to learn more about the red planet. In 1888, Italian astronomer Giovanni Schiaparelli produced images that showed a network of long, thin, dark lines crossing the surface of Mars. [C] He called these features *canali* in Italian, which became "canals" or "channels" in English. The strange appearance of the canals suggested to some scientists that they had been formed artificially rather than naturally. [D] The mystery deepened when Schiaparelli observed that many of the canals in the photographs were actually double.

63. Read the first sentence of a summary of the passage. Complete the summary by selecting the THREE answer choices that express the most important ideas in the passage. Some sentences do not belong in the summary because they express ideas that are not presented in the passage or are minor ideas in the passage. ***This question is worth 2 points.***

Scientists have long searched for evidence of water and life on Mars.

•
•
•

Answer Choices

Ⓐ Early photographs of Mars showed what appeared to be canals, polar ice caps, and ancient islands.

Ⓑ Dry streambeds, lakes, and seas suggest that Mars does not have enough water to support life.

Ⓒ The Martian atmosphere contains water vapor, and liquid water once flowed over the planet's surface.

Ⓓ Evaporates are mineral deposits that are left behind when liquid water turns to vapor.

Ⓔ Mineral deposits and a frozen sea provide evidence of water on Mars in the past and present.

Ⓕ Because Mars is so similar to Earth, scientists believe that humans will be able to live on Mars in the future.

How to Score 2–Point Questions	
Answers Correct	**Points Earned**
3	2
2	1
0–1	0

Answers are on page 304.

Record your Reading section score on page 380.

Disk 3, Track 1

LISTENING SECTION DIRECTIONS

The Listening section measures your ability to understand conversations and lectures in English. You will hear each conversation and lecture only one time. After each conversation or lecture, you will hear some questions about it. Answer the questions based on what the speakers state or imply.

You may take notes while you listen. You may use your notes to help you answer the questions.

In some questions, you will see this icon: . This means that you will hear, but not see, part of the question.

Some questions have special directions, which appear in a gray box. Most questions are worth one point. If a question is worth more than one point, the directions will indicate how many points you can receive.

You will now begin the first part of the Listening section.

Time – maximum of 60 minutes

Disk 3, Track 2

QUESTIONS 1–5

Conversation

1. Why does the student go to see his adviser?

   (A) To find out if he can change one of his classes
   (B) To ask her for a letter of recommendation
   (C) To check the time of his registration appointment
   (D) To learn if he still has required courses to take

2. Why does the adviser say this:

   (A) To invite the student to attend a meeting with her
   (B) To let the student know that she will have to leave soon
   (C) To announce that she will be speaking at a meeting
   (D) To explain why she cannot help the student right now

3. What does the student want to do next year?

   (A) Change his major field of study
   (B) Study at the university
   (C) Work as a weather forecaster
   (D) Become a professional golf player

4. In which subject areas must the student take courses next semester?

   Click on two answers.

   [A] Social science
   [B] Natural science
   [C] Humanities
   [D] Physical education

5. What does the student imply about golf?

   (A) Golf is his favorite leisure activity.
   (B) He enjoys playing golf with his boss.
   (C) He would like to know more about golf.
   (D) He has never played golf before.

Disk 3, Track 3

QUESTIONS 6–11

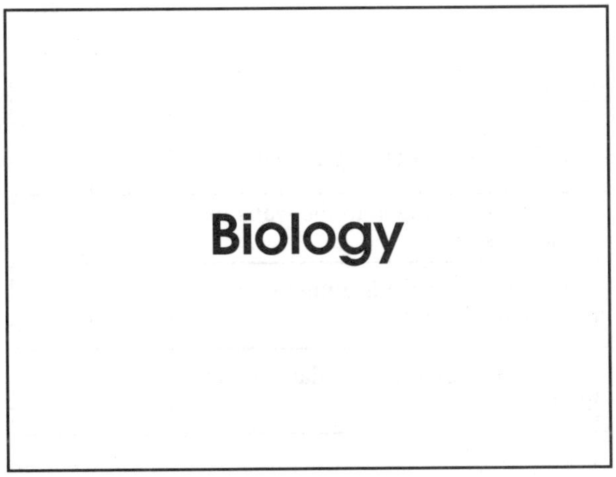

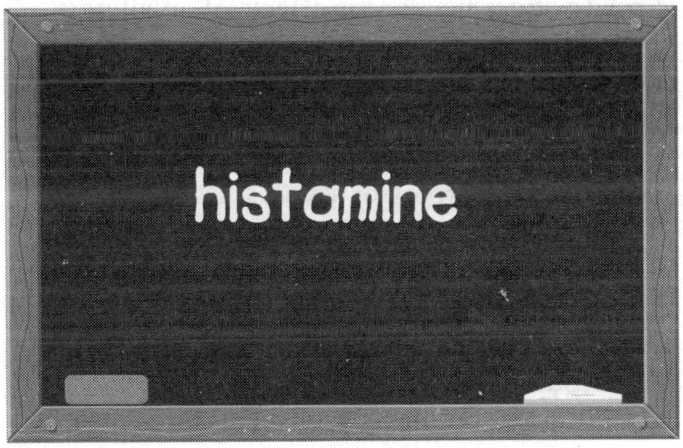

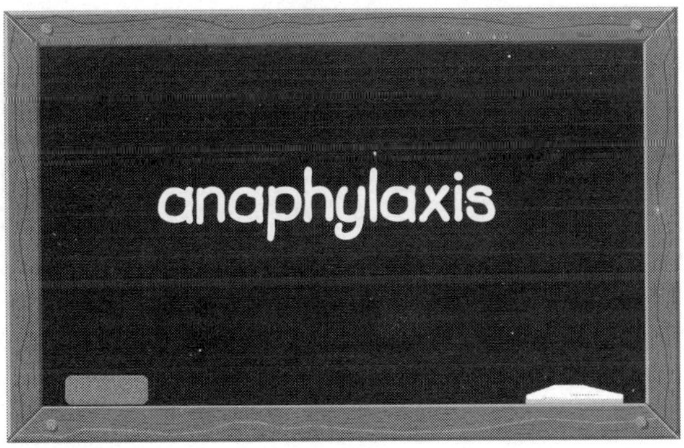

6. What is the lecture mainly about?

  (A) The components of the immune system
  (B) Why some people are immune from disease
  (C) A severe type of immune response
  (D) Dangers of different types of shock

7. According to the professor, what can initiate anaphylaxis?

  Click on two answers.

  [A] Alcohol
  [B] Bee venom
  [C] Peanuts
  [D] A virus

8. Why does the professor tell a story about a little girl at a birthday party?

  (A) To find out which students have children
  (B) To frighten the class with facts about bees
  (C) To change the topic of the discussion
  (D) To stress the serious effects of an allergy

9. Listen again to part of the lecture. Then answer the question.

  Why does the professor say this: 🎧

  (A) To stress the mysterious nature of severe immune responses
  (B) To argue that anaphylaxis is mainly the result of bad luck
  (C) To point out that scientists disagree over what causes allergies
  (D) To suggest that people are crazy to eat offending substances

10. The professor describes what happens during anaphylactic shock. Indicate whether each sentence below is a step in the process.

  For each sentence, click in the correct box.

	Yes	No
The chest feels tight and breathing is difficult.		
The face and throat begin to swell.		
Fatty particles attach to the walls of blood vessels.		
The body releases histamine into the bloodstream.		
The blood pressure rises dangerously high.		

11. What can be inferred about surviving anaphylaxis?

  (A) It is impossible for children to survive anaphylaxis.
  (B) Only a few people have ever survived anaphylaxis.
  (C) Survival depends on immediate medical treatment.
  (D) The professor knows someone who survived the disease.

Disk 3, Track 4

QUESTIONS 12–17

United States History

12. What is the talk mainly about?

- (A) American farm life in the early twentieth century
- (B) The history of a successful business innovation
- (C) Differences between the rural and urban way of life
- (D) The effects of mail–order catalogs on rural America

13. How did the mail–order business begin?

- (A) A businessman sent a catalog to a large number of farmers.
- (B) The railroads started delivering goods to isolated rural areas.
- (C) The post office added new services to promote ordering by mail.
- (D) A group of farmers organized a method of cooperative buying.

14. Why does the professor mention Rural Free Delivery and Parcel Post?

- (A) To give examples of early mail–order houses
- (B) To compare the benefits of two different types of services
- (C) To explain how these services helped the mail–order business
- (D) To describe the origins of the concept of customer service

15. According to the professor, what two factors led to the similarity of goods available nationwide?

Click on two answers.

- [A] The mass production of goods
- [B] The wide distribution of catalogs
- [C] The growing interest in regional styles
- [D] The desire to copy designer fashions

16. What does the professor mean when she says this: 🎧

- (A) Immigrants were required to buy a textbook to learn English.
- (B) Most of the people who used mail–order catalogs were immigrants.
- (C) The Sears catalog taught immigrants about American culture.
- (D) People immigrated to America for its economic opportunities.

17. Based on the information in the talk, would the professor most likely agree or disagree with each statement below?

For each sentence, click in the correct box.

	Agree	Disagree
Nineteenth–century farm families had the same cultural opportunities as city residents.		
Mail–order companies changed the lives of farm families across the country.		
Clothing ordered from mail–order catalogs was more fashionable than clothing bought in department stores.		
The Sears catalog provided an important illustration of American life.		

Disk 3, Track 5

QUESTIONS 18–22

Conversation

18. What is the main subject of the conversation?

(A) The importance of pure water
(B) Factors that affect the color of water
(C) How the human eye perceives color
(D) The colors of the light spectrum

19. What does the student mean when she says this:

(A) She does not believe that water is colorless.
(B) She has difficulty seeing certain colors.
(C) It is possible to see through water only if it is clear.
(D) It is interesting to look at things underwater.

20. Listen again to part of the conversation. Then answer the question.

Why does the student say this:

(A) To express her fear of very deep water
(B) To explain why she likes the color of the ocean
(C) To change the topic of the conversation
(D) To check her understanding of what the tutor said

21. According to the conversation, what factors influence the color of water?

Click on two answers.

[A] Waves on the surface
[B] The depth of the water
[C] Sediments in the water
[D] The water temperature

22. What can be inferred about a lake with brown water?

(A) The lake is not safe for swimming.
(B) The lake has a sandy bottom.
(C) The water contains suspended particles.
(D) The water is very deep in the center of the lake.

Disk 3, Track 6

QUESTIONS 23–28

23. According to the professor, how did children acquire their culture throughout most of history?

(A) By experiencing life in another country
(B) By watching cultural programs on television
(C) By going to the museum and the library
(D) By listening to parents and grandparents

24. What does the professor mean by the term "cultural narrator"?

(A) The voice that tells a story on a television program
(B) The medium that conveys a culture's values and beliefs
(C) A book that is considered a classic in its field
(D) A scholar who states theories about popular culture

25. According to the professor, why did Marshall McLuhan study popular culture?

(A) McLuhan wanted to understand the values of his students.
(B) McLuhan needed an interesting topic for his dissertation.
(C) McLuhan wanted to write stories for a popular magazine.
(D) McLuhan enjoyed watching television with his family.

26. What is the professor's opinion of *The Medium is the Message*?

(A) It is a good source of information about cultural history.
(B) Its ideas are becoming less relevant today than in the past.
(C) It was the first book to argue that television was bad for society.
(D) It will influence how the students think about communication.

27. Listen again to part of the lecture. Then answer the question.

Why does the professor say this:

(A) To compare different ways of conveying a message
(B) To explain an important theory of communications
(C) To show that miscommunication is a serious problem
(D) To introduce a controversial topic of conversation

28. Listen again to part of the lecture. Then answer the question.

What does the professor imply about the effects of the media on society?

(A) The media did not affect society before the twentieth century.
(B) Television has a mostly negative effect on human behavior.
(C) The media's effects are of widespread interest and concern.
(D) The Internet will be the most influential medium in the future.

Disk 3, Track 7

QUESTIONS 29–34

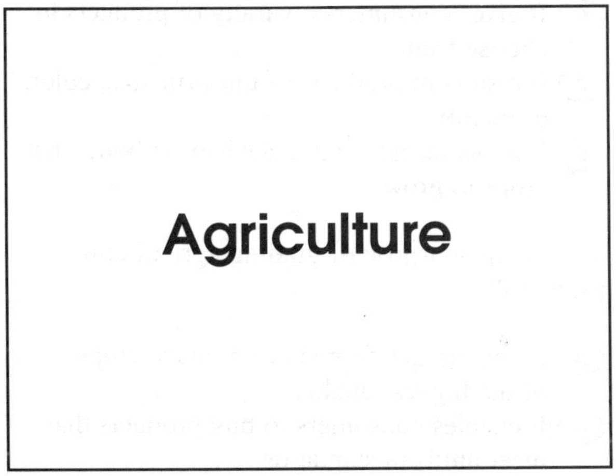

29. What does the professor mainly discuss?

(A) Recent advances in agricultural technology
(B) How farm products are supplied to consumers
(C) Methods that farmers use to increase production
(D) Ways of transporting farm products to stores

30. Why does the professor say this:

(A) To illustrate the unreasonable demands of the typical consumer
(B) To compare consumers in North America with those in other places
(C) To give examples of common agricultural products in North America
(D) To explain why agricultural marketing technology is necessary

31. Which of the following are examples of the marketing function of harvesting?

Click on two answers.

[A] Picking cotton
[B] Sorting eggs by size
[C] Moving corn to a grain elevator
[D] Milking cows

32. According to the professor, why is assembling an important function in agricultural marketing?

(A) It allows markets to deal efficiently with large quantities.
(B) It gives consumers a variety of products to choose from.
(C) It results in products of uniform size, color, or quality.
(D) It helps farmers make decisions about what crops to grow.

33. What is the purpose of grading agricultural products?

(A) It encourages farmers to produce crops of the highest quality.
(B) It enables consumers to buy products that meet uniform standards.
(C) It allows the government to regulate agricultural markets.
(D) It promotes the development of better marketing infrastructure.

34. Why does the professor say this:

(A) To show that agriculture involves taking risks
(B) To illustrate the function of transporting
(C) To compare various methods of harvesting
(D) To describe job opportunities in marketing

Stop

Answers are on page 307.

Record your Listening section score on page 381.

Disk 3, Track 8

SPEAKING SECTION DIRECTIONS

The Speaking section measures your ability to speak in English about a variety of topics. There are six questions in this section.

Questions 1 and 2 are independent tasks in which you will speak about familiar topics. Your rcsponses will be scored on your ability to speak clearly and coherently about the topics.

Questions 3 and 4 are integrated speaking tasks. You will read a passage, listen to a conversation or lecture, and then speak in response to a question about what you have read and heard. You will need to combine relevant information from the two sources to answer the question completely. Your responses will be scored on your ability to speak clearly and coherently and on your ability to accurately convey information about what you read and heard.

Questions 5 and 6 are integrated speaking tasks. You will listen to part of a conversation or lecture, and then speak in response to a question about what you have heard. Your responses will be scored on your ability to speak clearly and coherently and on your ability to accurately convcy information about what you heard.

You will hear each conversation and lecture only one time. You may take notes while you listen. You may use your notes to help you answer the questions.

Stop

QUESTION 1

In this question, you will be asked to talk about a familiar topic. After you hear the question, you will have 15 seconds to prepare your response and 45 seconds to speak.

Disk 3, Track 9

What is your favorite place to study? Describe it and explain why you like studying there. Include details and examples in your explanation.

Stop

Preparation Time – 15 seconds
Response Time – 45 seconds

QUESTION 2

In this question, you will be asked to give your opinion about a familiar topic. After you hear the question, you will have 15 seconds to prepare your response and 45 seconds to speak.

Disk 3, Track 10

Some people like humorous stories that make them laugh. Others prefer stories that are more serious and make them think. Which type of story do you prefer and why? Include details and examples in your explanation.

Stop

Preparation Time – 15 seconds
Response Time – 45 seconds

QUESTION 3

In this question, you will read a short passage about a campus situation, listen to a conversation, and then speak in response to a question about what you have read and heard. After you hear the question, you have 30 seconds to prepare your response and 60 seconds to speak.

Reading Time – 45 seconds

ANNOUNCEMENT FROM THE DEAN: NEW CREDIT REQUIREMENTS

The academic dean announces an important change to the university's core curriculum concerning the number of required credits in mathematics and writing. The mathematics requirement will increase from 1 to 2 courses (or a total of 7 credit hours). The writing requirement will increase from 2 to 3 courses (or a total of 9 credit hours). This change is in response to employers and graduate schools who state that students applying for employment or admission to graduate programs need strong skills in mathematics and writing. The new credit requirements will apply to all students who graduate after May 1 of next year.

Now cover the passage and listen to the recording. When you hear the question, begin preparing your response.

Disk 3, Track 11

The woman expresses her opinion about the new credit requirements. State her opinion and explain the reasons she gives for holding that opinion.

Stop

Preparation Time – 30 seconds
Response Time – 60 seconds

QUESTION 4

In this question, you will read a short passage on an academic subject, listen to a lecture on the same topic, and then speak in response to a question about what you have read and heard. After you hear the question, you have 30 seconds to prepare your response and 60 seconds to speak.

Reading Time – 45 seconds

SENSORY RECEPTORS

Sensations, or nerve impulses, begin with the excitation of sensory receptors, structures that detect changes in an animal's external and internal environment. Some sensory receptors are stimulated by physical bending or stretching caused by forms of mechanical energy such as pressure, touch, and motion. A common type of sensory receptor that detects motion is the hair cell. When hairs bend in one direction, they stretch the hair cell's membrane, sending a nerve impulse to the sensory areas of the brain. Hair cells can respond to the direction of motion as well as to its strength and speed.

Now cover the passage and listen to the recording. When you hear the question, begin preparing your response.

Disk 3, Track 12

Describe the whiskers of a cat, and explain how the whiskers function as sensory receptors.

Stop

Preparation Time – 30 seconds
Response Time – 60 seconds

QUESTION 5

In this question, you will listen to a conversation. You will then be asked to talk about the information in the conversation and to give your opinion about the ideas presented. After you hear the question, you have 20 seconds to prepare your response and 60 seconds to speak.

Disk 3, Track 13

Describe the woman's problem and the two suggestions the man makes about how to solve it. What do you think the woman should do, and why?

Stop

Preparation Time – 20 seconds
Response Time – 60 seconds

QUESTION 6

In this question, you will listen to part of a lecture. You will then be asked to summarize important information from the lecture. After you hear the question, you have 20 seconds to prepare your response and 60 seconds to speak.

Disk 3, Track 14

Using points and examples from the lecture, describe three types of learning disabilities, and explain how they can affect a child's ability to learn.

Stop

Preparation Time – 20 seconds
Response Time – 60 seconds

Key points for the Speaking responses are on page 309.

Each response earns a score of 1, 2, 3 or 4.

Record your total Speaking score on page 382.

Disk 3, Track 15

WRITING SECTION DIRECTIONS

The Writing section measures your ability to use writing to communicate in an academic environment. There are two writing questions.

Question 1 is an integrated writing task. You will read a passage, listen to a lecture, and then answer a question based on what you have read and heard. You have 20 minutes to plan and write your response.

Question 2 is an independent writing task. You will answer a question based on your own knowledge and experience. You have 30 minutes to plan and write your response.

Stop

QUESTION 1

For this task, you will write a response to a question about a reading passage and a lecture. You may take notes, and you may use your notes to help you write your response. Your response will be scored on the quality of your writing and on how well you connect the points in the lecture with points in the reading. Typically, an effective response will have 150 to 225 words.

Reading Time – 3 minutes

Spoken language is a complex sequence of sounds. When we know the language, we have no difficulty in distinguishing consonants from vowels and in separating the sounds into individual words. When we hear a language that we do not know, it is more difficult to distinguish single words.

The human voice is capable of making a very large number of sounds, but the sound system of each language restricts the number of acceptable sounds to a relatively small number. The sound stream of a language consists of separate, ordered parts: syllables, words, phrases, clauses, and sentences. Understanding and learning language comes naturally to us because the structure of language is so logical. Language has syntax, which means that syllables and words are organized into meaningful constructions. Syntax is a condition of all human languages. It controls the flow of information and expresses relationships. Linguistic syntax is most obvious at the phrase, clause, and sentence levels.

One of the most interesting aspects of language is how it changes over time. There can be changes in a language's sound system, such as a change in the pronunciation of a vowel. Such a change affects the "color" of the speech but has no effect on the meaning of a word. Change can also come in the creation of new words. Inventions, discoveries, and new contexts generate new words to describe them. Words also disappear as their relevant contexts disappear.

The vocabulary of a language has a great capacity to expand. The adoption of foreign words is part of the natural growth of almost any language. When language communities are forced together through political alliance or conquest, linguistic competition arises as two peoples try to converse. Often this results in a pidgin language, a mixing of words and expressions from the two languages.

Now listen to the recording. When you hear the question, begin your response. You may look at the passage during the writing time.

Disk 3, Track 16

Summarize the points made in the lecture, explaining how they are similar to points made in the reading.

Stop

Writing Time – 20 minutes

QUESTION 2

For this task, you will write an essay in response to a question that asks you to state and support your opinion on a topic. Your essay will be scored on the quality of your writing, including how well you organize and develop your ideas and how well you use language to express your ideas. Typically, an effective essay will have a minimum of 300 words.

Read the question below and make any notes that will help you plan your response. Then begin writing your essay.

> Some people think that scientists make the most important contributions to society. Other people think that the contributions of artists are the most important. Which position do you agree with? Give specific reasons and examples to support your answer.

Writing Time – 30 minutes

Key points for the Writing section are on page 310.

Each response earns a score of 1, 2, 3, 4 or 5.

Record your total Writing score on page 382.

TEST 4

READING SECTION DIRECTIONS

The Reading section measures your ability to read and understand passages in English. You will read three passages and answer questions about them. Answer all questions based on what is stated or implied in the passages.

Most questions are worth one point. The last question in each set is worth more than one point. For this question, the directions will indicate how many points you can receive.

Some passages have one or more words in bold type. For these bolded words, you will see a definition in a glossary at the end of the passage.

Allow 20 minutes to read each passage and answer the questions about it. You may now begin the first passage.

Time – 60 minutes

How Memory Works

1 Memory is the brain's ability to store and retrieve information related to previous experiences. Memory occurs in two stages: short–term and long–term. Short–term memory reflects an immediate sensory perception of an object or idea that occurs before the image is stored. Short–term memory enables you to dial a telephone number after looking it up but without looking at the number directly. If you call the number frequently, it becomes stored in long–term memory and can be recalled several weeks after you originally looked it up. Short–term memory and long–term memory can be thought of as memory structures, each varying as to how much information it can hold and for how long.

2 Memory relies on the ability to process information. Information processing begins with the environmental stimuli that you see, hear, smell, taste, and feel. These experiences are initially recorded in the brain's sensory register, which holds information just long enough (one to three seconds) for you to decide whether to process it further. Information that you do not selectively attend to will disappear from the system. However, if you recognize and attend to the information as meaningful or relevant, it is sent to short–term memory. Short–term memory can hold approximately seven unrelated bits of information at a time.

3 Short–term memory is often called working memory because it holds information that you are working with at a given moment, but only for about 20 seconds. Then, unless the information is processed further, it is quickly forgotten. For example, if you were asked to dial an unfamiliar telephone number, received a busy signal, and were then distracted by something else for 20 seconds, you probably would have forgotten the number at that point. Unless information in short–term memory is processed further, it does not make it to long–term memory.

4 Several control processes enable the transfer of information from short–term to long–term memory. One such process is rehearsal, or "practice makes perfect." Rehearsal is when you repeat something to yourself over and over. The purpose behind such behavior is usually to memorize information for later use, although sometimes it is simply to hold information in short–term memory for immediate use. For example, you may rehearse a telephone number by saying it aloud so you can redial it after getting a busy signal without having to look it up again in the phone book. Another process that enables the transfer of information to long–term memory is the association of new data with data previously learned and stored in long–term memory. Thus, it is easier to learn a new card game if you already have "card sense" from playing other games.

5 For cognitive psychologists, long–term memory is the most interesting of the memory structures, and most believe that the storage capacity of long–term memory is unlimited and contains a permanent record of everything you have learned. Long–term memory plays an influential role throughout the information processing system. The interests, attitudes, skills, and knowledge of the world existing in your long–term memory influence what you perceive and how you interpret your perceptions. They also affect whether you process information for short–term or long–term storage.

6 Long–term memory can hold recollections of personal experiences as well as factual knowledge acquired through other means such as reading. It also holds skills such as knowing how to ride a bicycle. In its ability to learn and remember, the brain can distinguish between facts and skills. When you acquire factual knowledge by memorizing dates, word definitions, formulas, and other information, you can consciously retrieve this fact memory from the data bank of your long–term memory. In contrast, skill memory usually involves motor activities that you learn by repetition without consciously remembering specific information. You perform learned motor skills, such as walking or riding a bicycle, without consciously recalling the individual steps required to do these tasks.

1. According to the passage, what must happen before information can be stored in memory?

   (A) The information must be pleasant.
   (B) An object or idea must be perceived.
   (C) An older memory must be replaced.
   (D) The information must be looked up.

2. The passage states that one difference between short–term memory and long–term memory is

   (A) the type of information they store
   (B) their importance in learning
   (C) the amount of information they hold
   (D) their location in the brain

3. The phrase attend to in paragraph 2 is closest in meaning to

   (A) reject
   (B) focus on
   (C) talk about
   (D) wait for

4. It can be inferred from paragraph 2 that something is NOT likely to be remembered if it is

   (A) not considered important
   (B) painful or embarrassing
   (C) related to previous experience
   (D) sent to short–term memory

5. The passage states that information can be lost from short–term memory when a person

   (A) does not know how to read
   (B) repeats the information over and over
   (C) processes the information further
   (D) is distracted for 20 seconds

6. The phrase make it to in paragraph 3 is closest in meaning to

   (A) disappear from
   (B) arrive at
   (C) respond to
   (D) seem like

7. Which sentence below best expresses the essential information in the highlighted sentence in paragraph 4? Incorrect choices change the meaning in important ways or leave out essential information.

   (A) Usually information is rehearsed so it can be used later, but sometimes it is rehearsed so it can be used right away.
   (B) There are several reasons for memorizing information; the most common reason is to improve short–term memory.
   (C) The belief that "practice makes perfect" causes people to repeat certain behavior even when the behavior is very complex.
   (D) It is fairly simple to keep information in short–term memory, but it is difficult to send it to long–term memory.

8. Why does the author mention "card sense" in paragraph 4?

   (A) To point out that playing cards requires a high level of thinking
   (B) To give an example of knowledge already stored in long–term memory
   (C) To compare learning a card game to remembering a telephone number
   (D) To explain why some card games are easier to learn than others

9. The word They in paragraph 5 refers to

   (A) cognitive psychologists
   (B) memory structures
   (C) interests, attitudes, skills, and knowledge of the world
   (D) what you perceive and how you interpret your perceptions

10. All of the following enhance the transfer of information from short–term memory to long–term memory EXCEPT

    (A) deciding that information is not meaningful or relevant
    (B) repeating information over and over to oneself
    (C) linking new information with data in long–term memory
    (D) performing a task frequently and repeatedly

TEST 4

11. What can be inferred from paragraph 6 about skill memory?

(A) It is more important than fact memory in everyday life.
(B) It exists in long–term memory because of repeated practice.
(C) It requires conscious effort to be retrieved from memory.
(D) It contains only the skills that people can perform well.

12. Look at the four squares, [A], [B], [C], and [D], which indicate where the following sentence could be added to the passage. Where would the sentence best fit?

One way of understanding the nature of long–term memory is to consider the types of information stored there.

[A] Long–term memory can hold recollections of personal experiences as well as factual knowledge acquired through other means such as reading. It also holds skills such as knowing how to ride a bicycle. [B] In its ability to learn and remember, the brain can distinguish between facts and skills. When you acquire factual knowledge by memorizing dates, word definitions, formulas, and other information, you can consciously retrieve this fact memory from the data bank of your long–term memory. [C] In contrast, skill memory usually involves motor activities that you learn by repetition without consciously remembering specific information. [D] You perform learned motor skills, such as walking or riding a bicycle, without consciously recalling the individual steps required to do these tasks.

13. Select the appropriate sentences from the answer choices and match them to the type of memory that they describe. TWO of the answer choices will NOT be used. ***This question is worth 4 points.***

Answer Choices

Ⓐ Inside this structure is a permanent record of everything you have learned.
Ⓑ It reflects sensory perceptions that occur before data are stored permanently.
Ⓒ Information is held here just long enough to be recognized.
Ⓓ It plays an influential role in the entire information processing system.
Ⓔ Information here affects how you interpret your perceptions.
Ⓕ This structure holds information that you are currently using.
Ⓖ It perceives a stimulus and sends it to the brain's sensory register.
Ⓗ Seven unrelated bits of information can be kept here for about twenty seconds.
Ⓘ It stores memories of personal experiences and factual knowledge.

Short–term Memory

•
•
•

Long–term Memory

•
•
•
•

How to Score 4–Point Questions	
Answers Correct	**Points Earned**
7	4
6	3
5	2
4	1
0–3	0

TEST 4

THE TRANSPORTATION REVOLUTION

1 By the close of the eighteenth century, the outlines of a world economy were clearly visible. Centered in Western Europe, it included Russia, India, the East Indies, the Middle East, northern and western Africa, and the Americas. Trade had increased greatly and shipping had grown in volume and speed, connecting the markets of the world more closely than ever before. The world market, however, was confined to the coasts and along rivers, and its effects were rarely felt a hundred miles inland. The expansion of economic activity into the interior, and its spread throughout China, Japan, Oceania, and Africa, was a major development of the nineteenth century. It was largely accomplished through a revolution in transportation, particularly the development of the steamship, canals, and railroads.

2 Since the fifteenth century, the wooden sailing ship had been the main instrument of European economic and political expansion. Sailing ships constantly grew in carrying capacity and speed with improvements in design, and they were built of easily available materials. The age of sailing ships reached its zenith in the middle of the nineteenth century, the era of the great ocean–plying **clippers** that carried the majority of international trade.

3 Before 1850, the bulk of internal trade was carried by water. In Western Europe, there had been several attempts to supplement the excellent river network with canals. However, it was the demands of the Industrial Revolution, particularly the need to transport huge quantities of coal, that stimulated large–scale canal building in the years 1760–1850, first in Britain and then in Western Europe and the United States. The introduction of steamboats gave an additional impetus to river navigation and canal construction. The steamship rose in stature in the 1870s, when technical progress reduced the amount of coal the steam engine consumed. Technical innovation, along with the completion of the Suez Canal in 1869, enabled the steamship to surpass the sailing ship as the chief instrument of international trade.

4 Methods of land transport continued to be slow, uncertain, and expensive until the boom in railroad construction at mid century. In 1840 there were 5,500 miles of rail track throughout the world; just twenty years later, there were 66,000 miles. Of these, 50 percent were in North America and 47 percent were in Europe. The rail lines built during that period served populated areas where considerable economic activity already existed, yet a global ideology of railroads gradually emerged: the belief that railroads could populate and bring wealth to undeveloped regions.

5 In Britain and the United States, private companies built hundreds of uncoordinated rail projects, but in continental Europe railroad construction became a concern of the state, which provided overall control and a large share of capital. Until 1914, the building of railroads remained the most important reason for the export of capital as well as the main method of developing new territories. British capital financed the majority of the railroads built in India, Canada, and Latin America. The U.S. transcontinental railroad played a key role in populating and developing huge tracts of land in North America, as did the Trans–Siberian Railway in Asia.

6 In the course of the nineteenth century, around 9 million square miles of land were settled in North and South America and Oceania. This was made possible by the decline in transportation costs, which greatly extended the area from which bulky products such as grains and minerals could be marketed. The introduction of refrigeration on railcars and steamers in the 1870s opened huge markets for meat, dairy products, and fruit in North America and Europe. The 1870s also saw the adoption of steel rails, electric signals, compressed–air brakes, and other inventions that made railroads a leading source of technical innovation in the nineteenth century.

7 In the world context, the rise of the railroad was inseparable from that of the steamship. The economic and geographic consequences of these two innovations complemented one another. Both had the effect of increasing the size of markets as well as the amount of economic activity worldwide.

Glossary:
clipper: a sailing ship that was built for great speed

14. Which sentence below best expresses the essential information in the highlighted sentence in paragraph 1? Incorrect choices change the meaning in important ways or leave out essential information.

    (A) International trade had to take place near oceans and rivers and did not extend to interior regions.
    (B) After several centuries of slow growth, the world economy was no longer confined by geography.
    (C) The effects of economic activity were felt everywhere, but especially along coasts and rivers.
    (D) World markets expanded rapidly, affecting people who lived hundreds of miles from the coast.

15. The word zenith in paragraph 2 is closest in meaning to

    (A) final goal
    (B) slow period
    (C) natural limit
    (D) high point

16. What factor led to an increase in canal building?

    (A) Competition among the world powers
    (B) The need to move large quantities of coal
    (C) Improvements in the design of sailing ships
    (D) An increase in the export of capital

17. The word impetus in paragraph 3 is closest in meaning to

    (A) push
    (B) style
    (C) shock
    (D) cost

18. Which of the following is given as a reason for the rise of the steamship over the sailing ship?

    (A) Wood for the construction of sailing ships became scarce.
    (B) The steamship could travel at faster speeds than the sailing ship.
    (C) Steamships were better than sailing ships at navigating canals.
    (D) Technical advances made the steamship require less coal.

19. The word boom in paragraph 4 is closest in meaning to

    (A) popular interest
    (B) loud noise
    (C) rapid growth
    (D) business opportunities

20. The word these in paragraph 4 refers to

    (A) methods of land transport
    (B) miles of rail track
    (C) rail lines
    (D) populated areas

21. According to the passage, what was a major result of railroad building in the nineteenth century?

    (A) The majority of wealth became concentrated in a few powerful nations.
    (B) Competition increased between private and state–owned companies.
    (C) There was an increase in the demand for an educated workforce.
    (D) Large parts of the world became populated and economically developed.

TEST 4

22. Why does the author mention refrigeration in paragraph 6?

(A) To show how the steam engine contributed to refrigeration
(B) To illustrate the standard of living of North America and Europe
(C) To give an example of an innovation that expanded markets
(D) To argue that refrigeration was the most important invention of the time

23. All of the following were effects of the transportation revolution EXCEPT

(A) the spread of trade to new regions
(B) innovations in technology
(C) population decline in major cities
(D) an increase in the size of world markets

24. It can be inferred from the passage that the author most likely believes which of the following about the transportation revolution of the nineteenth century?

(A) There will never again be so many developments in transportation in a single century.
(B) Improvements in transportation had a direct impact on world economics.
(C) The transportation revolution was part of a worldwide political revolution.
(D) Technical innovations of that time led to similar inventions in the next century.

25. Look at the four squares, [A], [B], [C], and [D], which indicate where the following sentence could be added to the passage. Where would the sentence best fit?

Railroad construction required enormous amounts of capital and was financed in diverse ways.

[A] In Britain and the United States, private companies built hundreds of uncoordinated rail projects, but in continental Europe railroad construction became a concern of the state, which provided overall control and a large share of capital. [B] Until 1914, the building of railroads remained the most important reason for the export of capital as well as the main method of developing new territories. [C] British capital financed the majority of the railroads built in India, Canada, and Latin America. [D] The U.S. transcontinental railroad played a key role in populating and developing huge tracts of land in North America, as did the Trans–Siberian Railway in Asia.

26. Read the first sentence of a summary of the passage. Complete the summary by selecting the THREE answer choices that express the most important ideas in the passage. Some sentences do not belong in the summary because they express ideas that are not presented in the passage or are minor ideas in the passage. ***This question is worth 2 points.***

A revolution in transportation took place in the nineteenth century.

•
•
•

Answer Choices

(A) Europe was the center of the world economy, but markets expanded to Asia, Africa, and the Americas.

(B) The Industrial Revolution created a demand for a system of canals.

(C) The sailing ship gave way to the steamship as the primary means of international trade.

(D) Steel rails, electric signals, and compressed–air brakes came into use during the 1870s.

(E) New methods of transportation required the development of better communications.

(F) Railroad construction led to technical innovation and the development of new territories.

How to Score 2–Point Questions	
Answers Correct	**Points Earned**
3	2
2	1
0–1	0

THE ART OF EMILY CARR

1 Born in 1871, Emily Carr grew up in Victoria, British Columbia, surrounded by a rugged landscape that fostered her passion for nature, animals, and painting. Carr started taking drawing lessons at the age of nine and decided to become an artist in her early teens. Before she was sixteen, both of her parents had died, so she lived with her sister until she went to art school in San Francisco. Later she studied in England and France before returning to Canada. Carr's early paintings were well received by local critics in Victoria and Vancouver, yet it was difficult to make a living from painting alone, so she supported herself by teaching children's art classes, raising dogs, and operating a boarding house.

2 Early in life, Carr developed an interest in painting the **aboriginal** culture of British Columbia. At the age of twenty–six, she made her first sketching trip to Ucluelet, an Indian Reserve on the west side of Vancouver Island. Her paintings of the First Nations people documented their fishing villages, totem poles, and life in the forest. Her fondness for aboriginal culture can be seen in *Totem Forest*, a series of totem poles painted in a bold style as Carr attempted to capture the spirit of the scene that would transcend its physical reality. The people of the villages affectionately called her "Klee Wyck," which means "the laughing one."

3 For the next forty years, Carr returned to the aboriginal villages to sketch and paint. These camping trips were unusual for a woman of her time, but to paint successfully Carr had to wrestle with the elements, with all of her senses alert. She drew inspiration from the cold, raw dampness of the coast, the sounds of the forest, and the sting of the smoke from campfires—experiences that she distilled to their essence in her large body of work.

4 Carr began to receive national recognition in 1927. At her first major exhibition outside of British Columbia, her paintings were shown in Toronto along with those of the **Group of Seven**. Carr met some of the Group when she traveled east for the show, and she liked what she saw of their work, especially the paintings of Lawren Harris. She eventually became a close friend of Harris and other prominent Canadian artists who treated her as a kindred spirit. The Toronto exhibition was a turning point for Carr, establishing her reputation as a leading figure in Canadian art. Encouraged by Harris, Carr revisited her earlier themes, creating the monumental paintings of totem poles that are her best–known works. She combined modernism with aboriginal form and color to create a powerful and unique visual landscape that captured the **transcendental** qualities of the wilderness.

5 At the age of seventy, Carr realized that the ancient First Nations culture might one day be lost, so she began to write stories about the beautiful, calm places of her earlier life among her aboriginal friends. As she lay in her bed, disabled by failing health, she recounted her days as Klee Wyck, which after forty years were still fresh in her mind because she had lived them so deeply at the time. In 1941 Carr published these stories in her first book, *Klee Wyck*, which united art and literature in a highly original way and won the Governor–General's award for general literature.

6 The art profession recognized Carr during her lifetime, and galleries in Vancouver, Toronto, Montreal, and Seattle displayed her paintings in solo exhibitions. While art historians have characterized her works as showing the influence of the Group of Seven, they also acknowledge that Carr produced paintings that were uniquely hers and credit her for raising Canadian art to a new height. The subjects Carr chose to paint, the region of the country in which she painted, and her own ideas about art combined to produce a vision that distinguished her from other artists. Carr's paintings endure as visual icons that Canadians can most easily associate with an individual artist, and for this reason she is the best–known woman artist in Canadian history.

Glossary:

aboriginal: existing in a region from the beginning; native
Group of Seven: a group of influential Canadian artists
transcendental: mystical; spiritual; supernatural

27. The word fostered in paragraph 1 is closest in meaning to

(A) inspired
(B) confused
(C) cured
(D) rivaled

28. The author connects all of the following to Emily Carr's early interest in art EXCEPT

(A) great love for nature
(B) teaching art to children
(C) birth into a family of artists
(D) interest in aboriginal culture

29. The author mentions fishing villages and totem poles in paragraph 2 as examples of

(A) places where Carr displayed her work
(B) topics that Carr liked to read about
(C) aboriginal culture that shocked Carr
(D) subjects that Carr painted frequently

30. The author points out that Carr's sketching trips to the forest

(A) introduced art to the aboriginal people
(B) were uncommon for a woman
(C) encouraged other artists to do the same
(D) caused her health to decline

31. In stating that Carr had to wrestle with the elements in paragraph 3, the author means that Carr needed to

(A) paint unusual subjects
(B) express her sense of humor
(C) experience her subjects directly
(D) struggle to support herself

32. Why does the author discuss the 1927 Toronto art exhibition in paragraph 4?

(A) It was the first time that Carr traveled outside of British Columbia.
(B) The exhibition introduced Carr to an entirely new style of painting.
(C) It was the first major exhibition of paintings by a Canadian woman.
(D) The exhibition established Carr's national reputation as an artist.

33. The word them in paragraph 5 refers to

(A) stories
(B) calm places
(C) her days as Klee Wyck
(D) art and literature

34. The word credit in paragraph 6 is closest in meaning to

(A) analyze
(B) blame
(C) tolerate
(D) praise

35. Which sentence below best expresses the essential information in the highlighted sentence in paragraph 6? Incorrect choices change the meaning in important ways or leave out essential information.

(A) It was very sad when Emily Carr could no longer paint, but she is still considered the best woman artist in Canada.
(B) Emily Carr remains Canada's most famous woman artist because her paintings are instantly recognized as hers.
(C) Most Canadians know about the visual icons of Emily Carr because they studied her paintings in art history class.
(D) Few people appreciated Emily Carr's paintings while she lived, but today most Canadians value her individuality.

36. According to the passage, what made Emily Carr's paintings unique?

(A) She rebelled against the popular style of the Group of Seven.
(B) She painted regional subjects in a bold and transcendental style.
(C) She combined light colors and deep shadows in an unusual way.
(D) She was the only Canadian painter who had no formal training.

37. It can be inferred from the passage that the author most likely believes which of the following about Emily Carr?

(A) Emily Carr deserves her position in Canadian cultural history.
(B) The Group of Seven was influenced by Emily Carr's vision.
(C) The paintings of Emily Carr are more important than her stories.
(D) Emily Carr's work has gone largely unnoticed until recently.

38. Look at the four squares, [A], [B], [C], and [D], which indicate where the following sentence could be added to the passage. Where would the sentence best fit?

Her later paintings applied the same intensity to the deep forests of British Columbia as did her earlier works.

[A] Carr began to receive national recognition in 1927. At her first major exhibition outside of British Columbia, her paintings were shown in Toronto along with those of the Group of Seven. Carr met some of the Group when she traveled east for the show, and she liked what she saw of their work, especially the paintings of Lawren Harris. [B] She eventually became a close friend of Harris and other prominent Canadian artists who treated her as a kindred spirit. [C] The Toronto exhibition was a turning point for Carr, establishing her reputation as a leading figure in Canadian art. Encouraged by Harris, Carr revisited her earlier themes, creating the monumental paintings of totem poles that are her best–known works. [D] She combined modernism with aboriginal form and color to create a powerful and unique visual landscape that captured the transcendental qualities of the wilderness.

39. Read the first sentence of a summary of the passage. Complete the summary by selecting the THREE answer choices that express the most important ideas in the passage. Some sentences do not belong in the summary because they express ideas that are not presented in the passage or are minor ideas in the passage. ***This question is worth 2 points.***

One of Canada's most prominent artists, Emily Carr, was born in British Columbia and worked there for most of her life.

•
•
•

Answer Choices

(A) Carr's struggle to support herself as an artist was long and frustrating.

(B) Carr documented the aboriginal culture of British Columbia in both paintings and stories.

(C) She became a close friend of Lawren Harris, a member of the Group of Seven.

(D) Monumental paintings of totem poles and forests are her most famous works.

(E) Carr's choice of subjects, bold style, and ideas about art made her vision unique.

(F) Some art historians have criticized Carr's depictions of aboriginal Canadian culture.

TEST 4

How to Score 2–Point Questions	
Answers Correct	**Points Earned**
3	2
2	1
0–1	0

Answers are on page 310.

Record your Reading section score on page 380.

Disk 4, Track 1

LISTENING SECTION DIRECTIONS

The Listening section measures your ability to understand conversations and lectures in English. You will hear each conversation and lecture only one time. After each conversation or lecture, you will hear some questions about it. Answer the questions based on what the speakers state or imply.

You may take notes while you listen. You may use your notes to help you answer the questions.

In some questions, you will see this icon: 🎧. This means that you will hear, but not see, part of the question.

Some questions have special directions, which appear in a gray box. Most questions are worth one point. If a question is worth more than one point, the directions will indicate how many points you can receive.

You will now begin the first part of the Listening section.

Time – maximum of 90 minutes

Disk 4, Track 2

QUESTIONS 1–5

Conversation

1. What are the students discussing?

Click on two answers.

A How they feel about their classes
B Applying for a job as a teaching assistant
C Not having enough time to study
D Stories from Russian history

2. Listen again to part of the conversation. Then answer the question.

Why does the woman say this:

(A) To request that the man speak more softly
(B) To express her dislike of thermodynamics
(C) To agree that lack of time is a problem
(D) To inform the man that she needs to leave

3. Why does the woman like her Russian history class?

(A) Her professor is a well–known Russian author.
(B) The discussions improve her ability to learn.
(C) All of the students in the class are from Russia.
(D) The assigned reading includes interesting stories.

4. What is the man's attitude toward discussion classes?

(A) He thinks that discussion classes are a good way to learn.
(B) He would like more time to prepare for the discussions.
(C) He finds that most of the discussions are boring.
(D) He does not like discussion classes as much as lectures.

5. What does the man suggest the woman do?

(A) Participate more in her discussion class
(B) Find out more about a job opening
(C) Quit her job in the pizza restaurant
(D) Try not to worry about her problems

Disk 4, Track 3

QUESTIONS 6–11

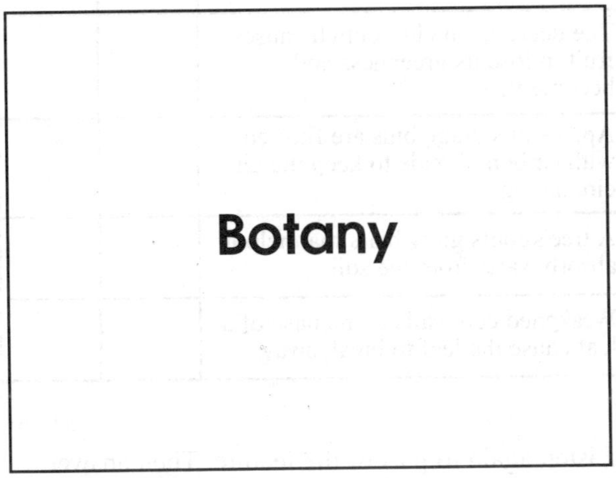

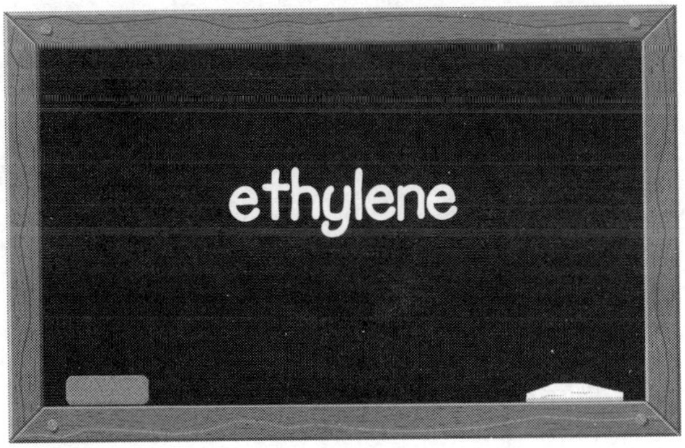

6. What is the lecture mainly about?

   (A) The role of ethylene in plant aging processes
   (B) The discovery of ethylene by fruit growers
   (C) Differences between ethylene and other hormones
   (D) How plant hormones influence growth

7. According to the professor, how is ethylene unique?

   (A) Ethylene is the only hormone that plants produce.
   (B) Ethylene is produced only in flowering plants.
   (C) Ethylene both stimulates and restricts plant growth.
   (D) Ethylene is the only plant hormone that is a gas.

8. According to the lecture, what are two effects of ethylene?

   Click on two answers.

   [A] Fruit becomes softer as it ripens.
   [B] Plants develop complex root systems.
   [C] Trees shed their leaves in the fall.
   [D] Flower buds open in the spring.

9. Listen again to part of the lecture. Then answer the question.

   Why does the professor say this: 🎧

   (A) To explain why she doesn't like apples
   (B) To describe a common disease of fruit
   (C) To summarize the chain reaction of ripening
   (D) To caution against eating unwashed fruit

10. Based on the information in the lecture, indicate whether each process below is related to the hormone ethylene.

    For each sentence, click in the correct box.

	Yes	No
The decrease in chlorophyll causes fruit to lose its greenness and become ripe.		
Apples in storage bins are flushed with carbon dioxide to keep the air circulating.		
A tree's roots grow hairs that help it absorb water from the soil.		
Weakened cell walls at the base of a leaf cause the leaf to break away.		

11. Listen again to part of the lecture. Then answer the question.

    What does the professor imply about the falling of leaves?

    (A) Leaves fall from old trees, but not from trees that are still young.
    (B) Both hormones and environmental factors cause leaves to fall.
    (C) The falling of leaves increases the tree's risk of getting a disease.
    (D) Spraying ethylene into an orchard will prevent leaves from falling.

Disk 4, Track 4

QUESTIONS 12–17

12. According to the discussion, what are the characteristics of a good manager?

Click on two answers.

A The ability to set goals
B Earning a high salary
C Knowledge of technology
D Achieving results

13. Why does the professor tell a story about May and Kay?

(A) To illustrate what a good manager does
(B) To inspire students to apply to top schools
(C) To explain how to write a business plan
(D) To compare good and bad study habits

14. What does the professor imply about the student named May?

(A) She should have asked a graduate student to be her tutor.
(B) She understood the principals of good management.
(C) She allowed events to keep her from reaching her goal.
(D) She studied very hard but had unusually bad luck.

15. In the story, what point does Kay illustrate?

(A) Management is a very difficult profession.
(B) Success is possible if you keep trying.
(C) Even average students can go to top schools.
(D) Some people have better luck than others.

16. Listen again to part of the discussion. Then answer the question.

Why does the professor ask this:

(A) He does not know whether May or Kay is a better manager.
(B) He disagrees with what the man says about May and Kay.
(C) He wants to invite either May or Kay as a guest speaker.
(D) He wants a more satisfactory response from the class.

17. What does the professor mean by this statement:

(A) Kay earned high grades in all of her management courses.
(B) Kay set goals and achieved results, as managers do.
(C) Kay acted independently without help from other people.
(D) Kay knew how to manage her time and money wisely.

Disk 4, Track 5

QUESTIONS 18–22

Conversation

18. Why does the student speak to the professor?

(A) He is applying for a job as her research assistant.
(B) He would like her advice about a research project.
(C) He wants to know her opinion of student activities.
(D) He is informing her of the masquerade ball.

19. What kind of information does the student want to obtain?

(A) Student attitudes about various campus events
(B) How to plan and organize a concert series
(C) Political beliefs of students and professors
(D) Which courses students find most interesting

20. According to the professor, what is one advantage of a survey?

(A) It is the least expensive method of research.
(B) It does not have to be conducted face–to–face.
(C) It provides more information than any other method.
(D) It is the most enjoyable method for the researcher.

21. Listen again to part of the conversation. Then answer the question.

Why does the professor ask this:

(A) To learn about the student's opinions
(B) To suggest possible research topics
(C) To give examples of poll questions
(D) To describe a survey that she wrote

22. How does the professor help the student?

Click on two answers.

[A] She gives him a copy of a sample survey.
[B] She recommends a useful book.
[C] She asks her assistant to help him.
[D] She agrees to review his survey draft.

Disk 4, Track 6

QUESTIONS 23–28

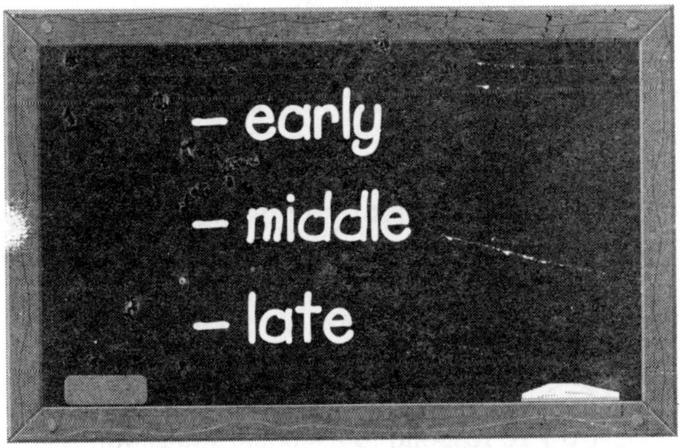

23. What aspect of adulthood does the professor mainly discuss?

(A) Biological changes related to the aging process
(B) Changes in roles and responsibilities during adulthood
(C) Differences between childhood and adulthood
(D) Cultural differences in attitudes toward older adults

24. Why does the professor discuss the "biological clock"?

(A) To review a term before the next test
(B) To compare different types of clocks
(C) To amuse students with a personal story
(D) To respond to a student's question

25. Why does the professor say this: 🎧

(A) To explain the concept of age norms
(B) To show that 20–year–olds have the most fun
(C) To describe cultural differences in aging
(D) To complain about abnormal behavior

26. Listen again to part of the lecture. Then answer the question.

What does the professor imply about age norms?

(A) Age norms for a 40–year–old are the same in every culture.
(B) An adult's status may be determined by age norms.
(C) It is young adults who define their society's age norms.
(D) Psychologists cannot explain why age norms exist.

27. Based on the information in the lecture, indicate whether each sentence below characterizes early adulthood, middle adulthood, or late adulthood.

For each sentence, click in the correct box.
This question is worth 2 points.

	Early adulthood	Middle adulthood	Late adulthood
The roles of spouse and parent generally begin now.			
This period is sometimes called the "sandwich generation."			
People gain more new roles now than at any other time.			
There is a decline in the number of social roles.			

28. What does the professor say about people who do not have children?

(A) They tend to become independent adults at a very young age.
(B) They follow the same basic stages of adulthood as other people.
(C) They do not have any social roles after they retire from work.
(D) They do not enjoy life as much as people with children do.

How to Score 2–Point Questions	
Answers Correct	**Points Earned**
4	2
3	1
0–2	0

Disk 4, Track 7

QUESTIONS 29–34

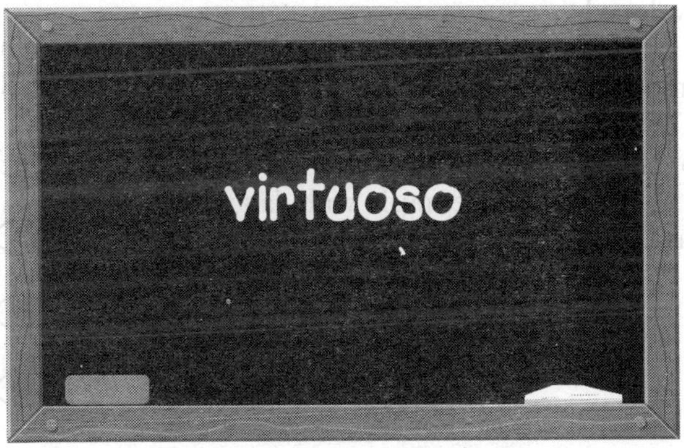

TEST 4

29. How does the professor develop the topic of Baroque music?

(A) By tracing the evolution of Baroque from earlier styles
(B) By describing features and forms of Baroque music
(C) By comparing Baroque music, architecture, and painting
(D) By explaining the philosophy of Baroque composers

30. What characterizes Baroque music?

Click on two answers.

[A] Expression of emotion
[B] Use of folk songs
[C] Emphasis on harmony
[D] Complex ornamentation

31. Why does the professor say this: 🎧

(A) To explain how new musical forms developed
(B) To quote the philosophy of a Baroque composer
(C) To emphasize the importance of a song's words
(D) To contrast Baroque music with dance music

32. Why does the professor discuss the instruments of the orchestra for Monteverdi's opera *Orfeo*?

(A) To compare the Baroque orchestra with the orchestra of today
(B) To give examples of instruments that Monteverdi invented
(C) To illustrate how different instruments helped to tell a story
(D) To explain why the orchestra was the center of Baroque music

33. What does the professor mean when she says this: 🎧

(A) Very few musicians were skilled enough to play Baroque concertos.
(B) Baroque composers had to earn money by playing in the orchestra.
(C) Musicians had to know how to play several different styles of music.
(D) Baroque musicians created new musical forms to display their ability.

34. What is the professor's opinion of the concertos called *The Four Seasons*?

(A) They are the world's most beautiful pieces of music.
(B) They are popular because they are easy to play.
(C) They are perfect examples of Baroque music.
(D) They are more complex than Monteverdi's operas.

Disk 4, Track 8

QUESTIONS 35–39

Conversation

35. What is the main purpose of the conversation?

   (A) The professor asked the student to come and talk to him.
   (B) The professor wants the student to be his teaching assistant.
   (C) The student wants a recommendation from the professor.
   (D) The student wants to discuss her research project.

36. Why does the student want to be a teacher?

   (A) She has an opportunity to teach a class about nature.
   (B) She enjoyed studying science when she was a child.
   (C) She is interested in the psychology of children's art.
   (D) She wants to make the professor proud of her.

37. Why does the student talk about being a camp counselor?

   (A) To summarize what she did in a psychology course
   (B) To describe her experience in working with children
   (C) To explain her interest in being a psychologist
   (D) To ask for the professor's help in getting a job

38. Listen again to part of the conversation. Then answer the question.

   Why does the professor say this:

   (A) He is thinking about what he will say in the recommendation.
   (B) He wants to know the student's opinion of his psychology class.
   (C) He needs the student's help in solving a difficult problem.
   (D) He would like to try something that he has never done before.

39. What will the professor probably include in the form that he fills out?

   (A) The student's examination scores
   (B) Slides of the student's artwork
   (C) A copy of the student's employment history
   (D) A description of the student's research report

Disk 4, Track 9

QUESTIONS 40–45

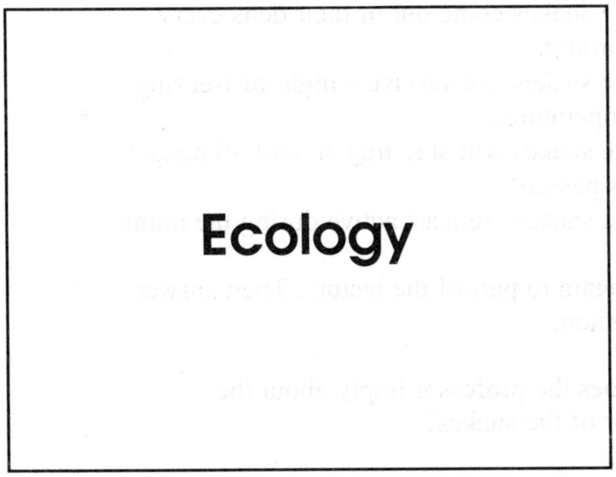

40. What is the main purpose of the lecture?

(A) To trace the natural history of Manitoba's Interlake region
(B) To describe the process of limestone formation
(C) To explain how one animal survives in its environment
(D) To persuade students that snakes are not dangerous

41. What natural features of Manitoba does the professor discuss?

Click on two answers.

[A] The large number of lakes
[B] The network of limestone caves
[C] The concentration of garter snakes
[D] The variety of snake species

42. Why does the professor say this: 🎧

(A) To praise the area's beautiful winter scenery
(B) To persuade students to build their own homes
(C) To describe the most common use of limestone
(D) To explain why so many snakes live in the region

43. How do the garter snakes deal with seasonal variations in temperature?

(A) They grow an extra layer of skin in winter and shed it in summer.
(B) They survive by migrating toward the south every winter.
(C) They move into the limestone pits to escape winter temperatures.
(D) They vary their food intake to maintain a constant body temperature.

44. Listen again to part of the lecture. Then answer the question.

What does the professor mean when he says this: 🎧

(A) The snakes come out of their dens every morning.
(B) The snakes can survive a night of freezing temperatures.
(C) The snakes will stay frozen until all danger has passed.
(D) The snakes are least active during the night.

45. Listen again to part of the lecture. Then answer the question.

What does the professor imply about the behavior of the snakes?

(A) The snakes' behavior is a warning signal to other animals.
(B) Temperature plays an important role in the snakes' behavior.
(C) Scientists can observe the snakes' behavior in their winter dens.
(D) The snakes are able to learn a variety of behavioral responses.

Disk 4, Track 10

QUESTIONS 46–51

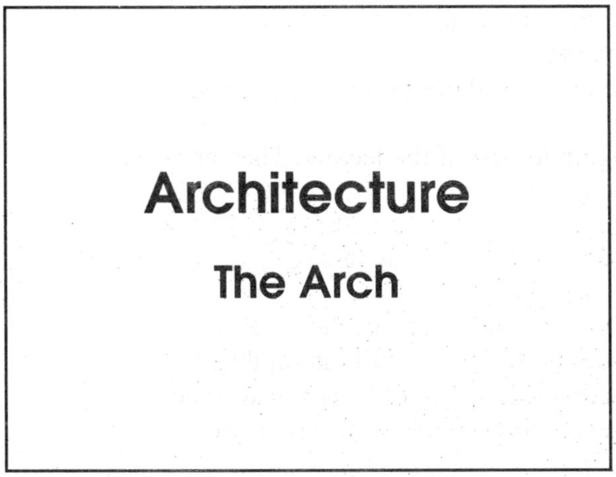

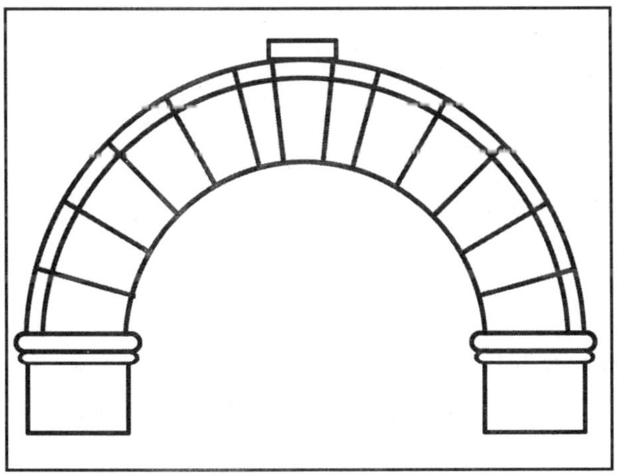

46. According to the professor, why was the arch an important development in architecture?

Click on two answers.

[A] The arch made Rome the greatest power on Earth.
[B] Wide openings could be spanned without using wood.
[C] There was no formal architecture before the arch.
[D] The arch led to a larger variety of buildings.

47. Listen again to part of the lecture. Then answer the question.

What does the professor imply about the public works projects of the Romans?

(A) The arch contributed to the success of these projects.
(B) The Romans were the first society to work on large projects.
(C) Each project developed a different style of architecture.
(D) The projects benefited only the wealthy citizens of Rome.

48. Identify the keystone in the drawing of the arch.

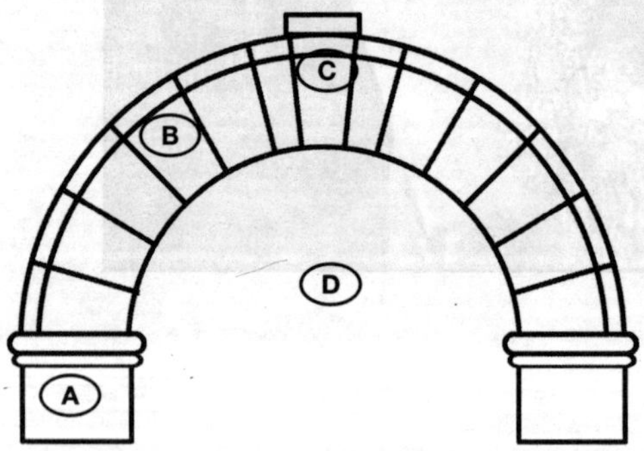

49. What reason is given for the stability of the arch?

(A) A concrete foundation supports the arch.
(B) The arch is built with wedge–shaped blocks.
(C) The Romans made a strong type of concrete.
(D) The pressure flows up to the keystone.

50. Listen again to part of the lecture. Then answer the question.

Why does the professor say this:

(A) To describe the shape of the arch
(B) To define the concept of lateral thrust
(C) To compare two types of physical force
(D) To explain why arches must be large

51. According to the professor, why are arches that are built today mostly decorative in function?

(A) Wedge–shaped blocks have become rare.
(B) Decorative arches provide work for bricklayers.
(C) Few architects like ancient construction techniques.
(D) Wide openings are now spanned with steel beams.

Stop

Answers are on page 313.

Record your Listening section score on page 381.

Disk 4, Track 11

SPEAKING SECTION DIRECTIONS

The Speaking section measures your ability to speak in English about a variety of topics. There are six questions in this section.

Questions 1 and 2 are independent tasks in which you will speak about familiar topics. Your responses will be scored on your ability to speak clearly and coherently about the topics.

Questions 3 and 4 are integrated speaking tasks. You will read a passage, listen to a conversation or lecture, and then speak in response to a question about what you have read and heard. You will need to combine relevant information from the two sources to answer the question completely. Your responses will be scored on your ability to speak clearly and coherently and on your ability to accurately convey information about what you read and heard.

Questions 5 and 6 are integrated speaking tasks. You will listen to part of a conversation or lecture, and then speak in response to a question about what you have heard. Your responses will be scored on your ability to speak clearly and coherently and on your ability to accurately convey information about what you heard.

You will hear each conversation and lecture only one time. You may take notes while you listen. You may use your notes to help you answer the questions.

Stop

QUESTION 1

In this question, you will be asked to talk about a familiar topic. After you hear the question, you will have 15 seconds to prepare your response and 45 seconds to speak.

Disk 4, Track 12

What is your most valuable possession? Describe it and explain why it is important to you. Include details and examples to support your explanation.

Stop

Preparation Time – 15 seconds
Response Time – 45 seconds

QUESTION 2

In this question, you will be asked to give your opinion about a familiar topic. After you hear the question, you will have 15 seconds to prepare your response and 45 seconds to speak.

Disk 4, Track 13

Some universities focus on having excellent libraries, laboratories, and other facilities. Others focus more on hiring the most successful and qualified professors. Which system do you think benefits students more, and why? Include details and examples in your explanation.

Stop

Preparation Time – 15 seconds
Response Time – 45 seconds

QUESTION 3

In this question, you will read a short passage about a campus situation, listen to a conversation, and then speak in response to a question about what you have read and heard. After you hear the question, you have 30 seconds to prepare your response and 60 seconds to speak.

Reading Time – 45 seconds

RESIDENT ASSISTANTS NEEDED FOR DORMITORIES ON CAMPUS

The University Housing Office is now accepting applications for the position of resident assistant (RA). Resident assistants must be full–time students in at least their second year at university and must live in the dormitory where they work as assistants to the Director of Housing. Responsibilities of RAs include checking new residents in and out of the dormitory, managing routine problems of residents, working four hours per week in the dormitory office, attending monthly meetings of all housing staff, and other related duties. Benefits include work experience and free residence in a private dormitory room.

Now cover the passage and listen to the recording. When you hear the question, begin preparing your response.

Disk 4, Track 14

The woman expresses her opinion about being a resident assistant. State her opinion and explain the reasons she gives for holding that opinion.

Stop

Preparation Time – 30 seconds
Response Time – 60 seconds

QUESTION 4

In this question, you will read a short passage on an academic subject, listen to a lecture on the same topic, and then speak in response to a question about what you have read and heard. After you hear the question, you have 30 seconds to prepare your response and 60 seconds to speak.

Reading Time – 45 seconds

THE HISTORY OF CLIMATE CHANGE

We know about past climate by studying the geological record and evidence of past glaciation. If we look at where the glaciers were, we can reconstruct a history of the ice ages that have affected our planet. Earth's climate is generally stable; however, average surface temperatures have varied throughout history. These temperature changes form a regular cycle that is approximately 100,000 years long. We are not entirely certain what caused the lower temperatures of Earth's ice ages, but we do know that the transition from the last ice age to the present warm period took thousands of years.

Now cover the passage and listen to the recording. When you hear the question, begin preparing your response.

Disk 4, Track 15

The professor discusses studies of the ice in Greenland. Explain how this research has advanced our understanding of past climate change.

Stop

Preparation Time – 30 seconds
Response Time – 60 seconds

QUESTION 5

In this question, you will listen to a conversation. You will then be asked to talk about the information in the conversation and to give your opinion about the ideas presented. After you hear the question, you have 20 seconds to prepare your response and 60 seconds to speak.

Disk 4, Track 16

The students discuss two possible solutions to the man's problem. Describe the problem. Then state which of the two solutions you prefer and explain why.

Stop

Preparation Time – 20 seconds
Response Time – 60 seconds

QUESTION 6

In this question, you will listen to part of a lecture. You will then be asked to summarize important information from the lecture. After you hear the question, you have 20 seconds to prepare your response and 60 seconds to speak.

Disk 4, Track 17

Using points and examples from the talk, explain how the two methods of food preservation keep food from spoiling.

Stop

Preparation Time – 20 seconds
Response Time – 60 seconds

Key points for the Speaking responses are on page 316.

Each response earns a score of 1, 2, 3 or 4.

Record your total Speaking score on page 382.

Disk 4, Track 18

WRITING SECTION DIRECTIONS

The Writing section measures your ability to use writing to communicate in an academic environment. There are two writing questions.

Question 1 is an integrated writing task. You will read a passage, listen to a lecture, and then answer a question based on what you have read and heard. You have 20 minutes to plan and write your response.

Question 2 is an independent writing task. You will answer a question based on your own knowledge and experience. You have 30 minutes to plan and write your response.

Stop

QUESTION 1

For this task, you will write a response to a question about a reading passage and a lecture. You may take notes, and you may use your notes to help you write your response. Your response will be scored on the quality of your writing and on how well you connect the points in the lecture with points in the reading. Typically, an effective response will have 150 to 225 words.

Reading Time – 3 minutes

The philosophy of realism promotes the idea of a universe that we can observe scientifically and understand objectively. The central idea of realism is that reality, knowledge, and facts are independent of the human mind. The real objects of the universe—stones, trees, animals—exist whether or not there is a human mind to know them.

Realists believe that anything that exists can be measured scientifically. Philosopher and mathematician Bertrand Russell believed that reason, logic, and the methods of science could be used to build a precise philosophy of reality. Russell felt that the universe is characterized by patterns that can be analyzed scientifically and verified mathematically. He believed that only science could claim to be real knowledge. According to Russell, we can get two types of data on reality: hard data and soft data. Hard data are the facts of the situation, facts that can withstand measurement and analysis. Soft data are such things as beliefs, passions, and emotions, which we can neither prove nor deny with certainty. Russell based his philosophy more on hard data that can be proven and less on soft data that are more difficult to prove. He argued that we should not believe something is real if it is based on soft data. Something is real only if hard data exist to support it.

Russell hoped that by using the methods of science, we could begin to solve large human problems such as poverty. He believed in knowledge and education as the keys to a better world. According to Russell, if we applied realist philosophy and scientific methods to education, we would achieve excellence in education, and ultimately we could eliminate problems such as poverty and create an ideal society.

Now listen to the recording. When you hear the question, begin your response. You may look at the passage during the writing time.

Disk 4, Track 19

Summarize the points made in the lecture, explaining how they contradict points made in the reading.

Stop

Writing Time – 20 minutes

QUESTION 2

For this task, you will write an essay in response to a question that asks you to state and support your opinion on a topic. Your essay will be scored on the quality of your writing, including how well you organize and develop your ideas and how well you use language to express your ideas. Typically, an effective essay will have a minimum of 300 words.

Read the question below and make any notes that will help you plan your response. Then begin writing your essay.

Do you agree or disagree with the following statement?

A university education should include an internship or some type of work experience.

Use specific reasons and examples to support your answer.

Writing Time – 30 minutes

Key points for the Writing section are on page 316.

Each response earns a score of 1, 2, 3, 4 or 5.

Record your total Writing score on page 382.

TEST 5

Reading Section Directions

The Reading section measures your ability to read and understand passages in English. You will read five passages and answer questions about them. Answer all questions based on what is stated or implied in the passages.

Most questions are worth one point. The last question in each set is worth more than one point. For this question, the directions will indicate how many points you can receive.

Some passages have one or more words in bold type. For these bolded words, you will see a definition in a glossary at the end of the passage.

Allow 20 minutes to read each passage and answer the questions about it. You may now begin the first passage.

Time – 100 minutes

POPULATION ECOLOGY

1 Population ecology is the science that measures changes in population size and composition and identifies the causes of these fluctuations. Population ecology is not concerned solely with the human population. In ecological terms, a population consists of the individuals of one species that simultaneously occupy the same general area, rely on the same resources, and are affected by similar environmental factors. The characteristics of a population are shaped by its size and by the interactions among individuals and between individuals and their environment.

2 Population size is a balance between factors that increase numbers and factors that decrease numbers. Some factors that increase populations are favorable light and temperature, adequate food supply, suitable habitat, ability to compete for resources, and ability to adapt to environmental change. Factors that decrease populations are insufficient or excessive light and temperature, inadequate food supply, unsuitable or destroyed habitat, too many competitors for resources, and inability to adapt to environmental change.

3 An important characteristic of any population is its density. Population density is the number of individuals per unit, such as the number of maple trees per square kilometer in a county. Ecologists can rarely determine population size by actually counting all individuals within geographical boundaries. Instead, they often use a variety of sampling techniques to estimate densities and total population sizes. In some cases, they estimate population size through indirect indicators, such as the number of nests or burrows, or signs such as tracks or droppings.

4 Another important population characteristic, dispersion, is the pattern of spacing among individuals within the population's geographical boundaries. Various species are distributed in their habitats in different ways to take better advantage of food supplies and shelter, and to avoid predators or find prey. Within a population's range, densities may vary greatly because not all areas provide equally suitable habitat, and also because individuals space themselves in relation to other members of the population.

5 Three possible patterns of dispersion are clumped, uniform, and random. A clumped dispersion pattern means that individuals are gathered in patches throughout their habitat. Clumping often results from the irregular distribution of resources needed for survival and reproduction. For example, fallen trees keep the forest floor moist, and many forest insects are clumped under logs where the humidity is to their liking. Clumping may also be associated with mating, safety, or other social behavior. Crane flies, for example, swarm in great numbers, a behavior that increases mating chances, and some fish swim in large schools so they are less likely to be eaten by predators.

6 A uniform or evenly spaced distribution results from direct interactions among individuals in the population. For example, regular spacing of plants may result from shading and competition for water. In animal populations, uniform distribution is usually caused by competition for some resource or by social interactions that set up individual territories for feeding, breeding, or resting.

7 Random spacing occurs in the absence of strong attraction or repulsion among individuals in a population. Overall, random patterns are rare in nature, with most populations showing a tendency toward either clumped or uniform distribution.

8 Populations change in size, structure, and distribution as they respond to changes in environmental conditions. Four main variables—births, deaths, immigration, and emigration—determine the rate of change in the size of the population over time. A change in the birth rate or death rate is the major way that most populations respond to changes in resource availability. Members of some animal species can avoid or reduce the effects of environmental stress by emigrating from one area and immigrating to another with more favorable environmental conditions, thus altering the population's dispersion.

1. Which sentence below best expresses the essential information in the highlighted sentence in paragraph 1? Incorrect choices change the meaning in important ways or leave out essential information.

   (A) Any species of life can be studied in population ecology.
   (B) Population ecologists care about the future of humanity.
   (C) The growth of the human population is a major concern.
   (D) Population ecology does not consider humans worthy of study.

2. According to the passage, which factor might cause the population of a species to decrease in size?

   (A) A favorable amount of light and water
   (B) An ability to hide from or defend against predators
   (C) A large number of other species competing for food
   (D) A greater number of births than deaths

3. Which of the following is an indirect indicator of a population's density?

   (A) The distribution of food in a given area
   (B) The number of nests in a given area
   (C) The number of births in a given period of time
   (D) The number of individuals counted in a given area

4. The distribution pattern of individuals within a population's geographical boundaries is known as

   (A) population ecology
   (B) population density
   (C) population change
   (D) population dispersion

5. The word range in paragraph 4 is closest in meaning to

   (A) territory
   (B) control
   (C) history
   (D) shelter

6. The word patches in paragraph 5 is closest in meaning to

   (A) dark places
   (B) family groups
   (C) warm spots
   (D) small areas

7. The word their in paragraph 5 refers to

   (A) resources
   (B) trees
   (C) insects
   (D) logs

8. All of the following are given as reasons for clumping EXCEPT

   (A) uneven resource distribution
   (B) territorial disputes
   (C) mating behavior
   (D) safety from predators

9. The phrase set up in paragraph 6 is closest in meaning to

   (A) forbid
   (B) establish
   (C) increase
   (D) conceal

10. Which of the following situations would be most likely to result in a uniform dispersion pattern?

    (A) Birds compete for a place to build their nests.
    (B) Fish swim in large schools to avoid predators.
    (C) Whales develop strong bonds among relatives.
    (D) Elephants form a circle to protect their young.

11. Why does the author mention immigration and emigration in paragraph 8?

    (A) To identify factors affecting population dispersion
    (B) To give examples of territorial behavior in animals
    (C) To show that populations balance themselves over time
    (D) To explain why animal populations are uniformly dispersed

TEST 5

12. Look at the four squares, **A**, **B**, **C**, and **D**, which indicate where the following sentence could be added to the passage. Where would the sentence best fit?

For example, they might estimate the number of black bears in a national park by counting individuals in a few sample plots representative of the whole park.

An important characteristic of any population is its density. **A** Population density is the number of individuals per unit, such as the number of maple trees per square kilometer in a county. **B** Ecologists can rarely determine population size by actually counting all individuals within geographical boundaries. **C** Instead, they often use a variety of sampling techniques to estimate densities and total population sizes. **D** In some cases, they estimate population size through indirect indicators, such as the number of nests or burrows, or signs such as tracks or droppings.

13. Read the first sentence of a summary of the passage. Complete the summary by selecting the THREE answer choices that express the most important ideas in the passage. Some sentences do not belong in the summary because they express ideas that are not presented in the passage or are minor ideas in the passage. ***This question is worth 2 points.***

Population ecology is the science of populations and the factors that influence them.

•
•
•

Answer Choices

(A) A population is affected by its size, density, and dispersion, as well as the relationships among its members.

(B) Dispersion of individuals in a population may be clumped, uniform, or random, as determined by environmental and social factors.

(C) Clumping is related to safety; for example, fish swim in large schools to reduce their chances of being eaten by predators.

(D) Most populations have either clumped or uniform distribution because random spacing is rare in nature.

(E) Populations change in density and dispersion as they respond to changes in environmental conditions and resource availability.

(F) If a population has an abundant food supply and a suitable habitat, it will not undergo evolutionary change.

How to Score 2–Point Questions	
Answers Correct	**Points Earned**
3	2
2	1
0–1	0

THE HISTORY OF COMMUNICATION TECHNOLOGY

1 Communication technology influences the ways in which we think about the world. It changes the things we think about, the symbols we use to form and communicate ideas, and the arenas in which our thoughts develop. In the history of communication, there have been many revolutionary technologies, among them the printing press in the fifteenth century and electronic media in the nineteenth century.

2 The development of writing was a major advancement in the ability to communicate over distances and to preserve information accurately. Writing conveyed knowledge of the arts and sciences, which provided foundations for other areas of investigation. However, before books and the printing press, written language was limited to a few clay tablets and parchment scrolls. It was not until books became available that writing made a major impact. For centuries, books were rare and expensive because each one was handwritten, a process that took several months. The printing press with movable type made it possible to produce hundreds of copies of a book in a single day.

3 The invention of the printing press in 1450 launched a new era in the technology of communication. The printing press opened to large groups of people a body of information that had previously been confined to the educated few. The printing press brought books to the common people, increasing the ranks of the literate. Rapid expansion of the arts and sciences and the use of printed materials required a higher level of education. Education became a formalized institution, and children earned adulthood by achieving literacy. The proliferation of books and reading changed how people thought and what they thought about. Reading entailed the linear organization of ideas, stimulating abstract thought and reasoning. The ability to read required a significant increase in a person's attention span, resulting in a higher degree of intellectual discipline. Higher rates of literacy led society to a broader, more global perspective.

4 Another significant revolution in communication technology began in the nineteenth century with the advent of electronic media. The invention of the telegraph in 1843 signaled a new era in communication technology, the electronic era—so called because the telegraph used electrical signals to carry information along an electrical wire. The telegraph fed society's growing appetite for immediate access to information, and it provided a foundation for successive technologies: the telephone in 1876, the phonograph in 1878, film and movies in the 1890s, radio in 1919, and television in 1925.

5 As with the earliest handwritten books, radio technology was at first restricted to the educated few, scientists and researchers, but later spread to the greater society. By the 1930s, the middle classes were listening to news, drama, comedy, and musical performances from thousands of miles away. Radio was the first mass broadcast medium and, together with television a few decades later, it was responsible for altering both the pattern and volume of information that flowed into people's homes.

6 The invention of electronic media changed communication more than any other technological event since the development of writing. The spread of electronic media occurred with a speed never seen before, thus intensifying commercial and social interaction. There was a tremendous shift in how people received the information that contributed to their understanding of the world. Voices or pictures could create ideas that appeared authentic—more so than ideas conveyed by the printed word. The graphic, intensely human nature of electronic media enhanced the belief that if it was on the air, it had to be true.

14. In stating that there have been many revolutionary technologies in paragraph 1, the author means that these technologies were very

(A) complex
(B) expensive
(C) influential
(D) controversial

15. Which of the following statements can be inferred from paragraph 1 about the history of communication?

(A) Certain advances in technology have greatly changed communication.
(B) People have both loved and feared new developments in technology.
(C) We do not know what people thought about before modern technology.
(D) The history of modern communication began in the fifteenth century.

16. According to the passage, at what point did writing begin to have a major effect on communication?

(A) When alphabets were developed
(B) When books became available
(C) When education was formalized
(D) When the telegraph was invented

17. The word one in paragraph 2 refers to

(A) clay tablet
(B) scroll
(C) book
(D) printing press

18. Which sentence below best expresses the essential information in the highlighted sentence in paragraph 3? Incorrect choices change the meaning in important ways or l eave out essential information.

(A) Numerous people had access to books and education because of the printing press.
(B) It took several people to operate a printing press, so the number of skilled workers grew rapidly.
(C) Previously forbidden books became available to people that could afford a private education.
(D) The printing press made it possible for books to include more information than ever before.

19. The word proliferation in paragraph 3 is closest in meaning to

(A) style
(B) expense
(C) control
(D) spread

20. The word signaled in paragraph 4 is closest in meaning to

(A) followed
(B) announced
(C) concluded
(D) delayed

21. According to the passage, how did the electronic era get its name?

(A) Electronics became a standard subject taught in schools.
(B) The discovery of electrons occurred during the period.
(C) Writers of the period predicted the invention of computers.
(D) The technology sent electrical signals along electrical wires.

22. All of the following are given as examples of electronic media EXCEPT

(A) the telegraph
(B) the computer
(C) movies
(D) radio

23. Why does the author compare books with radio technology in paragraph 5?

(A) To describe the influence of handwritten books on radio
(B) To explain how both changed patterns of information flow
(C) To show that both were initially confined to a few users
(D) To complain about the social restrictions imposed on radio

24. Look at the four squares, [A], [B], [C], and [D], which indicate where the following sentence could be added to the passage. Where would the sentence best fit?

The power of electronic technologies came from their ability to convey a sense of reality.

[A] The invention of electronic media changed communication more than any other technological event since the development of writing. [B] The spread of electronic media occurred with a speed never seen before, thus intensifying commercial and social interaction. There was a tremendous shift in how people received the information that contributed to their understanding of the world. [C] Voices or pictures could create ideas that appeared authentic—more so than ideas conveyed by the printed word. The graphic, intensely human nature of electronic media enhanced the belief that if it was on the air, it had to be true. [D]

25. Select the appropriate sentences from the answer choices and match them to the type of technology that they describe. TWO of the answer choices will NOT be used. ***This question is worth 3 points.***

Answer Choices

(A) This technology was introduced in the fifteenth century.
(B) Information was preserved on clay tablets and parchment scrolls.
(C) The first technology of this type was the telegraph.
(D) Multiple copies of a book could be produced quickly.
(E) The mass broadcast of voices and images became possible.
(F) Only a few wealthy people have benefited from this technology.
(G) Rates of literacy increased because of this technology.

Printing Press

Printing Press
•
•
•

Electronic Media

Electronic Media
•
•

How to Score 3–Point Questions	
Answers Correct	**Points Earned**
5	3
4	2
3	1
0–2	0

THE NORSE IN NORTH AMERICA

1 The Norse made the first documented European voyages to North America, and there is evidence of these visits in the medieval sagas, a collection of stories that tell the history of the Icelandic people. The Icelandic sagas relate how the Norse captain Leif Eriksson and his brother Thorvald were blown off course during a voyage from Norway to Greenland and landed to the west of Greenland, and also describe Thorfinn Karlsefni's attempt to colonize a place called Vinland. The sagas are a valuable source of details about these early voyages; however, historians have long expressed skepticism about their accuracy.

2 Norsemen ventured far from their homeland in Scandinavia to found settlements on the Greenland coast. One of them, the trader Bjarni Herjolfsson, was blown off course and subsequently discovered a wooded coastline, almost certainly that of Newfoundland. Although Herjolfsson did not go ashore, this discovery made him the first European to set eyes on the continent of North America.

3 Herjolfsson's account encouraged Leif Eriksson to undertake a southward voyage of exploration, starting around the year 1000. In the course of his travels, Eriksson landed in a place he called Stoneland, which was probably the rocky, barren Labrador coast of North America. Eriksson's party finally landed in Vinland, where they spent a winter in rough Viking huts in a seemingly frost–free land of abundant vines and wild grapes. They established the first European colony in North America at Vinland, the precise location of which remains a subject of scholarly dispute to this day. The Norsemen returned home in the spring, abandoning the rude settlement that, a few years later, would serve as home base for Thorfinn Karlsefni of Greenland.

4 Around 1004, the expedition led by Thorfinn Karlsefni set off southward, evidently with a longer stay in mind, as women and cattle accompanied the sailors. Karlsefni and his party passed two years in Vinland, exploring the coast and fighting the local aboriginal tribes, whom they called "skrelings." Thorfinn Karlsefni was killed in a bloody encounter with a native group, and continued threats from hostile tribes may have thwarted the Norse attempt at colonization. For some reason, they departed their settlement at Vinland, although Greenlanders continued to make occasional visits there in later years, using it as a fishing camp.

5 Until the twentieth century, the Icelandic sagas were the primary source of information about the Norse exploration of North America. They served as inspiration for Norwegian explorer and writer Helge Ingstad, who in the early 1960s traveled the coasts of eastern North America searching for evidence of Vinland. Encouraged by an alternative interpretation of "vin" as meaning "meadow" rather than vine or wine, he discovered a grassy site on the northern tip of Newfoundland that local people had believed was an aboriginal site haunted by ancient ghosts. There, Ingstad excavated the remains of eight **sod** huts, together with artifacts of Norse origin such as a bronze pin and sewing tools. He concluded that the grassland called L'Anse aux Meadows was, if not Vinland, then certainly a Norse settlement of some kind.

6 Huddled for protection from the wind, the cluster of sod–built structures at L'Anse aux Meadows was no temporary camp. Sod walls and sod roofs built over a timber frame indicated dwellings that were substantial enough for permanent occupation. The eight huts included three long, narrow buildings with features similar to those found in Norse structures in Greenland and Iceland. Other smaller buildings, probably used for storage and workshops, included a forge that used iron ore extracted from peat bogs—evidence of the first iron working in North America.

Glossary:

sod: soil held together by the roots of grass

26. What can be inferred from paragraph 1 about the Icelandic sagas?

    (A) They were not known outside of Iceland.
    (B) They were originally told in the form of songs.
    (C) They may not be historically accurate.
    (D) They inspired Leif Eriksson to explore Vinland.

27. The phrase set eyes on in paragraph 2 is closest in meaning to

    (A) colonize
    (B) observe
    (C) imagine
    (D) explore

28. According to the passage, who was probably the first European to step on the continent of North America?

    (A) Bjarni Herjolfsson
    (B) Leif Eriksson
    (C) Thorfinn Karlsefni
    (D) Helge Ingstad

29. The word abundant in paragraph 3 is closest in meaning to

    (A) numerous
    (B) tropical
    (C) familiar
    (D) poisonous

30. Which sentence below best expresses the essential information in the highlighted sentence in paragraph 3? Incorrect choices change the meaning in important ways or leave out essential information.

    (A) The Norse were the first Europeans to discover North America, but little evidence remains of their settlement at Vinland.
    (B) The location of Vinland, the first European colony in North America, was unknown until the twenty–first century.
    (C) The Europeans chose Vinland as the site of their first colony because it had perfect conditions for growing grapes.
    (D) Eriksson's Vinland was the first European colony in North America, but scholars still disagree over exactly where it was.

31. Why does the author mention women and cattle in paragraph 4?

    (A) To show the level of detail included in the sagas
    (B) To point out the peaceful intentions of the sailors
    (C) To provide evidence of a plan to start a colony
    (D) To describe the division of labor in Norse society

32. The word thwarted in paragraph 4 is closest in meaning to

    (A) preceded
    (B) ended
    (C) concealed
    (D) inspired

33. What became of Vinland after Thorfinn Karlsefni's party left?

    (A) Hostile native tribes destroyed the buildings.
    (B) It became a permanent colony a few years later.
    (C) Historians made no further mention of it.
    (D) It was sometimes used as a base for fishing.

34. What led to Helge Ingstad's discovery at L'Anse aux Meadows in the 1960s?

    (A) The account of Vinland's wild grapes in the sagas
    (B) The search for a favorable place for a colony
    (C) The idea that Vinland referred to a meadow
    (D) The interest in writing about a haunted place

35. The word those in paragraph 6 refers to

    (A) walls
    (B) roofs
    (C) huts
    (D) features

36. All of the following were discovered at L'Anse aux Meadows EXCEPT

(A) wild grapes
(B) huts made of sod
(C) sewing tools
(D) an iron forge

37. Look at the four squares, **A**, **B**, **C**, and **D**, which indicate where the following sentence could be added to the passage. Where would the sentence best fit?

He and his men then sailed south to Woodland, which could have been Newfoundland, Nova Scotia, or Maine, all of which are wooded.

Herjolfsson's account encouraged Leif Eriksson to undertake a southward voyage of exploration, starting around the year 1000. **A** In the course of his travels, Eriksson landed in a place he called Stoneland, which was probably the rocky, barren Labrador coast of North America. **B** Eriksson's party finally landed in Vinland, where they spent a winter in rough Viking huts in a seemingly frost–free land of abundant vines and wild grapes. **C** They established the first European colony in North America at Vinland, the precise location of which remains a subject of scholarly dispute to this day. **D** The Norsemen returned home in the spring, abandoning the rude settlement that, a few years later, would serve as home base for Thorfinn Karlsefni of Greenland.

38. Read the first sentence of a summary of the passage. Complete the summary by selecting the THREE answer choices that express the most important ideas in the passage. Some sentences do not belong in the summary because they express ideas that are not presented in the passage or are minor ideas in the passage. ***This question is worth 2 points.***

The Norse were the first Europeans to attempt to colonize North America.

•
•
•

Answer Choices

(A) The Icelandic sagas tell the story of how Leif Eriksson and his brother Thorvald were blown off course.

(B) A group of Norse explorers led by Leif Eriksson built a temporary colony at a place called Vinland.

(C) Norsemen from Greenland were able to travel to distant lands because they lived on preserved fish.

(D) Thorfinn Karlsefni established a colony at Vinland, but this settlement was abandoned a few years later.

(E) Evidence of an early Norse settlement was discovered at L'Anse aux Meadows in Newfoundland.

(F) A building with sod walls and a sod roof over a timber frame is strong enough for permanent occupation.

How to Score 2–Point Questions	
Answers Correct	**Points Earned**
3	2
2	1
0–1	0

THE FIVE–SEVEN SHIFT

1 All major theories of child psychology state that children undergo a major change between the ages of five and seven. In classical learning theory, this is a time when the simplest forms of learning give way to learning that involves more complex mental processes. According to psychologist Jean Piaget, the period from five to seven years old is a transition to operational thought, when children are able to move beyond using only their senses toward using a new set of rational–thinking skills. Because several **cognitive** changes occur in children between ages five and seven, this period is called the five–seven shift. The shift is biological in nature and involves fundamental growth in the brain and stabilization of brain–wave rhythms into a basically adult pattern. The five–seven shift involves many physical changes, such as the loss of the "baby teeth" and an increase in the rates of height acquired and weight gained.

2 By the time they are five years old, children can understand and use symbols. They have developed the ability to use words, gestures, and pictures to stand for "real life" objects, and they are skilled in deploying various symbol systems, such as language or drawing. However, a five–year–old child is able to focus attention on only one quality of an object at a time, such as the object's size or shape. The use of symbolization continues to evolve, reaching a peak around the age of seven or eight, when children become capable of concrete operations. When this happens, they can solve problems by using rational thought to make generalizations from their own experience.

3 By the age of seven or eight, a new set of abilities allows children to reason systematically about the world of objects, quantity, time, space, and causality. According to Piaget, this is because an "extra card" is added to the child's mental "computer" during the five–seven shift. The development of operational thought enables the child to appreciate the relations among a series of actions upon objects. For example, the child understands that a scene can be viewed from a different perspective and still contain the same elements. The child also understands that objects can be rearranged and still have the same quantity and that a substance can be changed in shape without its mass or volume being affected.

4 Piaget discovered the most widely known hallmark of the five–seven shift, an understanding of conservation, the idea that some properties stay the same despite changes in appearance. In one of Piaget's classic experiments on the conservation of quantity, the experimenter shows children of different ages two straight rows of coins, each with six coins pressed close together, beside each other on a table. The experimenter asks each child subject whether both rows have the same number of coins or whether one row has more. Then the experimenter spreads out the coins of one row to make the line look longer. The child must now say whether one row has more coins. Children younger than five years old cannot understand conservation, so they invariably say that the spread–out row has more coins than the other row.

5 Like most age–related tasks for children, there are other ways to set up the task. In a similar experiment, water is poured into two identical glasses until the child subject agrees that each contains an equal amount. Then the experimenter pours water from one of these glasses into a tall, thin glass. At that point, the child is asked whether one glass has more water than the other. Five–year–old children will say that there is more water in the tall, thin glass. When asked why they think that, many will confidently say, "Because it's taller." Older children, however, are likely to reply, "It looks like there's more water in this one because it's taller, but they're really the same." Such experiments show a difference between children of five years and children of eight years. The older children can solve the task promptly, easily, under a wide variety of conditions, and without being taught. The younger children, even if they are taught about conservation, cannot do what the five–seven shift will do for them naturally: provide them with a more developed brain.

Glossary:
cognitive: relating to mental processes

39. According to the passage, children between the ages of five and seven typically experience all of the following EXCEPT

    (A) development of rational thinking
    (B) an interest in morality and rules
    (C) important changes in the brain
    (D) an increase in the physical growth rate

40. What can be inferred from paragraph 1 about cognitive development during the five–seven shift?

    (A) It is a time when children start learning in very simple ways.
    (B) It is the most important period in the child's formal education.
    (C) It is a topic of disagreement among child psychologists.
    (D) It is related to biological developments in the child's brain.

41. Why does the author mention words, gestures, and pictures in paragraph 2?

    (A) To list things that are used in experiments with children
    (B) To give examples of symbols that children can understand
    (C) To compare different ways of illustrating a child's experience
    (D) To illustrate the concept of conservation of quantity

42. The word peak in paragraph 2 is closest in meaning to

    (A) large vocabulary
    (B) difficult period
    (C) high point
    (D) sudden reversal

43. According to the passage, a child who is capable of concrete operations can

    (A) perform tasks that may confuse an adult
    (B) install an extra card on a computer
    (C) make two rows of coins look the same
    (D) reason systematically about quantity and space

44. The word hallmark in paragraph 4 is closest in meaning to

    (A) characteristic
    (B) problem
    (C) disadvantage
    (D) experiment

45. The word each in paragraph 4 refers to

    (A) experiment
    (B) child
    (C) age
    (D) row

46. Which sentence below best expresses the essential information in the highlighted sentence in paragraph 4? Incorrect choices change the meaning in important ways or leave out essential information.

    (A) Before the age of five, children think the longer line has more coins because they are incapable of understanding conservation.
    (B) Five–year–old children do not understand the value of money, so they do not care if one line of coins is longer than another.
    (C) Because of the five–seven shift, children can understand why the longer row of coins is a better example of conservation.
    (D) Even if two rows of coins are different in length, very young children will say that both rows have the same number of coins.

47. In paragraph 5, the author describes an experiment in which water is poured into various glasses in order to

    (A) show how children approach difficult problems
    (B) recommend an experiment that can be done at home
    (C) give a variation on a classic experiment by Piaget
    (D) suggest an activity for parents and children

48. What can be inferred about children who easily solve the water task described in paragraph 5?

(A) They have already experienced the five–seven shift.
(B) They were taught about the concept of conservation.
(C) They had time to practice the task before the experiment.
(D) They are more intelligent than others of the same age.

49. Look at the four squares, **A**, **B**, **C**, and **D**, which indicate where the following sentence could be added to the passage. Where would the sentence best fit?

For instance, when sand is poured back and forth between containers of different sizes and shapes, the quantity of sand does not change.

Piaget discovered the most widely known hallmark of the five–seven shift, an understanding of conservation, the idea that some properties stay the same despite changes in appearance. **A** In one of Piaget's classic experiments on the conservation of quantity, the experimenter shows children of different ages two straight rows of coins, each with six coins pressed close together, beside each other on a table. **B** The experimenter asks each child subject whether both rows have the same number of coins or whether one row has more. Then the experimenter spreads out the coins of one row to make the line look longer. **C** The child must now say whether one row has more coins. Children younger than five years old cannot understand conservation, so they invariably say that the spread–out row has more coins than the other row. **D**

50. Select the appropriate sentences from the answer choices and match them to the period before or after the five–seven shift. TWO of the answer choices will NOT be used. ***This question is worth 3 points.***

Answer Choices

(A) The child's brain waves have rhythms similar to those of adults.
(B) The child's cognitive development cannot be measured scientifically.
(C) The child learns in simple ways and can focus on only one quality at a time.
(D) The child knows that the quantity stays the same when objects are rearranged.
(E) The child cannot distinguish between right and wrong.
(F) The child can quickly solve problems involving conservation.
(G) The child is not able to understand the conservation of quantity.

Before the Five–Seven Shift

•
•

After the Five–Seven Shift

•
•
•

How to Score 3–Point Questions	
Answers Correct	**Points Earned**
5	3
4	2
3	1
0–2	0

SOIL QUALITY

1 Soil is a renewable resource, but only on a very long time scale, as it takes hundreds or thousands of years for the natural processes of erosion, organic decay, and accumulation to create soils. Soil quality and the potential to produce crops can vary enormously from region to region and among various soil types.

2 One important factor affecting the productivity of soils over time is agriculture. Top–quality lands are brought into production earlier because of their higher potential to produce food. As more and more land has been brought under agricultural production, the average quality of land has decreased, reducing potential productivity per hectare. Crops deplete soil fertility by consuming nutrients, and this eventually reduces crop yields. Poor management practices lead to soil compaction and soil pollution as well as loss of soil cover. Without proper management and the constant addition of nutrients and energy in the form of fertilizers and irrigation, crop production falls over time.

3 Within the scientific community, there is little doubt that soil quality is diminishing in many areas around the world. Scientists have found that the quality of one quarter of the world's soils has experienced some **degradation**, and the pace of degradation has accelerated over the past 50 years. The loss of soil fertility has caused a slowing in the growth of agricultural productivity. Annual crops tend to degrade soils more than perennial crops, and common property lands generally suffer more degradation than private lands.

4 Today, irrigated cropland produces about one–third of the world's food. Approximately 18 percent of the world's cropland is irrigated, and scientists project this amount to double by 2020. Irrigation can increase crop yields per hectare to two or three times the yields of land watered only by rain. However, there are also some harmful side effects. Besides increasing crop productivity in the short run, irrigation can lead to sharp drops in crop productivity in the long run by causing excessive salt buildup and rising water tables.

5 One of the most critical soil quality problems related to irrigation is the increase in concentration of dissolved salts. This process, salinization, affects an estimated one–fourth of the world's irrigated cropland. In some places, irrigation water contains as much as 3.5 tons of salt per 1,000 cubic meters. As the water flows over and through the ground, it dissolves salts, increasing the salinity of the water. Since some crops require 6,000 to 10,000 cubic meters of water per hectare, land can receive tens of tons of salt per hectare. As the water evaporates, high concentrations of salts such as sodium chloride are left behind in the topsoil. Salt buildup can stunt crop growth, decrease yields, kill crop plants, and eventually make the land unproductive.

6 A problem that often accompanies salinization in dry regions is waterlogging, which often occurs when farmers apply heavy amounts of irrigation water in an attempt to prevent salts from accumulating. However, unless the water drains properly, it collects underground and gradually raises the water table closer to the surface, thereby bringing salts to the surface and concentrating them. Saltwater then envelops the fragile root systems of plants, killing the plants and converting fertile fields to wet deserts. This is a particularly serious problem in California's heavily irrigated San Joaquin Valley, where soils contain a clay layer that prevents water from flowing through the ground. Worldwide, at least one–tenth of all irrigated land is subject to waterlogging.

7 Another serious soil problem is erosion, the loss of soils from water and wind action. Soil erosion occurs on agricultural land without vegetative cover for protection or because of poor agricultural management. Scientists estimate that topsoil on cultivated land is being lost 16 to 300 times faster than it is being replaced. In many parts of the world, a shift away from traditional agricultural practices is placing greater pressure on the soil, which in turn is causing an increase in soil erosion rates. Studies in the United States suggest that the loss of just 2.5 centimeters of topsoil reduces corn and wheat yields by 6 percent.

Glossary:
degradation: loss of quality

51. According to the passage, all of the following contribute to soil degradation EXCEPT

(A) poor agricultural management
(B) rotation of annual crops
(C) accumulation of salts
(D) lack of water drainage

52. The word deplete in paragraph 2 is closest in meaning to

(A) reduce
(B) attract
(C) prepare
(D) create

53. Which sentence below best expresses the essential information in the highlighted sentence in paragraph 3? Incorrect choices change the meaning in important ways or leave out essential information.

(A) The scientific study of soils is improving soil quality in many regions worldwide.
(B) Few people would disagree that soil quality is as diminished as scientists say it is.
(C) The number of scientists who specialize in the study of soils has been decreasing.
(D) Most scientists agree that soil degradation is occurring in many parts of the world.

54. What can be inferred from paragraph 3 about annual crops and common property lands?

(A) They have been part of agriculture for only the past fifty years.
(B) They are not considered to be significant causes of soil degradation.
(C) They produce more income than perennial crops and private lands do.
(D) They may decrease soil fertility and agricultural productivity.

55. According to the passage, which of the following is a serious consequence of irrigation?

(A) Loss of fresh water for drinking
(B) Decrease in the level of rivers
(C) Excessive buildup of salts in the soil
(D) Increase in the rate of soil erosion

56. In what way is salinization a serious problem for agriculture?

(A) Soils with high salt concentrations are destructive to crop plants.
(B) Salinization can lead to soil compaction or to loss of soil cover.
(C) Excessive amounts of water are required to prevent salinization.
(D) Adding salt to fertilizer raises the operating costs of agriculture.

57. The word stunt in paragraph 5 is closest in meaning to

(A) speed
(B) hide
(C) cause
(D) limit

58. The term waterlogging in paragraph 6 means that

(A) logs are floating in water
(B) water is not available
(C) the soil holds too much water
(D) salts are removed from water

59. How are waterlogging and salinization related?

(A) Salinization occurs only where waterlogging is a problem.
(B) Waterlogging raises and concentrates salts near the surface.
(C) Farmers add salts to irrigation water as a way to fertilize soil.
(D) Both waterlogging and salinization contribute to soil erosion.

60. The word which in paragraph 7 refers to

(A) world
(B) practices
(C) pressure
(D) soil

61. Why does the author mention corn and wheat yields in paragraph 7?

(A) To illustrate the effect of a small amount of erosion
(B) To explain why erosion affects only certain crops
(C) To describe the result of a shift from traditional practices
(D) To show how poor management influences crop yields

62. Look at the four squares, [A], [B], [C], and [D], which indicate where the following sentence could be added to the passage. Where would the sentence best fit?

Unless they are flushed or drained from the soil, their buildup may cause a number of serious problems.

One of the most critical soil quality problems related to irrigation is the increase in concentration of dissolved salts. This process, salinization, affects an estimated one–fourth of the world's irrigated cropland. In some places, irrigation water contains as much as 3.5 tons of salt per 1,000 cubic meters. [A] As the water flows over and through the ground, it dissolves salts, increasing the salinity of the water. [B] Since some crops require 6,000 to 10,000 cubic meters of water per hectare, land can receive tens of tons of salt per hectare. [C] As the water evaporates, high concentrations of salts such as sodium chloride are left behind in the topsoil. [D] Salt buildup can stunt crop growth, decrease yields, kill crop plants, and eventually make the land unproductive.

63. Read the first sentence of a summary of the passage. Complete the summary by selecting the THREE answer choices that express the most important ideas in the passage. Some sentences do not belong in the summary because they express ideas that are not presented in the passage or are minor ideas in the passage. ***This question is worth 2 points.***

Several factors are responsible for the degradation of the world's soils.

•
•
•

Answer Choices

(A) Soils are created through the processes of erosion, organic decay, and accumulation.

(B) Contamination of the soil from air and water pollution is a growing threat.

(C) Agriculture and poor land management practices decrease the quality of soils over time.

(D) Irrigation can diminish soil productivity by causing salts and water to accumulate.

(E) The soils in the San Joaquin Valley contain a clay layer that contributes to waterlogging.

(F) The erosion of topsoil on agricultural lands is a growing problem that affects crop yields.

TEST 5

How to Score 2–Point Questions	
Answers Correct	**Points Earned**
3	2
2	1
0–1	0

Answers are on page 317.

Record your Reading section score on page 380.

Disk 5, Track 1

LISTENING SECTION DIRECTIONS

The Listening section measures your ability to understand conversations and lectures in English. You will hear each conversation and lecture only one time. After each conversation or lecture, you will hear some questions about it. Answer the questions based on what the speakers state or imply.

You may take notes while you listen. You may use your notes to help you answer the questions.

In some questions, you will see this icon: 🎧. This means that you will hear, but not see, part of the question.

Some questions have special directions, which appear in a gray box. Most questions are worth one point. If a question is worth more than one point, the directions will indicate how many points you can receive.

You will now begin the first part of the Listening section.

Time – maximum of 60 minutes

Disk 5, Track 2

QUESTIONS 1–5

1. Why does the woman go to the campus newspaper office?

   (A) She wants to thank the editor for helping her get a job.
   (B) She would like the editor's opinion of a story she wrote.
   (C) She is inquiring about writing arts reviews for the paper.
   (D) She is asking the editor to endorse a sample of her writing.

2. Why does the man say this: 🎧

   (A) To describe the type of story that the campus paper prints
   (B) To suggest that she change her academic major to journalism
   (C) To explain why the campus paper has an excellent reputation
   (D) To inform her that the paper does not need another reviewer

3. Listen again to part of the conversation. Then answer the question.

   What does the man mean when he says this: 🎧

   (A) He probably cannot offer her a job now.
   (B) The journalism department has strict rules.
   (C) He usually hires only journalism students.
   (D) The college may stop having a newspaper.

4. What does the man say about the city newspaper?

   (A) The city paper has a larger budget than the campus paper.
   (B) His former job was features editor for the city paper.
   (C) Sometimes the city paper prints stories written by students.
   (D) The city paper prefers writers who have a journalism degree.

5. What will the woman probably do?

   (A) Write concert and film reviews for the campus paper
   (B) Change her field of study from English to journalism
   (C) Go to the journalism department to ask for a job
   (D) Contact the city newspaper about writing book reviews

Disk 5, Track 3

QUESTIONS 6–11

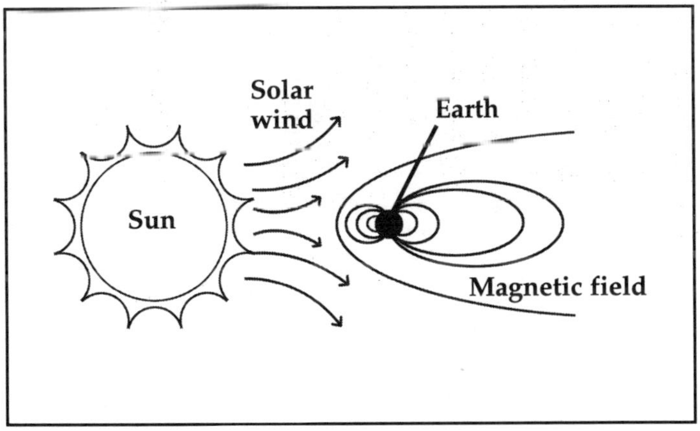

6. What aspect of the auroras does the professor mainly discuss?

   (A) Myths about the auroras
   (B) How to videotape the auroras
   (C) What causes the auroras
   (D) The beauty of the auroras

7. What colors are commonly seen in the auroras?

   Click on two answers.

   [A] Orange
   [B] Red
   [C] Green
   [D] Brown

8. Listen again to part of the lecture. Then answer the question.

   Why does the professor say this: 🎧

   (A) To compare the views from the North and South Poles
   (B) To explain why extremes of daylight exist at the poles
   (C) To point out where the auroras are most visible
   (D) To suggest taking a trip to the North or South Pole

9. Why does the professor say this: 🎧

   (A) To explain how the auroras are electrical in nature
   (B) To change the subject to something more interesting
   (C) To encourage the student to observe the auroras
   (D) To imply that the auroras contribute to global warming

10. The professor briefly explains how the auroras are formed. Indicate whether each sentence below is a part of the process.

    For each sentence, click in the correct box.

	Yes	No
Oxygen and nitrogen atoms in the ionosphere become "excited."		
Sunlight travels to Earth and is reflected back into space by clouds.		
Ionized atoms de–energize and emit radiation as visible light.		
The solar wind interacts with Earth's magnetic field.		

11. Listen again to part of the lecture. Then answer the question.

    What can be inferred about the auroras?

    (A) The auroras change in size and shape during the night.
    (B) The color of auroras is related to the type of gas involved.
    (C) The beauty of auroras is difficult to measure accurately.
    (D) The auroras are a possible source of nuclear energy.

Disk 5, Track 4

QUESTIONS 12–17

Political Science

Political Parties

12. How does the professor develop the topic of political parties?

 (A) By comparing the goals of different parties
 (B) By promoting the views of a specific party
 (C) By describing parties in a two–party system
 (D) By explaining how to organize a party

13. Listen again to part of the lecture. Then answer the question.

 Why does the professor say this: 🎧

 (A) To test the students' knowledge of parties
 (B) To find out which party the students support
 (C) To introduce a point that he will make
 (D) To show that all states have a two–party system

14. Listen again to part of the lecture. Then answer the question.

 What does the professor imply about political parties?

 (A) Parties make decisions based on the interests of several organizations.
 (B) Parties can never accomplish everything that they would like to do.
 (C) Parties carry on their work through the efforts of unpaid volunteers.
 (D) Parties are necessary in the exercise of democracy in national states.

15. Based on the information in the lecture, indicate whether each statement below describes political parties.

 For each sentence, click in the correct box.

	Yes	No
They are a group of people who come together mainly for amusement.		
They organize voters and compete for support on major issues.		
They are voluntary organizations of people who agree on public policies.		
They have research offices that develop positions on important issues.		

16. What does the professor mean when he says this: 🎧

 (A) It is possible to enjoy politics but dislike government at the same time.
 (B) A political party cares about major issues, but a government doesn't care.
 (C) Politics is about competition, while government is about responsibility.
 (D) Elections and government are like two sides of the same coin.

17. Why does the professor say this: 🎧

 (A) To show how major parties usually deal with the same issues
 (B) To suggest that both parties should give education more attention
 (C) To contrast the philosophy and methods of opposing parties
 (D) To point out which party is more concerned with education

Disk 5, Track 5

QUESTIONS 18–22

Conversation

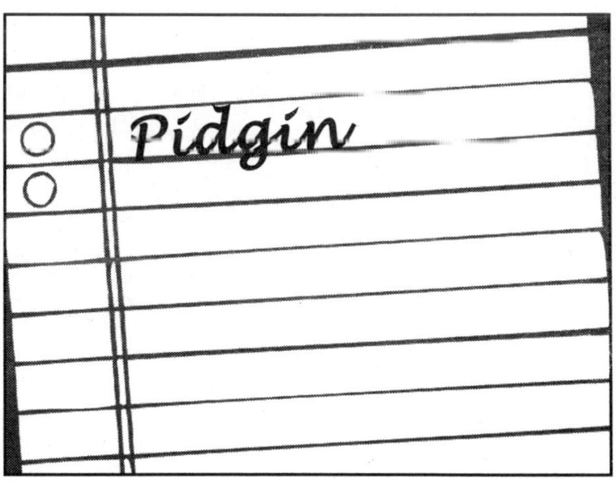

18. What are the students mainly discussing?

   (A) Languages that connect speakers of diverse languages
   (B) The evolution of the world's major languages
   (C) Why it is important to learn a second language
   (D) Similarities between linguistics and anthropology

19. What is the woman's attitude toward her linguistics class?

   (A) She thinks there is too much homework.
   (B) She is confused most of the time.
   (C) She thinks her professor is very nice.
   (D) She finds the lecture topics interesting.

20. According to the conversation, which languages are lingua francas?

   Click on two answers.

   [A] Italian
   [B] English
   [C] Polish
   [D] Swahili

21. Why does the woman say this:

   (A) To express amusement at the man's pronunciation
   (B) To give another word that has the same meaning
   (C) To correct the man's misunderstanding of a word
   (D) To help the man with a spelling problem

22. Based on the conversation, indicate whether each sentence below describes a lingua franca or a pidgin.

   For each sentence, click in the correct box.

	Lingua franca	**Pidgin**
It usually develops as a universal business language.		
It is a simplified language that blends two or more languages.		
It is the common language of many people who speak various languages.		
It is easy to learn because its grammar and vocabulary are simple.		

Disk 5, Track 6

QUESTIONS 23–28

Biology

23. What is the main idea of the talk?

Ⓐ Birds differ in appearance throughout the world.
Ⓑ The best diet for birds includes both seeds and insects.
Ⓒ The bird's bill is specialized to its preferred diet.
Ⓓ Birds have a variety of interesting behaviors.

24. Select the bird that is most likely a seed eater.

Ⓐ 
Ⓒ 
Ⓑ 
Ⓓ 

25. Listen again to part of the talk. Then answer the question.

Why does the professor say this:

Ⓐ To describe the nutritional benefits of flower nectar
Ⓑ To state that birds and their food evolved together
Ⓒ To compare the physical structure of birds and plants
Ⓓ To explain why birds need variety in their diet

26. Select the bird that is most likely a nectar drinker.

Ⓐ 
Ⓒ 
Ⓑ 
Ⓓ 

27. Listen again to part of the talk. Then answer the question.

What does the professor imply about hummingbirds?

Ⓐ They are a source of food for insects and spiders.
Ⓑ Their diet is not restricted to flower nectar.
Ⓒ They obtain protein from eating flower seeds.
Ⓓ Their behavior cannot be explained scientifically.

28. What physical features are characteristic of birds that eat insects?

Click on two answers.

[A] A thick, cone–shaped bill
[B] A slender, tweezer–like bill
[C] Strong jaw muscles
[D] A long, sticky tongue

Disk 5, Track 7

QUESTIONS 29–34

Chemistry

29. What is the main purpose of the talk?

Ⓐ To test the students' ability to understand chemistry
Ⓑ To explain different kinds of chemical processes
Ⓒ To list the jobs available to chemistry graduates
Ⓓ To introduce the students to the study of chemistry

30. According to the professor, why is chemistry sometimes called the central science?

Ⓐ Chemistry courses are the most difficult.
Ⓑ Chemical processes occur all around us.
Ⓒ Chemistry students have high status.
Ⓓ Chemists study how to control diseases.

31. Listen again to part of the talk. Then answer the question.

Why does the professor mention her former students?

Ⓐ To introduce basic skills that all chemists need
Ⓑ To make the study of chemistry more exciting
Ⓒ To give examples of successful graduates
Ⓓ To recommend former students as tutors

32. What does the professor imply about memorizing information?

Ⓐ It is the best strategy for earning high test scores.
Ⓑ It is difficult when the information is unfamiliar.
Ⓒ It is the only way to make chemistry interesting.
Ⓓ It is not the most important part of education.

33. Listen again to part of the talk. Then answer the question.

Why does the professor say this:

Ⓐ To emphasize the importance of doing homework regularly
Ⓑ To show that studying with others is useful in the sciences
Ⓒ To explain that every problem has only one correct answer
Ⓓ To encourage students to pursue graduate study in chemistry

34. What does the professor imply about making mistakes?

Ⓐ You should try not to make any mistakes.
Ⓑ It is dangerous to make mistakes in chemistry.
Ⓒ Mistakes can be a part of the learning process.
Ⓓ Professional chemists rarely make mistakes.

Stop

Answers are on page 320.

Record your Listening section score on page 381.

Disk 5, Track 8

SPEAKING SECTION DIRECTIONS

The Speaking section measures your ability to speak in English about a variety of topics. There are six questions in this section.

Questions 1 and 2 are independent tasks in which you will speak about familiar topics. Your responses will be scored on your ability to speak clearly and coherently about the topics.

Questions 3 and 4 are integrated speaking tasks. You will read a passage, listen to a conversation or lecture, and then speak in response to a question about what you have read and heard. You will need to combine relevant information from the two sources to answer the question completely. Your responses will be scored on your ability to speak clearly and coherently and on your ability to accurately convey information about what you read and heard.

Questions 5 and 6 are integrated speaking tasks. You will listen to part of a conversation or lecture, and then speak in response to a question about what you have heard. Your responses will be scored on your ability to speak clearly and coherently and on your ability to accurately convey information about what you heard.

You will hear each conversation and lecture only one time. You may take notes while you listen. You may use your notes to help you answer the questions.

Stop

QUESTION 1

In this question, you will be asked to talk about a familiar topic. After you hear the question, you will have 15 seconds to prepare your response and 45 seconds to speak.

Disk 5, Track 9

Describe an object, plant, or animal that represents your native country and explain its significance. Include details and examples to support your explanation.

Stop

Preparation Time – 15 seconds
Response Time – 45 seconds

QUESTION 2

In this question, you will be asked to give your opinion about a familiar topic. After you hear the question, you will have 15 seconds to prepare your response and 45 seconds to speak.

Disk 5, Track 10

Some universities are very large and have several thousand students. Others are small and have only a few thousand students. Which size of university do you think is better for students, and why? Include details and examples in your explanation.

Stop

Preparation Time – 15 seconds
Response Time – 45 seconds

QUESTION 3

In this question, you will read a short passage about a campus situation, listen to a conversation, and then speak in response to a question about what you have read and heard. After you hear the question, you have 30 seconds to prepare your response and 60 seconds to speak.

Reading Time – 45 seconds

SCIENCE SEMINAR

Any student is welcome to join the seminar section of our core science program. In the seminar, we read, discuss, and write about various topics in science and mathematics. We assume no background in mathematics or physics. We explore ideas about nature, history, and the philosophy of science, as well as methods of physics and mathematics. Readings and topics vary each term. Seminar students work together with beginning and advanced science students. Students earn 2 or 4 science credits by participating in one or two seminars each week and by completing short papers and online assignments.

Now cover the passage and listen to the recording. When you hear the question, begin preparing your response.

Disk 5, Track 11

The man expresses his opinion about the science seminar. State his opinion and explain the reasons he gives for holding that opinion.

Stop

Preparation Time – 30 seconds
Response Time – 60 seconds

QUESTION 4

In this question, you will read a short passage on an academic subject, listen to a lecture on the same topic, and then speak in response to a question about what you have read and heard. After you hear the question, you have 30 seconds to prepare your response and 60 seconds to speak.

Reading Time – 45 seconds

IMAGERY IN DANCE

Sometimes a dancer has the perfect experience in a dance class or performance. The dancer may describe it as effortless motion, kinetic flow, total body awareness, total freedom, inspiration, or pure joy in movement. Such a feeling occurs when the dancer's mind and body work together as a unit. Mental preparation, especially the use of imagery, is just as important as physical discipline for a dancer. The use of mental imagery helps dancers discover a whole new range of possibilities within their bodies. Imagery focuses the mind, increases expression, broadens technique, releases excess tension, and improves balance and coordination.

Now cover the passage and listen to the recording. When you hear the question, begin preparing your response.

Disk 5, Track 12

The instructor describes the use of imagery in dance. Explain how specific imagery can affect a dancer's experience and performance.

Stop

Preparation Time – 30 seconds
Response Time – 60 seconds

QUESTION 5

In this question, you will listen to a conversation. You will then be asked to talk about the information in the conversation and to give your opinion about the ideas presented. After you hear the question, you have 20 seconds to prepare your response and 60 seconds to speak.

Disk 5, Track 13

The students discuss two possible solutions to the woman's problem. Describe the problem. Then state which of the two solutions you prefer and explain why.

Stop

Preparation Time – 20 seconds
Response Time – 60 seconds

QUESTION 6

In this question, you will listen to part of a lecture. You will then be asked to summarize important information from the lecture. After you hear the question, you have 20 seconds to prepare your response and 60 seconds to speak.

Disk 5, Track 14

Using points and details from the lecture, explain the movement toward systemizing the home in the period described by the professor.

Stop

Preparation Time – 20 seconds
Response Time – 60 seconds

Key points for the Speaking responses are on page 322.

Each response earns a score of 1, 2, 3 or 4.

Record your total Speaking score on page 382.

Disk 5, Track 15

WRITING SECTION DIRECTIONS

The Writing section measures your ability to use writing to communicate in an academic environment. There are two writing questions.

Question 1 is an integrated writing task. You will read a passage, listen to a lecture, and then answer a question based on what you have read and heard. You have 20 minutes to plan and write your response.

Question 2 is an independent writing task. You will answer a question based on your own knowledge and experience. You have 30 minutes to plan and write your response.

Stop

QUESTION 1

For this task, you will write a response to a question about a reading passage and a lecture. You may take notes, and you may use your notes to help you write your response. Your response will be scored on the quality of your writing and on how well you connect the points in the lecture with points in the reading. Typically, an effective response will have 150 to 225 words.

Reading Time – 3 minutes

At the beginning of the twentieth century, French psychologist Alfred Binet devised the first test of human intelligence. The test consisted of problems of increasing difficulty that were designed to measure children's judgment, reasoning, and comprehension. Shortly after Binet's original work, psychologist Lewis Terman of Stanford University refined and standardized the test for American children. This test became known as the Stanford–Binet Intelligence Scale, which was first published in 1916 and revised several times after that.

Terman and his colleagues developed the idea of the IQ, or intelligence quotient. IQ is a measurement of general intelligence, a number representing the ratio of mental age (performance on the test) to actual chronological age in years. IQ has proven to be an accurate measurement of a child's potential to achieve in school and later in professional life. The most recent version of the Stanford–Binet test is still being used today and remains one of the world's most widely used and accurate tests of general intelligence. It has produced reliable results for individuals from age two through adulthood.

Intelligence testing has caused great excitement within the scientific community and the larger society. Many psychologists agree that intelligence testing is psychology's greatest achievement. Intelligence testing and IQ are important scientific developments with great social utility beyond the prediction of school achievement. Intelligence tests are now available to evaluate people for specific purposes, such as military service, placement in industrial organizations, and even social companionship.

Now listen to the recording. When you hear the question, begin your response. You may look at the passage during the writing time.

Disk 5, Track 16

Summarize the points made in the lecture you just heard, explaining how they cast doubt on points made in the reading.

Stop

Writing Time – 20 minutes

QUESTION 2

For this task, you will write an essay in response to a question that asks you to state and support your opinion on a topic. Your essay will be scored on the quality of your writing, including how well you organize and develop your ideas and how well you use language to express your ideas. Typically, an effective essay will have a minimum of 300 words.

Read the question below and make any notes that will help you plan your response. Then begin writing your essay.

> Do you agree or disagree with the following statement?
>
> **It is the responsibility of the government to provide health care to everyone living in that country.**
>
> Use specific reasons and examples to support your answer.

Writing Time – 30 minutes

Key points for the Writing section are on page 322.

Each response earns a score of 1, 2, 3, 4 or 5.

Record your total Writing score on page 382.

TEST 6

Reading Section Directions

The Reading section measures your ability to read and understand passages in English. You will read three passages and answer questions about them. Answer all questions based on what is stated or implied in the passages.

Most questions are worth one point. The last question in each set is worth more than one point. For this question, the directions will indicate how many points you can receive.

Some passages have one or more words in bold type. For these bolded words, you will see a definition in a glossary at the end of the passage.

Allow 20 minutes to read each passage and answer the questions about it. You may now begin the first passage.

Time – 60 minutes

MASS WASTING PROCESSES

1 The downslope movement of rock, mud, or other material under the influence of gravity is known as mass wasting. While the angle of the slope is a major factor in the potential for mass wasting, the slope is not the sole determiner of mass wasting events. Water plays a significant role, especially where it is plentiful during the rainy season. Earthquakes may cause rockslides, mudflows, and other mass movements. Factors such as the presence or absence of vegetation and human activities can also influence the potential for mass wasting.

2 One way to classify mass wasting processes is on the basis of the material involved, such as rock, debris, earth, or mud. The manner in which the material moves is also important and is generally described as a fall, a slide, or a flow. A fall occurs when weathering loosens boulders from cliffs or rock faces, causing the boulders to break away and fall. A slide takes place whenever material remains fairly coherent and moves along a well–defined surface. A flow involves the movement of debris containing a large amount of water.

3 Many mass wasting processes are described as slides. Rockslides occur when a coherent mass of rock breaks loose and slides down a slope as a unit. If the material involved is mostly separate pieces, it is called a debris slide. Slides are among the fastest and most destructive mass movements. Usually rockslides occur in a geologic setting where the rock layers are inclined, or where there are joints and fractures in the rock that are parallel to the slope. When such a rock unit is undercut at the base of the slope, it loses support and the rock eventually collapses. Rain or snowmelt can trigger a rockslide by wetting the underlying surface to the point that friction can no longer hold the rock in place. The fastest type of slide is a rock avalanche, in which a mass of rock literally floats on air as it moves downslope. The high speed of a rock avalanche is the result of air becoming trapped and compressed beneath the falling mass of debris, allowing it to move down the slope as a buoyant sheet.

4 Mudflows are relatively rapid mass wasting events that involve soil and a large amount of water. Because of their fluid properties, mudflows follow canyons and stream channels. Mudflows often take place in semiarid mountainous regions and on the slopes of some volcanoes. Although rainstorms in semiarid regions are infrequent, they are typically heavy when they occur. When a rainstorm or rapidly melting snow creates a sudden flood, large quantities of soil and loose rock are washed into nearby stream channels because there is usually little or no vegetation to anchor the surface material. The result is a flowing mass of well–mixed mud, soil, rock, and water. The consistency of the mudflow may be similar to that of wet concrete, or it may be a soupy mixture not much thicker than muddy water. The water content influences the rate of flow across the surface. When a mudflow is dense, it moves more slowly, but it can easily carry or push large boulders, trees, and even houses along with it.

5 In dry mountainous areas such as southern California, mudflows are a serious hazard to development on and near canyon hillsides. The removal of native vegetation by brush fires has increased the probability of these destructive events. Past mudflows have contributed to the buildup of fan–shaped deposits at canyon mouths. Such fans are relatively easy to build on and often have scenic views, so many have become desirable sites for residential development. However, because mudflows occur infrequently, homeowners are often unaware of the potential danger of building on the site of a previous mudflow.

6 Highly fluid, fast–flowing mudflows incorporate fine–grained sediment and are common after volcanic eruptions that produce large volumes of volcanic ash. Mudflows containing volcanic debris are called lahars, a word originating in Indonesia, a region that experiences many volcanic eruptions. Lahars occur when highly unstable layers of ash and debris become saturated with water and flow down steep volcanic slopes along stream channels. In the northwestern United States, the eruption of Mount St. Helens in 1980 created several lahars that raced down the valley of the Toutle River, altering the landscape in a relatively short period.

1. All of the following are given as factors in mass wasting EXCEPT

   (A) the angle of the slope
   (B) the presence of water
   (C) the absence of plants
   (D) the type of mineral

2. The name of a mass wasting process is a reflection of

   (A) the area in which the movement occurs
   (B) the material that is moved and the way it moves
   (C) the rate of movement relative to other processes
   (D) the mass and volume of the material involved

3. The word trigger in paragraph 3 is closest in meaning to

   (A) prevent
   (B) imitate
   (C) cause
   (D) decrease

4. Why does a rock avalanche move faster than other types of rockslides?

   (A) The rock moves over a layer of compressed air.
   (B) The rainfall is heavy where avalanches occur.
   (C) The rock breaks apart as it moves downslope.
   (D) The angle of the slope is almost vertical.

5. The word buoyant in paragraph 3 is closest in meaning to

   (A) floating
   (B) dangerous
   (C) heavy
   (D) sticky

6. The word anchor in paragraph 4 is closest in meaning to

   (A) push
   (B) replace
   (C) hold
   (D) improve

7. The word that in paragraph 4 refers to

   (A) result
   (B) consistency
   (C) mudflow
   (D) mixture

8. Which sentence below best expresses the essential information in the highlighted sentence in paragraph 5? Incorrect choices change the meaning in important ways or leave out essential information.

   (A) Fire has destroyed much of the original vegetation, so mudflows are now more likely.
   (B) More damage to vegetation is caused by brush fires than by any other natural event.
   (C) It is necessary to remove dead and damaged vegetation after a mudflow but not after a fire.
   (D) Fires occur frequently in areas where the vegetation has been cleared for development.

9. What can be inferred from paragraph 5 about mudflows in some parts of southern California?

   (A) Mudflows rarely occur more than once in the same location.
   (B) Mudflows cause the worst damage in areas that are heavily forested.
   (C) Mudflows occur more often than other natural disasters such as fires.
   (D) Mudflows are so dangerous because people do not expect them to occur.

10. It can be inferred from paragraph 6 that lahars

    (A) contain less water than other mudflows
    (B) occur in Indonesia
    (C) are relatively harmless events
    (D) cause volcanic eruptions

TEST 6

11. Why does the author use the word raced in paragraph 6 while describing the lahars caused by the eruption of Mount St. Helens?

(A) To show that lahars are faster than rock avalanches
(B) To state ironically that lahars do not actually move quickly
(C) To emphasize the fast speed of lahars
(D) To explain why people could not outrun the mudflows

12. Look at the four squares, [A], [B], [C], and [D], which indicate where the following sentence could be added to the passage. Where would the sentence best fit?

Thus, rockslides occur more frequently during the spring, when heavy rains and melting snow are most prevalent.

Many mass wasting processes are described as slides. Rockslides occur when a coherent mass of rock breaks loose and slides down a slope as a unit. [A] If the material involved is largely unconsolidated, it is called a debris slide. Slides are among the fastest and most destructive mass movements. Usually rockslides occur in a geologic setting where the rock layers are inclined, or where there are joints and fractures in the rock that are parallel to the slope. [B] When such a rock unit is undercut at the base of the slope, it loses support and the rock eventually collapses. Rain or snowmelt can trigger a rockslide by wetting the underlying surface to the point that friction can no longer hold the rock in place. [C] The fastest type of slide is a rock avalanche, in which a mass of rock literally floats on air as it moves downslope. The high speed of a rock avalanche is the result of air becoming trapped and compressed beneath the falling mass of debris, allowing it to move down the slope as a buoyant sheet. [D]

13. Select the appropriate phrases from the answer choices and match them to the type of mass wasting to which they refer. TWO of the answer choices will NOT be used. ***This question is worth 4 points.***

Answer Choices

(A) Occur when a mass of rock moves downslope as a unit
(B) Involve the mass movement of soil containing a large amount of water
(C) May have the consistency of wet concrete or soup
(D) Occur where sloping rock layers have cracks parallel to the slope
(E) Occur when a layer of snow breaks loose and moves rapidly downslope
(F) Include the transportation of organic materials by wind and water
(G) Float on a thin layer of air as they move rapidly down a mountain
(H) Move slowly but with enough force to carry away trees and houses
(I) Occur on slopes where layers of volcanic debris become extremely wet

Rockslides

•
•
•

Mudflows

•
•
•
•

How to Score 4–Point Questions	
Answers Correct	**Points Earned**
7	4
6	3
5	2
4	1
0–3	0

TEST 6

THE TRIANGLE FACTORY FIRE

1 The fire at the Triangle Waist Company in New York City was one of the worst workplace disasters in the history of labor. The incident highlighted the inhumane working conditions faced by many industrial workers, including low wages, excessively long hours, and an unsanitary and dangerous work environment. The Triangle Waist Company, a shirt factory, was a typical sweatshop in the heart of New York's garment district. Most of the workers were women, some as young as 15 years old, mostly recent Italian and European Jewish immigrants who had come to the United States with their families to seek a better life. Already struggling with a new language and culture, these workers could not speak out about working conditions for fear of losing their desperately needed jobs, and this forced them to endure exploitation by the factory owners.

2 On March 25, 1911, one of the five hundred employees of the Triangle Waist factory noticed that a rag bin near her eighth–floor workstation was on fire. She and her co–workers immediately tried to extinguish the flames, but their efforts proved futile, and piles of fabric ignited all over the eighth floor. The factory manager ordered his employees to unroll the fire extinguisher hose, but they found it rotted and useless. Panic erupted as the fire spread.

3 The shirt factory occupied the top three floors of the ten–story Asch Building. The seventy employees who worked on the tenth floor escaped the fire by way of the staircases or by climbing onto the roof, where students from New York University, located across the street, stretched ladders over to the Asch Building. The 260 workers on the ninth floor had the worst luck of all. Although the eighth–floor workers tried to warn them by telephone, the call did not reach them, and by the time the ninth–floor workers learned about the fire, their routes of escape were mostly blocked. When they found many of the exit doors locked, some managed to climb down the cables of the freight elevator. Others crammed into one narrow stairway. Still others climbed onto the single, inadequately constructed fire escape. However, the fire escape led nowhere, and it bent under the weight of hundreds of workers trying to escape. The spindly structure separated from the wall, falling to the ground and carrying many people with it.

4 To combat the disaster, the New York Fire Department sent thirty–five pieces of equipment, including a hook and ladder. The young women trapped on the ninth floor waited on the window ledges to be rescued, only to discover that the ladder, fully raised, stopped far below them at the sixth floor. Water from the hoses could not reach the top floors, and many workers chose to jump to their deaths rather than to burn alive. Within minutes, the factory was consumed by flame, killing 146 workers, mostly immigrant women. City officials set up a temporary morgue in a building on 26th Street, and over the next few days streams of survivors filed through the building to identify the dead.

5 The ten–story Asch Building was a firetrap typical of the working conditions of the period, and the Triangle fire tragically illustrated that fire inspections and safety precautions were very inadequate. The victims of the fire were trapped by the lack of fire escapes and by management's practice of locking the exit doors during work hours. The incident had a profound impact on women's unionism and job safety, affecting local and national politics in the process. An era of progressive reform began to sweep the nation, as people decided that government had a responsibility to ensure that private industry protected the welfare of workers. There was a public outcry for laws to regulate workplace safety. The New York Factory Investigating Commission was formed to examine the conditions in factories throughout the state, and their report led to many new regulations in the years following the fire.

6 The fire at the Triangle Waist Company highlighted the excesses of industrialism. The tragedy remains in the collective memory of the labor movement, and the victims of the tragedy are still honored as martyrs at the hands of industrial greed.

14. All of the following characterized the factory of the Triangle Waist Company EXCEPT

(A) unsafe working conditions
(B) a large number of female workers
(C) a strong labor union
(D) workrooms on three floors

15. Which sentence below best expresses the essential information in the highlighted sentence in paragraph 1? Incorrect choices change the meaning in important ways or leave out essential information.

(A) Because they did not speak the same language as the factory owners, the workers were not able to discuss conditions in the factory.
(B) Language and culture were serious problems in the workplace, but workers were even more afraid of being exploited by the factory owners.
(C) The factory owners forced the workers to learn a new language and culture because it was necessary for them to succeed in their jobs.
(D) The workers experienced cultural difficulties, poor conditions, and exploitation without complaint because they needed their jobs.

16. The word ignited in paragraph 2 is closest in meaning to

(A) disappeared
(B) caught fire
(C) exploded
(D) were thrown out

17. Why does the author mention the fire extinguisher hose in paragraph 2?

(A) To emphasize the unsafe working conditions
(B) To show the manager's leadership skills
(C) To illustrate the factory's modern technology
(D) To explain how the fire was eventually put out

18. According to the passage, how did many workers on the top floor manage to escape the fire?

(A) On the fire escape
(B) On the elevator
(C) On ladders
(D) On ropes

19. The phrase Still others in paragraph 3 refers to

(A) students from New York University
(B) eighth–floor workers
(C) ninth–floor workers
(D) routes of escape

20. The word spindly in paragraph 3 is closest in meaning to

(A) weak
(B) ugly
(C) wood
(D) tall

21. It can be inferred from paragraph 4 that

(A) New York had a well–equipped fire department
(B) fire fighters rescued everyone the ninth floor
(C) the women on the window ledges did not escape
(D) several workers took the stairs to the sixth floor

22. The author argues that the cause of the disaster was

(A) a careless worker with a cigarette
(B) the poor telephone system in the factory
(C) the slow response by the fire department
(D) the lack of fire safety measures

23. In stating that an era of progressive reform began to sweep the nation, the author means that

(A) more people criticized the government
(B) the idea of reform became widespread
(C) workers were required to join labor unions
(D) social reformers caused many problems

TEST 6

24. It can be inferred from the passage that the author most likely believes which of the following statements?

(A) The Triangle Waist Company had been a progressive business before the tragic fire.
(B) The owners of the Triangle factory did not know about the unsafe working conditions.
(C) The Triangle fire increased awareness of workplace safety and led to necessary reform.
(D) The government's job is to regulate the excesses and greed of labor unionism.

25. Look at the four squares, **A**, **B**, **C**, and **D**, which indicate where the following sentence could be added to the passage. Where would the sentence best fit?

The International Ladies Garment Workers Union increased its efforts to improve working conditions in factories.

A The ten–story Asch Building was a firetrap typical of the working conditions of the period, and the Triangle fire tragically illustrated that fire inspections and safety precautions were very inadequate. **B** The victims of the fire were trapped by the lack of fire escapes and by management's practice of locking the exit doors during work hours. The incident had a profound impact on women's unionism and job safety, affecting local and national politics in the process. **C** An era of progressive reform began to sweep the nation, as people decided that government had a responsibility to ensure that private industry protected the welfare of workers. **D** There was a public outcry for laws to regulate workplace safety. The New York Factory Investigating Commission was formed to examine the conditions in factories throughout the state, and their report led to many new regulations in the years following the fire.

26. Read the first sentence of a summary of the passage. Complete the summary by selecting the THREE answer choices that express the most important ideas in the passage. Some sentences do not belong in the summary because they express ideas that are not presented in the passage or are minor ideas in the passage. ***This question is worth 2 points.***

The 1911 fire at the Triangle Waist Company was one of the worst tragedies in labor history.

•
•
•

Answer Choices

(A) The garment industry in New York City employed a large number of Italian and Jewish workers.

(B) The fire occurred even though factory owners had invested a lot of money in fire safety equipment.

(C) The fire spread quickly through the factory, killing 146 workers who were mostly immigrant women.

(D) The tragedy exposed the unsafe working conditions and inadequate fire precautions of the time.

(E) After the fire, a group of labor unions assisted the survivors of the fire and families of fire victims.

(F) Public outrage about the fire led to a series of reforms, including laws to regulate workplace safety.

How to Score 2–Point Questions	
Answers Correct	**Points Earned**
3	2
2	1
0–1	0

DRAMA IN ANCIENT GREECE

1 Long before the ancient Greeks could read and write, they learned of their history and culture through epic poetry chanted by bards or singers. The bards chanted stories in standard musical phrases that were accompanied by musical instruments such as the lyre, a general name for any of several stringed instruments favored by the bards. The greatest bard, Homer, was a poet, singer and master of the lyre. According to tradition, Homer was a wandering minstrel who traveled from place to place chanting stories of gods and heroes. Another famous poet, singer, and lyre player was Sappho, who started a school for girls, where she taught the arts of music, poetry, and dance.

2 Greek civilization reached a golden age during the fifth century BC, when politics, philosophy, art, architecture, and theater thrived, as they never had before. As the Greeks took new pride in human achievements, they developed ideals of beauty, order, balance, and moderation throughout their culture, including music and drama.

3 Early drama was associated with the worship of the god Dionysus and was an outgrowth of the **choral** songs and dances performed in honor of the god. The famous outdoor Theater of Dionysus in Athens showed the importance of drama to the Greeks. It was situated on a hillside to take advantage of the natural slope and light, and it could accommodate an audience of 30,000 people. A **chorus** of singers, dancers, and musicians, led by a singer who stood on steps above them, performed stories that educated and entertained the audience while honoring the god.

4 The crucial innovation that turned choral performance into drama is attributed to Thespis, a poet who is said to have originated tragedy. As the chorus sang the story of a hero or god, Thespis would enter the theater as a masked actor. Between songs, he recited verses as a character in the story, and these spoken verses changed what had been a choral monologue into a dialogue between the actor and the chorus. The legacy of Thespis can be seen in the term "thespian," which now describes anything relating to drama.

5 Actors of that time wore a large mask made of linen or cork, inside which was a device like a speaking trumpet to amplify the voice. When the actor recited, it was in an exalted monotone, often to the accompaniment of flutes. The chorus enhanced the tragedy with various dances and songs, generally accompanied by the lyre. The actor chanted the lines of the lead character, while the chorus sang the narrative passages. Still, despite the attention the actor received, the chorus and its music continued to dominate dramatic performances with the combined power of singing and dancing.

6 Like Thespis, the playwright Aeschylus acted in his own plays, but he added a second masked actor. Now audience attention could be directed to the interplay between the two actors—action and reaction, question and answer, conflict or cooperation—rather than between the actor and chorus. A later playwright, Sophocles, added a third actor. This made possible not only three–way dramatic scenes but also plays with a large cast of characters, since the masks allowed an actor to play more than one part in different scenes. The addition of actors shifted the focus of drama away from the chorus toward the action and dialogue of the characters.

7 Playwrights continued to introduce innovations, but essentially they adhered to prescribed conventions. One of these conventions limited the number of scenes in a play to five. The drama always took place in one location and within a short span of time, sometimes a single day. Another convention reflected the society's sense of balance and order: bloody deeds rarely took place in front of the audience. Therefore, murders, suicides, and other acts of violence occurred offstage. The Greek concept of moderation is reflected in still another convention, in which any character who acted in an excess of passion was usually punished in the story.

Glossary:

choral: relating to a chorus, a group of singers or dancers who perform together
chorus: a group of singers or dancers who perform together

27. Which of the following statements can be inferred from paragraph 1?

(A) The bards of ancient Greece did not know how to read or write.
(B) Music and poetry were part of Greek culture from very early times.
(C) A bard had to be highly skilled in building musical instruments.
(D) Homer was very influential in the development of Western music.

28. According to the passage, what did Homer and Sappho have in common?

(A) Both started a school of the arts.
(B) Both lived in the same century.
(C) Both were skilled lyre players.
(D) Both acted in plays that they wrote.

29. Why does the author use the term golden age in discussing Greek civilization in the fifth century BC?

(A) To suggest that most of the ancient Greeks were wealthy
(B) To show that the period was a high point in Greek civilization
(C) To argue that Greece was the only society with a political system
(D) To explain why the population of Greece was growing rapidly

30. The word outgrowth in paragraph 3 is closest in meaning to

(A) separation
(B) contest
(C) contradiction
(D) product

31. According to the passage, all of the following characterized Greek drama EXCEPT

(A) an emphasis on costumes and makeup
(B) performances in an outdoor theater
(C) an actor or actors speaking in verse
(D) a chorus singing narrative passages

32. According to the passage, what major development changed choral performance into drama?

(A) The use of musical instruments
(B) Dances to honor the god Dionysus
(C) The addition of an actor who spoke
(D) A story that was written down

33. The word legacy in paragraph 4 is closest in meaning to

(A) tragedy
(B) contribution
(C) politics
(D) biography

34. The word which in paragraph 5 refers to

(A) mask
(B) linen
(C) cork
(D) trumpet

35. Which sentence below best expresses the essential information in the highlighted sentence in paragraph 5? Incorrect choices change the meaning in important ways or leave out essential information.

(A) The singers, dancers, and musicians remained at the center of drama, even though the actor was also important.
(B) There were several people in the chorus, but only one actor, and this is why the chorus was more interesting.
(C) Plays with singing and dancing were more popular with audiences than were plays with only actors reciting verses.
(D) The actor received very little attention because his voice was difficult to hear over the music and the chorus.

TEST 6

36. According to paragraph 6, what was the result of adding a second and a third actor?

(A) Playwrights were able to act in their own plays.
(B) The audience could understand the story more easily.
(C) The action could take place in more than one scene.
(D) The actors became more important than the chorus.

37. The phrase adhered to in paragraph 7 is closest in meaning to

(A) improved
(B) listed
(C) followed
(D) rejected

38. Look at the four squares, [A], [B], [C], and [D], which indicate where the following sentence could be added to the passage. Where would the sentence best fit?

The Greeks developed standard forms and dramatic conventions for both comedies and tragedies.

[A] Playwrights continued to introduce innovations, but essentially they adhered to prescribed conventions. One of these conventions limited the number of scenes in a play to five. [B] The drama always took place in one location and within a short span of time, sometimes a single day. [C] Another convention reflected the society's sense of balance and order: bloody deeds rarely took place in front of the audience. Therefore, murders, suicides, and other acts of violence occurred offstage. [D] The Greek concept of moderation is reflected in still another convention, in which any character who acted in an excess of passion was usually punished in the story.

39. Read the first sentence of a summary of the passage. Complete the summary by selecting the THREE answer choices that express the most important ideas in the passage. Some sentences do not belong in the summary because they express ideas that are not presented in the passage or are minor ideas in the passage. ***This question is worth 2 points.***

Drama was an important development of ancient Greek civilization.

•
•
•

Answer Choices

(A) Drama emerged from the poetry of the bards and from choral songs and dances in honor of the god Dionysus.

(B) Schools devoted to the arts were called music schools, which also taught politics and philosophy.

(C) The Theater of Dionysus, which could hold an audience of 30,000, was built in the open air on a hillside in Athens.

(D) The addition of masked actors shifted the focus of drama to the action and dialogue of the actors.

(E) Greek drama developed numerous conventions that reflected the ideals of balance, order, and moderation.

(F) Most tragedies contained violence, but a convention dictated that all violent acts take place offstage.

How to Score 2–Point Questions	
Answers Correct	**Points Earned**
3	2
2	1
0–1	0

Answers are on page 323.

Record your Reading section score on page 380.

TEST 6

Disk 6, Track 1

LISTENING SECTION DIRECTIONS

The Listening section measures your ability to understand conversations and lectures in English. You will hear each conversation and lecture only one time. After each conversation or lecture, you will hear some questions about it. Answer the questions based on what the speakers state or imply.

You may take notes while you listen. You may use your notes to help you answer the questions.

In some questions, you will see this icon: . This means that you will hear, but not see, part of the question.

Some questions have special directions, which appear in a gray box. Most questions are worth one point. If a question is worth more than one point, the directions will indicate how many points you can receive.

You will now begin the first part of the Listening section.

Time – maximum of 90 minutes

Disk 6, Track 2

QUESTIONS 1–5

1. What is the purpose of the conversation?

(A) The woman wants to make an appointment with the librarian.
(B) The woman is trying to reserve a book for her classmate.
(C) The woman is inquiring about the availability of study rooms.
(D) The woman wants to reserve a different room in the library.

2. Listen again to part of the conversation. Then answer the question.

Why does the man say this: 🎧

(A) To inform the woman that no rooms are available
(B) To encourage the woman to reserve a room now
(C) To recommend the rooms on the third floor
(D) To let the woman know which rooms are better

3. According to the man, why are so few study rooms available?

(A) There are more students now than in the previous year.
(B) Several rooms are being used as offices for library staff.
(C) There is a problem with students reserving more than one room.
(D) Some of the university buildings are still under construction.

4. Why does the woman need a study room?

(A) She is preparing for a final examination.
(B) Her professor requires everyone to have a study room.
(C) She does not have space to study in her apartment.
(D) She needs a place to meet with other students.

5. Why does the man say this: 🎧

(A) To tell the woman about the building that he works in
(B) To persuade the woman to accept a room in another building
(C) To describe an interesting aspect of the university layout
(D) To direct the woman to someone else who can help her

Disk 6, Track 3

QUESTIONS 6–11

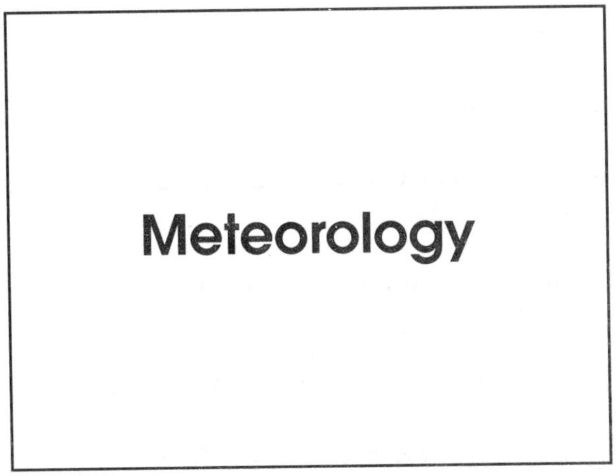

6. What is the talk mainly about?

(A) The dangers of driving in icy conditions
(B) The formation of ice from water vapor
(C) The various colors that ice crystals take
(D) The ice that falls to earth as precipitation

7. Why does the professor talk about her drive to school this morning?

(A) To give an example of a safe driving practice
(B) To encourage students to tell personal stories
(C) To describe the best way to get to campus
(D) To lead into the topic of discussion

8. The professor briefly explains how black ice forms. Indicate whether each sentence below is part of the process.

For each sentence, click in the correct box.

	Yes	No
Snow changes to ice on tree branches and other exposed surfaces.		
The air temperature is above freezing, but the ground temperature is below freezing.		
A thin layer of water vapor freezes on the surface of the highway.		
Pellets of ice develop from supercooled water droplets.		

9. Listen again to part of the discussion. Then answer the question.

Why does the professor say this:

(A) To warn students not to hang laundry outdoors
(B) To find out if the students wash their own clothes
(C) To illustrate the same phenomenon in a different way
(D) To point out a mystery that scientists cannot explain

10. Which of the following sentences illustrates sublimation?

(A) A thin layer of ice forms on the surface of a lake.
(B) Raindrops freeze when they touch the cold ground.
(C) Water vapor freezes on the surface of a sidewalk.
(D) All of the ice cubes in a glass of soda melt.

11. What factors cause frost to form in beautiful patterns on window glass?

Click on two answers.

[A] The glass is cold on the outside and warm on the inside.
[B] The temperature of the glass is below freezing.
[C] Impurities on the glass interfere with ice crystal growth.
[D] The window is on the north side of the house.

Disk 6, Track 4

QUESTIONS 12–17

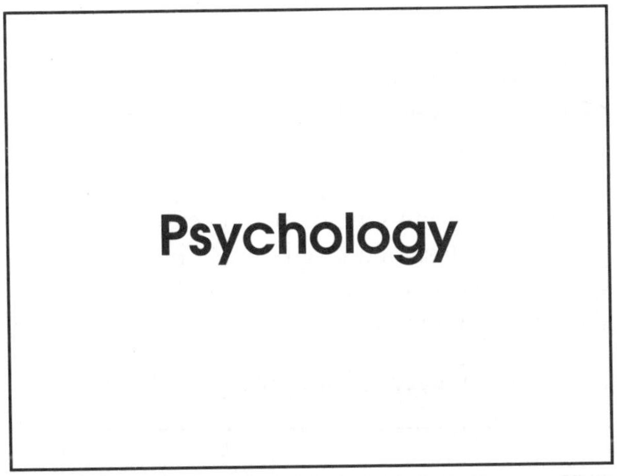

12. What topics does the professor discuss?

Click on two answers.

- [A] Social roles for grieving family and friends
- [B] Important events in the life of every family
- [C] Stages in the process of grieving a loss
- [D] Songs and prayers that are used at funerals

13. According to the professor, what important function do death rituals serve?

- (A) They explain the medical causes of a person's death.
- (B) They allow friends and family to get to know each other.
- (C) They help people accept practices of different cultures.
- (D) They provide a way to manage the grief caused by death.

14. Why does the professor say this: 🎧

- (A) To explain why people need to talk to psychologists
- (B) To give examples of cultural differences in grieving
- (C) To show that death causes people to do strange things
- (D) To describe the final stage in the process of grieving

15. According to the professor, why do death rituals include roles for friends?

- (A) Friends are more creative in performing rituals.
- (B) Friends give support and comfort to the family.
- (C) Friends are expected to pay the funeral expenses.
- (D) Friends experience less grief than the family does.

16. What does the professor imply about funerals and memorial services?

- (A) They are becoming a major expense for bereaved families.
- (B) They include three days of fasting and silent prayer.
- (C) They are part of a growing industry associated with death.
- (D) They help make the person's life and death meaningful.

17. The professor talks about the process of grieving the loss of a loved one. Indicate whether each sentence below describes a stage in the process.

For each sentence, click in the correct box.

	Yes	No
A widow develops an allergic reaction to a drug.		
There is a period of numbness and shock after a death.		
Someone yearns for a close friend who has died.		
A psychologist invents a model for dealing with loss.		
A survivor feels exhausted, depressed, or disorganized.		

Disk 6, Track 5

QUESTIONS 18–22

Conversation
Music Theory

18. What are the students mainly discussing?

Click on two answers.

[A] How music differs from noise
[B] Sounds made by musical instruments
[C] The phenomenon of antinoise
[D] Why some sounds are unpleasant

19. According to the conversation, what is noise?

(A) The complete absence of sound
(B) Patterns produced by sounds in nature
(C) Random sound with irregular waves
(D) Sounds made by a computer voice

20. Listen again to part of the conversation. Then answer the question.

Select the sentence that best expresses how the woman probably feels.

(A) "I'm frustrated because I don't understand."
(B) "I'm glad that you know so much about music."
(C) "I don't agree with what you are saying."
(D) "I wish that I knew how to play the drums."

21. How does the man help the woman understand the meaning of "antinoise"?

(A) By contrasting music and antinoise
(B) By reading a definition from the textbook
(C) By describing the sound of a drumbeat
(D) By telling her about a computer program

22. What will the woman probably do?

(A) Drop out of the music theory class
(B) Listen to recordings of various instruments
(C) Read the textbook before the next lecture
(D) Use a computer to search for information

Disk 6, Track 6

QUESTIONS 23–28

Art

Murals

23. Why is the class discussing the technical requirements of murals?

(A) They are preparing for an examination.
(B) They plan to visit some famous murals.
(C) They are helping to design a new building.
(D) They will be creating their own mural.

24. According to the discussion, what factors should be considered in planning a mural?

Click on two answers.

[A] The position of the observer
[B] The character of the artist
[C] The architecture of the room
[D] The colors of the paint

25. What does the instructor mean when she says this: 🎧

(A) A building with a mural will attract a lot of visitors.
(B) A mural serves the same purpose as other forms of art.
(C) The term "mural" has several different meanings.
(D) A mural is an expression of the building's character.

26. The instructor briefly explains how moisture damages a mural. Indicate whether each sentence below is a part of the process.

For each sentence, click in the correct box.

	Yes	No
Moisture seeps through the wall and dissolves salts in the wall material.		
The plaster dries more quickly than the paint.		
An air space between the interior and exterior walls insulates the mural.		
Dried salt deposits form a white film on the mural.		

27. What is the purpose of having an air space between the outer wall and the plaster?

(A) It will protect the plaster from temperature changes.
(B) It will give the mural a greater sense of depth.
(C) It will reduce the time needed for drying the plaster.
(D) It will eliminate the need to wash the wall frequently.

28. Why does the instructor say this: 🎧

(A) To explain how a wall can be made stronger
(B) To describe the process of framing a mural
(C) To explain how to create an insulating air space
(D) To describe a technique for texturing a plaster wall

Disk 6, Track 7

QUESTIONS 29–34

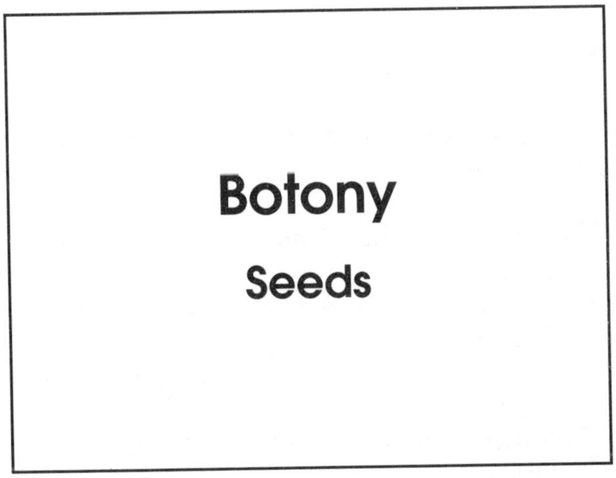

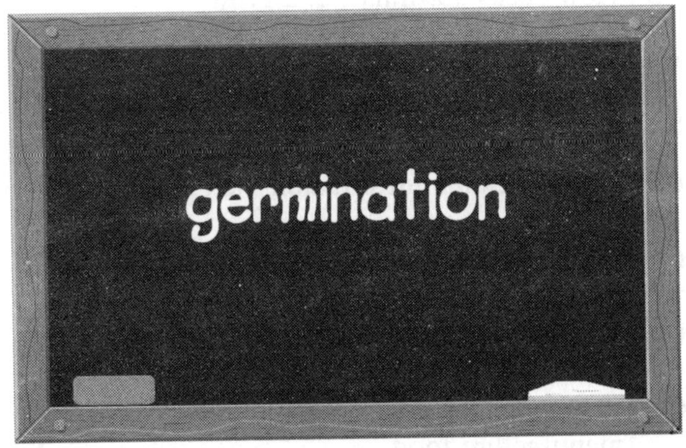

29. What aspect of seeds does the professor mainly discuss?

(A) Hereditary changes in seeds
(B) Ways that seeds are dispersed
(C) Genetic engineering of seeds
(D) How seeds germinate and grow

30. What role does heredity play in the life of a plant?

(A) It provides the information the plant needs to grow.
(B) It helps nutrients move up from the soil into the plant.
(C) It causes the seed to swell and burst out of its case.
(D) It supplies the energy required to manufacture food.

31. Listen again to part of the talk. Then answer the question.

Why does the professor say this: 🎧

(A) To point out the diversity of plant life
(B) To give an example of an environmental cue
(C) To compare different ecosystems where plants live
(D) To explain why few plants survive in the desert

32. What environmental factors are required for a seed to germinate?

Click on two answers.

[A] Heredity
[B] Water
[C] Organic fertilizer
[D] The proper temperature

33. How does a seed obtain the energy it needs for germination?

(A) It takes in nutrients through capillaries in its roots.
(B) It depends on the chemical energy from fertilizer.
(C) It converts the energy of food stored within itself.
(D) It uses solar energy collected through its leaves.

34. The professor explains how a seed becomes a young plant. Summarize the process by putting the events in order.

Drag each sentence to the space where it belongs.

(A) The plant collects sunlight for its growth energy.
(B) The embryonic root pushes outward into the soil.
(C) The seed takes in water and begins to swell.
(D) The tip of the shoot breaks through the soil's surface.

1	
2	
3	
4	

Disk 6, Track 8

QUESTIONS 35–39

TEST 6

35. Why does the student go to see the professor?

(A) He wants to hear the professor's comments about his term paper.
(B) He would like permission to change the topic of his research.
(C) He would like the professor to recommend him for a job.
(D) He needs the professor's advice about redesigning an organization.

36. According to the student, what is organizational redesign?

(A) Preparing materials that help people learn about an organization
(B) Writing an essay about why you want to work for an organization
(C) Keeping a record of people that join and leave an organization
(D) Changing an organization's goals, responsibilities and relationships

37. Listen again to part of the conversation. Then answer the question.

What does the professor imply about the student's paper?

(A) It is too short.
(B) It contains many errors.
(C) It lacks a clear focus.
(D) It has very few ideas.

38. What suggestions does the professor make for the student's paper?

Click on two answers.

[A] Explain why organizations need to be redesigned
[B] Focus on a few essential steps of organizational redesign
[C] Proofread the paper carefully and correct all mistakes
[D] Support his points with examples from a real organization

39. Why does the student mention the nursery business where his uncle works?

(A) To tell the professor where he would like to work
(B) To give an example that he might discuss in his paper
(C) To suggest a good place to shop for flowering shrubs
(D) To impress the professor with his family's success

Disk 6, Track 9

QUESTIONS 40–45

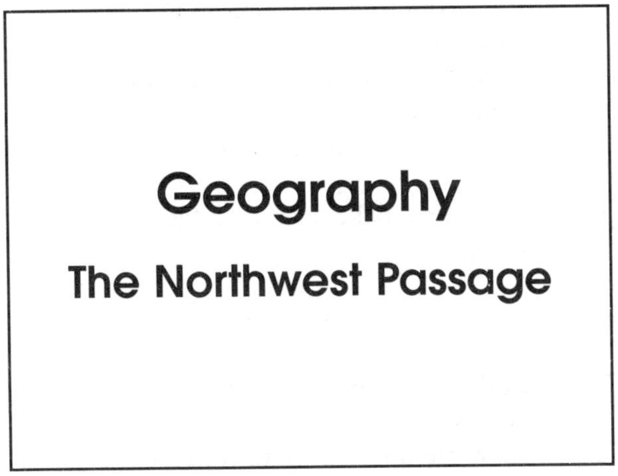

40. How does the professor organize the information that she presents?

(A) By comparing different reasons for exploring the Arctic Ocean
(B) By describing the past, present, and future of the Northwest Passage
(C) By explaining the causes of climate change in the Arctic region
(D) By listing popular tourist attractions in the Northwest Passage

41. According to the professor, why did European powers start looking for the Northwest Passage?

(A) They wanted to study the wildlife of the Arctic region.
(B) They were inspired by the idea of a New World.
(C) They hoped to find a plentiful source of oil.
(D) They wanted to establish a western route to Asia.

42. Why does the professor talk about Martin Frobisher and Henry Hudson?

(A) To give examples of early Arctic explorers
(B) To describe different routes for crossing the Arctic
(C) To compare the motivation of two adventurers
(D) To explain why one failed and the other succeeded

43. Listen again to part of the lecture. Then answer the question.

What can be inferred about the Northwest Passage?

(A) It takes a ship several weeks to navigate the passage.
(B) Ice makes the passage dangerous and unpredictable.
(C) The passage is no longer a practical trade route.
(D) Several ships make it through the passage every year.

44. Why does the professor say this:

(A) To explain why only icebreakers can cross the passage
(B) To show the difference between ice in winter and summer
(C) To illustrate changes in the ice covering the Arctic region
(D) To describe the dimensions of an average iceberg

45. According to the professor, what are the possible consequences of an increase in shipping in the Northwest Passage?

Click on two answers.

[A] Harm to wildlife
[B] An increase in piracy
[C] Noise pollution
[D] A major oil spill

Disk 6, Track 10

QUESTIONS 46–51

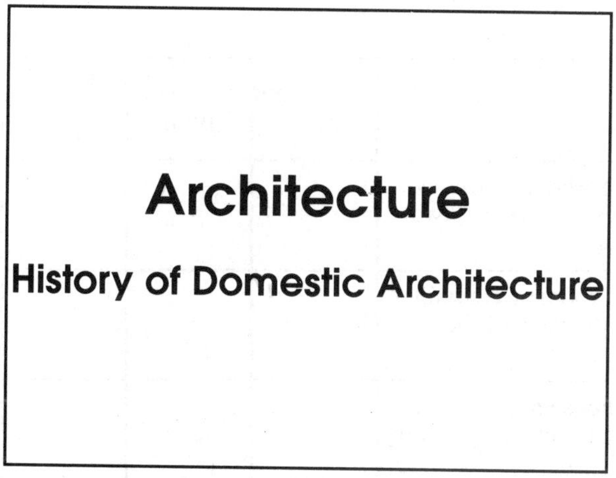

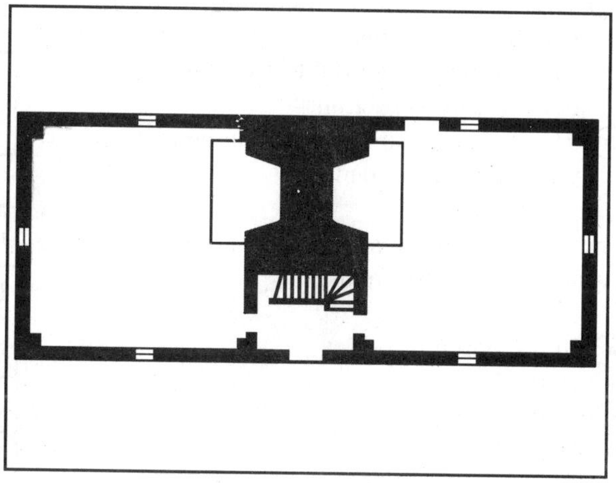

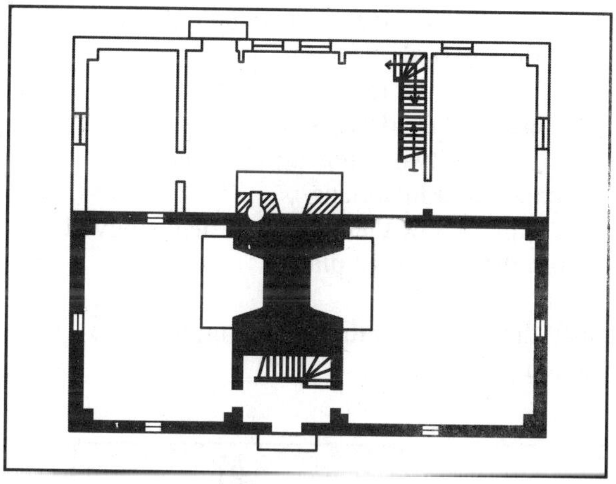

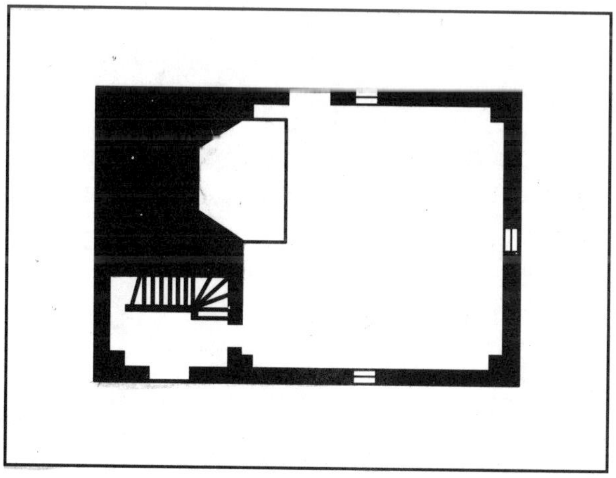

46. According to the speaker, why are seventeenth–century houses significant to architectural historians?

    (A) They are good examples of houses designed for the working class.
    (B) They give architects interesting ideas for new house designs.
    (C) They provide important information about domestic construction.
    (D) They are easy to find and can be restored without much expense.

47. Where was the main staircase located in a seventeenth–century house?

    (A) In the porch
    (B) In the hall
    (C) In the parlor
    (D) In the bedroom

48. Why does the speaker say this:

    (A) To illustrate the different social classes of the time period
    (B) To compare the function of the parlor in different house designs
    (C) To describe two opposing views held by architectural historians
    (D) To explain how the two–room plan evolved from the one–room plan

49. Identify the kitchen in the floor diagram of the added lean–to plan.

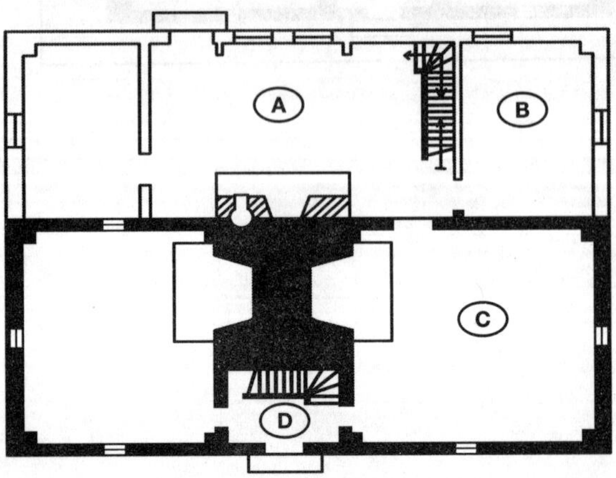

50. Based on the information in the talk, indicate whether each sentence below characterizes the one–room plan, the two–room plan or the added lean–to plan.

For each sentence, click in the correct box. This question is worth 2 points.

	One–room plan	**Two–room plan**	**Added lean–to plan**
There were two stories, and each story had two rooms.			
Extra rooms were built onto the back of the house.			
The house had one large space for cooking, dining, and living.			
A staircase led up from the kitchen to attic space for storage or sleeping.			

51. Why does the speaker say this:

    (A) Because only a few seventeenth–century houses have been studied
    (B) Because the earliest house plan continues to be built today
    (C) Because documents about colonial houses are difficult to read
    (D) Because plan type may not reveal exactly when a house was built

Stop

How to Score 2–Point Questions	
Answers Correct	**Points Earned**
4	2
3	1
0–2	0

Answers are on page 325.

Record your Listening section score on page 381.

Disk 6, Track 11

SPEAKING SECTION DIRECTIONS

The Speaking section measures your ability to speak in English about a variety of topics. There are six questions in this section.

Questions 1 and 2 are independent tasks in which you will speak about familiar topics. Your responses will be scored on your ability to speak clearly and coherently about the topics.

Questions 3 and 4 are integrated speaking tasks. You will read a passage, listen to a conversation or lecture, and then speak in response to a question about what you have read and heard. You will need to combine relevant information from the two sources to answer the question completely. Your responses will be scored on your ability to speak clearly and coherently and on your ability to accurately convey information about what you read and heard.

Questions 5 and 6 are integrated speaking tasks. You will listen to part of a conversation or lecture, and then speak in response to a question about what you have heard. Your responses will be scored on your ability to speak clearly and coherently and on your ability to accurately convey information about what you heard.

You will hear each conversation and lecture only one time. You may take notes while you listen. You may use your notes to help you answer the questions.

Stop

QUESTION 1

In this question, you will be asked to talk about a familiar topic. After you hear the question, you will have 15 seconds to prepare your response and 45 seconds to speak.

Disk 6, Track 12

> What is your idea of the perfect vacation? Describe it and explain why it would be the ideal vacation for you. Include details and examples in your explanation.

Stop

Preparation Time – 15 seconds
Response Time – 45 seconds

QUESTION 2

In this question, you will be asked to give your opinion about a familiar topic. After you hear the question, you will have 15 seconds to prepare your response and 45 seconds to speak.

Disk 6, Track 13

> Some students attend lecture classes in which only the teacher speaks. Other students have discussion classes in which everyone speaks. Which type of class do you think is better for students, and why? Include details and examples in your explanation.

Stop

Preparation Time – 15 seconds
Response Time – 45 seconds

Question 3

In this question, you will read a short passage about a campus situation, listen to a conversation, and then speak in response to a question about what you have read and heard. After you hear the question, you have 30 seconds to prepare your response and 60 seconds to speak.

Reading Time – 45 seconds

Notice of Increase in College Fees

The president of Springfield College announces a 10% increase in the student activity fee and a 10% increase in rent for all dormitory rooms and apartments on campus. The new fee schedule will take effect on August 25, the beginning of the new academic year. The fee increases will help the college to pay for a new gymnasium building on the north side of campus. The gymnasium will include a state–of–the–art workout room, racquetball courts, a dance and martial arts studio, and saunas for men and women. Architectural drawings of the new gymnasium are on display in the lobby of the library building.

Now cover the passage and listen to the recording. When you hear the question, begin preparing your response.

Disk 6, Track 14

The woman expresses her opinion about the fee increase. State her opinion and explain the reasons she gives for holding that opinion.

Stop

Preparation Time – 30 seconds
Response Time – 60 seconds

QUESTION 4

In this question, you will read a short passage on an academic subject, listen to a lecture on the same topic, and then speak in response to a question about what you have read and heard. After you hear the question, you have 30 seconds to prepare your response and 60 seconds to speak.

Reading Time – 45 seconds

THE UNIFORMITY OF GOODS

Starting in the nineteenth century, there was a movement toward uniformity in American production. Manufacturers tried to provide a common material experience so that all Americans could enjoy goods that were similar in style, quality, and price. Manufacturers expanded their production capabilities to regularize production and produce nearly uniform goods. The uniformity of products, or the belief that products were similar even when they were not, generally satisfied customers. Uniformity was achieved in several ways: through machine–based production, the identification of product type, the creation of brand names, and the establishment of standard sizes.

Now cover the passage and listen to the recording. When you hear the question, begin preparing your response.

Disk 6, Track 15

The professor discusses the history of the clothing industry. Explain how this industry contributed to the uniformity of goods.

Stop

Preparation Time – 30 seconds
Response Time – 60 seconds

QUESTION 5

In this question, you will listen to a conversation. You will then be asked to talk about the information in the conversation and to give your opinion about the ideas presented. After you hear the question, you have 20 seconds to prepare your response and 60 seconds to speak.

Disk 6, Track 16

Describe the woman's problem and the two suggestions the professor makes about how to deal with it. What do you think the woman should do, and why?

Stop

Preparation Time – 20 seconds
Response Time – 60 seconds

QUESTION 6

In this question, you will listen to part of a lecture. You will then be asked to summarize important information from the lecture. After you hear the question, you have 20 seconds to prepare your response and 60 seconds to speak.

Disk 6, Track 17

Using points and details from the talk, explain how sleep and problem solving are connected.

Stop

Preparation Time – 20 seconds
Response Time – 60 seconds

Key points for the Speaking responses are on page 328.

Each response earns a score of 1, 2, 3 or 4.

Record your total Speaking score on page 382.

Disk 6, Track 18

WRITING SECTION DIRECTIONS

The Writing section measures your ability to use writing to communicate in an academic environment. There are two writing questions.

Question 1 is an integrated writing task. You will read a passage, listen to a lecture, and then answer a question based on what you have read and heard. You have 20 minutes to plan and write your response.

Question 2 is an independent writing task. You will answer a question based on your own knowledge and experience. You have 30 minutes to plan and write your response.

Stop

QUESTION 1

For this task, you will write a response to a question about a reading passage and a lecture. You may take notes, and you may use your notes to help you write your response. Your response will be scored on the quality of your writing and on how well you connect the points in the lecture with points in the reading. Typically, an effective response will have 150 to 225 words.

Reading Time – 3 minutes

In animals and humans, genes determine the general size and shape of the organism, but there may also be variation in physical characteristics due to environmental influences. All organisms function most efficiently under certain environmental conditions; however, an individual organism may react to some change in the environment with responses that change the form or internal structure of the body.

An organism's environment includes nonliving factors such as temperature, water, and nutrients. The environment also includes biological factors: all the other organisms that are part of any individual's environment. Environmental stimuli can have important effects on individual organisms, groups, and whole populations.

The influence of environmental factors is particularly effective during the formative stages of life, both before and after birth. The experiences of early life determine the physical and mental attributes of the young and thereby determine the characteristics of the adult. Early influences can have favorable or unfavorable effects on the young organism's development. Environmental factors exert such a strong influence on development that some physical or mental characteristics are difficult or impossible to change later in life.

Research on many types of animals and observations of human life have revealed that early environmental influences affect an individual's initial rate of growth and resistance to various types of stress, as well as the ultimate body size of the adult. Environmental factors also affect learning ability and behavioral patterns in the young.

Now listen to the recording. When you hear the question, begin your response. You may look at the passage during the writing time.

Disk 6, Track 19

Summarize the points made in the lecture you just heard, explaining how they support points made in the reading.

Stop

Writing Time – 20 minutes

QUESTION 2

For this task, you will write an essay in response to a question that asks you to state and support your opinion on a topic. Your essay will be scored on the quality of your writing, including how well you organize and develop your ideas and how well you use language to express your ideas. Typically, an effective essay will have a minimum of 300 words.

Read the question below and make any notes that will help you plan your response. Then begin writing your essay.

> Some people think that earning a high salary is the most important thing about a job. Other people think that doing enjoyable work is more important, even if the job does not pay well. Which is more important to you: work that pays well or work that is enjoyable? Give specific reasons and examples to support your answer.

Writing Time – 30 minutes

Key points for the Writing section are on page 328.

Each response earns a score of 1, 2, 3, 4 or 5.

Record your total Writing score on page 382.

See pages [illegible] for the Writing scoring guidelines.

ANSWER KEY

For each answer, there is a short explanation followed by a number in parentheses. The number refers to the relevant unit in **Delta's Key to the Next Generation TOEFL® Test: Advanced Skill Practice for the iBT**, where you will find further discussion and examples of that particular skill and question type.

Delta's Key to the Next Generation TOEFL® Test: Advanced Skill Practice for the iBT
Skill Units

Reading

1.1 Understanding Facts and Details
1.2 Identifying Negative Facts
1.3 Locating Referents
1.4 Understanding Vocabulary in Context
1.5 Making Inferences
1.6 Determining Purpose
1.7 Recognizing Paraphrases
1.8 Recognizing Coherence
1.9 Summarizing Important Ideas
1.10 Organizing Information

Listening

2.1 Identifying the Topic and Main Idea
2.2 Listening for Details
2.3 Determining Attitude and Purpose
2.4 Making Inferences and Predictions
2.5 Categorizing Information
2.6 Summarizing a Process

Speaking

3.1 Independent Speaking: Developing a Topic
3.2 Independent Speaking: Stating and Supporting a Position
3.3 Speaking Clearly and Coherently
3.4 Evaluating Independent Speaking
3.5 Integrated Speaking: Connecting Information from Two Sources
3.6 Integrated Speaking: Taking Notes
3.7 Integrated Speaking: Developing a Topic
3.8 Integrated Speaking: Summarizing a Problem and Solutions
3.9 Integrated Speaking: Summarizing Important Ideas
3.10 Evaluating Integrated Speaking

Writing

4.1 Integrated Writing: Connecting Information from Two Sources
4.2 Integrated Writing: Taking Notes
4.3 Integrated Writing: Developing Ideas
4.4 Checking Sentence Structure
4.5 Evaluating the Response
4.6 Independent Writing: Prewriting
4.7 Independent Writing: Stating and Supporting an Opinion
4.8 Writing Coherently
4.9 Checking Sentence Variety and Word Choice
4.10 Evaluating the Essay

TEST 1

Reading (*p. 29*)

1. B The passage does not state that an unbroken prairie now extends from the western mountains to the eastern forest. All of the other answers are given: *...temperatures can vary widely from very hot in summer to bitter cold in winter; The wetlands were soon surrounded by fluttering waves of grasses: shortgrass, mixed grass, and tallgrass; An important feature of the northern Great Plains grasslands is the presence of millions of glacial depressions that are now small ponds known as prairie potholes.* (1.2)
2. B During the last century, large parts of the prairie have been converted to agricultural use. Clues: *One hundred years ago, the Great Plains grasslands were one vast, unbroken prairie. Much of the prairie is now farmland....* (1.1)
3. D *Alien* means *imported* in this context. Clues: *...virtually all the major native grasses have been replaced by alien species.* Imported grasses have replaced the original, native grasses. (1.4)
4. B The prairie potholes owe their origins mainly to the glaciers that melted at the end of the last Ice Age. Clues: *They were formed during the most recent Ice Age.... When the Ice Age ended around 12,000 years ago, the retreating glaciers created about 25 million depressions....* (1.1)
5. D *Today these small wetlands still cover the prairies...* is paraphrased in *...the small ponds remain; ...although much of the landscape...has been transformed to cropland and grassland for grazing* is paraphrased in *Even though a large portion of the prairies is used for crops and grazing....* (1.7)
6. A *Dot* means *cover* in this context. Clues: *Today these small wetlands still cover the prairies...; ...the seasonal wetlands that dot portions of Minnesota, Iowa....* (1.4)
7. B The author's purpose is to emphasize the area's value as a breeding ground for ducks. Clues: *...serves as an important breeding area for more than 300 bird species, including large numbers of migrating shorebirds and waterfowl; Every spring, birds arrive in great numbers...to mate in the seasonal wetlands...; Prairie pothole country produces half of North America's 35 to 40 million ducks....* (1.6)

ANSWER KEY

8. D A carbon sink removes carbon dioxide naturally from the atmosphere. Clue: ...*a vast carbon sink: a natural sponge that absorbs carbon dioxide emissions from cars, factories, and power plants.* (1.1)

9. C The referent of *this* is something that scientists have termed "carbon sequestration." The previous sentence states that *carbon dioxide is captured naturally and stored in trees, soil, and plants.* Logic tells you that *this* refers to *the capture and storage of carbon dioxide in trees, soil, and plants.* (1.3)

10. A You can infer that carbon sequestration in the prairie pothole region depends on the land not being disturbed by agriculture. Clues: ...*prairie potholes hold an average of 2.5 tons of carbon per acre per year when not being farmed;* ...*if the entire pothole region in the United States and Canada were to stop being farmed, the region would store about 400 million tons of carbon over 10 years....* (1.5)

11. C *Offset* means *counteract* in this context. Clues: ...*the region would store about 400 million tons of carbon over 10 years—the equivalent of taking almost 4 million cars off the road. Thus, preserving the potholes could be a way to offset greenhouse gas emissions that are warming the planet.* The prefix *counter–* = against; preserving the potholes would act against greenhouse gases such as carbon dioxide. (1.4)

12. A In the added sentence, *Today* is a time expression that logically follows *One hundred years ago* in the previous sentence. In the added sentence, *however* is a transition that shows contrast between *the Great Plains grasslands were one vast, unbroken prairie* in the previous sentence and *the original grassland associations of plants and animals have been almost completely destroyed* in the added sentence. (1.8)

13. B, C, E Key information: *Much of the prairie is now farmland...dominated by monocultures of cereal grains; In areas given over to grazing lands...virtually all the major native grasses have been replaced by alien species; An important feature of the northern Great Plains grasslands is the presence of millions of glacial depressions that are now small ponds known as prairie potholes;* ...*serves as an important breeding area for more than 300 bird species...;* ...*the prairie pothole region is potentially a vast carbon sink....* Answer (A) is not mentioned; answers (D) and (F) are minor ideas. (1.9)

14. B The author makes the point that monarchs did not have real power but were symbols of national unity. Clues: ...*while monarchs remained symbols of national unity, real power had passed to constitutional assemblies.* (1.1)

15. A *Survived* means *remained* in this context. Clues: *At the start of the twentieth century, monarchs ruled over most of the world, but by the middle of the century, only a handful remained;* ...*while monarchs remained symbols of national unity...; It lasted longer in the few small states...;* the stem *–viv–* = alive. (1.4)

16. B The referent of *The term* is something that applies to a broad group of states with a parliamentary or representative political tradition. The subject of the previous sentence is *liberal democracy.* Logic tells you that *The term* refers to *liberal democracy.* (1.3)

17. A The author's purpose is to contrast two concepts of where political authority rests. In liberal democracies, *political authority rests in the people acting through elected representatives.* In people's democracies, political authority rests in the Communist party. Clues: *Liberal democracies differ from...in which the Communist party holds the ultimate authority.* (1.6)

18. C *Pattern* means *model* in this context. Clues: ...*some form of liberal democracy...;* ...*with the executive power vested in a cabinet responsible to the parliament....* The passage describes various forms or models of democracies: people's democracies, parliamentary democracies, and presidential democracies. (1.4)

19. D The passage mentions a bill of rights stated in a constitution as a limit on state control. Clues: *The liberal democratic state claimed the right to control every aspect of human life...except where limits on state control were directly stated in a bill of rights in a democratic constitution....* (1.1)

20. D Every democratic state changed during the twentieth century in the way that state activity expanded to promote the well being of the people. Clues: *The expansion of state activity and extension of state services involved a new view of legislation and its role in society. The passing of laws came to be seen as a way to promote the well being of the people.* (1.1)

21. C *In these cases, some form of totalitarian dictatorship emerged...* is paraphrased in *Totalitarian dictatorships took over some democracies...;* ...*replacing popular sovereignty with the total power of the state* is paraphrased in ...*took over some democracies with the idea that the state, not the people, held all power.* (1.7)

22. B The authority of the people through elected representatives is not a characteristic of authoritarian governments; it is a characteristic of liberal democracies. All of the other answers are given: ...*a system that prohibited parties opposed to the regime...;* ...*a head of state or leader with exceptional powers...;* ...*a bureaucratic administration that was in no way subject to popular control.* (1.2)

23. A You can infer that the author believes there was a general movement away from monarchy toward democracy, with some cases of authoritarian rule. Clues: *In most states where monarchical authority was removed, some form of liberal democracy took its place; The trend toward liberal democracy continued throughout the century, but at various times there was also a tendency toward a revival of authoritarian rule.* (1.5)

24. D In the added sentence, *for example* is a transition that introduces the example of the British Parliament passing more laws in the first half of the twentieth century than in all its previous history. This example develops the idea that *the number of new laws increased immensely*, mentioned in the previous sentence. (1.8)

25. A, E Monarchy: *...a monarch, whose right to rule is generally hereditary and lifelong; Monarchy survived as a form in Europe only where the king or queen functioned as the symbolic head of a parliamentary state....*
B, F Liberal Democracy: *...an elected executive is responsible to the will of the people as a whole; The doctrine that all of the people had effective authority, or sovereignty, became the basis for the functioning of democratic states. This doctrine of popular sovereignty....*
D Dictatorship: *...some form of totalitarian dictatorship emerged, replacing popular sovereignty with the total power of the state; ...a head of state or leader with exceptional powers, with a party to support him.* Answers (C) and (G) are not mentioned. (1.10)

26. B The author's purpose is to emphasize the close connection between smell and the brain. Clues: *Smell is the most direct of all the senses; The olfactory nerve, which manages the perception of smells, is essentially an extension of the brain; ...a direct link from receptors at the top of the nose to the portion of the brain....* (1.6)

27. A *Detects* means *notices* in this context. Clues: *...receptors at the top of the nose...; ...olfactory system detects certain airborne chemicals that enter the nose...; ...chemical information....* The prefix *de–* = from. The olfactory system notices information from chemicals that enter the nose. (1.4)

28. D The color of the olfactory region at the upper end of each nostril shows the strength of the ability to smell. Clues: *The shade of yellow indicates the strength of the sense of smell...; Animals have a very strong sense of smell, so their olfactory regions are dark yellow to reddish brown....* (1.1)

29. B *Diffuse* means *flow* in this context. Clues: *When an odorous substance enters the nose...; Odor molecules diffuse into this region...; ...odor molecules float up into the nasal cavity....* (1.4)

30. C When the cilia of the olfactory receptor cells absorb odor molecules, the olfactory nerve sends impulses to the brain. Clues: *Odor molecules diffuse into this region and are absorbed by the cilia of the olfactory receptor cells; The receptor cells alert the olfactory nerve, which sends impulses to the brain's olfactory bulb, or smell center.* (1.1)

31. B *Integrates* means *connects* in this context. Clues: *The limbic system of the brain integrates memory, emotion, and behavior; ...a group of related* The prefix *inte–/inter–* = between. The paragraph discusses how the brain makes connections between memory, emotion, and behavior. (1.4)

32. B The passage does not state that the scent is transmitted to the other sensory organs. All of the other answers are given: *When we inhale a scent, receptors in the brain's limbic center compare the odor entering our nose to odors stored in our memory; ...memories associated with those odors are stimulated; ...it triggers powerful images and emotions.* (1.2)

33. A The author's purpose is to give examples of smells that can trigger memories and emotions. The smells of crayons and grass can call up memories of childhood. Clues: *A smell can be overwhelmingly nostalgic because it triggers powerful images and emotions.* (1.6)

34. C *What we see and hear may fade quickly in short–term memory...* is paraphrased in *...while sights and sounds may be held only briefly; ...but what we smell is sent directly to long–term memory* is paraphrased in *Smells go straight to long–term memory....* (1.7)

35. C The referent of *which* is something that was presented both with and without scents. The sentence discusses a study in which children memorized a word list. Logic tells you that *which* refers to *list*. (1.3)

36. B You can infer that scents can strengthen the ability to hold new information in the memory. Clues: *Smells can...stimulate learning and retention; The children recalled words on the list more easily and with higher accuracy when the list was given with scents than without....* (1.5)

37. A In the added sentence, *One of these structures* refers to *a group of related nervous system structures*, mentioned in the previous sentence. The added sentence gives the example of *central processing unit* to develop the idea of a group of related nervous system structures. (1.8)

38. B, C, F Key information: *The olfactory nerve provides a direct link from receptors at the top of the nose to the portion of the brain that controls memory, emotion, and behavior; The limbic system of the brain integrates memory, emotion...; ...receptors in the brain's limbic center compare the odor entering our nose to odors stored in our memory; ...memories associated with those odors are stimulated. Scent may be the strongest trigger of memory and emotions; Smells can increase alertness and stimulate learning and retention.* Answers (A), (D) and (E) are minor ideas. (1.9)

39. A *Maliciously* means *destructively* in this context. Clues: *...sometimes maliciously but usually with results that are positive. But* shows contrast, indicating that *maliciously* is the opposite of *with results that are positive*. The prefix *mal–* = bad. (1.4)

40. D *When he plays tricks, he performs important cultural tasks that benefit humans...* is paraphrased in *...his tricks contribute positively to human culture; ...for this reason the trickster is a significant figure in world mythology* is paraphrased in *The trickster is an important mythological character because....* (1.7)

41. A The author's purpose is to illustrate two different views of the trickster–hero. Clues: *In different cultures, the trickster and the hero are combined in various ways. In Greek mythology...usually portrayed as an intellectual. In many Native American stories...usually more of a jokester or a prankster than an intellectual.* (1.6)

42. C *Pranks* means *mischievous acts* in this context. Clues: *...one who tricks others...; ...trickster...; ...acts out of passion and impulse; ...behavior....* (1.4)

43. C The referent of *both* is something for which the trickster is responsible. The sentence discusses *good* and *evil*. Logic tells you that *both* refers to *good* and *evil*. (1.3)

ANSWER KEY

44. D Awareness of good and evil is not a trait of the trickster; in fact, the trickster *knows neither good nor evil*. All of the other answers are given: *...the trickster is a god, spirit, human, or animal who breaks the rules...; ...occasionally disguises himself in female form; ...the greatest shapeshifter of all and can change into anything...; ...superior to man because of his superhuman qualities...; ...possesses some magical powers.* (1.2)

45. B Native American stories with a trickster–hero are usually about the creation or transformation of the world. Clue: *In Native American mythology, the majority of trickster myths concern the creation or transformation of the earth.* (1.1)

46. C In the story about Raven, the trickster steals the sun from the gods. Clues: *Raven knows the gods are protective of their possessions, so he devises a trick; ...flies off carrying the ball of light in his beak. He hangs the ball—the sun—in the sky, bringing light to the world.* (1.1)

47. B *Savior* means *one who rescues others from harm* in this context. Clues: *...leads the human race to a new and better world; ...whose great gift to humans is showing them new ways of knowing and doing. Savior* is a noun form of the verb *save*. (1.4)

48. C You can infer that the author believes the trickster serves as an explanation for creation, change and renewal. Clues: *...the majority of trickster myths concern the creation or transformation of the earth; ...there is darkness at the beginning of the world, so Raven decides he will find light; ...the trickster is a savior whose great gift to humans is showing them new ways of knowing and doing.* (1.5)

49. A The added sentence compares Raven and Coyote, developing the idea that *Coyote's character is similar to that of Raven's*, mentioned in the previous sentence. The added sentence introduces the idea of events that benefit humanity, which the next sentence develops with the example *Coyote steals fire from a group of "fire beings" and gives it to humans.* (1.8)

50. B, E, G Raven: *Raven is the greatest shapeshifter of all and can change into anything to get what he wants; ...watches each day as the chief god's daughter draws water from a nearby lake. He magically transforms himself into a pinyon seed and falls into the girl's drinking cup; ...tricks the elder gods into revealing where they hide a shining ball of light; He hangs the ball—the sun—in the sky, bringing light to the world.*

A, F Coyote: *...Coyote wants to make human life more interesting, so he introduces sickness, sorrow, and death; ...by causing the flood, Coyote leads the human race to a new and better world.* Answers (C) and (D) describe neither Raven nor Coyote. (1.10)

51. C *Furnished* means *provided* in this context. Clues: *...by providing meat, milk, and fertilizer...; ...main source of animal protein...; ...also furnished wool, leather, and land transport.* (1.4)

52. C Small animals do not have the ability to pull a plow. Clues: *...livestock helped to feed more people...by pulling plows; ...they also furnished wool, leather, and land transport; Many of these small animals provided food, clothing, or warmth. However, none of them pulled plows...none carried riders....* (1.1)

53. A You can infer that relatively few species of large mammals have the necessary characteristics for domestication. Clues: *Humans have domesticated only a few species of large animals...; Early herding societies quickly domesticated all large mammal species that were suitable for domestication.* (1.5)

54. D Early humans domesticated all suitable large mammal species within a few thousand years after farming and herding began. Clues: *Early herding societies quickly domesticated all large mammal species that were suitable for domestication; ...these species were domesticated...within the first few thousand years of the origins of farming–herding societies....* (1.1)

55. C Domesticated animals differ from their wild ancestors because animals' evolutionary responses in captivity differ from those in the wild. Clues: *Truly domesticated animals differ in many ways from their wild ancestors. These differences result from...evolutionary responses of animals to the forces of natural selection operating in human environments rather than in wild environments.* (1.1)

56. B *A candidate for domestication must be primarily a herbivore...* is paraphrased in *Herbivorous animals are likely to be domesticated...; ...because it takes less plant biomass to feed a plant eater than it does to feed a carnivore that consumes plant eaters* is paraphrased in *...because they eat less plant matter than what carnivores consume indirectly.* (1.1)

57. D The author's purpose is to give examples of animals that grow too slowly for domestication. Clues: *A candidate must...also grow quickly. That eliminates gorillas and elephants....* (1.6)

58. C *Disqualify* means *reject* in this context. Clues: *...certain qualities disqualify a wild animal for domestication; ...cannot have...; ...characteristics that eliminate....* The paragraph discusses characteristics that are not desirable for domestication; any of these qualities would reject an animal for domestication. (1.4)

59. A *Panics* means *feels terror* in this context. Clues: *The animal cannot be so nervous...; ...react to danger from predators or humans...; ...programmed for instant flight when they perceive danger.* (1.4)

60. D You can infer that deer and antelope have not successfully been domesticated. Clues: *The animal cannot be so nervous that it panics around humans; Some species are nervous, fast, and programmed for instant flight when they perceive danger; Most species of deer and antelope are of the former type....* (1.5)

61. B Unpredictable behavior is not a characteristic favorable to domestication. In fact, it is a quality that would disqualify an animal for domestication. All of the other answers are given: *A candidate must not only weigh an average of over 100 pounds but also grow quickly; ...candidates for domestication must be able to breed successfully in captivity; ...living in a herd, maintaining a dominance hierarchy in the herd....* (1.2)

62. C The added sentence gives more information about *Eurasia*, mentioned in the previous sentence. The added sentence introduces the idea of Eurasia having *a great many large mammal species,* which the next sentence develops further. (1.8)

63. A, D, E Key information: *Large domestic animals became the societies' main source of animal protein...; Early herding societies quickly domesticated all large mammal species that were suitable for domestication; To be domesticated, a wild species must possess several characteristics. A candidate for domestication must be primarily a herbivore...; Almost all domesticated large mammals are species whose wild ancestors share three social characteristics: living in a herd....* Answers (B) and (F) are minor ideas; answer (C) is not mentioned. (1.9)

LISTENING (*p. 50*)

1. D The man needs to replace his identification card. He says *Excuse me. Is this where I can get a student ID?; I need to, um, replace my old one.* (2.1)
2. C The man's dog destroyed his student ID card. The man says *I need to, um, replace my old one. You'll never believe it, but my dog ate it.* (2.3)
3. B The man wants to replace his student ID card. He says *So, I thought I'd better get a new one so I can keep riding the bus for free.* You can infer that there is no bus fare if you have a student ID. (2.4)
4. A The woman says *If you want an unofficial transcript, you can use the computers in the information center to get a printout; Unofficial is free.* (2.2)
5. A, D The man wants a new student ID card, so you can predict that he will have his picture taken. The woman says *...you take your receipt down to the photo shop, and they'll take your picture and make your new card.* You can also predict that the man will request an official copy of his transcript. He says *I'm applying for a scholarship, so could I have the form for an official transcript?* (2.4)
6. C The professor's purpose is to state that Wilson first proposed the theory of plate tectonics. The professor says *This theory is called plate tectonics. It was first put forth in 1963 by a Canadian geophysicist by the name of Tuzo Wilson.* (2.3)
7. A The professor says *Most of the world's earthquakes and volcanoes occur at plate boundaries; ...because plate boundaries are where a great deal of friction and stress occur.* (2.2)
8. C The professor says *This process of rock being "swallowed" or forced back into the earth's mantle is called subduction.* (2.2)
9. D The professor says *...rock is melted and forced back into the mantle—at trenches. This process of rock being "swallowed" or forced back into the earth's mantle is called subduction; ...lava that rises and spreads from the oceanic ridges sinks again elsewhere in subduction zones, which are nearly identical with the ocean trenches.* (2.2)
10. D The professor's purpose is to introduce a phenomenon that he intends to explain. After the professor asks the question, he answers by saying *Sea floor spreading doesn't cause an increase in the earth's surface. And why not? Because the lava that rises and spreads from the oceanic ridges sinks again elsewhere in subduction zones, which are nearly identical with the ocean trenches.* (2.3)
11. B, C Chains of volcanic islands are associated with subduction zones: *Subduction zones...are usually associated with the rows of volcanic islands that accompany the oceanic trenches.* The sliding of one plate under another occurs at subduction zones: *This is where a subducted plate is thought to have disappeared beneath the North American plate....* (2.2)
12. C The main purpose of the talk is to trace the evolution of home design. Key phrases: *The human habit of building homes has a long history. Anthropologists think home building began...; ...the first solid dwellings probably evolved; The box shape was a major development in home construction.* (2.3)
13. C–A–D–B The professor says *(1) ...home building began with very simple round huts...; ...tree branches were leaned up against one another...then the frame was covered with leaves...; (2) Round huts progressed from being temporary shelters...into stronger, more permanent structures built of stone; (3) The box shape was a major development in home construction. By making the sides of the house rectangular, and then covering the four walls with a roof...; (4) After the room came the multi–unit dwelling: the apartment house.* (2.6)
14. D The professor says *By making the sides of the house rectangular, and then covering the four walls with a roof, it was possible to place structures next to one another, and to join them with doorways. Thus, the room was invented.* (2.2)
15. B, C The outer boundary still exists in the homes of today: *The homes of today still contain some ancient features. Around the house itself there's an outer perimeter—the symbolic boundary of the ancient home territory.* The garden exists in the homes of today: *Inside the boundary, we find...the garden, where we—like our ancestors—grow a few fruits and vegetables.* (2.2)
16. B The professor's purpose is to explain how walls determine who may enter a room. Walls are boundaries that divide the home into public and private spaces. The professor says *Each room you come to becomes more private and less available to outsiders.* (2.3)
17. C The professor implies that the rooms inside the homes of today are arranged to progress from public to private. The professor says *Each room you come to becomes more private and less available to outsiders. Guests are allowed to enter the living room. Closer friends can go farther; ...somewhere less accessible in our home—this is where we find the bedrooms and bathrooms, the most private rooms of our home.* (2.4)
18. C The students mainly discuss a major epidemic of influenza. The woman says *OK, so we're going to look at the influenza epidemic of 1918 and, uh, probably its effects, like how many people got the flu.* (2.1)

19. C The woman mentions her great–grandfather because he was affected by the 1918 epidemic. The woman says *My great–grandfather could remember the flu epidemic. He was born in 1910, so he was eight years old at the time. He remembered that there were a lot of funerals. His baby sister and his best friend died of the flu, and that made an impression on him.* (2.3)

20. B The man says *What I found out was, it was the army that first noticed large numbers of men getting sick, and it was the army that first started reporting statistics about how many people were affected.* (2.2)

21. A, D You can predict that the students will include statistics on other major disease epidemics. The man says *I wonder how the flu statistics compare with the statistics for other major epidemics, you know, like AIDS and tuberculosis or other flu epidemics.* The woman replies *I don't know, but I'll try to find out. That might be good to include in our report.* You can also predict that they will include the connection between World War I and influenza. The man says *I think we should also talk about the connection between the flu and World War I.* The woman replies *I like what you're saying about focusing on the war and the global aspects.* (2.4)

22. B The students agree to meet again to discuss their research. The woman says *Why don't we meet again and talk about what we have? Can you meet again on Thursday?* The man replies *...yeah, sure, that's fine with me.* (2.2)

23. B The class mainly discusses the regulation of business by government. The professor says *The economic role of the government has grown tremendously over the past century, as more and more corporate activities have come under regulation; These are all reasons why we have government regulation of business; ...a whole set of industries has come under government regulation....* (2.1)

24. C The students' purpose is to give reasons why governments regulate corporations. The professor asks *The economic role of the government has grown tremendously over the past century, as more and more corporate activities have come under regulation. Why has this happened?* The students respond to the professor's question. (2.3)

25. A, C Governments influence economic activity through taxation and spending: *Taxes encourage or discourage certain kinds of economic activity; Government spending—the government gives business incentives to produce certain goods or services; Governments intervene in economic activity through taxation and spending.* (2.2)

26. D The professor's purpose is to explain the origins of government regulation. Key phrases: *Beginning in the late 1800s...; The government started to use its power...; One of the first things the government did....* (2.3)

27. B The professor says *There are a number of laws regulating food and cosmetics; ...laws that protect all of society...regulations for air and water pollution, and for storage and disposal of hazardous materials like nuclear waste; ...safety standards for automobiles and consumer products...; All of these are forms of social regulation.* (2.2)

28. A The professor says *The general public has come to accept—and even expect—these limits on capitalism.* You can infer that many people agree that the government should regulate business. (2.4)

29. D The professor compares cardiac muscle and skeletal muscle. The professor says *...skeletal muscle controls body movements, and cardiac muscle controls the body's blood flow. Skeletal muscle is found throughout the body, but cardiac muscle is found only in one place—the heart; Like skeletal muscle, cardiac muscle is striated; Cardiac muscle cells can generate impulses without any input from the nervous system. In contrast to this, skeletal muscles don't contract unless the nervous system tells them to.* (2.1)

30. A The professor's purpose is to introduce the topic of cardiac muscle, which the rest of the lecture develops. The professor answers her own question by saying *It's possible because of the specialized type of muscle—cardiac muscle—that makes up the heart tissue....* (2.3)

31. C The professor's purpose is to review material the class has already studied. The professor says *...let's back up a bit,* indicating that what she says next will review something that they have already discussed. (2.3)

32. ✓ Skeletal muscle: These muscles are connected to the bones, which move when the muscles contract: *Skeletal muscles are attached to the bones, and they move the bones by contracting.*

✓ Cardiac muscle: When this type of muscle contracts, blood moves throughout the body: *...a series of contractions in the cardiac muscle. When the heart's walls contract, they force blood out of the chambers and into the next chamber or the large blood vessels that lead to the rest of your body.*

✓ Skeletal muscle: To contract, this type of muscle must be stimulated by a motor neuron: *A skeletal muscle contracts only when it's stimulated by a motor neuron.*

✓ Cardiac muscle: These muscle cells can generate electrical impulses without input from the nervous system: *Cardiac muscle cells can generate impulses on their own, without any input from the nervous system.*

✓ Cardiac muscle: This muscle cannot stop to rest without serious consequences for the body: *...your cardiac muscle can never stop and take a rest. If your heart stops beating, you have very little time—only a matter of minutes—for it to start up again before all your other body systems are permanently damaged or stop functioning altogether.* (2.5)

33. D The professor says *...an electrical impulse generated in one part of the heart will spread to all the cardiac muscle cells. Thus, the whole heart will contract.* (2.2)

34. B The professor says *Electrically, they're set up so, so that sodium and calcium—positive ions—change places with potassium—a negative ion—across the cell membrane; When sodium, calcium, and potassium ions move into or out of a cardiac cell, it causes the muscle to contract.* You can infer that the contraction of cardiac muscle depends on the action of sodium, calcium, and potassium. (2.4)

SPEAKING (p. 63)

1. Responses will vary. (3.1–3.4)
2. Responses will vary. (3.1–3.4)
3. Key points:
    - Students must buy a parking permit to park a vehicle on campus, and they must park in the new parking lot. The man does not like the parking policy.
    - One reason he gives is that the cost of a parking permit is too high; the cost has increased since last year.
    - Another reason is that the faculty and staff can park on campus for free, but students must pay, which is not fair.
    - Another reason is that students have to park in the new parking lot, which is far away from the classrooms. (3.5–3.7, 3.10)
4. Key points:
    - Pavlov's experiments with dogs showed that when a bell was rung each time a dog was fed, the dog would associate the sound of the bell with food. The dog responded by drooling, a behavior called a conditioned reflex that occurred because the dog was trained by the sound of the bell.
    - Pavlov's experiments contributed to the concept of environmental conditioning, a central idea in behaviorism. Behaviorists believe that behavior is the result of conditioning, or careful control of the environment.
    - Pavlov's experiments support the idea that behavior is not based on something inside a dog or a person; rather, behavior is the result of conditioning.
    - Pavlov's experiments support the belief that it is possible to determine the laws of behavior and to control behavior. (3.5–3.7, 3.10)
5. Key points:
    - The woman's problem is that she was not able to register for the economics class she needs for graduation because all sections of the course were already full.
    - The man suggests that she take the course in the summer.
    - The man suggests that she take the course in the spring at the community college because she might be able to fit an evening course into her schedule. (3.8, 3.10)
6. Key points:
    - Problems that threaten the world's oceans include overfishing, pollution, climate change, and loss of habitat.
    - A cause of overfishing is bottom trawling; effects are destruction of habitat and fish declines, particularly in several groundfish species. Another effect is the decline in numbers of large ocean predators.
    - A cause of pollution is erosion from the land that puts silt into the ocean; an effect is loss of marine life close to shores. Other causes of pollution are ships, boats, and seaplanes that put oil and other petroleum products into the water.
    - Climate change causes disease outbreaks in ocean environments, affecting marine life such as corals and oysters. Melting ice may have an effect on the breeding patterns and survival of polar bears. (3.9, 3.10)

WRITING (p. 69)

1. Key points:
    - According to the lecture, the idea that certain foods have super powers is exaggerated, misleading, and questioned by nutrition scientists. This casts doubt on the point in the reading that the concept of superpower foods is supported by research.
    - The lecture states that the research on blueberries and brain function was conducted only on rats and mice, not humans, so we cannot say the results are true for humans. This casts doubt on the point in the reading that blueberries have a positive effect on the human brain.
    - The lecture states that there is no direct proof that tomatoes, broccoli, and cabbage will prevent cancer. This casts doubt on the point in the reading that these vegetables help prevent cancer.
    - The lecture states that a recent review of the evidence on garlic shows its effects to be unclear. This casts doubt on the point in the reading that garlic reduces blood cholesterol and fights the common cold. (4.1–4.5)
2. Responses will vary. (4.6–4.10)

TEST 2

READING (p. 73)

1. C The passage states that the main goal of the Dada movement was to destroy traditional standards of art. Clues: *Dada was a subversive movement in the arts...; ...attempted to discover authentic reality through the destruction of traditional culture and aesthetic forms; Dadaists on both sides of the Atlantic had one goal in common: to demolish current aesthetic standards.* (1.1)
2. A The author's purpose is to explain the origin of the name "Dada." Clues: *The knife pointed to the word dada, a French baby–talk word for a hobby–horse... an appropriate term for their anti–art.* (1.6)
3. C The Dadaists mocked society by using "found" objects in works of art. Clues: *Dadaists used absurdity to create artworks that mocked society yet defied intellectual analysis, such as the use of "found" objects in sculptures and installations.* (1.1)
4. B *Forerunner* means *earliest artist* in this context. Clues: *The forerunner of the Dadaists, and ultimately their leading member...; ...in 1913 created his first "ready–made,"....* The prefix *fore–* = before; Duchamp's first "ready–made" appeared just before the Dada movement was founded in 1916. (1.4)
5. C The passage does not give a soup can as an example of a "ready–made." All of the other answers are given: *...his first "ready–made," the Bicycle Wheel, consisting of a wheel mounted on the seat of a stool; ...ready–mades—manufactured objects that he selected and exhibited—including a bottle rack and a comb.* (1.2)
6. C The referent of *them* is something that the young artists of the Pop movement embraced. The first part of the sentence mentions *ordinary things.* Logic tells you that *them* refers to *ordinary things.* (1.3)
7. D You can infer that the Pop artists succeeded in changing ideas about art. Clues: *...the barrier between "high" and "low" art collapsed, which...the Pop artists attained with an energy not seen before.* (1.5)
8. B *Pop art caught on quickly...eagerly consumed by the masses* is paraphrased in *The public enthusiastically accepted Pop art...; ...it was art about mass consumption...* is paraphrased in *...which portrayed commercial culture.* (1.7)
9. C Roy Lichtenstein created works based on the work of other artists, such as comic strip artists, and on other styles, such as Cubism and Art Deco. Clues: *Lichtenstein painted enlarged copies of the least "arty" things he could find: romance and adventure comic strips; Lichtenstein also painted other pictorial styles, including blowups of other artists' brushstrokes and parodies of Cubism and Art Deco.* (1.1)
10. D *Took on* means *responded to* in this context. Clues: *...took on the mind–numbing overload of American mass culture; ...mimic the condition of mass advertising; ...felt this and embodied it.* Warhol's art was a response to American mass culture. (1.4)
11. A *Glut* means *excess* in this context. Clues: *...images that become meaningless by being repeated again and again....* (1.4)
12. A In the added sentence, *the crisis* refers to *the First World War*, mentioned in the previous sentence. The added sentence further develops the idea in the previous sentence that *Dada was the first expression of protest against the war.* (1.8)
13. B, E, H Dada: *Dada was a subversive movement in the arts...; ...an appropriate term for their anti–art; The Dada movement extended to literature and music...; Dada emerged from despair over the First World War...; ...protest against the war; ...the use of "found" objects in sculptures and installations; ...shocked the art establishment with these ready–mades....*

    A, D, F, I Pop Art: *Pop artists were curious about the commercial media of ads, billboards, newsprint, television, and all aspects of popular culture; ...considered Pop to be the culture of the mass media...; The subject matter of Pop art was derivative, depicting something that had already been published or produced...; ...the first American artist to react to comic strips, finding beauty in these crude designs...; The thirty–two soup cans are about sameness: same brand...; ...a famous brand name or the image of a famous person....* Answers (C) and (G) describe neither Dada nor Pop Art. (1.10)
14. A The author makes the point that deforestation in North America occurred mostly within a single century. Clues: *...in the eighteenth century, almost one–third of that area was covered with old–growth forests; ...nearly 90 percent of the land was thick with forests...; By the end of the nineteenth century, after several decades of intensive deforestation, only half of the original forests remained.* (1.1)
15. B The passage does not state that an increase in forest fires contributed to deforestation. All of the other answers are given: *Land for agriculture came almost exclusively from clearing forests; ...iron makers relied on charcoal, or charred wood, to fire their furnaces; The river steamboats that came into operation after 1830 had a voracious appetite for wood.* (1.2)
16. B The referent of *they* is something that was reduced to concentrated carbon. The previous clause states that charcoal burners made charcoal by burning logs. Logic tells you that *they* refers to *logs*.
17. D The author's purpose is to emphasize that large areas of woodland were eliminated. In this context, *toll* refers to loss because many trees had to be cut to make charcoal. Clues: *...countless acres were cut to feed the furnaces of the iron industry.* (1.6)
18. B *Voracious* means *greedy* in this context. Clues: *...contributed greatly to deforestation; ...a voracious appetite for wood; ...consumption of wood on riverboats continued to increase...; ...stripped of their forests.* (1.4)
19. C *"Wood hawks"* means *people who sold wood* in this context. Clues: *The wood was supplied by thousands of...stacks of cut firewood.* (1.4)
20. D *Surged* means *increased* in this context. Clues: *...immigration and westward expansion surged... railroads swept over the continent; Railroads in the United States and Canada stretched from coast to coast....* (1.4)

21. C You can infer that "iron horses" were steam engines that moved trains. Clues: *...hardwood was the preferred fuel of the "iron horses,"...; Not only did wood fuel the steam engines....* (1.5)

22. D *More than four out of five of the houses constructed in the early nineteenth century—from log cabins to clapboard cottages...* is paraphrased in *...the vast majority of houses built in the early nineteenth century; ...were built mainly of wood and roofed with wooden shingles* is paraphrased in *Wood was the primary construction material....* (1.7)

23. D You can infer that home heating was a major reason for cutting trees in the early nineteenth century. Clues: *Two–thirds of all households in North America were heated by open, wood–burning fireplaces, and it took between 10 and 20 acres of forest to keep a single fireplace burning for one year.* (1.5)

24. C The tremendous increase in the production of lumber was primarily due to innovations in technology. Clues: *...the annual production of lumber rose from 1.6 million to 8 billion board feet. This increase was made possible by the widespread application of steam power. Wood–fueled steam engines...; Railroad lines...; These innovations had their greatest impact....* (1.1)

25. A The added sentence introduces the idea that the timber industry led all others in the exploitation of North American forests. The rest of the paragraph develops this idea with facts and details: *...the timber industry continued to supply the single most valuable raw material...; ...the annual production of lumber rose...; ...the widespread application of steam power.* (1.8)

26. B, C, F Key information: *The demand for farmland and timber continued to soar...more than 100 million acres of old–growth forest had been cut or burned off...; ...iron makers relied on charcoal, or charred wood, to fire their furnaces; ...countless acres were cut to feed the furnaces of the iron industry; The river steamboats...had a voracious appetite for wood; ...the "iron horses," which required the cutting of 215,000 acres of woodland...; More than four out of five of the houses constructed in the early nineteenth century...were built mainly of wood and roofed with wooden shingles; ...the annual production of lumber rose...; This increase was made possible by the widespread application of steam power; ...the technology of the timber industry had triumphed over the natural abundance of the forests, and woodlands that had once seemed endless were now depleted.* Answers (A) and (D) are minor ideas; answer (E) is not mentioned.

27. D *Only in recent years have health professionals begun to realize...* is paraphrased in *Health professionals have just started to understand...; ...the prevalence and severity of sleep deprivation in the working population* is paraphrased in *...that sleep deprivation in workers is a serious problem.* (1.7)

28. C The passage does not give boring work as a cause of sleep deprivation. All of the other answers are given: *A significant number of people work at night, work long shifts, or suffer from...jet lag.* (1.2)

29. C *Deprived of* means *kept from* in this context. Clues: *...sleep deprivation...; ...work at night, work long shifts, or suffer from insomnia or jet lag; ...deprived of sleep because they work too hard, stay out too late, or try to do too many things in a day; ...sleep six hours or less....* (1.4)

30. B *Adversely* means *negatively* in this context. Clues: *...certain patterns of electrical and chemical activity that occur during sleep are interrupted and the brain cannot function normally.* The passage mainly discusses the negative effects of sleep deprivation. (1.4)

31. D The purpose of the study was to determine the effects of sleep deprivation on brain activity. Clues: *The scans recorded each subject's brain activity from a rested state through various stages of sleep deprivation....* (1.1)

32. C The referent of *others* is something in which there was decreased activity. The sentence states that the images showed *increased activity in some regions of the brain and decreased activity in others.* Logic tells you that *others* refers to *regions of the brain.* (1.3)

33. B The researchers learned that subjects who had gone several hours without sleep had no activity in part of the brain during verbal tasks. Clues: *...the temporal lobe of the brain, the region involved in language processing, was activated during verbal tasks in rested subjects but not in sleep–deprived subjects; ...after several hours without sleep, there was no activity within this region.* (1.1)

34. B The author's purpose is to compare the effects of sleep deprivation and alcohol. Clues: *...researchers reported that sleep deprivation had some of the same hazardous effects as being drunk; ...people who drove after being awake for 17 to 19 hours performed worse than those with a blood alcohol level of .05 percent....* (1.6)

35. A You can infer that medical personnel and other emergency workers are at risk for experiencing anxiety and depression. Clues: *Drivers who get too little sleep may have higher levels of stress, anxiety and depression.... These dangers affect not only drivers but also people who work long shifts or night shifts, such as medical personnel and other emergency workers.* (1.5)

36. C Sleep deprivation can affect the body's immune system by reducing the body's ability to make or use insulin. Clues: *Sleep deprivation has been linked to a decrease in the body's production of hormones such as insulin; ...the pancreas does not make enough insulin or the body is unable to use the insulin that is present.* (1.1)

37. D *Setting the stage* means *providing the conditions* in this context. Clues: *Sleep deprivation weakens the immune system, making an individual more prone to diseases...; ...glucose builds up in the bloodstream, setting the stage for diabetes and heart disease.* (1.4)

38. B The added sentence introduces the topic of drivers, which the next sentence develops by discussing a *study of drivers.* (1.8)

39. C, E, F Key information: *...the brain is adversely affected by sleep deprivation because certain patterns of electrical and chemical activity that occur during sleep are interrupted and the brain cannot function normally; ...after several hours without sleep, there was no activity within this region. The effects of the inactivity included slurred speech...; ...getting fewer than six hours of sleep a night can impair... coordination, reaction time, and judgment...; In one study of drivers, researchers reported that sleep deprivation had some of the same hazardous effects as being drunk; The dangers of sleep deprivation...undermine all areas of an individual's physical and mental health; Sleep deprivation weakens the immune system, making an individual more prone to diseases....* Answers (A) and (D) are minor ideas; answer (B) is not mentioned. (1.9)

LISTENING (p. 86)

1. C The students mainly discuss the man's upcoming art show. The woman says *Hey, I heard about your senior thesis show in Gallery Two! That's great! I'm so proud of you, Malcolm.* The man then talks about his sculpture, which will be in the show. (2.1)
2. A The woman asks if she can bring her roommate to the opening reception. The man tells her to bring all her friends because *more* people will be *merrier* (more fun). You can infer that the man hopes that a lot of people come to the opening reception. (2.4)
3. B, D The man's sculpture includes boxes of different colors: *This time it's three boxes—one red, one blue, and one black.* It also includes different styles of music: *There's a different style of music for each color. The red box plays Dixieland jazz, the blue one plays solo saxophone, and the black one is all sad violins.* (2.2)
4. C The man says *Actually, I read an article on this topic about a year ago...; ...this study about the moods of music...showed that people sort of think of different kinds of music—the different sounds and tones of music—in terms of colors.* (2.2)
5. B The woman's purpose is to explain a possible use of her photograph. She is talking about a black and white photograph of *benches covered in snow*, which might appear in next year's catalog because *the dean liked it.* (2.3)
6. B, C The professor discusses how glaciers are created: *You might expect that heavy snowfall is the main requirement for the formation of a glacier; For a glacier to form, the snow can't melt.* The professor also discusses the movement of glaciers: *...part of the ice moves over the edge of the hollow and starts moving down the valley. Large glaciers usually move faster than small ones. Also, the movement is faster in the summer...; Most valley glaciers move at a rate of....* (2.1)
7. A The professor says *Snowfall alone isn't enough. For a glacier to form, the snow can't melt. It has to be conserved; ...there are massive ice sheets because the snow that does fall is conserved and transformed into ice.* (2.2)
8. C The professor's purpose is to describe conditions that lead to glacier formation. The professor is talking about the role of snow in glacier formation. She describes places in high mountains where snow accumulates, leading to glacier formation. (2.3)
9. ✓ No: Precipitation falls as freezing rain or ice pellets: Not supported by the information in the lecture.
   ✓ Yes: Snow accumulates and gradually turns into ice: *As snow accumulates in a hollow, it's gradually converted to ice.*
   ✓ No: Minerals in the meltwater change the texture of snowflakes: Not supported by the information in the lecture.
   ✓ Yes: Snow crystals become rounded and coarse, like grains of sugar: *Gradually, over time, the snowflakes change into grains. They become rounded and granular, like the grains of coarse sugar.*
   ✓ Yes: Weight and movement compress the air out of ice crystals: *In the end, it's pure ice, with all the air squeezed out. The flow of the glacier down the mountain contributes to crystal growth, as the movement helps to compress the air out.* (2.6)
10. A The professor says *Most valley glaciers move at a rate of... oh ... between a few inches and a few feet a day. But some glaciers—called surging glaciers—can travel as much as 300 feet a day.* (2.2)
11. B The professor says that glaciers in warmer climates *cause more erosion, more carving out of the valley floor* and that they have an *impact on the landscape.* You can infer that glaciers in warmer climates can change the shape of a mountain valley. (2.4)
12. A The professor implies that each design gives the audience a different experience. The professor says *Each of these styles has advantages and disadvantages, and each is good for certain types of plays.* Then he discusses how each stage design affects the experience of the audience. (2.4)
13. C The professor says *However, the proscenium arch also creates a distancing effect—which is...a disadvantage for others; ...for some plays—for, example, close-up views of real life—the proscenium is sort of a barrier between the actors and the audience.* (2.2)
14. B The professor says *...there's been a movement to bring theater closer to real life...a movement toward more informal, more intimate theater. Thus, we have the arena stage...; The actors are in the center, so everyone in the audience can be close to them. The effect is a sense of intimacy, a kind of closeness that comes whenever people form a circle.* You can infer that an intimate drama about everyday life would best be produced on an arena stage. (2.4)
15. C The professor's purpose is to describe the origins of the arena stage. The professor says *The arena is the oldest style of theater.* Then he mentions *early theatrical performances* such as *ceremonies, rituals, and dances*, which all took place in a circle. (2.3)
16. D The professor says *The third design—the thrust stage—falls somewhere between the proscenium and the arena styles. In the thrust stage theater, the audience sits on three sides or in a half-circle, around a stage that sticks out into the center.* (2.2)

17. A, D The thrust stage combines the advantages of the other two styles: *The thrust stage is kind of a compromise between the proscenium and the arena styles. It combines the scenic features of the proscenium theater with the intimacy of the arena stage.* Many great plays were written for the thrust stage: *...the fact that so many great dramatic works were written for it gives the thrust stage a prominent position among the other major forms.* (2.2)

18. C The student wants to discuss the topic of her research. The professor says *...you wanted to talk about your research?; You're studying goose populations, right?* The student says *Well, I was anyway. That's what I wanted to talk to you about. I think I want to go in a different direction.* (2.3)

19. B The student's purpose is to explain why she wants to change the focus of her research. In her research into problems concerning geese, the student found an article that sent her *off in a different direction.* As a result, she wants to change her focus to the problem of geese and airplane accidents. (2.3)

20. A The professor means that results are tragic when airplanes strike birds. The woman tells about an airplane accident in which *several geese were sucked into two of the engines*, causing a crash in which *the whole crew was killed.* The professor responds by saying *Birds and planes don't mix*, emphasizing the tragic results of such encounters between birds and planes. (2.4)

21. A, D Peregrine falcons naturally prey on geese and ducks: *...the right kind of bird can keep the wrong kind of bird away, so they started using peregrine falcons to patrol the runways; Mostly it was geese and ducks, because it's near a wetland. But now, since they started the falcon program, and since falcons are predators, there haven't been any bird–aircraft collisions that required any repairs!* Peregrine falcons can fly faster than any other bird: *They can exceed 200 miles per hour in a dive—faster than any other living creature.* (2.2)

22. D The student's opinion is that the falcon program is interesting because it uses biology to solve a problem. She says *The falcons get the credit for keeping the geese and ducks away. It's an interesting solution to the problem, I mean, adding a predator to change the biology of the runway.* (2.3)

23. B The professor mainly discusses how a market economy works. The professor says *In this course, we'll look at the basic problems every economy must face. We'll focus on the modern industrial economy...; We'll examine the market mechanism, how the problems of production are solved through a system of markets and prices.* (2.1)

24. D The professor's purpose is to contrast a pure market economy with a mixed economy. First, the professor mentions the government's *important role in regulating business activity* in a mixed economy. Then she states that a pure market system would have *no government intervention*, showing the contrast between the two systems. (2.3)

25. C The professor means that consumers use their money like votes to buy goods. The professor continues by saying *They use their money like votes to buy what they want. My votes compete with your votes over the goods we both want to buy.* (2.4)

26. B The professor says *The lower the price, the more they'll buy. So you can see there's a definite relationship between the price of a good and the quantity demanded; But when the price falls, demand increases, as more people will be willing and able to buy it at a lower price.* (2.2)

27. D The professor implies that the supply of a good is directly related to its price. Businesses must make a profit, so when the price of a good is high, producers will supply more of it because they will make a higher profit. However, when the price is low, producers will supply a different, more profitable good. (2.4)

28. A The professor says *Tomorrow we'll look at just how supply and demand work in a real–world mixed economy. We'll see how the market price of a good is a function of supply and demand....* You can predict that the next lecture will be about examples of how supply and demand affect prices. (2.4)

29. C The main idea of the talk is that fire revitalizes the forest and promotes a diversity of life. The instructor says *Without fire, ecosystems can stagnate and lose their diversity of life; Now we know that fire is a natural agent that rejuvenates a forest.* (2.1)

30. A The instructor means that fire prevention has actually damaged the forest ecosystem. The previous forest policy was to eliminate forest fires. Preventing fires saved trees *but at the expense of the forest community* because periodic fires are natural and benefit the forest as a whole. (2.4)

31. A, C Periodic fire is necessary to forest ecosystems because it releases nutrients into the soil. The instructor says *Fire removes nutrients from standing dead trees and returns them to the earth, where they become available to the root systems of new trees.* Fire also controls insect pests that harm trees. The instructor says *Fire is nature's way of controlling insect infestations; ...the heat kills off great numbers of beetles and larvae, providing a natural method of pest control.* (2.2)

32. B The instructor says *The exclusion of fire from the ecosystem is creating unhealthy, overcrowded forests that contain more fuel for larger, more severe fires; ...the flames were fed by dead wood and combustible debris that had accumulated on the forest floor over years of fire suppression.* (2.2)

33. B The instructor says *Prescribed fire, or controlled fire...; ...prescribed burns are carried out every three to five years in one of the national forests. These controlled burns....* (2.2)

34. D The instructor's purpose is to give examples of the negative effects of fire. The instructor says *...fire has consequences* (negative effects), and then he lists *smoky, hazy skies and patches of blackened forest*, and *the risk of a fire becoming too large* as examples. (2.3)

35. C The man needs help in improving his study skills. He says *...I'm taking some difficult courses this semester and I have a lot of reading to do. I just feel like I need to bone up on my study skills, you know, learn how to study better.* (2.3)

36. A The woman suggests that the man attend one of the special workshops. She says *You could take one of our special workshops. There are several of these each week. The workshops in study skills and time management are especially popular.* (2.2)

37. B The woman says *We have several workshops. All of them are two hours long. Most are held in the evening, but there's a couple that are on the weekend.* (2.2)

38. D The man's purpose is to express pleasure that the workshops are free. The woman says *All of the workshops are free to students.* The man replies *Hey, that's not a bad deal,* meaning it is a good idea. (2.3)

39. B The man is interested in taking a workshop in study skills. The woman says *...there's a sheet there for every workshop offered this semester, and that's how you sign up.* You can predict that the man will look at the workshops that are available. (2.4)

40. B The professor mainly presents a comparison of two philosophers. The professor says *...two of the world's great educational philosophers, Confucius and Dewey; ...both of these thinkers held some interesting—and amazingly parallel—ideas about teaching and learning; As was the case with Confucius, some of Dewey's ideas were considered revolutionary; Despite the centuries that separated them, Confucius and Dewey held some similar ideas about knowledge, teaching, and learning.* (2.1)

41. A The professor's purpose is to illustrate Confucius's respect for tradition. The quote states that Confucius valued the wisdom of the ancients and illustrates his belief that teachers should continue the ancient tradition. (2.3)

42. D The professor says *Confucius was a revolutionary because he believed that there should be no distinction of social class in education. He believed that education should be, um, not just for the privileged class, but for any boy or girl who was able and willing to learn.* (2.2)

43. C The professor says *...pragmatism was highly influential in several fields...especially education. One of its leading thinkers was the American philosopher John Dewey.* (2.2)

44. C, D The idea that the education of the individual will benefit society is important in both philosophies: *Dewey believed that the cultivation of the individual would benefit society as a whole...; This is similar to the Confucian idea...that the greatness of individuals is necessary for social order.* Another important idea is that education is a combination of knowledge and experience: *Confucius believed that the processes of teaching and learning stimulate each other; ...the ideal teacher is one who goes over what he's already learned and gains some new understanding from the experience. Compare this to Dewey's idea that education is a continuously constructive process, with experience and knowledge building on each other.* (2.2)

45. A The professor implies that Confucius and Dewey had similar ideas about the continuous nature of learning. Confucius believed that reviewing past learning can produce *some new understanding.* Dewey believed that education is *a continuously constructive process* and that experience and knowledge build on each other. (2.4)

46. B, D The professor discusses behaviors that help prey avoid predators: *Prey species have adaptations, too—physical and behavioral adaptations that enable them to elude predators and avoid being eaten; ...hiding...; ...escaping..., ...running away...; ...alarm call...; ...mobbing.* The professor also discusses defensive coloration: *Some animals rely on defensive coloration; Another defensive adaptation is warning coloration.* (2.1)

47. C The professor's purpose is to illustrate a disadvantage of an active anti–predator response. The professor says *Fleeing—running away—is the most direct anti–predator response, but it requires the animal to expend a lot of energy.* She then gives the example of a rabbit running away from a lynx. (2.3)

48. B The professor says *During mobbing, the prey turns the tables and attacks the predator; The chickadee starts scolding the owl...; The other birds chase, dive–bomb, or surround the owl, usually vocalizing loudly.* (2.2)

49. A The professor's purpose is to explain why camouflage is not a perfect defense. *Once the bird learns the moth's identity, it has a search image for it, and the moth's disguise is useless* means that the moth's camouflage is not effective after the bird learns that some leaves are actually moths. The bird will then search for moths that look like leaves. (2.3)

50. C The professor means that some birds appear able to manage the poison of bees and wasps. Many birds eat bees and wasps, *perhaps after learning to cope with their chemical defenses*, which suggests that birds may develop ways to counteract the insects' chemical weapons. (2.4)

51. ✓ Chemical weapons: A toad squirts a nerve poison from glands on its back: *...poisonous toads and frogs—can synthesize toxins that attack the nervous system of predators.*

✓ Camouflage: A fish cannot be seen against rocks of the same color: *...camouflage, which makes prey difficult to spot against a background of similar color.*

✓ Warning coloration: A bird avoids eating a black and yellow striped wasp: *...young warblers leave wasps alone because the birds recognize the danger in the black and yellow stripes of the wasp.*

✓ Camouflage: An insect disguises itself to look like a leaf: *Moths that camouflage themselves to match a leaf stand a good chance of not being seen....* (2.5)

SPEAKING (p. 106)

1. Responses will vary. (3.1–3.4)
2. Responses will vary. (3.1–3.4)
3. Key points:
    - The students have a choice of several different formats for presenting their projects to the class. The man prefers the format of a Web page.
    - One reason he gives is that knowing how to build a Web page is a skill that will help in their careers.
    - Another reason is that they can be more creative and make their report more interesting.
    - Another reason is that their classmates are already users of the Web, so a Web page is a natural choice. (3.5–3.7, 3.10)
4. Key points:
    - Women report more conflict between work and family roles. For women, there is less of a boundary between family and work. Women do more of the childcare and housework than their husbands do. They are more likely to stop working when their children are young, or more likely to stay home with a sick child. Women are more likely to feel overworked and stressed–out.
    - Men do not experience the same degree of role conflict or overload as women do. For men, work and family are more separated. The roles of husband and father are very important to men, and men carry emotional distress from the family into the workplace. Men are more likely to have an argument at work after having an argument at home.
    - Women do more of the work at home after their husbands have a hard day at work, but fewer men do more work at home after their wives have a hard day at work. (3.5–3.7, 3.10)
5. Key points:
    - The man's problem is that he cannot decide whether to go to the beach with his family or to go on a research trip to the rainforest during spring break.
    - The woman suggests that he explain to his family that he has a great opportunity to do some research and might not get another opportunity like this.
    - The woman suggests that he think about his future and how the experience in the rainforest might help him when he looks for a job after graduation. (3.8, 3.10)
6. Key points:
    - The human hand made the development of human culture possible. The human hand is a tool, a toolmaker, and an extension of the brain.
    - The power of the human hand comes from the way the brain controls and coordinates its actions with signals from the eyes.
    - The hand is capable of brute strength and can perform hard physical labor. It is also capable of delicate tasks and is sensitive to slight changes in form and texture.
    - Two important characteristics of the hand are the opposable thumb and the double grip. The opposable thumb allows the thumb to touch every part of every finger on the same hand. The double grip allows us to hold two balls separately in one hand. (3.9, 3.10)

WRITING (p. 112)

1. Key points:
    - The lecture states that hydropower facilities are not always convenient for everyone because some people are forced to move when a dam is built in their community. This contrasts with the point in the reading that hydropower reservoirs contribute to the local economy and quality of life.
    - The lecture states that hydroelectricity causes long–term environmental hazards and toxic waste in the buildup of silt behind the dams, which will eventually be expensive to clean up. This contrasts with the point in the reading that hydroelectricity is "clean and green" because it does not release greenhouse gases into the atmosphere nor produce waste that requires special containment.
    - The lecture states that the huge dams built for hydroelectricity remove water needed for healthy river ecosystems, harming bird and fish populations. This contrasts with the point in the reading that hydroelectricity is "clean and green."
    - The lecture states that even though water is a naturally recurring resource, the water supply is subject to natural conditions that make water as a source of fuel unreliable in the long run. This contrasts with the point in the reading that the earth's water cycle naturally replenishes the supply of fuel water. (4.1–4.5)
2. Responses will vary. (4.6–4.10)

TEST 3

READING (p. 117)

1. B Thick walls of stone or brick were typical of tall buildings before the nineteenth century. Clues: *Until the nineteenth century, most tall buildings were constructed of load–bearing masonry walls. Masonry walls had to be thick...; Stoneworkers built these walls by placing stone upon stone or brick upon brick....* (1.1)
2. C *Force* means *load* in this context. Clues: *...load–bearing masonry walls; ...support a building's great weight; ...the major vertical force of buildings was supported by thick masonry walls.* (1.4)
3. A The passage does not state that sturdy walls made of stone or brick were a benefit of iron–frame construction; in fact, such walls characterized masonry construction. All of the other answers are given: *The introduction of metal construction made it possible to build larger interior spaces with fewer columns than before; An interior wrought iron skeleton supported all of the building's weight; ...walls that once bore weight evolved into thin curtain walls that would allow more windows.* (1.2)
4. B *As masonry yielded to concrete...* is paraphrased in *...now they were...made of concrete...*; *...walls that once bore weight...* is paraphrased in *Walls used to be made of load–bearing masonry...*; *...evolved into thin curtain walls that would allow more windows* is paraphrased in *...now they were thin..., so more windows were possible.* (1.7)
5. B It is true that the earliest skyscrapers were eight or more stories high. Clues: *...taller buildings that quickly became known as skyscrapers; Buildings of eight or more stories quickly transformed the city skyline....* (1.1)
6. D The author's purpose is to show how an innovation contributed to architecture. Clues: *The invention of the mechanical elevator made it possible to construct even taller buildings; The elevator made the upper floors as rentable as the first floor, liberating architecture from dependence on stairways and human muscle.* (1.6)
7. D *Rentable* means *desirable* in this context. Clues: *The elevator made the upper floors as rentable as the first floor....* The elevator meant that people no longer had to climb numerous stairways to the upper floors. Thus, people desired (wanted) to rent the upper floors as much as the first floor. (1.4)
8. A The referent of *they* is something that erased the traditional architectural distinctions separating the different parts of a building. The subject of the previous clause is *innovations*. Logic tells you that *they* refers to *innovations*. (1.3)
9. D *Refined* means *improved* in this context. Clues: *Construction techniques were refined and extended...to produce... "true skyscrapers," buildings over twenty stories high.* The paragraph describes improvements in materials and techniques that enabled buildings to be taller than ever before. (1.4)
10. A Steel replaced iron in the construction of skyscrapers because steel is stronger than iron and resists fatigue better. Clues: *...steel T–beams and I–beams replaced iron in these new structures; Steel...exceeds both masonry and iron in tension and compression strength as well as resistance to fatigue.* (1.1)
11. B You can infer that the author believes cast iron technology and the elevator made the skyscraper possible. Clues: *Skyscrapers differed from previous tall structures with their use of technical innovations such as cast iron and the elevator. The development of cast iron technology...made modern plumbing possible. Cast iron pipes, fittings, and valves could deliver pressurized water to the many floors of tall buildings...; The invention of the mechanical elevator made it possible to construct even taller buildings. Before the elevator, office buildings were rarely more than four or five stories high.* (1.5)
12. B The added sentence discusses *plumbing*, a topic introduced in the previous sentence. The added sentence states that *Sophisticated plumbing was needed to service bathrooms and also to heat buildings*, which the next sentence develops further by stating that *pipes, fittings, and valves could deliver pressurized water to the many floors of tall buildings.* (1.8)
13. B, D, F Key information: *...an alternative was emerging that would eliminate the need for exterior weight–bearing walls: a three–dimensional grid of metal beams and columns; An interior wrought iron skeleton supported all of the building's weight. Exterior walls of reinforced concrete acted mainly as weatherproofing; The invention of the mechanical elevator made it possible to construct even taller buildings; ... "true skyscrapers," buildings over twenty stories high. The invention of steel was particularly significant, as steel T–beams and I–beams replaced iron in these new structures.* Answers (A), (C), and (E) are minor ideas. (1.9)
14. D The passage does not state that the concept of systems involves the origin of the scientific method. All of the other answers are given: *...scientists use the word "system" to describe a collection of several components that are linked to one another by functional relationships; ...the components of a system, their relationships with one another, and their relationships with other systems.* (1.2)
15. C *Although each science has its own systems with their own subject matter and networks of relationships...* is paraphrased in *System components and relationships differ for each science, yet...*; *...the formal characteristics of systems are similar for all sciences* is paraphrased in *...systems in all sciences share similar properties.* (1.7)
16. C The referent of *them* is something among which there are relations or forces. The last part of the sentence discusses the *elements* involved in systems, and the relations or forces among these elements. Logic tells you that *them* refers to *elements*. (1.3)
17. B *Exhausted* means *used* in this context. Clues: *The energy supply of a closed system is limited and is progressively used up...; The ability of the system to function decreases as the available energy is exhausted.* The prefix *ex–* = out. (1.4)

18. A The example of a mill wheel illustrates the point that the energy supply of a closed system is limited. Clues: *The energy supply of a closed system is limited and is progressively used up by the processes operating within the system; Without any additional energy supplied from the outside, the system's processes stop altogether...; Once the container of water is empty, the wheel no longer turns because there is no water to turn it.* (1.1)

19. C The Earth system as a whole is a closed system because no mass crosses the system boundary, but some energy does. Clues: *...many define closed systems more broadly as those allowing energy but not mass to cross the system boundary. By this definition, the Earth system as a whole is a closed system; ...energy passes across the Earth's system boundary, but mass does not, making it a closed system.* (1.1)

20. A You can infer that living organisms are part of a larger system that receives and gives off energy. Clues: *Living organisms are open systems; Each open system is part of a larger system that receives and gives off energy.* (1.5)

21. D *Dries up* means *stops flowing* in this context. Clues: *...the energy supply is halted...; ...for example, the stream to the reservoir supplying the mill dries up for a long period...; The water in the reservoir is used up...* (1.4)

22. B You can infer that the mill wheel is temporarily a closed system during long dry periods, when there is no new water supply. Clues: *These can behave as closed systems temporarily if the energy supply is halted for a period. If, for example, the stream to the reservoir supplying the mill dries up for a long period...; The water in the reservoir is used up, and if the dry period is long enough, the mill wheel stops turning.* (1.5)

23. B The author's purpose is to illustrate the point that open systems are part of larger systems. The stream–reservoir–mill system is an open system when the stream flows again because the water comes from the surroundings—from the Earth's larger water systems. Clues: *...the stream–reservoir–mill system is itself a part of the Earth's much larger systems of water circulation and water budget....* (1.6)

24. A In the added sentence, *For example* is a transition that introduces the example of hot tea in a vacuum bottle. The hot tea *does not interact with the environment outside the bottle*, which illustrates the idea that *A closed system is isolated from its surroundings*, stated in the previous sentence. (1.8)

25. B, E Closed System: *The energy supply of a closed system is limited and is progressively used up by the processes operating within the system; ...not mass to cross the system boundary; ...no mass is exchanged between the Earth system and the rest of the universe.*

C, D, G Open System: *In an open system, energy and mass can be transferred between the system and its surroundings; ...relationships exist between the components of a system and its surroundings...; Each open system is part of a larger system that receives and gives off energy; ...the energy is continually resupplied from sources outside the system.* Answers (A) and (F) describe neither closed systems nor open systems. (1.10)

26. C The author makes the point that average levels of life satisfaction are similar for every age group. Clues: *...average levels of life satisfaction do not change significantly with age. Generally speaking, older adults are as satisfied with their lives as are younger or middle–aged adults.* (1.1)

27. B The passage does not state that age is a predictor of life satisfaction. In fact, *average levels of life satisfaction do not change significantly with age.* All of the other answers are given: *One such predictor is health...; Another predictor of life satisfaction is a feeling of being in charge of one's own life...; The largest predictor of life satisfaction appears to be the adequacy of social relationships, especially marriage and family relationships.* (1.2)

28. B *In charge of* means *responsible for* in this context. Clues: *...a sense of authority over one's own decisions; ...feel that they have some choices and options....* People who feel in charge of their lives feel responsible for their own decisions. (1.4)

29. C The referent of *problem* is something that signals a loss of control over the lives of older adults. The sentence states that older adults experience financial strain. Logic tells you that *problem* refers to *financial strain.* (1.3)

30. D *Adequacy* means *quality* in this context. Clues: *...perceived quality....* (1.4)

31. A You can infer that close social relationships are likely to influence long–term health and happiness. Clues: *The largest predictor of life satisfaction appears to be the adequacy of social relationships, especially marriage and family relationships; The quality of social support available in one's key relationships affects the ability to handle stress and life changes as well as one's ongoing level of life satisfaction.* (1.5)

32. D The author says that people who are well adjusted and successful at midlife probably had positive personal qualities as young adults. Clues: *Well–adjusted or successful middle–aged adults began adulthood with more personal resources, including better psychological and physical health at college age; ...had been practical and well organized...had shown greater intellectual competence.* (1.1)

33. B *However, no measure of early family environment or early adult competence...* is paraphrased in *Neither family background nor qualities of early adulthood...; ...remained a significant predictor of psychological well being at the end of middle age* is paraphrased in *...can predict life satisfaction beyond middle age.* (1.7)

34. A The author's purpose is to illustrate a point about satisfaction late in life. Clues: *...what did predict success and well being at age 65 was..., Late–life success is related more directly to...; ...that determines long–term life satisfaction.* (1.6)

35. C *Preordained* means *determined* in this context. Clues: *...a successful adult life is not something preordained from childhood or early adulthood but rather something created out of the opportunities available...; ...it is what one does with the experiences...that determines long–term life satisfaction.* The prefix *pre–* = before. (1.4)

ANSWER KEY

36. A You can infer that the author believes long–term life satisfaction is affected by the decisions made throughout adulthood. Clues: *...it is what one does with the experiences—both positive and negative—that determines long–term life satisfaction. The choices that people make in early adulthood help shape who they are at midlife, and those midlife qualities in turn influence who they become later in life.* (1.5)

37. B The added sentence further develops the idea that *the happiest and most successful middle–aged adults had grown up in warm, supportive, intellectually stimulating families*, mentioned in the previous sentence. (1.8)

38. B, C, F Key information: *...certain factors are reliable predictors of life satisfaction. One such predictor is health...; Another predictor of life satisfaction is a feeling of being in charge of one's own life and a sense of authority over one's own decisions; The largest predictor of life satisfaction appears to be the adequacy of social relationships...; The perceived quality rather than the quantity of social interactions is most strongly related to happiness; The choices that people make in early adulthood help shape who they are at midlife, and those midlife qualities in turn influence who they become later in life.* Answers (A) and (E) are minor ideas; answer (D) is not mentioned. (1.9)

39. C The author's purpose is to support the idea that film is an illusion. Clues: *Film is an illusion because the moving pictures seen on the screen are not moving at all; They appear to be moving because....* (1.6)

40. A *Catch up with* means *hurry to process* in this context. Clues: *...the image persists in the brain's visual center for a fraction of a second. Then, the next frame comes along and the brain has to catch up with the new image.* As the brain hurries to process each image, one image blends into the next image, so we think we see a moving picture. (1.4)

41. B The author primarily defines special effects as techniques and devices to create illusions in film. Clues: *Another illusion of film is known collectively as special effects, the tricks and techniques that filmmakers use....* (1.1)

42. B *Rolls* means *operates* in this context. Clues: *...a scene is filmed, the camera is stopped...and then the camera rolls again.* (1.4)

43. D *Simulate* means *create the appearance of* in this context. Clues: *...create an illusion...; ...feathers or plastic chips to simulate snow, and wires to create the illusion that people are flying.* (1.4)

44. C You can infer that silent films used sound effects to make scenes more convincing. Clues: *Many sound effects are mechanical effects; During the silent film era, the music machine called the Kinematophone was popular because it could produce the sounds of sirens, sleigh bells, gunfire, baby cries, and kisses....* (1.5)

45. B Filming each half of a frame separately would not necessarily involve mechanical effects but would involve optical effects. All of the other answers are given: *...wires to create the illusion that people are flying; ...a vibrating sheet of metal sounds like thunder; ...tiny copies of buildings or cities.* (1.2)

46. D *To reduce the cost of studio sets or location photography...* is paraphrased in *...thus making filming less expensive*; *...special–effects technicians create painted or projected backgrounds, which replace the set or add to it* is paraphrased in *Painted and projected backgrounds are special effects that improve or replace sets....* (1.7)

47. B The referent of *which* is something that was filled with small charges of flash powder. The sentence states that carpenters drilled small holes. Holes can be filled. Logic tells you that *which* refers to *holes*. (1.3)

48. A The author makes the point that *King Kong* combined two different types of special effects. Clues: *Sometimes optical and mechanical effects are used together; ...a tiny movable model of the ape...; ...stop–motion photography....* (1.1)

49. B In the added sentence, *another example* is a transition that introduces the example of an actor appearing to take off his head. This example naturally follows the example *an actor's clothes keep returning to his body*, mentioned in the previous sentence. (1.8)

50. C, E Optical Effects: *One category of special effects is called optical or visual effects, tricks made with the camera; Stop–motion photography can create the illusion of an actor disappearing on screen.*

A, D, G Mechanical Effects: *Mechanical effects are objects or devices used during the filming to create an illusion...; Other mechanical effects are puppets, robots...tiny copies of buildings or cities; ...small contact–rigged explosives...; In a 1916 silent film...mechanical effects created the appearance of an enemy invasion of the California seacoast.* Answer (B) describes persistence of vision; answer (F) describes computer graphics. (1.10)

51. C Whether signs of water indicate that life has existed on Mars has been a major focus of research about Mars. Most of the passage discusses evidence of water on Mars. Clues: *The presence or absence of water has a direct bearing on the possibility of life on other planets; ...Mars was an obvious target in the search for life; ...all of the available evidence does suggest that Mars meets all the requirements that are needed for life to exist.* (1.1)

52. B Astronomers of the nineteenth and twentieth centuries studied Mars mainly through photographic images. Clues: *New photographic technology offered a way for astronomers to learn more about the red planet; Other photographic images of Mars revealed...; ...a good photographic plate of the near–infrared spectrum of Mars.* (1.1)

53. D You can infer that Schiaparelli's observation of canals on Mars led to new questions about intelligent life on Mars. Clues: *The strange appearance of the canals suggested to some scientists that they had been formed artificially rather than naturally. The mystery deepened....* (1.5)

54. B The discovery of ancient islands in a dry streambed led some scientists to think that the Martian atmosphere had produced heavy rains in the past. Clues: *...features that appeared to be ancient islands located in what was now a dry streambed. When the islands were first discovered, some scientists speculated that a thick water–laden atmosphere capable of generating heavy rains had once existed on Mars.* (1.1)
55. A *Today, the presence of water vapor in the Martian atmosphere is generally accepted...* is paraphrased in *Most scientists believe there is water vapor in the Martian atmosphere...*; *...as is the belief that the atmosphere was once much denser than it is now, with a much greater abundance of water vapor* is paraphrased in *...which is now less dense than it was in the past.* (1.7)
56. C *Filled up* means *became wet* in this context. Clues: *...water was once common...*; *...shallow lakes or seas that dried out and then filled up again.* The next sentence mentions *dry stages*, which implies that there were wet stages and dry stages. (1.4)
57. B *Habitable* means *suitable for life* in this context. Clues: *...seas and lakes extended across hundreds of thousands of square miles, creating habitable conditions....* A major idea in the passage is that the presence of water may indicate the possibility of life on Mars. (1.4)
58. C Layers of rock on the Martian plains are evidence that water was present there for a long time. Clues: *Rocks that clearly formed in water extend throughout 300 meters of layered materials in several locations across the Martian plains. The layers were built up over time, which means water was present, at least temporarily, for extended periods on ancient Mars.* (1.1)
59. D Evidence of lava flows does not indicate the presence of water on Mars. All of the other answers are given: *Other photographic images of Mars revealed its seasonally changing polar ice caps...*; *...in 1963, a team of astronomers obtained a good photographic plate...*; *...water vapor lines could be seen*; *...clay and gypsum deposits that were formed by water in the soil.* (1.2)
60. A *Ingredient* means *factor* in this context. Clues: *Liquid water is the key ingredient for life as we know it*; *...the requirements that are needed for life to exist.* (1.4)
61. B The author's purpose is to point out that Mars has the conditions for life to exist. Life exists on Earth, and since *Mars is most like Earth*, life may have existed on Mars. Clues: *...all of the available evidence does suggest that Mars meets all the requirements that are needed for life to exist.* (1.6)
62. B In the added sentence, *Astronomers already knew that Mars had some kind of atmosphere* logically follows *Mars was an obvious target in the search for life* in the previous sentence. (1.8)
63. A, C, E Key information: *...images that showed a network of long, thin, dark lines crossing the surface of Mars; ... "canals" or "channels"...*; *Other photographic images of Mars revealed its seasonally changing polar ice caps and features that appeared to be ancient islands...*; *...the presence of water vapor in the Martian atmosphere is generally accepted...*; *...liquid water once flowed over the planet; Evidence of water includes the presence of various minerals...*; *...water was present...on ancient Mars*; *...astronomers have discovered a frozen sea....* Answers (B) and (D) are minor ideas; answer (F) is not mentioned. (1.9)

LISTENING (*p. 138*)

1. D The student's purpose is to learn if he still has required courses to take. The student says *...I wanted to check with you to see if there are any courses I still need before I transfer. I think I've filled all the requirements, but I, uh, just wanted to make sure before I register.* (2.3)
2. B The adviser's purpose is to let the student know that she will have to leave soon. The student asks the adviser if she is busy, and she tells him about *a meeting at two–thirty*. She says that she has *a few minutes* before she must leave for the meeting. (2.3)
3. B The student says *...I hope to transfer to the university next year.* (2.2)
4. B, D The student must take a course in natural science: *You're required to have at least one more natural science course before you can transfer.* He must also take a course in physical education: *...it looks like you also need two credits in physical education; You're required to have four credits, and you've only got two so far.* (2.2)
5. C The student implies that he would like to know more about golf. He says *I've only played a couple of times, but I need to do better than that. My boss plays golf and he's always talking about it. It would be nice to know what he's talking about!* (2.4)
6. C The professor mainly discusses a severe type of immune response called anaphylaxis. The professor says *A massive allergic reaction to a sting is known as anaphylaxis; Anaphylaxis is actually a disease, a severe form of allergic over–response by the immune system when it's suddenly faced with a foreign substance.* (2.1)
7. B, C Bee venom can initiate anaphylaxis: *One type of immune response has to do with bees...*; *But stings and bites usually aren't dangerous... unless you have an allergic reaction to the venom.* Peanuts can initiate anaphylaxis: *No one who was with her at the time knew she was allergic to peanuts, so they didn't know why she suddenly went into respiratory distress. The reason, of course, was anaphylaxis.* (2.2)

8. D The professor's purpose is to stress the serious effects of an allergy. The professor says *...that's what happened last year to a little girl who ate a peanut cookie at a birthday party. No one who was with her at the time knew she was allergic to peanuts, so they didn't know why she suddenly went into respiratory distress. The reason, of course, was anaphylaxis. But by the time the medics got there, it was too late, and the girl died.* (2.3)

9. A The professor's purpose is to stress the mysterious nature of severe immune responses. Scientists do not understand why some immune systems *go crazy*, or *overreact* to an offending substance, while other immune systems do not. (2.3)

10. ✓ Yes: The chest feels tight and breathing is difficult: *The chest feels tight, and the person has trouble breathing....*
    ✓ Yes: The face and throat begin to swell: *The tissues of the face and throat may swell up.*
    ✓ No: Fatty particles attach to the walls of blood vessels: Not supported by the information in the lecture.
    ✓ Yes: The body releases histamine into the bloodstream: *This sets off a whole series of reactions involving the release of histamine into the bloodstream.*
    ✓ No: The blood pressure rises dangerously high: *The blood pressure drops dangerously low.* (2.6)

11. C The professor says *With anaphylaxis, a few minutes can make the difference between life and death, so the keys to survival are being prepared and acting quickly.* You can infer that survival depends on immediate medical treatment. (2.4)

12. D The professor mainly discusses the effects of mail–order catalogs on rural America. The professor says *Farm families were isolated, often with limited funds, and few could afford the time or the expense of shopping in the city. But all of this changed with the introduction of the mail–order catalog; The Sears catalog sold food, clothing, machinery, tools, stoves—anything and everything a farm family might need.* (2.1)

13. A The professor says *In 1872, a Chicago merchant named Montgomery Ward began sending copies of a catalog to thousands of farmers in the Midwest; This is how Montgomery Ward and Company became the nation's first mail–order company.* (2.2)

14. C The professor's purpose is to explain how these services helped the mail–order business. The professor says *The mail–order business spread rapidly, largely because of improvements in postal services. The post office established Rural Free Delivery...and Parcel Post...; These new services greatly contributed to the success of mail–order houses.* (2.3)

15. A, B The mass production of goods and the wide distribution of catalogs led to the similarity of goods available nationwide: *The wide distribution of the Sears catalog had another interesting effect. The Sears catalog had a lot to do with the similarity of goods available nationwide. Of course, this was also due to the mass–production of goods; The two factors working together—mass production and nationwide distribution—tended to minimize regional differences in clothing styles.* (2.2)

16. C The professor means that the Sears catalog taught immigrants about American culture. The purpose of a textbook is to teach, and the Sears catalog was like a textbook because it taught immigrants *how to dress, how to furnish their homes, and...how to cook American food.* (2.4)

17. ✓ Disagree: Nineteenth–century farm families had the same cultural opportunities as city residents: *...farm families felt that they weren't keeping up with the urban population, which had electric lights, telephones, and access to the latest goods in department stores. Farm families were isolated, often with limited funds, and few could afford the time or the expense of shopping in the city.*
    ✓ Agree: Mail–order companies changed the lives of farm families across the country: *This contact with the outside world broke their isolation and changed the outlook of rural America. Thanks to the mail–order houses of Montgomery Ward and Sears and Roebuck, no farm was too isolated to be aware of the latest clothing, furniture, farm equipment, music, and literature.*
    ✓ Disagree: Clothing ordered from mail–order catalogs was more fashionable than clothing bought in department stores: *Sears didn't pretend to be a leader in fashion, but it did try to provide what average Americans wanted.*
    ✓ Agree: The Sears catalog provided an important illustration of American life: *And for immigrants who wanted to become Americans, the Sears catalog was a textbook. Here they learned how to dress, how to furnish their homes, and...how to cook American food.* (2.4)

18. B The speakers mainly discuss factors that affect the color of water. The student asks *...why is water blue, like blue glass?* The tutor says *It's because water transmits light of every color, but it's clearest for colors with shorter wavelengths; Well, there are actually lots of factors that affect the color of water.* (2.1)

19. A The student means that she does not believe that water is colorless. She *was taught that water doesn't have a color*, but her *own eyes* tell her *otherwise*. Her eyes tell her that water does have a color. (2.4)

20. D The student's purpose is to check her understanding of what the tutor said. She says *So, that means....* Then she repeats the tutor's explanation in her own words to check whether she understands correctly. (2.3)

21. B, C One factor that influences the color of water is its depth: *...there are actually lots of factors that affect the color of water; Such as...how deep the water is?; Right.* Another factor is sediments in the water: *That's another factor that affects the color of water—sediments. Even the cleanest, purest mountain lake contains a lot of tiny particles that scatter light.* (2.2)

22. C The tutor says *Lakes fed by glaciers get their colors from the fine, suspended silt in the water...; Some water is green and some is brown, depending on the mineral content.* You can infer that a lake with brown water contains suspended particles. (2.4)

23. D The professor says *Throughout most of human history, a society's culture was defined and communicated primarily through the family; Parents and grandparents had the job of passing on the culture's history and traditions.* (2.2)

24. B By "cultural narrator," the professor means the medium that conveys a culture's values and beliefs. The professor says *The cultural narrator helped to sustain the society through the preservation of vital cultural information. Until the mid–twentieth century, the family was the medium by which culture was passed along.* (2.4)

25. A The professor says *He couldn't figure out their interests and values, why they spoke and acted and felt the way they did. So, he set out to learn more about the values of his students by studying their popular culture....* (2.2)

26. D The professor's opinion is that *The Medium is the Message* will influence how the students think about communication. The professor says *It's a book—and an idea—that you'll come back to over and over again, and reading it will probably change your view of how we communicate.* (2.3)

27. B The professor's purpose is to explain an important theory of communications, specifically the meaning of McLuhan's theory that the medium is the message. (2.3)

28. C The professor implies that the media's effects are of widespread interest and concern. The professor says that researchers are interested in the effects of television on human behavior. He says *...there are a growing number of issues and new questions* that require study of *the relationship of the media to human development.* (2.4)

29. B The professor mainly discusses how farm products are supplied to consumers. The professor says *Marketing is supplying people with goods and services—what people want, in the form they want it, and when they want it; Marketing links the producer with the consumer; The focus of agricultural marketing technology is on meeting consumer demand.* (2.1)

30. D The professor's purpose is to explain why agricultural marketing technology is necessary. Agricultural marketing technology meets consumer demand by getting farm products ready for consumers and delivering the products in the form and quantities that consumers want, when consumers want them. (2.3)

31. A, D Picking cotton and milking cows are examples of the marketing function of harvesting: *Harvesting includes a wide variety of activities—for example, ...picking cotton, ...milking cows....* (2.2)

32. A The professor says *A very important function that comes after harvesting is assembling; Assembling is gathering large quantities together to make marketing more efficient. Marketing professionals want to deal with large volumes, and some farms don't have large enough volumes, so they have to combine their product with the product of other farms.* (2.2)

33. B The professor says *Another function is grading, which is sorting products for uniformity; When people buy eggs, they kind of want a uniform size—not a mixture of small, medium, and large eggs.* (2.2)

34. B The professor's purpose is to illustrate the function of transporting, *moving the product from one place to another.* (2.3)

SPEAKING (*p. 151*)

1. Responses will vary. (3.1–3.4)
2. Responses will vary. (3.1–3.4)
3. Key points:
    - The university is raising the credit requirements in mathematics and writing. The woman supports the new requirements.
    - One reason she gives is that the dean thinks students need more math and writing, and the dean knows what he is talking about.
    - Another reason is that businesses need good mathematics and writing skills; these skills affect a company's reputation.
    - Another reason is that graduate schools want good writers because graduate students have to do a lot of writing. (3.5–3.7, 3.10)
4. Key points:
    - The whiskers of a cat are long, stiff, coarse, highly touch–sensitive hairs on the cat's face (lips, cheeks, and chin) that are twice as thick as the hairs in the cat's coat.
    - The whiskers are sensory receptors that can detect the slightest movement, including air currents. The whiskers provide the brain with information on the cat's surroundings.
    - The cat uses its whiskers to sense and investigate close objects. The whiskers can detect air currents deflected by objects—the reason that the cat can feel its way around in the dark without touching objects. (3.5–3.7, 3.10)
5. Key points:
    - The woman's problem is that she would like to go to a special event (panel discussion) that evening, but she already has plans to meet with her tutor and study for a test.
    - The man suggests that she try to change the meeting time with her tutor.
    - The man suggests that she find someone with a VCR who can record the panel discussion for her. (3.8, 3.10)
6. Key points:
    - One type of learning disability is dyslexia, in which a child perceives the letters in words as backwards, upside down, or sideways. This disability affects the child's ability to learn to read and write.
    - A second learning disability is difficulty with translating thoughts into writing. This disability causes a child to become blocked and unable to write, to write very slowly, to have poor handwriting, or to have difficulty with spelling.
    - A third learning disability is attention deficit disorder, the inability to focus on a task for a long period of time. This disability causes a child to have trouble sitting still, paying attention, and controlling impulses.
    - Learning disabilities affect a child's ability to keep up with classmates, to remember, and to concentrate. Learning disabilities cause problems with reading, writing, and math skills. (3.9, 3.10)

Writing (p. 157)

1. Key points:
    - The lecture compares music to spoken language regarding sound system, syntax, and change over time.
    - The lecture states that music is a sound sequence made up of separate, ordered parts: chords, measures, phrases, and tunes. This is similar to the point in the reading that spoken language is a sequence of sounds consisting of separate, ordered parts: syllables, words, phrases, clauses, and sentences.
    - The lecture states that the sound system of a musical language defines and limits musical sounds. This is similar to the point in the reading that the sound system of each language restricts the number of acceptable sounds.
    - Music has syntax, relationships between parts, to control and order the flow of sound and to allow us to process it. This is similar to the point in the reading that language has syntax to organize and control information, and to express relationships.
    - Music changes and evolves over time, and different musical languages can influence each other. This is similar to the point in the reading that language changes over time, and a language can adopt foreign words or mix with another language. (4.1–4.5)
2. Responses will vary. (4.6–4.10)

TEST 4

Reading (p. 161)

1. B Before information can be stored in memory, an object or idea must be perceived. Clues: *…an immediate sensory perception of an object or idea that occurs before the image is stored.* (1.1)
2. C One difference between short–term memory and long–term memory is the amount of information they hold. Clues: *Short–term memory and long–term memory can be thought of as memory structures, each varying as to how much information it can hold….* (1.1)
3. B *Attend to* means *focus on* in this context. Clues: *…recognize…; …meaningful or relevant….* Information must be recognized as meaningful if it is to be processed further. If you do not focus on the information as being meaningful or relevant, it will not be stored in memory. (1.4)
4. A You can infer that something is not likely to be remembered if it is not considered important. Clues: *Information that you do not selectively attend to will disappear from the system. However, if you recognize and attend to the information as meaningful or relevant, it is sent to short–term memory.* (1.5)
5. D Information can be lost from short–term memory when a person is distracted for 20 seconds. Clues: *…were then distracted by something else for 20 seconds, you probably would have forgotten the number at that point.* (1.1)
6. B *Make it to* means *arrive at* in this context. Clues: *…unless the information is processed further, it is quickly forgotten; Unless information in short–term memory is processed further, it does not make it to long–term memory.* If something is not processed any more, it disappears or is forgotten; thus, it does not arrive at long–term memory. (1.4)
7. A *The purpose behind such behavior is usually…* is paraphrased in *Usually information is rehearsed so…; …to memorize information for later use…* is paraphrased in *…so it can be used later…; …although sometimes it is simply to hold information in short–term memory for immediate use* is paraphrased in *…but sometimes it is rehearsed so it can be used right away.* (1.7)
8. B The author's purpose is to give an example of knowledge already stored in long–term memory. "Card sense" is the previously learned information about other card games, which is stored in long–term memory. Clues: *…association of new data with data previously learned and stored in long–term memory; …"card sense" from playing other games.* (1.6)
9. C The referent of *They* is something that affects whether you process information for short–term or long–term storage. The subject of the previous sentence is *interests, attitudes, skills, and knowledge of the world.* Logic tells you that *They* refers to *interests, attitudes, skills, and knowledge of the world.* (1.3)

10. A Deciding that information is not meaningful or relevant does not enhance the transfer of information from short–term memory to long–term memory; in fact, it decreases the likelihood of the information being sent to memory at all. All of the other answers are given: *Several control processes enable the transfer of information from short–term to long–term memory. One such process is rehearsal... Rehearsal is when you repeat something to yourself over and over; Another process that enables the transfer of information to long–term memory is the association of new data with data previously learned and stored in long–term memory; ...skill memory usually involves motor activities that you learn by repetition....* (1.2)

11. B You can infer that skill memory exists in long–term memory because of repeated practice. Clues: *Long–term memory...; ...holds skills such as knowing how to ride a bicycle; ...skill memory usually involves motor activities that you learn by repetition....* (1.5)

12. A The added sentence introduces the topic of *the types of information stored* in long–term memory. The next two sentences develop this topic with details: *...recollections of personal experiences...; ...factual knowledge acquired through other means...; ...skills....* (1.8)

13. B, F, H Short–term Memory: *Short–term memory reflects an immediate sensory perception of an object or idea that occurs before the image is stored; Short–term memory is often called working memory because it holds information that you are working with at a given moment, but only for about 20 seconds; Short–term memory can hold approximately seven unrelated bits of information at a time.*

A, D, E, I Long–term Memory: *...the storage capacity of long–term memory is unlimited and contains a permanent record of everything you have learned; Long–term memory plays an influential role throughout the information processing system; ...influence what you perceive and how you interpret your perceptions; Long–term memory can hold recollections of personal experiences as well as factual knowledge....* Answer (C) describes the sensory register; answer (G) describes any of the senses. (1.10)

14. A *The world market...was confined to the coasts and along rivers...* is paraphrased in *International trade had to take place near oceans and rivers...; ...and its effects were rarely felt a hundred miles inland* is paraphrased in *...and did not extend to interior regions.* (1.7)

15. D *Zenith* means *high point* in this context. Clues: *...the main instrument...; The age of sailing ships reached its zenith...the era of the great ocean–plying clippers that carried the majority of international trade.* (1.4)

16. B The need to move large quantities of coal led to an increase in canal building. Clues: *...it was the demands of the Industrial Revolution, particularly the need to transport huge quantities of coal, that stimulated large–scale canal building....* (1.1)

17. A *Impetus* means *push* in this context. Clues: *...the demands of the Industrial Revolution...; ...stimulated large–scale canal building...; ...an additional impetus to river navigation and canal construction.* (1.4)

18. D A reason given for the rise of the steamship over the sailing ship was that technical advances made the steamship require less coal. Clues: *The steamship rose in stature in the 1870s, when technical progress reduced the amount of coal the steam engine consumed. Technical innovation... enabled the steamship to surpass the sailing ship as the chief instrument of international trade.* (1.1)

19. C *Boom* means *rapid growth* in this context. Clues: *...slow, uncertain, and expensive until...; In 1840 there were 5,500 miles of rail track throughout the world; just twenty years later, there were 66,000 miles.* (1.4)

20. B The referent of *these* is something of which 50 percent were in North America and 47 percent were in Europe. The previous sentence discusses the *miles of rail track* in the world. Logic tells you that *these* refers to *miles of rail track.* (1.3)

21. D A major result of railroad building in the nineteenth century was that large parts of the world became populated and economically developed. Clues: *...the building of railroads remained...the main method of developing new territories; The U.S. transcontinental railroad played a key role in populating and developing huge tracts of land in North America, as did the Trans–Siberian Railway in Asia.* (1.1)

22. C The author's purpose is to give an example of an innovation that expanded markets. Clues: *...opened huge markets for meat, dairy products, and fruit in North America and Europe.* (1.6)

23. C The passage does not state that population decline in major cities was an effect of the transportation revolution. All of the other answers are given: *The expansion of economic activity...and its spread...; ...was largely accomplished through a revolution in transportation...; ...inventions that made railroads a leading source of technical innovation in the nineteenth century; ...the railroad...the steamship; ...these two innovations...; ...the effect of increasing the size of markets as well as the amount of economic activity worldwide.* (1.2)

24. B You can infer that the author believes improvements in transportation had a direct impact on world economics. Clues: *The expansion of economic activity into the interior...was a major development of the nineteenth century. It was largely accomplished through a revolution in transportation...; In the course of the nineteenth century, around 9 million square miles of land were settled in North and South America and Oceania. This was made possible by the decline in transportation costs...; ...the rise of the railroad...the steamship; Both had the effect of increasing the size of markets as well as the amount of economic activity worldwide.* (1.5)

25. A The added sentence introduces the topic of how railroad construction was financed. The rest of the paragraph develops this topic with facts and details: *...private companies...; ...a concern of the state...; British capital financed the majority of the railroads....* (1.8)

26. B, C, F Key information: *...it was the demands of the Industrial Revolution...that stimulated large-scale canal building...; The introduction of steamboats gave an additional impetus to river navigation and canal construction; ...the steamship to surpass the sailing ship as the chief instrument of international trade; ...the building of railroads remained...the main method of developing new territories; ...the adoption of steel rails, electric signals, compressed–air brakes, and other inventions that made railroads a leading source of technical innovation....* Answers (A) and (D) are minor ideas; answer (E) is not mentioned. (1.9)

27. A *Fostered* means *inspired* in this context. Clues: *...a rugged landscape...; ...her passion for nature, animals, and painting; ...decided to become an artist....* The British Columbia landscape inspired Carr and became the subject of her paintings. (1.4)

28. C The author does not connect birth into a family of artists to Emily Carr's early interest in art. All of the other answers are given: *...a rugged landscape that fostered her passion for nature, animals, and painting; ...she supported herself by teaching children's art classes...; Early in life, Carr developed an interest in painting the aboriginal culture....* (1.2)

29. D Fishing villages and totem poles are subjects that Carr painted frequently. Clues: *Her paintings of the First Nations people documented their fishing villages, totem poles...; ...a series of totem poles painted in a bold style....* (1.1)

30. B The author points out that Carr's sketching trips to the forest were uncommon for a woman. Clues: *...Carr returned to the aboriginal villages to sketch and paint. These camping trips were unusual for a woman of her time....* (1.1)

31. C The author means that Carr needed to experience her subjects directly. Clues: *...with all of her senses alert; ...drew inspiration from the cold, raw dampness of the coast, the sounds of the forest, and the sting of the smoke from campfires—experiences....* (1.4)

32. D The author's purpose is to show that the exhibition established Carr's national reputation as an artist. Clues: *Carr began to receive national recognition in 1927. At her first major exhibition outside of British Columbia...; The Toronto exhibition was a turning point for Carr, establishing her reputation as a leading figure in Canadian art.* (1.6)

33. C The referent of *them* is something that Carr had lived deeply and which were still fresh in her mind. The sentence states that Carr *recounted her days as Klee Wyck* forty years earlier. Logic tells you that *them* refers to *her days as Klee Wyck.* (1.3)

34. D *Credit* means *praise* in this context. Clues: *...recognized Carr...; ...raising Canadian art to a new height; ...combined to produce a vision....* In general, the passage praises Carr's contributions to Canadian art. (1.4)

35. B *Carr's paintings endure as visual icons that Canadians can most easily associate with an individual artist...* is paraphrased in *...her paintings are instantly recognized as hers; ...for this reason she is the best–known woman artist in Canadian history* is paraphrased in *Emily Carr remains Canada's most famous woman artist because...* (1.7)

36. B Emily Carr's paintings were unique because she painted regional subjects in a bold and transcendental style. Clues: *...a series of totem poles painted in a bold style as Carr attempted to capture the spirit of the scene that would transcend its physical reality; ...a powerful and unique visual landscape that captured the transcendental qualities of the wilderness; The subjects Carr chose to paint, the region of the country in which she painted, and her own ideas about art combined to produce a vision that distinguished her from other artists.* (1.1)

37. A You can infer that the author believes Emily Carr deserves her position in Canadian cultural history. Clues: *She combined modernism with aboriginal form and color to create a powerful and unique visual landscape that captured the transcendental qualities of the wilderness; ...her first book, Klee Wyck...united art and literature in a highly original way...; The subjects Carr chose to paint, the region of the country in which she painted, and her own ideas about art combined to produce a vision that distinguished her from other artists; ...she is the best–known woman artist in Canadian history.* (1.5)

38. D In the added sentence, *Her later paintings* refers to *the monumental paintings of totem poles that are her best–known works*, mentioned in the previous sentence. The added sentence compares her later paintings to her earlier works, which further develops the idea that *Carr revisited her earlier themes*, mentioned in the previous sentence. The next sentence further develops the topic of her later paintings. (1.8)

39. B, D, E Key information: *...developed an interest in painting the aboriginal culture of British Columbia; Her paintings of the First Nations people documented their fishing villages, totem poles, and life in the forest; ...she began to write stories about the beautiful, calm places of her earlier life among her aboriginal friends; ...monumental paintings of totem poles that are her best–known works; ...a powerful and unique visual landscape that captured the transcendental qualities of the wilderness; The subjects Carr chose to paint...and her own ideas about art combined to produce a vision that distinguished her from other artists.* Answers (A) and (C) are minor ideas; answer (F) is not mentioned. (1.9)

LISTENING (*p. 174*)

1. A, C The students discuss how they feel about their classes. The woman asks *How do you like your classes this semester?* The man replies *Not bad, I guess. Thermodynamics is the hardest.* The man asks *How are your classes?* The woman replies *Pretty good, actually. All of my professors are great, and I really like my discussion class in Russian history.* The students also discuss not having enough time to study. The man says *It takes a long time for me to do the problems, and then I don't have enough time to do the reading for English and history. There just aren't enough hours in a day.* The woman says *I hear you; ...I'd end up working 25 hours a week. I never had enough time to study.* (2.1)
2. C The woman's purpose is to agree that lack of time is a problem. The man says *There just aren't enough hours in a day.* The woman replies *I hear you*, an expression of agreement. (2.3)
3. B The woman says *I like the discussions because we can go beyond the lecture and the reading; ...I get a lot out of the discussions. I think I learn more, you know, when I get a chance to talk about Russian history. I certainly remember more of the details. And that sure helped me on the first test.* (2.2)
4. D The man says *...I've never cared for discussion classes. I prefer the lecture format. I'd rather listen to my professor than to my classmates.* (2.3)
5. B The man suggests that the woman find out more about a job opening. He says *Hey, I know just the job for you! I saw—there's a notice on the job board in the Student Center—I just saw it today. There's a job opening for host of the graduate student lounge.* (2.4)
6. A The professor mainly discusses the role of ethylene in plant aging processes. The professor says *Several of the processes related to growth and aging in plants involve the effects of hormones. Today I'll talk about two aging processes—the ripening of fruit and the falling of leaves in autumn. These processes involve a hormone called ethylene.* (2.1)
7. D The professor says *Ethylene is unique among plant hormones because it's the only hormone that's a gas.* (2.2)
8. A, C One effect of ethylene is that fruit becomes softer as it ripens: *One example of the aging process is the ripening of fruit. The ripening of fruit involves several changes in structure and metabolism; One change is the weakening of cell walls, which softens the fruit.* Another effect is that trees shed their leaves in the fall: *Another aging process in plants where ethylene plays a role is the falling of leaves in autumn* (2.2)
9. C The professor's purpose is to summarize the chain reaction of ripening. The release of ethylene causes fruit to ripen, which then causes the release of more ethylene, which then causes the ripening to spread from fruit to fruit. Thus, one bad (rotten) apple causes other apples to spoil, as the signal to ripen increases and spreads. (2.3)
10. ✓ Yes: The decrease in chlorophyll causes fruit to lose its greenness and become ripe: *...the decrease in chlorophyll content, which causes the fruit to lose its greenness.*
    ✓ Yes: Apples in storage bins are flushed with carbon dioxide to keep the air circulating: *...storage facilities have to slow down the ripening caused by natural ethylene. For example, apples are stored in bins that are flushed with carbon dioxide. Circulating the air with carbon dioxide prevents ethylene from accumulating....*
    ✓ No: A tree's roots grow hairs that help it absorb water from the soil: Not supported by the information in the lecture.
    ✓ Yes: Weakened cell walls at the base of a leaf cause the leaf to break away: *As the influence of ethylene becomes stronger, the cells start producing enzymes that weaken the cell walls of the breaking layer. Finally, with the help of wind or rain, the leaf breaks away at that layer and falls from the tree.* (2.6)
11. B The professor implies that both hormones and environmental factors cause leaves to fall. The falling of leaves involves the hormones *ethylene and auxin*. Environmental factors such as *wind or rain* also play a role. (2.4)
12. A, D The professor says *A manager has the ability to set goals, and then to accomplish what he or she sets out to do. Business managers shoot for results. This means that once you set your business plan and budget for the year, you have to achieve the sales, the market share, the earnings—whatever you set out to do.* (2.2)
13. A The professor's purpose is to illustrate what a good manager does. The professor says *But good managers have to adjust to changing circumstances. ...but let me share a story I tell all my students. It's about two promising young people of equal intelligence and ability. Both are college students, and both want to go on to a top graduate school of business.* (2.3)
14. C The professor implies that May allowed events to keep her from reaching her goal. The professor says *But then one year she gets the flu before final exams, and she performs poorly on her exams; But something always happens to wreck May's plans.* (2.4)
15. B The professor says *After trying several different approaches—studying harder, reading more, asking for help—what she ends up doing is finding a graduate student to tutor her. She works long and thinks hard. And, of course, you know the end of the story: Kay gets her A.* You can infer that Kay illustrates the point that success is possible if you keep trying. (2.4)
16. D The professor wants a more satisfactory response from the class. The professor asks *Now, what kind of manager is each student*, but the students do not answer the question sufficiently. The professor repeats the question by asking *But who's the better manager: May or Kay?* After that, the students give more satisfactory responses to the professor's question. (2.3)

17. B The professor means that Kay set goals and achieved results, as managers do. The professor's main point is that managers set goals and achieve results, and Kay's actions illustrate this. The professor says *She had grasped the essentials of good business management—not because she worked so hard, but because when one action failed, she tried another, and another, until she achieved her goal. That is what managers do.* (2.4)

18. B The student would like the professor's advice about a research project. The student says ...*Student Activities is trying to find out what students think about the different events we sponsor. So I'm designing a study for them, and I was wondering if I could get your advice.* (2.3)

19. A The student says *Well, like I said, we want to find out what students like and don't like about our events—like the concerts we have, the masquerade ball, the spring picnic, and so on.* (2.2)

20. B The professor says *A survey can be highly structured and doesn't require a face–to–face situation, so that's an advantage. You could do a survey in the form of a printed questionnaire, or you could also do it over the telephone.* (2.2)

21. C The professor's purpose is to give examples of poll questions. The professor says ...*a poll is much simpler in design. A poll is simply a headcount. The respondents are presented with a limited number of options.* Then she gives examples of poll questions. (2.3)

22. B, D The professor helps the student by recommending a useful book: ...*there's an excellent book that explains the pluses and minuses of each of these methods. It's called How to Measure Attitudes....* The professor also agrees to review the student's survey draft. The student asks ...*if we decide to go with a printed survey...would you be willing to look at my draft first?* The professor replies *Of course. You could just slip it into my mailbox, or stop by anytime during my office hours.* (2.2)

23. B The professor mainly discusses changes in roles and responsibilities during adulthood. The professor says *We all change over the course of our adulthood; A lot of the changes in adulthood involve social relationships and responsibilities.* (2.1)

24. D The professor's purpose is to respond to a student's question. The student asks ...*is what you're talking about—I mean these changes we experience—are they part of our biological clock?* The professor replies *I'm glad you brought up the biological clock.* (2.3)

25. A The professor's purpose is to explain the concept of age norms. He says *Virtually all societies are organized into age strata, periods in life with norms for...expectations, demands, social roles and responsibilities.* Then he illustrates age norms by mentioning our different expectations of *20–year–olds, 40–year–olds, and 70–year–olds.* (2.3)

26. B The professor implies that an adult's status may be determined by age norms. Age norms are different expectations of and attitudes toward different age groups. The professor illustrates age norms by stating *For example, an older adult might be seen as having more—or less—status than a young adult....* (2.4)

27. ✓ Early adulthood: The roles of spouse and parent generally begin now: *Young adults also acquire the role of spouse, as most first marriages occur during early adulthood. A major new role is that of parent.*

✓ Middle adulthood: This period is sometimes called the "sandwich generation": *This is the "sandwich generation," because people in middle adulthood are sandwiched between the needs of their children and the needs of their aging parents.*

✓ Early adulthood: People gain more new roles now than at any other time: *Early adulthood is when more new social roles are acquired than at any other time of life.*

✓ Late adulthood: There is a decline in the number of social roles: *Late adulthood is normally marked by a decline in the number of social roles.* (2.5)

28. B The professor says *They follow the basic pattern of adulthood. By this I mean, they add new roles in early adulthood, change roles in middle adulthood, and shed roles in late adulthood.* (2.2)

29. B The professor describes features and forms of Baroque music. The professor says *One of the most striking features of the Baroque style is its expressiveness; Baroque music is known for its virtuoso instrumental music; It was in the Baroque era that some of the forms we know today began to take shape: the opera, the sonata, and the concerto; The music is characterized by its dazzling virtuosity and ornamentation.* (2.1)

30. A, D Baroque music is characterized by its expression of emotion: *One of the most striking features of the Baroque style is its expressiveness. Baroque music is a vigorous style combining imagination with great feeling.* Complex ornamentation is another characteristic: ...*Baroque music has more ornament. Trills and grace notes—little twists on notes...; The music is characterized by its dazzling virtuosity and ornamentation.* (2.2)

31. A The professor's purpose is to explain how new musical forms developed. The rise of instrumental music freed music from having to move to speech rhythms. The professor names new musical forms that emerged: *the opera, the sonata, and the concerto.* (2.3) .

32. C The professor's purpose is to illustrate how different instruments helped to tell a story. The professor says *With these instruments, Monteverdi told the Greek legend of Orpheus. The instruments dramatized the story's characters and plot. For example, the high flute and a small violin accompanied the shepherd, brasses and organ music suggested the underworld, and so forth.* (2.3)

33. D The professor means that Baroque musicians created new musical forms to display their ability. The *concerto and the sonata* were new musical forms that allowed *musicians to show off their skills*, or to display their ability. (2.4)

34. C The professor's opinion is that *The Four Seasons* are perfect examples of Baroque music. The professor says *They are pure, quintessential Baroque music—descriptive, expressive, elaborate—and with virtuoso violin playing.* (2.3)

35. C The student wants a recommendation from the professor. The student says *...I've decided to apply to the teacher certification program, and I wondered—I'd like it if you would, um, recommend me for the program.* (2.3)

36. B The student says *...I've known for a long time that I wanted to be a teacher, ever since I was in sixth grade myself. I loved science when I was a kid—still love science—and ... I guess I, um, want to share my love of science with kids.* (2.2)

37. B The student's purpose is to describe her experience in working with children. The student says *I've worked with kids before—as a camp counselor for two summers—teaching nature classes and leading nature hikes and stuff like that—and I just had so much fun with the kids! I think I'm a pretty good counselor, and I love being in the woods myself.* (2.3)

38. A The professor is thinking about what he will say in the recommendation. The student has asked for a recommendation, so the professor asks her to talk about what she did in his course. He wants the student to remind him of her work so that he can *get a handle on it*, or remember what she did so he can write about it in the recommendation. (2.3)

39. D The student talks about a report she gave in the professor's class, and the professor says *Yes, I recall. Your report was very well done. I remember it well, and I'll mention it in my letter.* You can infer that he will include a description of the student's research report in the form that he fills out. (2.4)

40. C The main purpose of the lecture is to explain how one animal, the red–sided garter snake, survives in its environment. The professor says *Animals interact with their environment in a number of ways...; The migration of garter snakes to the limestone pits is an example of a behavioral mechanism for dealing with seasonal variations in temperature. Moving to a new location is an animal's quickest response to an unfavorable change in the environment. By gathering in a mass below the frost line, the snakes are able to survive the harsh prairie winter.* (2.3)

41. B, C The professor discusses the network of limestone caves: *The limestone pits in Manitoba's Interlake region are like nothing else in the world.* He also discusses the concentration of garter snakes: *This is the world's largest concentration of snakes. Tens of thousands of these snakes congregate at the surface of their winter dens each year.* (2.2)

42. D The professor's purpose is to explain why so many snakes live in the region. The snakes are drawn to the region because the limestone pits provide *winter dens* where they can escape the cold winter temperatures, making the region *an ideal home* for them. (2.3)

43. C The professor says *The migration of garter snakes to the limestone pits is an example of a behavioral mechanism for dealing with seasonal variations in temperature; By gathering in a mass below the frost line, the snakes are able to survive the harsh prairie winter.* (2.2)

44. B The professor means that the snakes can survive a night of freezing temperatures. The snakes have the *ability to endure short freezes*, which means they can tolerate freezing temperatures for a short time. This ability *will get them through till morning*, which means the snakes can survive for one night. (2.4)

45. B The professor implies that temperature plays an important role in the snakes' behavior. Temperature causes a *physiological–behavioral response* in the snakes. Freezing temperatures are a *signal* for the snakes *to alter their behavior, to move and find a warmer place.* (2.4)

46. B, D The arch was an important development because wide openings could be spanned without using wood: *The invention of the arch made it possible to span wide openings without large timbers.* Also, the arch led to a larger variety of buildings: *They perfected a system of arch and vault construction. As a result, a larger variety of buildings appeared, each with a form suited to its function.* (2.2)

47. A The professor implies that the arch contributed to the success of these projects. The public works projects of the Romans all *utilized the arch.* The arch enabled the Romans to *supply their vast public baths and fill the water needs of their citizens.* (2.4)

48. C The professor says *The block at the highest point—the center of the arch—is called the keystone. The keystone is the most important block because it holds the other blocks in place. The keystone locks the other stones together.* (2.2)

49. B The professor says *The round arch is extremely strong and stable. It's primarily the wedge shape of the blocks that gives the arch its stability. The wedge–shaped blocks are locked together tightly, transferring their weight downward on either side.* (2.2)

50. B The professor's purpose is to define the concept of lateral thrust. Lateral thrust is the sideways pressure that supports the arch on each side. (2.3)

51. D The professor says *...behind all that beautiful brickwork is a system of steel beams. The beams are doing the real work of holding up the building. The brick arches are just for show. Steel beams for wide spans have reduced the arch to a mostly decorative function.* (2.2)

SPEAKING (p. 193)

1. Responses will vary. (3.1–3.4)
2. Responses will vary. (3.1–3.4)
3. Key points:
    - The man is thinking of applying to be a resident assistant (RA). The woman does not support this idea.
    - One reason she gives is that her friend was an RA, and the position took a lot of her time because other students interrupted her often, so she could not study in her room.
    - Another reason is that the stress of being an RA had a negative effect on her schoolwork.
    - Another reason is that RAs have other related duties, which could mean almost anything. (3.5–3.7, 3.10)
4. Key points:
    - Studies of the ice in Greenland show us that climate change has occurred in cycles but also challenge theories that climate change has always been gradual.
    - The ice cores are evidence of a flickering climate: sudden swings from warm to cold, and back again within a short period.
    - The layers in the ice tell the history of the ice ages on Earth.
    - The ice cores show that there was a period of global warming in the past, and that this warming occurred very rapidly in several sudden jumps.
    - The ice cores show that the change from the latest ice age to the present warm period might have taken less than a human lifetime, rather than occurring gradually over thousands of years. (3.5–3.7, 3.10)
5. Key points:
    - The man's problem is that the bus company is going to cancel the bus that goes to his neighborhood, so he will have no way to get to school.
    - One possible solution is to carpool with another student who drives a car.
    - Another solution is to move closer to campus. (3.8, 3.10)
6. Key points:
    - Food preservation prevents or slows the natural decay that is caused by microorganisms (bacteria, molds, and yeasts) in the food.
    - Drying is a method in which food is exposed to warm air. Drying removes water in the food that would otherwise cause it to spoil. The microorganisms that cause spoilage need water to grow, so removing the water will stop the microorganisms from growing.
    - Curing is a method in which ingredients such as salt, sugar, spices, or lemon juice are added to food. Salt slows the growth of microorganisms and removes some of the water from the food. Sugar counteracts the hardening that salt may cause. Lemon or lime juice preserves raw fish for a short time without removing all the moisture. (3.9, 3.10)

WRITING (p. 199)

1. Key points:
    - The lecture states that the philosophy of realism ignores passion, emotion, and feeling, which are parts of the total human experience. This contradicts the point in the reading that beliefs, passions, and emotions are soft data, which we can not prove with certainty.
    - The lecture states that such things as passions, feelings, and the psychological causes of poverty cannot be measured scientifically or reduced to mathematics. This contradicts the point in the reading that anything that exists can be measured scientifically and verified mathematically.
    - The lecture states that realism has led to an educational system based on standardized tests, which dehumanize people because they do not respect passion, emotion, and feeling. This contradicts the point in the reading that realist philosophy and scientific methods can achieve excellence in education.
    - The lecture states that the realist ideal of our technological society shows little respect for the unity of knowledge, mentioning that scientists might work on biological weapons without knowing it. This contradicts the point in the reading that realism and scientific methods can lead us to the creation of an ideal society. (4.1–4.5)
2. Responses will vary. (4.6–4.10)

TEST 5

Reading (*p. 203*)

1. A *Population ecology is…concerned…with…* is paraphrased in *…can be studied in population ecology; …not…solely with the human population* is paraphrased in *Any species of life…* (1.7)
2. C A large number of other species competing for food might cause the population of a species to decrease in size. Clues: *Factors that decrease populations are…too many competitors for resources….* (1.1)
3. B The number of nests in a given area is an indirect indicator of a population's density. Clues: *…indirect indicators, such as the number of nests….* (1.1)
4. D The distribution pattern of individuals within a population's geographical boundaries is called population dispersion. Clues: *…dispersion, is the pattern of spacing among individuals within the population's geographical boundaries.* (1.1)
5. A *Range* means *territory* in this context. Clues: *…within the population's geographical boundaries; …habitats…; …areas….* (1.4)
6. D *Patches* means *small areas* in this context. Clues: *...gathered...; clumped under logs...; …swarm in great numbers...; …swim in large schools....* A patch is a small piece or part of something; in this context, it is a small part of a habitat. (1.4)
7. C The referent of *their* is something that likes the humidity under logs. The clause states that many forest insects are clumped under logs. Logic tells you that *their* refers to *forest insects.* (1.3)
8. B The passage does not give territorial disputes as a reason for clumping. All of the other answers are given: *Clumping often results from the irregular distribution of resources…; Clumping may also be associated with mating, safety… Crane flies, for example, swarm in great numbers, a behavior that increases mating chances, and some fish swim in large schools so they are less likely to be eaten by predators.* (1.2)
9. B *Set up* means *establish* in this context. Clues: *…uniform distribution is usually caused…by social interactions that set up individual territories for feeding, breeding, or resting.* Animals establish territories that result in uniform spacing of individuals. (1.4)
10. A You can infer that birds competing for a place to build their nests would probably result in a uniform dispersion pattern. Clues: *In animal populations, uniform distribution is usually caused by competition for some resource or by social interactions that set up individual territories for feeding, breeding, or resting.* (1.5)
11. A The author's purpose is to identify factors affecting population dispersion. Clues: *…by emigrating from one area and immigrating to another with more favorable environmental conditions, thus altering the population's dispersion.* (1.6)
12. D In the added sentence, *For example* is a transition that introduces the example of one of the *sampling techniques to estimate densities and total population sizes*, mentioned in the previous sentence. In the added sentence, *they* refers to *Ecologists* in a previous sentence. (1.8)
13. A, B, E Key information: *The characteristics of a population are shaped by its size and by the interactions among individuals and between individuals and their environment; An important characteristic of any population is its density; Another important population characteristic, dispersion…; Three possible patterns of dispersion are clumped, uniform, and random; …often results from the irregular distribution of resources…; …may also be associated with mating, safety, or other social behavior; Populations change in size, structure, and distribution as they respond to changes in environmental conditions.* Answers (C) and (D) are minor ideas; answer (F) is not mentioned. (1.9)
14. C The author means that many technologies were very influential. Clues: *Communication technology influences the ways in which we think about the world. It changes the things we think about….* (1.4)
15. A You can infer that certain advances in technology have greatly changed communication. Clues: *Communication technology influences…; It changes…; In the history of communication, there have been many revolutionary technologies….* (1.5)
16. B Writing began to have a major effect on communication when books became available. Clues: *…before books and the printing press, written language was limited…; It was not until books became available that writing made a major impact.* (1.1)
17. C The referent of *one* is something that was handwritten. The subject of the sentence is *books*. Logic tells you that *one* refers to *book.* (1.3)
18. A *The printing press opened to large groups of people…* is paraphrased in *Numerous people had access to…because of the printing press*; *…a body of information that had previously been confined to the educated few* is paraphrased in *…books and education….* (1.7)
19. D *Proliferation* means *spread* in this context. Clues: *The printing press brought books to the common people, increasing the ranks of the literate.* The prefix *pro–* = forward. (1.4)
20. B *Signaled* means *announced* in this context. Clues: *…significant revolution in communication technology began…; …invention of the telegraph… a new era in communication technology.* (1.4)
21. D The electronic era got its name from the fact that technology sent electrical signals along electrical wires. Clues: *…the electronic era—so called because the telegraph used electrical signals to carry information along an electrical wire.* (1.1)
22. B The passage does not give the computer as an example of electronic media. All of the other answers are given: *…the electronic era—so called because the telegraph used electrical signals to carry information along an electrical wire; …movies…radio….* (1.2)
23. C The author's purpose is to show that both were initially confined to a few users. Clues: *As with the earliest handwritten books, radio technology was at first restricted to the educated few….* (1.6)

24. C The added sentence introduces the idea that electronic technologies had an *ability to convey a sense of reality*. The next sentence develops this idea with the idea that *Voices or pictures could create ideas that appeared authentic*. (1.8)

25. A, D, G Printing Press: *...the printing press in the fifteenth century...; The printing press with movable type made it possible to produce hundreds of copies of a book in a single day; The printing press brought books to the common people, increasing the ranks of the literate.*

C, E Electronic Media: *The invention of the telegraph in 1843 signaled a new era in communication technology, the electronic era...; Radio was the first mass broadcast medium...; Voices or pictures....* Answers (B) and (F) describe neither the printing press nor electronic media. (1.10)

26. C You can infer that the Icelandic sagas may not be historically accurate. Clues: *...historians have long expressed skepticism about their accuracy.* (1.5)

27. B *Set eyes on* means *observe* in this context. Clues: *...discovered...; ...did not go ashore...; ...the first European to set eyes on the continent of North America.* Herjolfsson discovered the continent, but did not go ashore (walk on land). He was the first to see, or observe, North America. (1.4)

28. B Leif Eriksson was probably the first European to step on the continent of North America. Clues: *...Eriksson landed in a place he called Stoneland, which was probably the rocky, barren Labrador coast of North America.* (1.1)

29. A *Abundant* means *numerous* in this context. Clues: *...Vinland...; ...land of abundant vines and wild grapes.* Eriksson may have named the place Vinland because there were a lot of vines and grapes there. (1.4)

30. D *They established the first European colony in North America at Vinland...* is paraphrased in *Eriksson's Vinland was the first European colony in North America...; ...the precise location of which remains a subject of scholarly dispute to this day* is paraphrased in *...but scholars still disagree over exactly where it was.* (1.7)

31. C The author's purpose is to provide evidence of a plan to start a colony. Clues: *...evidently with a longer stay in mind...; ...the Norse attempt at colonization.* (1.6)

32. B *Thwarted* means *ended* in this context. Clues: *...continued threats from hostile tribes may have thwarted the Norse attempt at colonization; ...departed their settlement....* (1.4)

33. D Vinland was sometimes used as a base for fishing after Thorfinn Karlsefni's party left. Clues: *...they departed their settlement at Vinland...continued to make occasional visits there in later years, using it as a fishing camp.* (1.1)

34. C The idea that Vinland referred to a meadow led to Helge Ingstad's discovery at L'Anse aux Meadows. Clues: *Encouraged by an alternative interpretation of "vin" as meaning "meadow"....* (1.1)

35. D The referent of *those* is something found in Norse structures in Greenland and Iceland. The referent of *those* is compared to *features* in three buildings at L'Anse aux Meadows. Logic tells you that *those* refers to *features*. (1.3)

36. A The passage does not state that wild grapes were discovered at L'Anse aux Meadows. All of the other answers are given: *...sod huts...; ...sewing tools...; ...a forge...evidence of the first iron working....* (1.2)

37. B In the added sentence, *He* refers to *Eriksson* in the previous sentence. In the added sentence, the time marker *then* and the idea *then sailed south to Woodland* logically follow *landed in a place he called Stoneland* in the previous sentence. In the next sentence, *Eriksson's party finally landed in Vinland* follows the added sentence in time order. (1.8)

38. B, D, E Key information: *Eriksson's party finally landed in Vinland, where they spent a winter...; They established the first European colony in North America at Vinland...; Karlsefni and his party passed two years in Vinland...; ...a grassy site on the northern tip of Newfoundland...; ...the grassland called L'Anse aux Meadows was...certainly a Norse settlement of some kind.* Answers (A) and (F) are minor ideas; answer (C) is not mentioned. (1.9)

39. B The passage does not state that children between the ages of five and seven typically experience an interest in morality and rules. All of the other answers are given: *...the period from five to seven years old is a transition to operational thought...a new set of rational–thinking skills; ...fundamental growth in the brain and stabilization of brain–wave rhythms...; ...an increase in the rates of height acquired and weight gained.* (1.2)

40. D You can infer that cognitive development during the five–seven shift is related to biological developments in the child's brain. Clues: *Because several cognitive changes occur in children between ages five and seven, this period is called the five–seven shift. The shift is biological in nature and involves fundamental growth in the brain and stabilization of brain–wave rhythms into a basically adult pattern.* (1.5)

41. B The author's purpose is to give examples of symbols that children can understand. Clues: *...children can understand and use symbols. They have developed the ability to use words, gestures, and pictures to stand for "real life" objects....* (1.6)

42. C *Peak* means *high point* in this context. Clues: *...continues to evolve, reaching a peak...; ...become capable of concrete operations.* (1.4)

43. D A child who is capable of concrete operations can reason systematically about quantity and space. Clues: *...children become capable of concrete operations. When this happens, they can solve problems by using rational thought...; ...a new set of abilities allows children to reason systematically about the world of objects, quantity...space....* (1.1)

44. A *Hallmark* means *characteristic* in this context. Clues: *...the most widely known hallmark of the five–seven shift, an understanding of conservation....* The passage discusses several characteristics of the five–seven shift; the ability to understand conservation is a well known characteristic. (1.4)

45. D The referent of *each* is something with six coins pressed close together, beside each other on a table. The sentence discusses an experiment with *two straight rows of coins*. Logic tells you that *each* refers to *row*. (1.3)

46. A *Children younger than five years old...* is paraphrased in *Before the age of five...*; *...cannot understand conservation...* is paraphrased in *...they are incapable of understanding conservation*; *...so they invariably say that the spread–out row has more coins than the other row* is paraphrased in *...children think the longer line has more coins because....* (1.7)

47. C The author's purpose is to give a variation on a classic experiment by Piaget. In the previous paragraph, the author describes one of Piaget's classic experiments on the conservation of quantity. Then the author describes another variation of the experiment. Clues: *...there are other ways to set up the task. In a similar experiment....* (1.6)

48. A You can infer that children who easily solve the water task have already experienced the five–seven shift. Solving the task shows that they understand conservation, which means they have reached the level of development resulting from the five–seven shift. Clues: *Such experiments show a difference between children of five years and children of eight years. The older children can solve the task promptly...; The younger children...cannot do what the five–seven shift will do for them naturally....* (1.5)

49. A In the added sentence, *For instance* is a transition that introduces an example of conservation, mentioned in the previous sentence. In the added sentence, the fact that *when sand is poured back and forth between containers of different sizes and shapes, the quantity of sand does not change* illustrates the idea that *some properties stay the same despite changes in appearance*, mentioned in the previous sentence. (1.8)

50. C, G Before the Five–Seven Shift: *...the simplest forms of learning...; ...a five–year–old child is able to focus attention on only one quality of an object at a time...; Children younger than five years old cannot understand conservation....*

A, D, F After the Five–Seven Shift: *The shift is biological in nature and involves...stabilization of brain–wave rhythms in a basically adult pattern; The child also understands that objects can be rearranged and still have the same quantity...; The older children can solve the task promptly....* Answer (B) is inaccurate both before and after the five–seven shift; answer (E) is not mentioned. (1.10)

51. B The passage does not state that rotation of annual crops contributes to soil degradation. All of the other answers are given: *One important factor affecting the productivity of soils over time is agriculture; Poor management practices lead to soil compaction and soil pollution as well as loss of soil cover; One of the most critical soil quality problems related to irrigation is the increase in concentration of dissolved salts; ...unless the water drains properly, it collects underground and gradually raises the water table closer to the surface....* (1.2)

52. A *Deplete* means *reduce* in this context. Clues: *...the average quality of land has decreased, reducing potential productivity...; Crops deplete soil fertility by consuming nutrients, and this eventually reduces crop yields.* The prefix *de–* = down, away. (1.4)

53. D *Within the scientific community, there is little doubt...* is paraphrased in *Most scientists agree...*; *...that soil quality is diminishing in many areas around the world* is paraphrased in *...that soil degradation is occurring in many parts of the world.* (1.7)

54. D You can infer that annual crops and common property lands may decrease soil fertility and agricultural productivity. Clues: *The loss of soil fertility has caused a slowing in the growth of agricultural productivity; Annual crops tend to degrade soils more...common property lands generally suffer more degradation....* (1.5)

55. C Excessive buildup of salts in the soil is a serious consequence of irrigation. Clues: *...irrigation can lead to sharp drops in crop productivity in the long run by causing excessive salt buildup...; One of the most critical soil quality problems related to irrigation is the increase in concentration of dissolved salts.* (1.1)

56. A Salinization is a serious problem for agriculture because soils with high salt concentrations are destructive to crop plants. Clues: *...the increase in concentration of dissolved salts. This process, salinization...; Salt buildup can stunt crop growth, decrease yields, kill crop plants....* (1.1)

57. D *Stunt* means *limit* in this context. Clues: *Salt buildup can stunt crop growth, decrease yields, kill crop plants, and eventually make the land unproductive.* In general, salt buildup is harmful. (1.4)

58. C *Waterlogging* means that the soil holds too much water. Clues: *...farmers apply heavy amounts of irrigation water...; ...unless the water drains properly, it collects underground and gradually raises the water table closer to the surface...; ...wet deserts; ...prevents water from flowing through the ground. (1.4)*

59. B Waterlogging and salinization are related in that waterlogging raises and concentrates salts near the surface. Clues: *...unless the water drains properly, it collects underground and gradually raises the water table closer to the surface, thereby bringing salts to the surface and concentrating them* (1.1)

60. C The referent of *which* is something that is causing an increase in soil erosion rates. Logic tells you that *which* refers to *pressure* on the soil. (1.3)

61. A The author's purpose is to illustrate the effect of a small amount of erosion, only 2.5 centimeters of topsoil. Clues: *...the loss of just 2.5 centimeters of topsoil reduces corn and wheat yields by 6 percent.* (1.6)

62. D In the added sentence, *they* and *their* refer to *salts such as sodium chloride* in the previous sentence. The added sentence introduces the topic of *a number of serious problems* caused by salt buildup, which the next sentence develops with examples: *...stunt crop growth, decrease yields, kill crop plants, and eventually make the land unproductive.* (1.8)

63. C, D, F Key information: *One important factor affecting the productivity of soils over time is agriculture; Poor management practices lead to soil compaction and soil pollution as well as loss of soil cover; ...irrigation can lead to sharp drops in crop productivity in the long run by causing excessive salt buildup and rising water tables; One of the most critical soil quality problems related to irrigation is the increase in concentration of dissolved salts; Another serious soil problem is erosion...; ...the loss of just 2.5 centimeters of topsoil reduces corn and wheat yields....* Answers (A) and (E) are minor ideas; answer (B) is not mentioned. (1.9)

LISTENING (*p. 224*)

1. C The woman is inquiring about writing arts reviews for the paper. She says *...I'm interested in writing for the campus paper; I'm interested—I'd like to write arts reviews, stories about...concerts and films and events in the arts.* (2.3)
2. D The man's purpose is to inform her that the paper does not need another reviewer. The woman wants to write arts reviews, but the man says they already have *a couple of journalism students who write reviews.* He explains further by saying *You see, we're not a big paper to start out with, and the administration just cut our funding, and there are lots of students who want to write for us, so I'm afraid it's pretty competitive.* (2.3)
3. A The man means that he probably cannot offer her a job now. The woman wants to write reviews for the campus paper, but the man says he *couldn't guarantee anything (a job) at present.* He explains further by saying *...our budget was cut, and we had to reduce the size of our paper.* (2.4)
4. C The city newspaper is called *The Clarion*. The man says *If you really want to write reviews, you should send something to The Clarion; They sometimes print reviews by students.* (2.2)
5. D The woman wants to write reviews for a newspaper, and the man advises her to send some of her writing to the city newspaper, *The Clarion*. The woman says *Thanks! I really appreciate the information; Actually, I would be very interested in writing book reviews.* You can predict that she will contact the city newspaper about writing book reviews. (2.4)
6. C The professor mainly discusses what causes the auroras. The professor says *The auroras are the result of a complex interaction between the solar wind and the Earth's magnetic field. Here's what happens.* (2.1)
7. B, C Red and green are commonly seen in the auroras. The professor says *An early twentieth–century explorer wrote about the "bloody red" and "ghostly green" lights; Most of the time they're greenish–yellow, but sometimes they take colors from violet to red.* (2.2)
8. C The professor's purpose is to point out where the auroras are most visible. The professor says *They're most often seen near the North and South Poles....* (2.3)
9. A The professor's purpose is to explain how the auroras are electrical in nature. The student says *it sounds kind of like electricity*, and the professor responds by explaining how electricity is generated by the solar wind, carrying a stream of charged particles and moving across Earth's magnetic field. (2.3)
10. ✓ Yes: Oxygen and nitrogen atoms in the ionosphere become "excited": *...oxygen and nitrogen atoms in the ionosphere become "excited," or ionized.*
    ✓ No: Sunlight travels to Earth and is reflected back into space by clouds: Not mentioned in the lecture.
    ✓ Yes: Ionized atoms de–energize and emit radiation as visible light: *The auroras happen when these ionized atoms return to their normal state from their excited, energized states; ...as they do so, they emit radiation. Part of this radiation is visible light....*
    ✓ Yes: The solar wind interacts with Earth's magnetic field: *The auroras are the result of a complex interaction between the solar wind and the Earth's magnetic field.* (2.6)
11. B The professor says *Oxygen releases either dark red or ghostly green. Nitrogen emits rosy pink or magenta.* You can infer that the color of auroras is related to the type of gas involved. (2.4)
12. C The professor describes political parties in a two–party system. The professor says *The democratic institutions of these countries operate essentially on a two–party system. Why a two–party system? Or, should I say why has the two–party system prevailed in so many democratic states?; In every democratic society, there are generally two dominant parties...; The two parties have lasted so long because they have the ability to adjust to changes in events and in public opinion.* (2.1)
13. C The professor's purpose is to introduce a point that he will make. The professor's point is that the two–party system has succeeded in democratic states because *the essence of politics is debate*, so there must be another party to debate with. (2.3)
14. A The professor implies that parties make decisions based on the interests of several organizations. He says that parties *are closely associated with* various groups and organizations that *want to influence the decisions of the state*, implying that these organizations influence the decisions made by parties. (2.4)
15. ✓ No: They are a group of people who come together mainly for amusement: Not supported by the information in the lecture.
    ✓ Yes: They organize voters and compete for support on major issues: *...political parties that organize voters and compete for support on issues.*
    ✓ Yes: They are voluntary organizations of people who agree on public policies: *Political parties are voluntary organizations...made up of people who agree to some degree on public policies.*
    ✓ Yes: They have research offices that develop positions on important issues: *Parties maintain research offices and establish connections with press and citizens groups. This is how political parties develop information and thinking on major issues.* (2.5)

16. C The professor means that politics is about competition, while government is about responsibility. The professor says that politics is like a game with *winners and losers* and that politics is based on competition. However, government must be responsible, and *collaboration and compromise are necessary because the job has got to get done.* (2.4)

17. A The professor's purpose is to show how major parties usually deal with the same issues. The professor says *...the party platforms tend to balance each other in the types of issues they take up*, and he mentions education reform as an example of an issue that both parties deal with. (2.3)

18. A The students mainly discuss languages that connect speakers of diverse languages. The students say *A lingua franca is sort of common language used by people who speak different languages; That language that connects them all is a lingua franca; That makes sense—kind of a universal business language; ...any language can be a lingua franca if it connects lots of people who speak different languages.* (2.1)

19. D The woman finds the lecture topics interesting. She says *My linguistics class is really getting good. Today the lecture was about the social aspects of language, like slang and accents, and stuff. But the thing that really intrigues me is something called a lingua franca.* (2.3)

20. B, D English and Swahili are lingua francas. The speakers say *...English is a lingua franca because English is an international business language; English is definitely a lingua franca. In East Africa, Swahili is a lingua franca that's understood in every marketplace.* (2.2)

21. C The woman's purpose is to correct the man's misunderstanding of a word. The man thinks that the word for a type of language is "pigeon," like the bird of that name. The woman corrects his misunderstanding by showing him the correct word, "pidgin." (2.3)

22. ✓ Lingua franca: It usually develops as a universal business language: *...countries with ports on the Mediterranean needed a common trade language. So a new language sort of evolved; Most of the time lingua francas have been trade languages.*

✓ Pidgin: It is a simplified language that blends two or more languages: *A "pidgin" is a type of language. It's a simplified language that's a mixture of two or more languages. It has words from both languages.*

✓ Lingua franca: It is the common language of many people who speak various languages: *A lingua franca is sort of common language used by people who speak different languages*

✓ Pidgin: It is easy to learn because its grammar and vocabulary are simple: *Pidgins have a simple grammar and vocabulary, so they're easy to learn.* (2.5)

23. C The main idea of the talk is that the bird's bill is specialized to its preferred diet. The professor says *The bird's bill is highly modified for a variety of activities—such as cutting and crushing seeds, probing tree crevices for insects, drinking nectar from flowers, catching fish, and so on; Different birds have evolved different bill types to assist in their feeding. What I mean is, the shape of the bird's bill is specially adapted to specific foods.* (2.1)

24. B The professor says *A large number of birds are primarily seed eaters. These birds typically have stout, cone–shaped bills....* You can infer that the seed eater is the bird with the cone–shaped bill. (2.4)

25. B The professor's purpose is to state that birds and their food evolved together. Some birds drink the nectar of flowers. *The co–evolution of birds and flowers* means that birds and flowers evolved alongside each other. (2.3)

26. C The professor says *Birds who drink nectar have long, narrow bills....* You can infer that the nectar drinker is the bird with the long, narrow bill that can reach the nectar at the bottom of the flower. (2.4)

27. B The professor implies that the diet of hummingbirds is not restricted to flower nectar because *hummingbirds will also grab any insect they meet.* In addition to nectar, hummingbirds eat *insects and spiders*. (2.4)

28. B, D Birds that eat insects have a slender, tweezer–like bill: *Birds that eat insects collect their food in a number of ways. The warblers have short, slender, tweezer–like bills, that they sort of use like tweezers to pick small insects off leaves and twigs.* Insect eaters also have a long, sticky tongue: *The insect eater's tongue—like the bill—is specialized to the bird's diet. The tongue of some woodpeckers is long, sticky....* (2.2)

29. D The main purpose of the talk is to introduce the students to the study of chemistry. The professor says *Chemistry is the science that deals with the materials of the universe and the changes these materials go through; Chemistry courses have a reputation for being difficult; Don't expect to understand everything right away; To solve a typical chemistry problem...; It takes time to learn chemistry.* (2.3)

30. B The professor says *Chemistry is sometimes called the central science. This isn't surprising, since most of the processes going on around us involve chemical changes.* She then lists examples of chemical processes. (2.2)

31. A The professor's purpose is to introduce basic skills that all chemists need: *an understanding of the fundamentals, the ability to solve problems, and the ability to communicate.* (2.3)

32. D The professor implies that memorizing information is not the most important part of education. The professor says *Some people think education is just storing information in the brain. A lot of students just want to memorize lists of facts...; Memorizing facts is important, but it's just the beginning of education; Analytical thinking is the center of education.* (2.4)

33. B The professor's purpose is to show that studying with others is useful in the sciences. She recommends working with a classmate on the homework problems because that is *a good way to learn about how scientists work together.* (2.3)

34. C The professor implies that mistakes can be a part of the learning process. The professor says *You might feel frustrated when you make a mistake. Just keep working—and learning from your mistakes—and you'll make steady progress* (2.4)

ANSWER KEY

SPEAKING (p. 237)

1. Responses will vary. (3.1–3.4)
2. Responses will vary. (3.1–3.4)
3. Key points:
    - The science seminar is a course in which students who are not science majors can study with science students. The man wants to enroll in the seminar.
    - One reason he gives is that he needs science credits and can earn credits that count toward the science requirement.
    - Another reason is that he lost interest in science because most science classes are boring, but the seminar seems different and more interesting and might help him to like science again.
    - Another reason is that he will have the opportunity to study with advanced science students. (3.5–3.7, 3.10)
4. Key points:
    - One kind of imagery is visualization, or using your mind's eye, to focus on a specific part of your body as you perform a dance step. If you change the focus to a different body part, it will change how you perform the step.
    - The image of a leaf can help you develop an awareness that will fill your whole body. Identifying with the leaf allows the image to control your expression.
    - Images of water include slicing through water like a ship, splashing through water, and moving underwater like a fish. Using different images of water will give you a wider range of techniques for expressing yourself, will increase your sense of mental clarity, and may even result in fewer muscle aches afterward. (3.5–3.7, 3.10)
5. Key points:
    - The woman's problem is that she is very busy with schoolwork and her duties as president of a student club. Her courses are difficult; she is worried about her grades and afraid that she might fail one course.
    - One possible solution is to quit the club.
    - Another solution is to ask other members of the club to help her with her duties. (3.8, 3.10)
6. Key points:
    - The movement toward systemizing the home was an attempt to make the home rational, scientific, and well organized.
    - The rooms in the home were designed and organized according to function. The kitchen and the living room each had several distinct functions. The dining room, bedrooms, and bath had built–in cabinets and closets. The hallway organized the flow of traffic.
    - Domestic science and home economics were established as fields of study at technical colleges.
    - The home was thought of as a factory. Women became production experts whose goals were the increase of efficiency and the reduction of boring labor. New technology, such as the washing machine and the vacuum cleaner, enhanced human performance in the home. (3.9, 3.10)

WRITING (p. 243)

1. Key points:
    - The lecture states that intelligence tests alone, particularly IQ tests, cannot predict greatness or achievement in life. This casts doubt on the point in the reading that IQ is an accurate measurement of a child's potential to achieve in school and later in professional life.
    - The lecture states that many psychologists think that most intelligence tests are really just testing a child's ability to do well in school. This casts doubt on the point in the reading that intelligence tests can evaluate people for purposes such as the military, placement in industrial organizations, and social companionship.
    - The lecture states that the concept of IQ is useful in identifying "school–house intelligence," but IQ cannot explain the source of original ideas and beautiful creations. This casts doubt on the point in the reading that IQ is a measurement of general intelligence.
    - The lecture states that a new theory of intelligence considers a person's motivation and creativity more important than a high IQ in predicting achievement. This casts doubt on the point in the reading that IQ is an accurate measurement of the potential to achieve in school and in professional life. (4.1–4.5)
2. Responses will vary. (4.6–4.10)

TEST 6

READING (*p. 247*)

1. D The passage does not give the type of mineral as a factor in mass wasting. All of the other answers are given: *...the angle of the slope is a major factor in the potential for mass wasting...; Water plays a significant role...; ...absence of vegetation....* (1.2)
2. B The name of a mass wasting process is a reflection of the material that is moved and the way it moves. Clues: *One way to classify mass wasting processes is on the basis of the material involved...rock, debris, earth, or mud. The manner in which the material moves is also important...a fall, a slide, or a flow.* (1.1)
3. C *Trigger* means *cause* in this context. Clues: *Rain or snowmelt can trigger a rockslide by wetting the underlying surface...can no longer hold the rock in place.* The water from the rain or snowmelt causes a rockslide to occur. (1.4)
4. A A rock avalanche moves faster than other types of rockslides because the rock moves over a layer of compressed air. Clues: *The fastest type of slide is a rock avalanche, in which a mass of rock literally floats on air as it moves downslope. The high speed of a rock avalanche is the result of air becoming trapped and compressed beneath the falling mass of debris....* (1.1)
5. A *Buoyant* means *floating* in this context. Clues: *...a mass of rock literally floats on air as it moves downslope; ...air becoming trapped and compressed beneath the falling mass of debris....* (1.4)
6. C *Anchor* means *hold* in this context. Clues: *...rainstorms in semiarid regions...; When a rainstorm or rapidly melting snow creates a sudden flood, large quantities of soil and loose rock are washed into nearby stream channels because there is usually little or no vegetation to anchor the surface material.* (1.4)
7. B The referent of *that* is something of wet concrete to which the consistency of the mudflow may be similar. Logic tells you that *that* refers to *consistency*. (1.3)
8. A *The removal of native vegetation by brush fires* is paraphrased in *Fire has destroyed much of the original vegetation...; ...has increased the probability of these destructive events* is paraphrased in *...so mudflows are now more likely*. (1.7)
9. D You can infer that mudflows are so dangerous because people do not expect them to occur. Clues: *...mudflows are a serious hazard to development on and near canyon hillsides; ...because mudflows occur infrequently, homeowners are often unaware of the potential danger of building on the site of a previous mudflow.* (1.5)
10. B You can infer that lahars occur in Indonesia. Clues: *Mudflows containing volcanic debris are called lahars, a word originating in Indonesia, a region that experiences many volcanic eruptions.* (1.5)
11. C The author's purpose is to emphasize the fast speed of lahars. Clues: *...altering the landscape in a relatively short period.* One meaning of *race* is to move at a high speed. (1.6)
12. C In the added sentence, *Thus* is a transition that shows result. *Thus* links *Rain or snowmelt can trigger a rockslide* in the previous sentence with *rockslides occur more frequently during the spring, when heavy rains and melting snow are most prevalent* in the added sentence. (1.8)
13. A, D, G Rockslides: *Rockslides occur when a coherent mass of rock breaks loose and slides down a slope as a unit; ...where there are joints and fractures in the rock that are parallel to the slope; ...a mass of rock literally floats on air as it moves downslope.*

    B, C, H, I Mudflows: *Mudflows...involve soil and a large amount of water; The consistency of the mudflow may be similar to that of wet concrete, or it may be a soupy mixture...; When a mudflow is dense, it moves more slowly, but it can easily carry or push large boulders, trees, and even houses along with it; Mudflows containing volcanic debris are called lahars...; Lahars occur when highly unstable layers of ash and debris become saturated with water....* Answers (E) and (F) refer to neither rockslides nor mudflows. (1.10)
14. C The passage does not state that a strong labor union was a characteristic of the Triangle Waist Company's factory. All of the other answers are given: *...the inhumane working conditions...an unsanitary and dangerous work environment; Most of the workers were women...; The shirt factory occupied the top three floors....* (1.2)
15. D *Already struggling with a new language and culture...* is paraphrased in *The workers experienced cultural difficulties...; ...these workers could not speak out about working conditions for fear of losing their desperately needed jobs...* is paraphrased in *...without complaint because they needed their jobs; ...and this forced them to endure exploitation by the factory owners* is paraphrased in *...poor conditions, and exploitation....* (1.7)
16. B *Ignited* means *caught fire* in this context. Clues: *...a rag bin...was on fire; ...tried to extinguish the flames, but their efforts proved futile...; ...the fire spread.* (1.4)
17. A The author's purpose is to emphasize the unsafe working conditions. Clues: *The incident highlighted the inhumane working conditions faced by many industrial workers, including...an unsanitary and dangerous work environment; ...they found it rotted and useless.* (1.6)
18. C Many workers on the top floor managed to escape the fire on ladders. Clues: *...the ten–story Asch Building; The seventy employees who worked on the tenth floor escaped the fire...by climbing onto the roof, where students from New York University, located across the street, stretched ladders over to the Asch Building.* (1.1)
19. C The referent of *Still others* is something or someone that climbed onto the fire escape. The previous three sentences discuss the efforts of the *ninth–floor workers* to escape the fire, and the pronouns *their, they, some,* and *Others* in these sentences refer to *ninth–floor workers*. Logic tells you that *Still others* also refers to *ninth–floor workers*. (1.3)

20. A *Spindly* means *weak* in this context. Clues: *...inadequately constructed fire escape; ...it bent under the weight of hundreds of workers...; ...separated from the wall, falling to the ground....* (1.4)

21. C You can infer that the women on the window ledges did not escape. Clues: *The young women trapped on the ninth floor waited on the window ledges to be rescued, only to discover that the ladder, fully raised, stopped far below them at the sixth floor; ...killing 146 workers, mostly immigrant women.* (1.5)

22. D The author argues that the cause of the disaster was the lack of fire safety measures. Clues: *...the Triangle fire tragically illustrated that fire inspections and safety precautions were very inadequate. The victims of the fire were trapped by the lack of fire escapes....* (1.1)

23. B The statement that an era of progressive reform began to *sweep the nation* means that the idea of reform became widespread. Clues: *The incident had a profound impact...affecting local and national politics in the process; ...people decided that government had a responsibility...; ...a public outcry for laws to regulate workplace safety.* (1.4)

24. C You can infer that the author believes the Triangle fire increased awareness of workplace safety and led to necessary reform. Clues: *The incident had a profound impact on...job safety...; An era of progressive reform began to sweep the nation...; There was a public outcry for laws to regulate workplace safety; ...led to many new regulations in the years following the fire.* (1.5)

25. C The added sentence further develops the idea that *The incident had a profound impact on women's unionism and job safety*, mentioned in the previous sentence. (1.8)

26. C, D, F Key information: *Within minutes, the factory was consumed by flame, killing 146 workers, mostly immigrant women; The incident highlighted the inhumane working conditions faced by many industrial workers, including...dangerous work environment; ...the Triangle fire tragically illustrated that fire inspections and safety precautions were very inadequate; There was a public outcry for laws to regulate workplace safety; ...their report led to many new regulations in the years following the fire.* Answer (A) is a minor idea; answers (B) and (E) are not mentioned. (1.9)

27. B You can infer that music and poetry were part of Greek culture from very early times. Clues: *Long before the ancient Greeks could read and write, they learned of their history and culture through epic poetry...; The bards chanted stories in standard musical phrases that were accompanied by musical instruments such as the lyre....* (1.5)

28. C Both Homer and Sappho were skilled lyre players. Clues: *Homer, was a...master of the lyre; Another famous...lyre player was Sappho....* (1.1)

29. B The author's purpose is to show that the period was a high point in Greek civilization. Clues: *...during the fifth century BC, when politics, philosophy, art, architecture, and theater thrived, as they never had before.* (1.6)

30. D *Outgrowth* means *product* in this context. Clues: *Early drama...was an outgrowth of the choral songs and dances...; A chorus of singers, dancers, and musicians...performed stories that educated and entertained the audience....* The prefix *out–* = beyond. Drama was a new product that developed from choral songs and dances and grew beyond them. (1.4)

31. A The passage does not state that an emphasis on costumes and makeup characterized Greek drama. All of the other answers are given: *The famous outdoor Theater of Dionysus in Athens showed the importance of drama to the Greeks; ...a masked actor; ...recited verses as a character in the story...spoken verses...; ...the chorus sang the narrative passages.* (1.2)

32. C The addition of an actor who spoke was a major development that changed choral performance into drama. Clues: *The crucial innovation that turned choral performance into drama is attributed to Thespis...; Thespis would enter the theater as a masked actor; ...he recited verses...and these spoken verses changed what had been a choral monologue into a dialogue between the actor and the chorus.* (1.1)

33. B *Legacy* means *contribution* in this context. Clues: *The crucial innovation that turned choral performance into drama is attributed to Thespis...; ...the term "thespian," which now describes anything relating to drama.* The actor's contribution to drama is honored by a word derived from his name. (1.4)

34. A The referent of *which* is something with a device like a speaking trumpet inside. Logic tells you that *which* refers to *mask.* (1.3)

35. A *Still, despite the attention the actor received...* is paraphrased in *...even though the actor was also important*; *...the chorus and its music continued to dominate dramatic performances with the combined power of singing and dancing* is paraphrased in *The singers, dancers, and musicians remained at the center of drama....* (1.7)

36. D Adding a second and a third actor led to the actors becoming more important than the chorus. Clues: *Now audience attention could be directed to the interplay between the two actors...; The addition of actors shifted the focus of drama away from the chorus toward the action and dialogue of the characters.* (1.1)

37. C *Adhered to* means *followed* in this context. Clues: *Playwrights continued to introduce innovations, but essentially they adhered to prescribed conventions. But* shows contrast between the idea of introducing innovations (new developments) and adhering to prescribed conventions (established practices or rules). (1.4)

38. A The added sentence introduces the topic of *standard forms* and *dramatic conventions*, which the rest of the paragraph develops with examples: *One of these conventions...; The drama always took place...; Another convention...; ...still another convention....* (1.8)

39. A, D, E Key information: *...they learned of their history and culture through epic poetry chanted by bards or singers; Early drama was associated with the worship of the god Dionysus and was an outgrowth of the choral songs and dances performed in honor of the god; ...enter the theater as a masked actor; ...recited verses as a character in the story...; The addition of actors shifted the focus of drama away from the chorus toward the action and dialogue of the characters; ...they adhered to prescribed conventions; Another convention reflected the society's sense of balance and order...; The Greek concept of moderation is reflected in still another convention....* Answer (B) is not mentioned; answers (C) and F) are minor ideas. (1.9)

LISTENING (*p. 260*)

1. C The woman is inquiring about the availability of study rooms. The woman says *Could you please tell me if there are any study rooms here in the library?* (2.3)
2. B The man's purpose is to encourage the woman to reserve a room now because *most of the rooms have already been reserved* and some are *already completely booked for the quarter*. (2.3)
3. A The man says *Enrollment is up 12 percent over last year, and it really makes a difference.* (2.2)
4. D The woman says *Well, actually it's for me and two of my classmates. We're working on a presentation together, and we need a quiet space to meet and talk.* (2.2)
5. B The man's purpose is to persuade the woman to accept a room in another building, the Communications Building, because most of the rooms in the library have already been reserved. The man asks *Does it matter if it's in the Communications Building? They have some rooms over there.* Then he emphasizes that the Communications Building is very close to the library. (2.3)
6. B The professor mainly discusses the formation of ice from water vapor, specifically the formation of black ice. The professor says *...black ice can form on the highway...; The black ice formed when evaporation on the wet surface of the pavement—it was mist, actually, water vapor—when the mist was exposed to above-freezing air temperatures; ...this then froze the very thin layer of mist on the surface of the pavement.* (2.1)
7. D The professor's purpose is to lead into the topic of discussion, black ice and how it forms. The professor says *...I had a rather close call when I was getting on the expressway; ...I ran into a patch of black ice.* (2.3)
8. ✓ No: Snow changes to ice on tree branches and other exposed surfaces: Snow is not mentioned in the talk.
   ✓ Yes: The air temperature is above freezing, but the ground temperature is below freezing: *However, black ice can form on the highway when the air temperature is slightly above freezing but the ground temperature is below freezing.*
   ✓ Yes: A thin layer of water vapor freezes on the surface of the highway: *The evaporation lowered the surface temperature to below freezing, and this then froze the very thin layer of mist on the surface of the pavement.*
   ✓ No: Pellets of ice develop from supercooled water droplets: Not mentioned in the talk. (2.6)
9. C The professor's purpose is to illustrate the same phenomenon in a different way. The phenomenon is the formation of ice from water vapor even when it is not freezing outside. Black ice is one example; the freezing of wet laundry is another example. (2.3)
10. C The professor says *Sublimation is when water changes state from a gas directly to a solid...; Ice formed in this way—by sublimation—forms directly from water vapor, or mist, which is a gas.* (2.2)
11. B, C Frost forms in beautiful patterns on window glass when the temperature of the glass is below freezing: *It can look like delicate feathery patterns of crystals on your windowpane...; ...the temperature of the window glass has to be below freezing.* Another factor is impurities on the glass: *...the beautiful patterns of window frost are due to its slightly curved crystals, because of organic impurities on the glass—dust and dirt—that interfere with crystal growth.* (2.2)
12. A, C The professor discusses social roles for grieving family and friends: *Death rituals give the bereaved family and friends specific roles to play.* He also discusses stages in the process of grieving a loss: *One theory states that there are four stages of grieving: numbness, yearning, despair, and reorganization.* (2.1)
13. D The professor says *Every culture has some set of rituals associated with death. These rituals serve an important function, and are a way for societies to control the grief caused by death.* (2.2)
14. B The professor's purpose is to give examples of cultural differences in grieving. There are differences in the type of ceremony held, such as a *wake*, *shiva*, or *memorial service*. There are also differences in *how the bereaved persons should act*, such as how much emotion should be shown. (2.3)
15. B The professor says *The rituals also have roles for friends, who often act as support givers. For example, friends may bring food to the home of the bereaved family, or drop in to offer help, or send flowers or sympathy cards.* (2.2)
16. D The professor implies that funerals and memorial services help make the person's life and death meaningful. The professor says *Rituals can also give meaning to the death by emphasizing the life of the person who died; Reviewing the life and accomplishments of the loved one—sharing stories and memories with family and friends—this makes the death easier for the survivors to accept.* (2.4)

17. ✓ No: A widow develops an allergic reaction to a drug: Not supported by the information in the lecture.
✓ Yes: There is a period of numbness and shock after a death: *In the first stage, the bereaved person feels numbness—a lack of feeling. Or he or she feels shock....*
✓ Yes: Someone yearns for a close friend who has died: *In the second stage—yearning—the bereaved person yearns for and may actively search for the lost one.*
✓ No: A psychologist invents a model for dealing with loss: The stage theory model is discussed in the lecture, but the model is not a stage in the grieving process.
✓ Yes: A survivor feels exhausted, depressed, or disorganized: *The third stage is when the person feels great despair, exhaustion, depression...; He or she may feel disorganized....* (2.6)

18. A, C The students discuss how music differs from noise: *...what is the difference between music and noise?; ...how's a sound that's noise different from a sound that's music?; Noise is different from music because it doesn't have a pattern.* They also discuss the phenomenon of antinoise: *The other thing I didn't get was what he said about antinoise; ...the result is antinoise—silence.* (2.1)

19. C The man says *Do you remember how he said that noise is a random sound?; Well, it's a random sound that has irregular sound waves.* (2.2)

20. A The woman says *But why is the sound of a drumbeat noise instead of music? Isn't a drumbeat a note?* You can infer that she feels frustrated because she does not understand the difference between music and noise. (2.4)

21. D The woman asks *Antinoise is silence?* The man replies *Right! And there's a computer program that proves this.* (2.1)

22. C The man says *...it's better to do the reading before the lectures....* The woman says *Yeah, you're right. I guess have some catching up to do.* You can predict that she will read the textbook before the next lecture. (2.4)

23. D The class will be creating their own mural. The instructor says *I know you're all excited about our class project. But before we get started on the design of our mural, let's review some of the technical requirements for murals.* (2.3)

24. A, C In planning a mural, the position of the observer should be considered: *We want people to take in our mural—all of it—from a moving position, since they'll be observing it as they walk through the lobby to the elevators.* The architecture of the room should also be considered: *A mural is an integral part of the building. If it's painted in an existing building, like ours will be, it should be planned to fit into the architectural design....* (2.2)

25. D The instructor means that a mural is an expression of the building's character. The instructor points out that the term "mural" suggests a *feeling, nature,* or *quality* that is *appropriate to the architecture*, and that a mural is *an integral part of the building*. This description relates to the essential character of the building. (2.4)

26. ✓ Yes: Moisture seeps through the wall and dissolves salts in the wall material: *When water leaks through a wall, it may dissolve the salts that are in the building materials.*
✓ No: The plaster dries more quickly than the paint: Not mentioned in the discussion.
✓ No: An air space between the interior and exterior walls insulates the mural: *...an air space of one–half to one inch between the outer and inner walls. That's enough to protect our mural from moisture....*
✓ Yes: Dried salt deposits form a white film on the mural: *When the moisture dries, the salts are deposited in the form of white, moldy–looking film on the surface of the plaster.* (2.6)

27. A The student says *We could create an air space between the outer wall of the building and the plaster; The air space would have an insulating effect. What I mean is, it would slow down any temperature changes on the plaster.* (2.2)

28. C The instructor's purpose is to explain how to create an insulating air space between the outer and inner walls. The instructor describes how to *build another wall on top of* strips of wood attached to the inside surface of the wall. The mural will be painted on this new wall. (2.3)

29. D The professor mainly discusses how seeds germinate and grow. The professor says *Our study of the life cycle of a plant usually starts with the germination of a seed; The germination of a seed is a critical stage in the plant's life cycle.* (2.1)

30. A The professor says *Heredity determines what the plant will look like, how it will grow, and what kind of seeds it will bear. Inside the seed is all the genetic information the plant needs to grow to maturity.* (2.2)

31. B The professor's purpose is to give an example of an environmental cue. The professor explains that some seeds require a *specific environmental cue* for germination. Then he gives the example of a heavy rainfall, an environmental cue that causes desert plants to germinate. (2.3)

32. B, D Water is an environmental factor that seeds require for germination: *Water is a basic requirement, and no seed will germinate unless it absorbs water.* Another factor is the proper temperature: *Germination also requires a certain combination of temperature and light...; Each plant species has an ideal temperature at which the largest number of seeds will germinate.* (2.2)

33. C The professor says *For a seed to sprout and grow, it needs a great deal of energy. Seeds get this energy by converting the energy of their stored fuel molecules....* (2.2)

34. C–B–D–A The professor says *(1) When the embryo takes in water, it often swells to several times its original size; (2) The first organ to emerge from the germinating seed is the embryonic root. The root pushes outward into the soil...; (3) The tip of the shoot has to break through the soil surface; (4) ...it unfolds its solar collectors, its first leaves; ...now it draws most of its growth energy directly from the sun.* (2.6)

35. A The student wants to hear the professor's comments about his term paper. He asks *...did you get a chance to read the draft of my term paper yet?* (2.3)
36. D The student says *It's changing the goals, responsibilities, and relationships within an organization.* (2.2)
37. C The professor implies that the student's paper lacks a clear focus. The professor says *What you end up with is lots of ideas, some of them overlapping and duplicating each other. What you need to do is narrow this down to the three or four ... or five steps that you believe are necessary for redesigning an organization.* (2.4)
38. B, D The professor suggests that the student focus on a few essential steps of organizational redesign: *What you need to do is narrow this down to the three or four ... or five steps that you believe are necessary for redesigning an organization.* She also suggests that he support his points with examples from a real organization: *It would also be good to illustrate your points with examples from a real organization...; You need to focus on three or four essential steps for organizational redesign and then illustrate them with a real–world example of what a real business could do, or has done, along these lines.* (2.2)
39. B The student's purpose is to give an example that he might discuss in his paper. He says *I actually thought of an example, but I don't know if it's right for this paper. It's a nursery business...; It's a business I actually know. My uncle is the superintendent there.* (2.3)
40. B The professor describes the past, present, and future of the Northwest Passage. The professor says *For the next 500 years, they nudged their ships through the Arctic waters, looking for the Northwest Passage; The Northwest Passage wasn't crossed until almost 300 years later...; In the summer of 2000...; For the past few summers now...; Climate experts now predict that, in 50 years or less, the passage will be free of ice throughout the summer.* (2.1)
41. D The professor says *It was the promise of wealth that first drew European powers to look for a westward route to Asia; So, they began to search for a way around the northern edge of the continent, a Northwest Passage that would link the Atlantic to the Pacific.* (2.2)
42. A The professor's purpose is to give examples of early Arctic explorers. The professor says *The Englishman Martin Frobisher spent several years exploring what is now Canada and searching for wealth in the Arctic; In 1607, Henry Hudson began his exploration of the Canadian Arctic.* (2.3)
43. B The professor calls the Northwest Passage *a deadly maze of sea ice, narrow straits, and oddly shaped islands.* She also says *The passage changes from year to year, and even from week to week.* You can infer that ice makes the passage dangerous and unpredictable. (2.4)
44. C The professor's purpose is to illustrate changes in the ice covering the Arctic region. The ice is disappearing and getting thinner as a result of a temperature rise of 3 to 4 degrees. (2.3)
45. A, D One possible consequence of an increase in shipping in the Northwest Passage is harm to wildlife: *There are potential consequences to shipping in the passage. Ships could disrupt the polar bears and bowhead whales that live there. There could be an increase in the smuggling of polar bear hides and walrus tusks.* Another possible consequence is a major oil spill: *The biggest concern, however, is the threat of an oil spill from a supertanker. An oil spill would damage this pristine region and be extremely difficult to clean up.* (2.2)
46. C The speaker says *These early houses of New England are the greatest single source of knowledge about domestic architecture of the seventeenth century, particularly about details of plan and construction.* (2.2)
47. A The speaker says *In the porch, there was a steep staircase built up against a massive chimney; The staircase in the porch led to one large sleeping room upstairs.* (2.2)
48. D The speaker's purpose is to explain how the two–room plan evolved from the one–room plan. The speaker says *The second house design was the two–room plan, which was simply the one–room plan with a parlor added at the other side of the chimney and porch.* Then he explains how *the parlor was actually built onto an older one–room house* in early examples of the two–room design. In later examples, *both rooms were built at the same time*, showing the evolution of the design. (2.3)
49. A The speaker says *The added space was used as a kitchen. The cooking was done in a fireplace added to the back of the central chimney structure.* (2.2)
50. ✓ Two–room plan: There were two stories, and each story had two rooms: *...the two–room plan, which was simply the one–room plan with a parlor added...; Upstairs, there were two sleeping rooms....*
    ✓ Added lean–to plan: Extra rooms were built onto the back of the house: *...the added lean–to plan, was the result of an addition at the back of the house...; The added space was used as a kitchen; There were two more rooms built on either side of the kitchen.*
    ✓ One–room plan: The house had one large space for cooking, dining, and living: *The large main room was a combination living–dining–cooking room called the "hall."*
    ✓ Added lean–to plan: A staircase led up from the kitchen to attic space for storage or sleeping: *Above the kitchen, under the lean–to roof, there was attic space for storage or more sleeping rooms, which you reached by a staircase leading up from the kitchen.* (2.5)
51. D The speaker makes the statement because plan type may not reveal exactly when a house was built. He says that plan type *is not a perfect indicator of the house's age.* Since the one–room plan *continued to be built throughout the seventeenth century*, one cannot use plan type alone to determine exactly when a one–room house was built. (2.3)

ANSWER KEY

SPEAKING (p. 280)

1. Responses will vary. (3.1–3.4)
2. Responses will vary. (3.1–3.4)
3. Key points:
   - The college has announced fee increases that will help pay for a new gymnasium. The woman supports the fee increases.
   - One reason she gives is that it is the first fee increase since she has been a student, and a 10 percent increase is not too bad.
   - Another reason is that every student will benefit from the new gymnasium, which will be better than the old, small, crowded gym.
   - Another reason is that the fee increases will cost her less money than she would have to pay to join a health club in town. (3.5–3.7, 3.10)
4. Key points:
   - The uniformity of goods was achieved through machine–based production, the identification of product type, the creation of brand names, and the establishment of standard sizes.
   - The men's clothing industry contributed to the establishment of standard sizes. This began during a war, when the army needed large numbers of uniforms for soldiers.
   - After the war, there was a large demand for clothing for returning soldiers, so manufacturers increased production, using standardized sizes and better sewing machines.
   - Soon American men could buy mass–produced, ready–to–wear suits, shirts, hats, and shoes with well–known brand names. Women could buy ready–made clothing from mail–order catalogs and department stores.
   - The shirtwaist (blouse) was one of the earliest mass–produced garments for women. The shirtwaist was produced in standard sizes and was popular with women of all social classes. (3.5–3.7, 3.10)
5. Key points:
   - The woman's problem is that she has not yet decided whether to look for a job or go to graduate school after her graduation.
   - The professor suggests that if she decides to go to graduate school, she should apply early. She should research graduate programs and learn about admissions requirements.
   - The professor suggests that if she decides to look for a job, she should write a résumé of her qualifications and work experience. (3.8, 3.10)
6. Key points:
   - Studies on sleep show that our brains continue to work on problems while we are sleeping. The right answer to a problem might come to us more easily after eight hours of sleep.
   - Creativity and problem solving seem to be directly linked to getting enough sleep. One study showed that students who had eight hours of sleep were three times more likely to solve a mathematical problem than were students who had less sleep.
   - Research indicates that the brain reorganizes and restructures our memories during deep sleep. This restructuring of memories seems to help our creativity and problem–solving ability. (3.9, 3.10)

WRITING (p. 286)

1. Key points:
   - The lecture states that any kind of stimulation of the young shortly after birth will affect the rate of growth and the resistance to stress. Stimulation can have positive or negative results. This supports the point in the reading that the influence of environmental factors is particularly effective during the formative stages of life. It also supports the point that early influences can have favorable or unfavorable effects on the young organism's development.
   - The lecture states that malnutrition early in life can have lifelong consequences; for example, deer born when food is scarce will remain relatively small, even if their adult diet improves. This supports the point in the reading that environmental factors exert such a strong influence on development that some physical characteristics are difficult or impossible to change later in life.
   - The lecture states that the eating habits acquired early in life tend to last throughout life; for example, rats that are used to eating a low–protein diet will continue to do so by choice. This supports the point in the reading that environmental factors exert such a strong influence on development that some mental characteristics are difficult or impossible to change later in life.
   - The lecture states that poor nutrition in children affects their mental development and their ability to learn in school. This supports the point in the reading that environmental factors affect learning ability and behavioral patterns in the young. (4.1–4.5)
2. Responses will vary. (4.6–4.10)

AUDIO SCRIPTS

TEST 1

Disk 1, Track 1

LISTENING SECTION DIRECTIONS (*p. 50*)

The Listening section measures your ability to understand conversations and lectures in English. You will hear each conversation and lecture only one time. After each conversation or lecture, you will hear some questions about it. Answer the questions based on what the speakers state or imply.

You may take notes while you listen. You may use your notes to help you answer the questions.

In some questions, you will see this icon: 🎧. This means that you will hear, but not see, part of the question.

Some questions have special directions, which appear in a gray box. Most questions are worth one point. If a question is worth more than one point, the directions will indicate how many points you can receive.

You will now begin the first part of the Listening section.

Disk 1, Track 2

Questions 1 through 5. Listen to a conversation in a college office.

M: Excuse me. Is this where I can get a student ID?
W: Yes, we do make ID cards here—actually downstairs in the photo shop—but this is where you start.
M: I need to, um, replace my old one. You'll never believe it, but my dog ate it.
W: You're kidding! I've never heard that one before! Usually dogs prefer homework.
M: Well, not my dog. He's particular about his food.
W: I hope it didn't hurt him. Did he swallow it whole?
M: Nah, he's all right. He just chewed it up. So, I thought I'd better get a new one so I can keep riding the bus for free.
W: There's a twenty dollar fee for a replacement ID.
M: OK. Where do I pay?
W: At the cashier's office. But first you need to fill out this form. And I need to see your driver's license or some other form of ID.
M: OK, so I just fill out this form and give it back to you?
W: Yeah, and then I have to check your status in the database so I can order the ID. It only takes a minute or so. Then you go up to the cashier to pay. After that, you take your receipt down to the photo shop, and they'll take your picture and make your new card.
M: OK. Oh, by the way, is it possible to get a copy of my transcript?
W: Sure. If you want an unofficial transcript, you can use the computers in the information center to get a printout. You could also do that through our Web site. But if you want an official transcript, you need to fill out a request form and pay five dollars for each copy you want. It takes about five days to process your request.
M: What's the difference between official and unofficial?
W: An unofficial transcript is, like, if you just wanted it for your own use, or if it doesn't have to be in a sealed envelope. Unofficial is free. An official transcript is in a sealed envelope with the college seal. If you need a transcript to transfer to another school, or to, uh, apply for a scholarship, then you need an official transcript.
M: I'm applying for a scholarship, so could I have the form for an official transcript? Looks like I'd better fill that out, too.
W: Here you go.
M: Thanks.

1. What problem does the man have?
2. Why does the man talk about his dog?
3. Listen again to part of the conversation. Then answer the question.
   "Nah, he's all right. He just chewed it up. So, I thought I'd better get a new one so I can keep riding the bus for free."
   What can be inferred about riding the bus?
4. What is one difference between an unofficial transcript and an official transcript?
5. What will the man probably do?

Disk 1, Track 3

Questions 6 through 11. Listen to part of a lecture in a geology class. The professor is talking about plate tectonics.

We currently believe that the earth's crust—the rocky part of the earth—is composed of several large, rigid plates. These plates are being created at some edges and being destroyed at others. They're also moving across the earth. This theory is called plate tectonics. It was first put forth in 1963 by a Canadian geophysicist by the name of Tuzo Wilson.

Tuzo Wilson was instrumental in advancing the theory of plate tectonics. He suggested that the Hawaiian and other volcanic island chains might have formed as a result of the movement of a plate over a motionless "hotspot" in the earth's mantle. Hundreds of studies have proved that Wilson was right. However, in the early 1960s, his idea was considered so radical that his "hotspot" manuscript was initially rejected by all the major international scientific journals.

Basically, plates are areas of the earth's crust that move as a unit. At the present time, there are eight large plates, as well as a similar number of smaller plates.

According to the theory of plate tectonics, a plate has three kinds of boundaries with other plates: oceanic ridges, oceanic trenches, and transform faults. Most of the world's earthquakes and volcanoes occur at plate boundaries. This is what you'd expect because plate boundaries are where a great deal of friction and stress occur.

At plate boundaries, a couple of things can happen. One is that rock is forced up from the mantle in molten form as lava—at ridges. Another is that rock is melted and forced back into the mantle—at trenches. This process of rock being "swallowed" or forced back into the earth's mantle is called subduction. During subduction, as a plate dives into the depths, we think part of it finds its way back to the surface in the form of volcanoes.

The theory of plate tectonics and the discovery of sea floor spreading have confirmed the theory of continental drift, the movement of continents. Sea floor spreading was discovered in the North Atlantic, and soon afterward in all other oceans. What we found is that—in the areas around oceanic ridges—the deep sea floor is formed by rising lava, which then spreads out sideways in both directions.

So, does the spreading of the ocean floor mean that the surface of the earth is increasing? No, not in the least. Sea floor spreading doesn't cause an increase in the earth's surface. And why not? Because the lava that rises and spreads from the oceanic ridges sinks again elsewhere in subduction zones, which are nearly identical with the ocean trenches.

Subduction zones are areas of frequent earthquakes and are usually associated with the rows of volcanic islands that accompany the oceanic trenches. Subduction is currently happening beneath island arcs, like Japan. Subduction is also taking place on the Pacific Northwest Coast of North America, beyond the end of the San Andreas Fault. This is where a subducted plate is thought to have disappeared beneath the North American plate in recent geological time, leaving the volcanoes of the Cascade Range as evidence of its past existence.

6. Why does the professor talk about Tuzo Wilson?
7. Why do earthquakes and volcanoes occur at plate boundaries?
8. What is subduction?
9. Identify the area in the diagram where subduction occurs.
10. Listen again to part of the lecture. Then answer the question.
    "So, does the spreading of the ocean floor mean that the surface of the earth is increasing? No, not in the least. Sea floor spreading doesn't cause an increase in the earth's surface. And why not? Because the lava that rises and spreads from the oceanic ridges sinks again elsewhere in subduction zones, which are nearly identical with the ocean trenches."
    Why does the professor ask this:
    "So, does the spreading of the ocean floor mean that the surface of the earth is increasing?"
11. Which of the following are associated with subduction zones?

Disk 1, Track 4

Questions 12 through 17. Listen to part of a talk in an anthropology class.

Human beings, like all animals, are territorial. The center of our territory is the home. Think about it. The home is where we spend most of our time. We begin and end our day there. We eat and sleep and bathe … and relax … and play with our children there … and are most comfortable there. We keep our possessions there. We furnish our homes as an expression of our taste. We say—and generally believe—that "There's no place like home" and "Home is where the heart is."

The human habit of building homes has a long history. Anthropologists think home building began with very simple round huts, similar to the shelters still built in parts of Africa today. Round huts probably started out like this: tree branches were leaned up against one another like the ribs of an umbrella; then the frame was covered with leaves or animal skins.

It's from these round, tent–like structures that the first solid dwellings probably evolved. As the tents became larger and more elaborate, they became the center of family life, and the place where the family's possessions could be kept. In other words, these structures became home, the heart of the human territory. Round huts progressed from being temporary shelters, made of wood and skins and leaves, into stronger, more permanent structures built of stone.

But even though stone structures were stronger, there was still a problem: the round shape made it difficult to combine it with other structures. This difficulty was overcome with the development of the cube, or box shape. The box shape was a major development in home construction. By making the sides of the house rectangular, and then covering the four walls with a roof, it was possible to place structures next to one another, and to join them with doorways. Thus, the room was invented.

After the room came the multi–unit dwelling: the apartment house. Nearly ten thousand years ago, this method of building led to the construction of clusters of rectangular buildings that made up the first complex human settlements. Today the box shape not only survives but also remains the basis of our domestic dwellings.

The homes of today still contain some ancient features. Around the house itself there's an outer perimeter—the symbolic boundary of the ancient home territory. Today the boundary is often marked by a barrier, like a fence, a wall, or a hedge. Inside the boundary, we find the yard—where we keep our dogs—and the garden, where we—like our ancestors—grow a few fruits and vegetables. We surround our home with a grass lawn, like our ancestors surrounded theirs with pastures for their livestock.

Today, humans are more sociable than in ancient times, and so we allow others to enter the home territory, especially the outer boundary. For example, we let people bring letters and packages to our door. Sometimes we let outsiders enter the first of the private areas, the hallway, which is inside the solid wall of the home itself. But beyond the hallway, there are more boundaries. Each room you come to becomes more private and less available to outsiders.

Guests are allowed to enter the living room. Closer friends can go farther. We tell our closest friends to "make yourself at home" and allow them into the rooms where we cook and eat and pursue our hobbies. But … up the stairs … or down the hall … somewhere less accessible in our home—this is where we find the bedrooms and bathrooms, the most private rooms of our home. These rooms are where we, the owners of the territory, feel most secure. This is where we retreat, like any animal to its den, whenever we are at our most vulnerable—for example, when we're sleeping, bathing, or when we're sick.

12. What is the main purpose of the talk?
13. The professor briefly describes developments in home building. Put the developments in the order in which they occurred.
14. According to the professor, why was the box shape a major development in home building?
15. According to the professor, what ancient features still exist in the homes of today?
16. Why does the professor say this:
    "Sometimes we let outsiders enter the first of the private areas, the hallway, which is inside the solid wall of the home itself. But beyond the hallway, there are more boundaries. Each room you come to becomes more private and less available to outsiders."
17. What does the professor imply about the rooms inside the homes of today?

Disk 1, Track 5

Questions 18 through 22. Listen to part of a conversation between two students. They are planning an oral report for their history class.

W: OK, so we're going to look at the influenza epidemic of 1918 and, uh, probably its effects, like how many people got the flu.
M: The numbers should be fairly easy to find.
W: Actually, I have some numbers already. Let me see … OK. From spring 1918 to winter 1919, 25 percent of Americans—one out of every four people—contracted the flu … and about 3 percent of the people who got the flu died from it.
M: Wow. One–fourth of the population got sick. That's a lot. It must've had a pretty bad effect on the workforce and productivity. Imagine if one–fourth of the people didn't show up for work. Doctors and hospitals must have been overwhelmed.
W: Here's some more interesting numbers: 675,000 Americans died from influenza, but only 116,000 died in World War I. That means that the war killed only about … what … about one–sixth of the people who died of the flu.
M: I wonder how the flu statistics compare with the statistics for other major epidemics, you know, like AIDS and tuberculosis … or other flu epidemics. I think there were other flu epidemics later, after 1918.
W: Hmm. I don't know, but I'll try to find out. That might be good to include in our report.
M: So, we can talk about the flu and its effects on society and the economy, you know, and … uh compare it to other epidemics. What else should we do?
W: I think we should tell stories about its effects on real people. My great–grandfather could remember the flu epidemic. He was born in 1910, so he was eight years old at the time. He remembered that there were a lot of funerals. His baby sister and his best friend died of the flu, and that made an impression on him.
M: Wow. Did your great–grandfather get the flu?
W: You know, I'm not really sure … he never said if he got sick. Well, I mean, if he did, he survived it and lived to be 91.
M: You could tell the story about your great–grandfather. You know … that might be a great way to start our presentation.
W: Yeah? Maybe. It might get our audience's attention.
M: I think we should also talk about the connection between the flu and World War I. That was the first global war, and it was the first global epidemic in recorded history. I've done some reading about that. What I found out was, it was the army that first noticed large numbers of men getting sick, and it was the army that first started reporting statistics about how many people were affected. You can imagine how fast influenza spread among soldiers living in close quarters, and traveling to other countries.
W: Wow. OK … ah … we've got some pretty good ideas. I like what you're saying about focusing on the war and the global aspects.
M: I'll do a little more research and see what else I can find.
W: Good. I will, too. I'll look for stuff about other epidemics. Why don't we meet again and talk about what we have? Can you meet again on Thursday?
M: Uh … yeah, sure, that's fine with me.

18. What are the students mainly discussing?
19. Why does the woman mention her great–grandfather?
20. According to the man, what group first reported large numbers of influenza cases?
21. What information will the students probably include in their report?
22. What do the students agree to do?

Disk 1, Track 6

Questions 23 through 28. Listen to part of a discussion in an economics class.

M1: The large economic unit called the "corporation" has come to define business activity in a modern industrial–service economy. Even a mid–sized corporation employs thousands of people, serves hundreds of thousands of customers, and controls assets and does business amounting to several million dollars. The growing power of corporations has brought increased intervention by the only body with sufficient strength and scope to match corporate power. And what body is this? What has enough power to control the corporation?
W: The government.
M1: Yes. The federal government. The economic role of the government has grown tremendously over the past century, as more and more corporate activities have come under regulation. Why has this happened?
M2: Well, to prevent fraud against stockholders, for one thing. Also, to protect customers from fraud, like false advertising.
W: To protect the workers. For example, laws against child labor … and unsafe working conditions.
M1: Yes. These are all reasons why we have government regulation of business. Not just in this country, but in most advanced industrial and service economies, governments have taken on an increasing role in economic affairs. Let's take a minute to review what we talked about last time. What are the methods that governments use to influence economic activities? Elizabeth?
W: Taxes. Taxes encourage or discourage certain kinds of economic activity. Taxes are also a way for the government to get money to spend on programs.
M1: That's right. So … OK, there's taxes and … what else? Joshua?
M2: Government spending—the government gives business incentives to produce certain goods or services. Also … uh … spending could take the form of a tax break, or it could be a direct payment, like a government contract, or a grant or a subsidy.
M1: Yes, that's right. Governments intervene in economic activity through taxation and spending. A third method, of course, what we've just been talking about: regulation. There's been a tremendous increase in the laws and regulations governing the economic affairs of complex societies like ours. Beginning in the late 1800s, our political leaders rejected the idea that "government governs best which governs least." The government started to use its power to police the economic system. One of the first things the government did was to limit the exercise of monopoly power by regulating railroads and public utilities. After that, the government began regulating utility rates—costs for telephone, electricity, fuel, and so on. Since then, a whole set of industries has come

AUDIO SCRIPTS

under government regulation: financial markets, the airlines, trucking, barge and water traffic, oil and natural gas pipelines, and so on. Also, in recent decades there's been a rapid growth of social regulation. What do I mean by social regulation?

W: Uh … things like … like laws that require a food package to list all the ingredients?

M1: Yes, that's a good example. There are a number of laws regulating food and cosmetics. Social regulation also includes the laws that were first passed to protect workers in mines, and then workers in general. Now there are laws that protect all of society—for example, regulations for air and water pollution, and for storage and disposal of hazardous materials like nuclear waste. There are also safety standards for automobiles and consumer products, such as car seats for babies. All of these are forms of social regulation. We've come a long way since the days of laissez–faire capitalism, when business ran free and unchecked by government. When the political leaders of the nineteenth century first started proposing
regulation of business, this was considered a radical idea. However, with the passage of time, the radical ideas of that era became the accepted convictions of today. The general public has come to accept—and even expect—these limits on capitalism.

23. What is the discussion mainly about?
24. Why do the students say this:
"Well, to prevent fraud against stockholders, for one thing. Also, to protect customers from fraud, like false advertising."
"To protect the workers. For example, laws against child labor … and unsafe working conditions."
25. According to the discussion, governments influence economic activity through which methods?
26. Listen again to part of the discussion. Then answer the question.
"Beginning in the late 1800s, our political leaders rejected the idea that 'government governs best which governs least.' The government started to use its power to police the economic system. One of the first things the government did was to limit the exercise of monopoly power by regulating railroads and public utilities."
Why does the professor say this:
"Beginning in the late 1800s, our political leaders rejected the idea that 'government governs best which governs least.'"
27. According to the professor, what is the function of social regulation?
28. Listen again to part of the discussion. Then answer the question.
"When the political leaders of the nineteenth century first started proposing regulation of business, this was considered a radical idea. However, with the passage of time, the radical ideas of that era became the accepted convictions of today. The general public has come to accept—and even expect—these limits on capitalism."
What can be inferred about government regulation of business?

Disk 1, Track 7

Questions 29 through 34. Listen to part of a lecture in a biology class. The professor is talking about cardiac muscle.

Every minute of every day, blood flows through every corner of your body. The flow of blood brings oxygen and other nutrients to your tissues. Then it loads up the waste products of your metabolism and carries them away. This system of nutrient exchange is what keeps your organs and tissues alive. It's made possible only because of the steady beating of your heart—the driving force of your circulatory system.

How can your heart keep beating and beating, never stopping, and rarely getting out of sync? It's possible because of the specialized type of muscle—cardiac muscle—that makes up the heart tissue, and also because of the action of specialized electrical pathways that run through the heart's walls.

Before I go into cardiac muscle, let's back up a bit. You may recall from last time that the action of a muscle is always to contract. Muscles can extend only passively. They extend as they relax between contractions. You'll also recall that the human body has different types of muscles. For example, skeletal muscle controls body movements, and cardiac muscle controls the body's blood flow. Skeletal muscle is found throughout the body, but cardiac muscle is found only in one place—the heart.

Skeletal muscles get their name from the fact that their movement is based on the contraction of muscles working against the skeleton. Skeletal muscles are attached to the bones, and they move the bones by contracting.

A skeletal muscle consists of a bundle of long fibers running the length of the muscle. The bundles of fibers are arranged in a regular pattern—a repeating pattern of light and dark bands. This pattern is called striation, and skeletal muscle is also known as striated muscle. When a muscle contracts, the length of each bundle is reduced. A skeletal muscle contracts only when it's stimulated by a motor neuron.

Cardiac muscle, on the other hand, contracts rhythmically all on its own. Cardiac muscle cells can generate impulses on their own, without any input from the nervous system. They can do this because of complex chemical and electrical changes involving sodium, calcium, and potassium, each of which carries an electrical charge.

Like skeletal muscle, cardiac muscle is striated. However, the membranes between cardiac muscle cells contain specialized regions that provide direct electrical contact among cells. What this means is, an electrical impulse generated in one part of the heart will spread to all the cardiac muscle cells. Thus, the whole heart will contract. Cardiac muscle cells can generate impulses without any input from the nervous system. In contrast to this, skeletal muscles don't contract unless the nervous system tells them to.

A single cardiac muscle cell will "beat" even when it's isolated from the heart and placed in cell culture in the laboratory. If you removed a little piece of muscle from your heart and put it in a dish, you would see it continue to contract. That's because cardiac muscle cells have something called an action potential. Electrically, they're set up so, so that sodium and calcium—positive ions—change places with potassium—a negative ion—across the cell membrane. This happens automatically, over and over again. When sodium, calcium, and potassium ions move into or out of a cardiac cell, it causes the muscle to contract.

What we think of as a heartbeat is really a series of contractions in the cardiac muscle. When the heart's walls contract, they force blood out of the chambers and into the next chamber or the large blood vessels that lead to the rest of your body. Every day, your heart contracts 100,000 times or more, pumping more than 2,000 gallons of blood.

But, unlike the skeletal muscles in your body, your cardiac muscle can never stop and take a rest. If your heart stops beating, you have very little time—only a matter of minutes—for it to start up again before all your other body systems are permanently damaged or stop functioning altogether.

29. How does the professor develop the topic of cardiac muscle?
30. Why does the professor say this:
"How can your heart keep beating and beating, never stopping, and rarely getting out of sync?"
31. Why does the professor say this:
"Before I go into cardiac muscle, let's back up a bit."
32. Based on the information in the lecture, indicate whether each sentence below describes skeletal muscle or cardiac muscle.
33. What happens when an electrical impulse generated in one part of the heart spreads to all the cardiac muscle cells?
34. Listen again to part of the lecture. Then answer the question.
"If you removed a little piece of muscle from your heart and put it in a dish, you would see it continue to contract. That's because cardiac muscle cells have something called an action potential. Electrically, they're set up so, so that sodium and calcium—positive ions—change places with potassium—a negative ion—across the cell membrane. This happens automatically, over and over again. When sodium, calcium, and potassium ions move into or out of a cardiac cell, it causes the muscle to contract."
What can be inferred about the contraction of cardiac muscle?

Disk 1, Track 8

SPEAKING SECTION DIRECTIONS (*p. 63*)

The Speaking section measures your ability to speak in English about a variety of topics. There are six questions in this section.

Questions 1 and 2 are independent tasks in which you will speak about familiar topics. Your responses will be scored on your ability to speak clearly and coherently about the topics.

Questions 3 and 4 are integrated speaking tasks. You will read a passage, listen to a conversation or lecture, and then speak in response to a question about what you have read and heard. Y ou will need to combine relevant information from the two sources to answer the question completely. Your responses will be scored on your ability to speak clearly and coherently and on your ability to accurately convey information about what you read and heard.

Questions 5 and 6 are integrated speaking tasks. You will listen to part of a conversation or lecture, and then speak in response to a question about what you have heard. Your responses will be scored on your ability to speak clearly and coherently and on your ability to accurately convey information about what you heard.

You will hear each conversation and lecture only one time. You may take notes while you listen. You may use your notes to help you answer the questions.

Disk 1, Track 9

Describe the qualities of a good teacher and explain why these qualities are effective. Include details and examples to support your explanation.

Disk 1, Track 10

Some people like to cook their own meals at home. Others prefer to eat in a restaurant or a cafeteria. Which do you prefer and why? Include details and examples in your explanation.

Disk 1, Track 11

Now listen to two students as they discuss parking on campus.

W: So, Julian, are you all ready to start another year?
M: Almost. I've still got to get a parking permit, but I was a little shocked to see how much they cost this year. Last year it was only thirty–five dollars a quarter to park on campus, but now it's fifty! That's a big increase. The annual permits went up too.
W: That's probably because the college built that big new parking lot.
M: Yeah, and they're making the students pay for it. The faculty and staff can park on campus for free—and they get to park next to the main building in the old lot—but we have to park in the new lot. And we're hit with a big fee increase. It's not fair!
W: I'm glad I take the bus.
M: I don't even understand why they had to build that new parking lot. It's bigger than they really need, and it's so far away from everything. It takes a long time to walk from the parking lot to where most of the classrooms are. And they want us to pay more for the privilege!

The man expresses his opinion about parking on campus. State his opinion and explain the reasons he gives for holding that opinion.

Disk 1, Track 12

Now listen to part of a talk in a psychology class.

One of the earliest behaviorists is Ivan Pavlov, an experimental psychologist noted for his studies of the reflex reaction in humans and animals. A reflex is an involuntary action of the body, such as a sneeze, a blink, or a hiccup. Pavlov did a series of experiments using dogs. He found that when a bell is rung each time a dog is fed, the dog starts to associate the sound of the bell with food. Consequently, whenever the bell rings, the dog expects food. The dog salivates and drools, and there is an increase in the flow of his stomach juices. The dog's bodily response to the bell is a conditioned reflex, a behavior that occurs because the dog has been trained by the sound of the bell.

Pavlov's experiments with dogs and discovery of the conditioned reflex contributed to the development of behaviorism. The dog's bodily response—its behavior—does not come from something inside the dog. Rather, the behavior is the result of conditioning, the careful control of the dog's environment. Pavlov argued that the dog's behavior—drooling—was strictly a reaction to the environmental stimulus of the bell.

Describe Pavlov's experiments with dogs, and explain how these experiments contributed to the psychology of behaviorism.

Disk 1, Track 13

Now listen to a conversation between two students.

M: So, have your registered for Spring Quarter yet?
W: Yes, but unfortunately I didn't get all the classes I wanted, like the economics course I still need for graduation. All sections of that course were completely filled up. I couldn't believe it!
M: Really? That's too bad. Can you take the course in summer?
W: Hmm, I don't know. I'll have to ask my adviser if I can do that and still start business school in the fall. But I don't think I'll be able to take any classes at all this summer.
M: Why not? Summer is usually a good time to go to school, and the classes usually don't fill up.
W: But I'll be working six days a week at my parents' restaurant this summer. That won't leave me with any time to study.
M: Then why not take the economics course in the spring anyway? It's probably offered at the community college.
W: Oh yeah? I didn't think of that. But aren't a lot of the classes at the community college given in the evening?
M: Yeah, but so what? It might be easier to fit an evening class into your schedule.
W: Hmm, maybe that's true. Well, I'll have to decide on it soon because I need this course to graduate.

Describe the woman's problem and the two suggestions the man makes about how to solve it. Then state which of the two solutions you prefer and explain why.

Disk 1, Track 14

Now listen to part of a lecture in a marine biology class. The professor is discussing problems that threaten the world's oceans.

A major study shows that the world's oceans face several serious problems related to overfishing, pollution, climate change, and loss of habitat.

At least one–third of the fish stocks are "overfished." This includes several groundfish species that will take decades to recover. The estimated number of large ocean predators—tuna, marlin, sharks, and halibut—has fallen 90 percent globally in half a century. One reason for overfishing is bottom trawling, the practice of dragging nets along the sea bottom to catch huge quantities of fish. Bottom fishing with nets can destroy habitat and contribute to fish declines.

Pollution is a serious and growing danger. Land–based pollution in the form of erosion puts silt into the ocean, killing marine life close to shores. Cargo ships, container ships, and cruise ships dump at least 65 million gallons of petroleum products a year into the seas. Even small amounts of oil can damage sensitive marine environments. Scientists estimate that nearly 30 million gallons of petroleum seep into North American waters every year, most of it from runoff, seaplanes, and small boats.

Climate change is causing new disease outbreaks in ocean environments, affecting everything from coral reefs to oysters. Diseases threaten many corals in the Pacific. Since coral reefs provide rich habitat for fish, the loss of coral contributes to fish declines. Climate change also hurts large mammals that depend on fish. In the Arctic, melting ice may be preventing polar bears from reaching their fishing areas, and this affects their breeding patterns and the survival of their young cubs.

Using examples and details from the lecture, describe the causes and effects of problems that threaten the world's oceans.

Disk 1, Track 15

WRITING SECTION DIRECTIONS (*p. 69*)

The Writing section measures your ability to use writing to communicate in an academic environment. There are two writing questions.

Question 1 is an integrated writing task. You will read a passage, listen to a lecture, and then answer a question based on what you have read and heard. You have 20 minutes to plan and write your response.

Question 2 is an independent writing task. You will answer a question based on your own knowledge and experience. You have 30 minutes to plan and write your response.

Disk 1, Track 16

Now listen to part of a lecture about the same topic.

The idea that some foods are better than others has been around for a long time. But the idea that certain foods have super powers is a big exaggeration. Several leading nutrition scientists question the evidence on some of these claims—and for good reason. The whole concept of superpower foods is far–fetched.

For instance, while the research on blueberries and brain function is very exciting, this work has so far been conducted only on animals. The studies were conducted on rats and mice, not humans. There are no completed studies that show comparable results in people. Until we have data on humans, we can't go around telling people that blueberries have super powers.

While the evidence in the article isn't exactly wrong, it tends to be misleading because it doesn't differentiate between direct evidence and stuff that's pretty speculative. For example, it's a good idea to eat tomatoes because they're full of nutrients, but we can't promise that people who eat them aren't going to get cancer. The same is true for broccoli and other vegetables in the cabbage family. They might prevent colon cancer, but we don't yet have direct proof of this.

Another thing, the statement that garlic has the power to lower cholesterol probably isn't true. According to a more recent review of the evidence, the effect of garlic on cholesterol is unclear. While garlic may produce a drop in cholesterol for the first three months, the decline disappears after six months.

What I'm saying is, no food has magic powers. You have to realize that a lot of these so–called "studies" are poorly designed and unscientific. So when you read claims about certain foods, you have to be careful to distinguish direct, scientific evidence from simplifications, opinions, and misleading statements.

Summarize the points made in the lecture you just heard, explaining how they cast doubt on points made in the reading.

TEST 2

Disk 2, Track 1

LISTENING SECTION DIRECTIONS (*p. 86*)

The Listening section measures your ability to understand conversations and lectures in English. You will hear each conversation and lecture only one time. After each conversation or lecture, you will hear some questions about it. Answer the questions based on what the speakers state or imply.

You may take notes while you listen. You may use your notes to help you answer the questions.

In some questions, you will see this icon: 🎧. This means that you will hear, but not see, part of the question.

Some questions have special directions, which appear in a gray box. Most questions are worth one point. If a question is worth more than one point, the directions will indicate how many points you can receive.

You will now begin the first part of the Listening section.

Disk 2, Track 2

Questions 1 through 5. Listen to a conversation between two students.

W: Hey, I heard about your senior thesis show in Gallery Two! That's great! I'm so proud of you, Malcolm!

M: Thanks. Yeah, I can hardly believe it myself. I've still got a lot to do before the opening, though.

W: When's the opening?

M: Friday night. There's going to be a reception starting at four o'clock. I hope to see you there.

W: That's great! I'll be there. Will there be food?

M: Of course there'll be food! It's an opening reception! The Friends of the Gallery are paying for it all.

W: I'll definitely be there! Can I bring my roommate? She's an artist, too, a painter.

M: Bring all your friends, as many as you like. The more, the merrier.

W: Great! So … tell me about your piece. It's a sculpture, right?

M: Yeah, it's three pieces actually, but they're all connected. You've seen my boxes before, right?

W: Uh … yeah, I remember one box you did that was all different shades of white.

M: Yeah, that was last year. Well, I'm still into monochrome. This time it's three boxes—one red, one blue, and one black. And it's sort of multimedia because there's music involved.

W: No kidding! I'm intrigued. How did you do the music?

M: It wasn't easy, believe me. Each box has a miniature CD player built into it, hidden out of sight. There's a different style of music for each color. The red box plays Dixieland jazz, the blue one plays solo saxophone, and the black one is all sad violins.

W: So, your message is about the colors of the music.

M: Yes. Actually, I read an article on this topic about a year ago, and I think I've been carrying this idea around in my head ever since. There was this study about the moods of music, and it, um, showed that people sort of think of different kinds of music—the different sounds and tones of music—in terms of colors. People see lively music as red, and romantic music as blue, and sad music as black.

W: And so you found a way to put all of it—color, music, form—all in your thesis. Well done, Malcolm! I can't wait to see these boxes, and hear them too! It sounds awesome.

M: Thanks. I'm pleased that Gallery Two is showing it. So, what have you been up to? How's your photography?

W: OK, I guess. I sent some of my pictures to the campus magazine, but they were rejected. I might have a picture in next year's catalog, though—it's a shot I took of the … you know the stone benches in front of the nursing school?

M: Uh-huh.

W: Well, it's a black and white shot of the benches covered in snow. The dean liked it, and they might use it in the catalog.

M: Cool!

W: Well, I've got to go, got class in a few minutes. It was great running into you. I'll see you Friday!

M: Great! See you later!

1. What are the students mainly discussing?
2. How does the man probably feel when he says this: "Bring all your friends, as many as you like. The more, the merrier."
3. Which features are included in the man's sculpture?
4. How did the man get the idea for his sculpture?
5. Why does the woman say this: "Well, it's a black and white shot of the benches covered in snow. The dean liked it, and they might use it in the catalog."

Disk 2, Track 3

Questions 6 through 11. Listen to part of a lecture in a geology class.

You might expect that heavy snowfall is the main requirement for the formation of a glacier. But if you stop and think about it, you'll realize there are lots of areas of the world that receive huge amounts of snow but have no glaciers. Snowfall alone isn't enough. For a glacier to form, the snow can't melt. It has to be conserved. In the extremely cold Arctic and Antarctic, there are large areas that receive minimal precipitation and actually qualify as desert. Although there's little snow, there are massive ice sheets because the snow that does fall is conserved and transformed into ice.

Of course, lots of places do get large amounts of snow, and they do have glaciers … high mountains, for example. In high mountains where the climate is humid and cold, snowfall is frequent. Above the snowline, the annual snowfall exceeds the annual melting, so snow builds up. The accumulation is thickest in the hollows at the heads of valleys, because these locations are relatively high and cool, and are protected from sun and wind.

As snow accumulates in a hollow, it's gradually converted to ice. First, the fragile snow crystals break as they're compressed by the weight of more snow settling on top of them. There's some melting and refreezing because of compaction, earth heat, and seasonal temperature fluctuations. So, the snow crystals are broken, then they're wetted by meltwater, and refrozen, over and over again.

Gradually, over time, the snowflakes change into grains. They become rounded and granular, like the grains of coarse sugar. There are pockets of air between the grains, connecting the grains to one another. This old snow, called "firn," is generally created after one complete winter–summer cycle.

Firn is actually bits of ice. The firn begins to re–crystallize, and eventually, it combines and crystallizes into solid ice—a glacier. What happens is, the small grains coalesce to form large interlocking crystals of ice, with air trapped as bubbles inside the crystals. In the end, it's pure ice, with all the air squeezed out. The flow of the glacier down the mountain contributes to crystal growth, as the movement helps to compress the air out.

As the hollow in the valley head fills with snow turning to ice, the hollow enlarges, and the rock walls are carved out by shifting ice. As new snow is added, the lower part of the snow–and–ice mass bulges out, kind of like a mud pie. As the mass continues to bulge, part of the ice moves over the edge of the hollow and starts moving down the valley. Large glaciers usually move faster than small ones. Also, the movement is faster in the summer, when more meltwater is present beneath and around the ice mass to lubricate it and buoy it up.

Most valley glaciers move at a rate of ... oh ... between a few inches and a few feet a day. But some glaciers—called surging glaciers—can travel as much as 300 feet a day. There are at least 200 of these surging glaciers in Alaska and the Northwest Territories. The surging is caused by a number of conditions, like ... oh ... sudden adjustment to an increase in the snow load on top, or, more likely, an increase in the production of meltwater due to a rise in temperature. Glaciers that have more meltwater are better lubricated and tend to move faster than drier ones. In very cold climates, glaciers are quite dry because of the lack of melting. The amount of water is slight, so the glacier does not slide as quickly.

In warmer climates, glaciers are better lubricated with meltwater. They also cause more erosion, more carving out of the valley floor. This is because during the melt–freeze cycle, parts of the glacier freeze to the bottom and sides of the valley, and then, as the ice moves on, large chunks of glacier pluck out rock. So you can see why glaciers in warmer climates have a greater impact on the landscape than those in very cold climates.

6. What is the lecture mainly about?
7. What point does the professor make about the snow that forms a glacier?
8. Listen again to part of the lecture. Then answer the question.
   "In high mountains where the climate is humid and cold, snowfall is frequent. Above the snowline, the annual snowfall exceeds the annual melting, so snow builds up. The accumulation is thickest in the hollows at the heads of valleys, because these locations are relatively high and cool, and are protected from sun and wind."
   Why does the professor say this:
   "The accumulation is thickest in the hollows at the heads of valleys, because these locations are relatively high and cool, and are protected from sun and wind."
9. The professor briefly explains a process that occurs in mountain valleys. Indicate whether each sentence below is a stage in the process.
10. Why are some glaciers called surging glaciers?
11. Listen again to part of the lecture. Then answer the question.
   "In warmer climates, glaciers are better lubricated with meltwater. They also cause more erosion, more carving out of the valley floor. This is because during the melt–freeze cycle, parts of the glacier freeze to the bottom and sides of the valley, and then, as the ice moves on, large chunks of glacier pluck out rock. So you can see why glaciers in warmer climates have a greater impact on the landscape than those in very cold climates."
   What can be inferred about glaciers in warmer climates?

Disk 2, Track 4

Questions 12 through 17. Listen to part of a talk in a theater class. The professor is talking about stages.

Throughout the long history of theater, three basic types of stages have prevailed. Each of these styles has advantages and disadvantages, and each is good for certain types of plays. Let's take a look at the three styles and see why each has been so successful. The three designs are (1) the proscenium or picture–frame stage, (2) the arena or circle stage, and (3) the thrust stage with three–quarter seating.

The first design, the proscenium stage, gets its name from the proscenium arch, the frame that sort of outlines the stage and separates it from the audience. The proscenium stage is also called the picture–frame stage because it looks like a large picture frame that the audience looks through to see the action of the play. The seats for the audience all face in the same direction, toward the stage at the front end of the theater.

The stage area of proscenium theaters is usually deep, and this allows for elaborate scenery and scene changes. Scenery pieces—called backdrops—are hung on ropes or cables at the rear, in layers, one behind the other. They're called backdrops because they can be dropped into position and then raised again as necessary. The number of different backdrops possible allows the scene designer to create an extremely realistic set.

However, the proscenium arch also creates a distancing effect—which is an advantage for certain types of drama, but a disadvantage for others. The proscenium works really well for large–scale productions with lots of characters and action, but for some plays—for, example, close–up views of real life—the proscenium is sort of a barrier between the actors and the audience.

Next, the arena stage. In the past half–century, there's been a movement to bring theater closer to real life ... a movement toward more informal, more intimate theater. Thus, we have the arena stage—also called the circle theater or theater–in–the–round. In the arena theater, the stage is in the center of a square or circle, with seats for the audience around it on all sides. The actors are in the center, so everyone in the audience can be close to them. The effect is a sense of intimacy, a kind of closeness that comes whenever people form a circle.

The arena is the oldest style of theater. It's interesting to note that almost all early theatrical performances were "in the round," as ceremonies, rituals, and dances in all parts of the world took place in a circle.

One disadvantage of the arena theater is that, while its design allows for intimacy, it also makes it impossible to have elaborate scenery or scene changes. This lack of flexibility is one reason why the third style of theater has become very popular again.

The third design—the thrust stage—falls somewhere between the proscenium and the arena styles. In the thrust stage theater, the audience sits on three sides or in a half–circle, around a stage that sticks out into the center. Behind the stage is a stage house from which the actors enter and exit, and scenery is changed. The thrust stage is kind of a compromise between the proscenium and the arena styles. It combines the scenic features of the proscenium theater with the intimacy of the arena stage.

The formal English theaters of Shakespeare's day were thrust stage theaters, and today it's the most widely used of all the designs. Its advantages are obvious. It has the intimacy of three–quarter seating around the actors, and the stage house at the rear makes scene changes possible. Also, the fact that so many great dramatic works were written for it gives the thrust stage a prominent position among the other major forms.

12. What does the professor imply about the various types of stages?
13. Which of the following is a disadvantage of the proscenium stage?
14. Which type of performance would probably best be produced on an arena stage?
15. Why does the professor say this:
"It's interesting to note that almost all early theatrical performances were 'in the round,' as ceremonies, rituals, and dances in all parts of the world took place in a circle."
16. Which diagram represents the thrust stage theater?
17. According to the professor, why is the thrust stage theater the most widely used of the three designs?

Disk 2, Track 5

Questions 18 through 22. Listen to a conversation between a student and a professor.

W: Dr. Marshall?
M: Hello, Gloria. Is it … uh … you wanted to talk about your research?
W: Yes. Is this a good time?
M: Sure, sure. How's it coming along? You're studying goose populations, right?
W: That's right. Well, I was anyway. That's what I wanted to talk to you about. I think I want to go in a different direction.
M: Oh …?
W: You see … it's like this. I've done a lot of Internet searches, and I've, uh, come up with some articles about geese, mostly about problems in urban areas, like city parks. But there was this one story that kind of got me off in a different direction. I found out about this accident that happened in Alaska when some geese got sucked into an airplane.
M: Really? When did that happen?
W: About six years ago. It was a pretty bad accident, too. It was a military jet, and several geese were sucked into two of the engines right after takeoff. The jet crashed, and the whole crew was killed.
M: Birds and planes don't mix—that's for sure.
W: For sure. Well, anyway this article got me thinking about birds and plane accidents, so I started … uh … researching that, and I found out it's a pretty serious problem around airports.
M: Hmm. I can see why.
W: It's a big problem especially if the airport is surrounded by bird habitat, like wheat fields or wetlands. It's a big problem that I never knew about before. And then I learned about this program that uses biology to solve the problem.
M: Oh? How so?
W: Well, the air force figured out that the right kind of bird can keep the wrong kind of bird away, so they started using peregrine falcons to patrol the runways. This one air force base used to shoot the birds that were always hanging around the runway. Mostly it was geese and ducks, because it's near a wetland. But now, since they started the falcon program, and since falcons are predators, there haven't been any bird–aircraft collisions that required any repairs!
M: That's amazing! Well, not really, when you consider the peregrine falcon's reputation as a predator. They can exceed 200 miles per hour in a dive—faster than any other living creature. I imagine just the sight of these birds is enough to discourage any other birds from coming anywhere near the airfield.
W: It's true. The falcons and their trainers patrol the runways several times a day, during the lulls between takeoffs and landings. And after six months of falcon protection, they found that the cost of the program itself was only seven percent of the amount they'd been spending on bird–airplane damage.
M: So, the benefits of this natural method of bird control are obvious.
W: Right. The falcons get the credit for keeping the geese and the ducks away. It's an interesting solution to the problem, I mean, adding a predator to change the biology of the runway.
M: Well, I think your research has taken a very meaningful turn. You're still studying problem geese, but you've just found an interesting angle in the way the problem's being dealt with. Keep going with it.
W: Oh, good. I'm glad you think it's OK. Thanks, Dr. Marshall. I appreciate your time.
M: All right. Good luck.

18. Why does the student go to see her professor?
19. Listen again to part of the conversation. Then answer the question.
"You see … it's like this. I've done a lot of Internet searches, and I've, uh, come up with some articles about geese, mostly about problems in urban areas, like city parks. But there was this one story that kind of got me off in a different direction. I found out about this accident that happened in Alaska when some geese got sucked into an airplane."
Why does the student say this:
"But there was this one story that kind of got me off in a different direction."
20. What does the professor mean when he says this:
"Birds and planes don't mix—that's for sure."
21. According to the conversation, which statements about peregrine falcons are true?
22. What is the student's opinion of the falcon program?

Disk 2, Track 6

Questions 23 through 28. Listen to part of a lecture in an economics class.

In this course, we'll look at the basic problems every economy must face. We'll focus on the modern industrial economy, and how it solves the problems of what, how, and for whom goods are produced. We'll examine the market mechanism, how the problems of production are solved through a system of markets and prices.

The market system isn't perfect. In fact, it's far from perfect, but it's one way to solve the problems of production. Let me just say one thing before we go on. No human economy today is purely a market economy. What we have in most capitalist societies today is known as a mixed economy.

In a mixed economy, the markets and the government share economic control over the direction of the market. The government has an important role in regulating business activity. A pure market system would have no government intervention—just consumers and businesses interacting through markets to determine the answers to the basic questions of economic organization.

OK. It's essential to understand how a pure market system works. Basically, it works like this: consumers are kind of like voters. They use their money like votes to buy what they want. My votes compete with your votes over the goods we both want to buy. The consumers with the most dollar votes have the most influence over what gets produced and to whom goods go. In economics, the consumer is king.

The consumer is like a king—or a dictator, really, if we're talking about a pure market system. In a pure market, the consumer would dictate the type and quantity and price of the goods that get produced. Of course, it's not exactly like that in the real world because real consumers don't always have complete information about goods, and, of course, real consumers can be influenced by advertising.

OK. Let's take a look at how the consumer's money votes operate in the marketplace. What I mean is, we'll examine the theory of the two central economic forces: supply and demand, and how they influence each other and are eventually brought into balance by the price of the good.

First, let's consider demand. In economics, "demand" refers to the amount of a good or service that people are ready to buy. Generally speaking, the quantity that people will buy depends on the price. The higher the price of a good, the less of it people will buy. The lower the price, the more they'll buy. So you can see there's a definite relationship between the price of a good and the quantity demanded. The connection between price and quantity is clear. When the price of a good is raised, consumer demand for it goes down. But when the price falls, demand increases, as more people will be willing and able to buy it at a lower price.

OK. That's demand. Now, what about supply? In economics, "supply" means how much of a good producers are willing to supply. Goods are supplied by businesses. Businesses—if they're competitive—they don't supply goods for fun. They supply goods for profit. They'll supply more of a good when the price is high because it's more profitable to do so. But when the price is low, producers will choose to supply some other more profitable good instead.

I've just given you the briefest summary of market economics. Tomorrow we'll look at just how supply and demand work in a real–world mixed economy. We'll see how the market price of a good is a function of supply and demand … how the price is a sort of agreement between the people who sell a good and the people who buy it.

23. What is the lecture mainly about?
24. Listen again to part of the lecture. Then answer the question.
"In a mixed economy, the markets and the government share economic control over the direction of the market. The government has an important role in regulating business activity. A pure market system would have no government intervention—just consumers and businesses interacting through markets to determine the answers to the basic questions of economic organization."
Why does the professor say this:
"A pure market system would have no government intervention—just consumers and businesses interacting through markets to determine the answers to the basic questions of economic organization."
25. What does the professor mean when she says this:
"…consumers are kind of like voters."
26. According to the professor, why does the demand for a good increase when the price decreases?
27. Listen again to part of the lecture. Then answer the question.
"Businesses—if they're competitive—they don't supply goods for fun. They supply goods for profit. They'll supply more of a good when the price is high because it's more profitable to do so. But when the price is low, producers will choose to supply some other more profitable good instead."
What does the professor imply about the supply of a good?
28. What will the next lecture probably be about?

Disk 2, Track 7

Questions 29 through 34. Listen to part of a talk in a forestry class. The instructor is discussing forest fire.

We all know that change is a fact of life. For North American forests, change often comes in the form of fire. After thousands of years of living with fire, many plant and animal species have come to depend on its periodic presence. Without fire, ecosystems can stagnate and lose their diversity of life.

In the past, before we understood the role that fire plays in the natural life cycle of our forests, our goal was to prevent or contain all forest fires. For almost ninety years, our land management agencies tried to eliminate fires. In many cases, we protected the trees, but at the expense of the forest community. Now we know that fire is a natural agent that rejuvenates a forest. And we know that fire suppression can actually threaten the lives of healthy trees. So, today our policy is to allow natural fires to burn under close observation and to set "prescribed" fires under carefully controlled conditions.

Research shows that forests go through natural fire cycles. Periodic fires are necessary for several reasons. Fire removes nutrients from standing dead trees and returns them to the earth, where they become available to the root systems of new trees. Fire also opens the forest to sunlight. Openings in the tree cover benefit a variety of wildlife by stimulating the growth of lush green plants, which are eaten by several species of animals.

Fire is nature's way of controlling insect infestations. By contrast, fire suppression preserves dead wood that harbors insect pests, like the larvae of the mountain pine beetle. These beetle larvae feed on the inner bark of some trees, which blocks the flow of nutrients and eventually kills the trees. When dead trees burn during periodic outbreaks of fire, the heat kills off great numbers of beetles and larvae, providing a natural method of pest control.

The exclusion of fire from the ecosystem is creating unhealthy, overcrowded forests that contain more fuel for larger, more severe fires. For example, when a huge fire threatened a grove of giant sequoias in California, observers noted that the flames were fed by dead wood and combustible debris that had accumulated on the forest floor over years of fire suppression.

A large–scale, intense forest fire causes more significant impacts to water, soil, and air resources than a managed prescribed fire. Prescribed fire, or controlled fire, has several purposes. Chiefly, it reduces the hazard of more serious wildfires by periodically burning accumulated weeds, brush, and other plants. If done carefully, prescribed burning also releases nutrients back into the soil and controls insect pests. In Florida, prescribed burns are carried out every three to five years in one of the national forests. These controlled burns keep the forest open and reduce the growth of problem species.

We recognize that fire is a natural and revitalizing process that enhances the diversity of the forest. However, we also know that fire has consequences. There may be smoky, hazy skies and patches of blackened forest for a long time after a fire. There's also the risk of a fire becoming too large and threatening inhabited areas. But we have to accept these realities if our forests are to retain their ecological balance.

29. What is the main idea of the talk?
30. Listen again to part of the talk. Then answer the question.
"In the past, before we understood the role that fire plays in the natural life cycle of our forests, our goal was to prevent or contain all forest fires. For almost ninety years, our land management agencies tried to eliminate fires. In many cases, we protected the trees, but at the expense of the forest community."
What does the instructor mean by this statement:
"In many cases, we protected the trees, but at the expense of the forest community."
31. According to the instructor, why is periodic fire necessary to forest ecosystems?
32. According to the instructor, how does the elimination of fire endanger the forest?
33. What is prescribed fire?
34. Why does the instructor say this:
"We recognize that fire is a natural and revitalizing process that enhances the diversity of the forest. However, we also know that fire has consequences. There may be smoky, hazy skies and patches of blackened forest for a long time after a fire. There's also the risk of a fire becoming too large and threatening inhabited areas."

Disk 2, Track 8

Questions 35 through 39. Listen to a conversation in the learning resource center of a university.

M: Hello.
W: Hello.
M: Um … I heard that the learning resource center has some kind of class on how to get help with studying for a test.
W: Uh–huh. We do have special workshops, but we don't really have any classes that deal with just test preparation. But we do have tutors for particular subject areas. What test are you studying for?
M: Uh … not any test in particular. But I, uh, I'm taking some difficult courses this semester and I have a lot of reading to do. I just feel like I need to bone up on my study skills, you know, learn how to study better.
W: Uh–huh.
M: I spend a lot of time studying but still have trouble organizing my notes and stuff. I was hoping I could get some help with that.
W: OK. You could take one of our special workshops. There are several of these each week. The workshops in study skills and time management are especially popular. Would you be interested in doing something like that?
M: Yeah, I would.
W: OK. We have several workshops. All of them are two hours long. Most are held in the evening, but there's a couple that are on the weekend.
M: Yeah, I see that. Evenings would be good for me because I work on weekends. Um … so the classes are just two–hour workshops that just meet once? Or does a class continue every week?
W: They're just one–time workshops. I mean, except for the class called Super Student. That one runs for three Wednesday nights, starting next week.
M: Super Student? I get it … it makes you like Superman.
W: Well, I don't know about that!
M: So, um, how does this work? Do you have to register for these workshops?
W: Yes, but it's only a matter of signing up. Do you see that board over there? The white board next to it, just to the right of the computers?
M: Uh–huh.
W: Well, there's a sheet there for every workshop offered this semester, and that's how you sign up. Some of the workshops are given more than once. You just write your name in any available space, under a particular date and time. When there are no more spaces left, that means the class is closed. We have to have a limit 'cause there's only so much space in our classroom.
M: How much does a workshop cost?
W: There isn't any cost. All of the workshops are free to students.
M: Hey, that's not a bad deal. OK, thanks for the info. I guess I'll see if there's any workshop that looks good.
W: I'll be right here if you have any more questions.
M: OK. Thanks.

35. Why does the man go to the learning resource center?
36. What does the woman suggest the man do?
37. When do most of the special workshops take place?
38. Listen again to part of the conversation. Then answer the question.
"There isn't any cost. All of the workshops are free to students."
"Hey, that's not a bad deal."
Why does the man say this:
"Hey, that's not a bad deal."
39. What will the man probably do next?

Disk 2, Track 9

Questions 40 through 45. Listen to part of a lecture in a philosophy class.

M: More than two thousand years separated two of the world's great educational philosophers, Confucius and Dewey. Yet, despite their, uh, separation in time and space, both of these thinkers held some interesting—and amazingly parallel—ideas about teaching and learning. Confucius lived during the sixth century B.C., during China's Classical Age, and is generally held to be China's greatest and most influential philosopher. Confucius was, and still is, considered both reactionary and revolutionary. He's reactionary because his perspective looked to the past, to the wisdom of the ancients. Confucius felt that his role as a teacher was to carry on the ancient tradition, rather than to create something new. He said, "I transmit, but do not create; I have faith in and love for ancient studies." During his lifetime, Confucius studied and commented on several texts of the ancient tradition, including the books known as the Six Classics. Yes, Tracy?

W: If Confucius just studied the ancient books, why was he considered a philosopher? I mean, he didn't create anything new. He just talked about other people's work.

M: The way he looked to the past, his focus on the classical texts—that's the reactionary side of Confucianism.

W: OK, but if he didn't create anything new, how does this make him a revolutionary?

M: Confucius was a revolutionary because he believed that there should be no distinction of social class in education. He believed that education should be, um, not just for the privileged class, but for any boy or girl who was able and willing to learn. Confucius stressed education for practical use because he believed the goal of education is to improve all of humanity. This aspect of Confucianism shares a core belief with the Western philosophy of pragmatism. According to pragmatism, the value of knowledge is a function of its practical outcome, that is, its usefulness to both the individual and the society. In the early twentieth century, pragmatism was highly influential in several fields—like government, business, but especially education. One of its leading thinkers was the American philosopher John Dewey. Like Confucius, Dewey was a scholar and educator whose ideas have had a tremendous impact, both in his time and beyond. Like Confucius, Dewey has a place among our greatest thinkers. As was the case with Confucius, some of Dewey's ideas were considered revolutionary. Dewey's ideas about individuality and social progress were radical in the early twentieth century. Dewey believed that the cultivation of the individual would benefit society as a whole, and therefore, the education of individual students is good for social progress. This is similar to the Confucian idea that if a man is true to his inner self, he will achieve true greatness, and that the greatness of individuals is necessary for social order. Despite the centuries that separated them, Confucius and Dewey held some similar ideas about knowledge, teaching, and learning. Confucius believed that the processes of teaching and learning stimulate each other. Teaching is half of learning, and the ideal teacher is one who goes over what he's already learned and gains some new understanding from the experience. Compare this to Dewey's idea that education is a continuously constructive process, with experience and knowledge building on each other.

40. Which of the following best describes the organization of the lecture?
41. Listen again to part of the lecture. Then answer the question.
"Confucius was, and still is, considered both reactionary and revolutionary. He's reactionary because his perspective looked to the past, to the wisdom of the ancients. Confucius felt that his role as a teacher was to carry on the ancient tradition, rather than to create something new. He said, 'I transmit, but do not create; I have faith in and love for ancient studies.'"
Why does the professor quote Confucius?
42. According to the professor, in what way was Confucius a revolutionary?
43. With which philosophy is John Dewey associated?
44. Which ideas are important in the philosophy of both Confucius and Dewey?
45. Listen again to part of the lecture. Then answer the question.
"Confucius believed that the processes of teaching and learning stimulate each other. Teaching is half of learning, and the ideal teacher is one who goes over what he's already learned and gains some new understanding from the experience. Compare this to Dewey's idea that education is a continuously constructive process, with experience and knowledge building on each other."
What does the professor imply about Confucius and Dewey?

Disk 2, Track 10

Questions 46 through 51. Listen to part of a lecture in a zoology class. The professor is talking about animal defenses.

One of the most important relationships between different animal species is predation—the predator–prey interaction, in which a predator eats a prey. Predator species have several adaptations that help them catch prey species. Prey species have adaptations, too—physical and behavioral adaptations that enable them to elude predators and avoid being eaten. These defensive adaptations evolved in prey species through repeated encounters with predators over evolutionary time.

Some animal defenses are passive, such as hiding. Some defenses are active, such as escaping. Fleeing—running away—is the most direct anti–predator response, but it requires the animal to expend a lot of energy. A rabbit uses up a lot of energy running away from a lynx. Many animals avoid expending too much energy by escaping into a shelter.

Several prey species have some sort of vocalization—an alarm call—to announce the presence of a predator. The alarm call often triggers a behavioral defense called mobbing. During mobbing, the prey turns the tables and attacks the predator. For example, when a chickadee spots a threat—say, an owl—it calls out the alarm. The chickadee starts scolding the owl, sometimes actually striking it from behind. Birds of other species may fly in to investigate, and often participate in the mobbing. The other birds chase, dive–bomb, or surround the owl, usually vocalizing loudly. Their intent is to encourage the "enemy" to move on to another area.

Some animals rely on defensive coloration. A well–known example of defensive coloration is camouflage, which makes prey difficult to spot against a background of similar color. All a camouflaged animal has to do is remain still to avoid being seen. Thus, camouflage is probably the most effective passive defense. Incidentally, some predators also use camouflage, especially predators who lie in wait for prey and have to blend into their environment.

Moths that camouflage themselves to match a leaf stand a good chance of not being seen by moth–eating birds, unless, of course, the moths become so populous that a bird is likely to come across one by accident. Once the bird learns the moth's identity, it has a search image for it, and the moth's disguise is useless. Looking like a leaf is then no advantage because the bird will start pecking at leaves in the hope that they are moths, and it will keep doing it as long as a sufficient number do turn out to be moths.

Another animal defense is the use of chemical weapons. We're all familiar with the chemical weapon of the skunk. Some animals—like poisonous toads and frogs—can synthesize toxins that attack the nervous system of predators. Other animals acquire chemical defenses passively. For example, some caterpillars acquire poison from the plants they eat. Then, when a bird eats the caterpillar, the bird quickly vomits. After that, the bird will avoid eating that kind of caterpillar. Some birds can remember bad–tasting meals a year later.

Another defensive adaptation is warning coloration. Animals with effective chemical defenses are often brightly colored, and there is evidence that predators are more cautious in dealing with bright color patterns in potential prey. This is probably because a lot of poisonous or bad–tasting animals are colored brightly, with black and yellow, or black and red stripes.

Warning coloration quickly trains predators to avoid eating these brightly–colored animals. Some birds have an instinctive tendency to avoid eating insects with warning coloration. For example, young warblers leave wasps alone because the birds recognize the danger in the black and yellow stripes of the wasp. However, warning coloration is not an absolute defense, as there is also evidence showing that many birds occasionally feed on bees and wasps, perhaps after learning to cope with their chemical defenses.

46. What topics does the professor mainly discuss?
47. Why does the professor say this:
    "A rabbit uses up a lot of energy running away from a lynx."
48. What takes place during a mobbing event?
49. Listen again to part of the lecture. Then answer the question.
    "Moths that camouflage themselves to match a leaf stand a good chance of not being seen by moth–eating birds, unless, of course, the moths become so populous that a bird is likely to come across one by accident. Once the bird learns the moth's identity, it has a search image for it, and the moth's disguise is useless."
    Why does the professor say this:
    "Once the bird learns the moth's identity, it has a search image for it, and the moth's disguise is useless."
50. What does the professor mean when she says this:
    "However, warning coloration is not an absolute defense, as there is also evidence showing that many birds occasionally feed on bees and wasps, perhaps after learning to cope with their chemical defenses."
51. Based on the information in the lecture, indicate whether each situation below involves camouflage, chemical weapons, or warning coloration.

Disk 2, Track 11

SPEAKING SECTION DIRECTIONS (*p. 106*)

The Speaking section measures your ability to speak in English about a variety of topics. There are six questions in this section.

Questions 1 and 2 are independent tasks in which you will speak about familiar topics. Your responses will be scored on your ability to speak clearly and coherently about the topics.

Questions 3 and 4 are integrated speaking tasks. You will read a passage, listen to a conversation or lecture, and then speak in response to a question about what you have read and heard. You will need to combine relevant information from the two sources to answer the question completely. Your responses will be scored on your ability to speak clearly and coherently and on your ability to accurately convey information about what you read and heard.

Questions 5 and 6 are integrated speaking tasks. You will listen to part of a conversation or lecture, and then speak in response to a question about what you have heard. Your responses will be scored on your ability to speak clearly and coherently and on your ability to accurately convey information about what you heard.

You will hear each conversation and lecture only one time. You may take notes while you listen. You may use your notes to help you answer the questions.

Disk 2, Track 12

What is your favorite style of dress? Describe this clothing style and explain why it appeals to you. Include details and examples in your explanation.

Disk 2, Track 13

Some students learn better by reading. Others learn more from listening to a teacher. Which way of learning is better for you, and why? Include details and examples to support your explanation.

Disk 2, Track 14

Now listen to two students as they discuss their project report.

M: We should decide the format of our presentation ahead of time, even before we do the formal written part.

W. I think we should do an oral report to the class. You and Steve and I could each talk about one part of our project.

M: But we've already done lots of oral reports. Why don't we do something different this time? I'd like to do a Web page. Steve already knows how to do it, and, besides, knowing how to build a Web page is a good skill to have. It will help us in our careers.

W: Hmm. You're probably right about that.

M: We could be more creative. We could include text from our written report and graphics to make it more interesting. A Web page is the best way to show the results of our survey. And, you know, our classmates are already big users of e–mail and the Web, so isn't this a natural choice for us?

W: Hmm. Maybe. But won't it take a lot of time to do?
M: Not really. Let's talk to Steve. He's done it before.
W: OK. Let's see what he thinks.

The man expresses his preference for the format they should use for their project report. State his preference and explain the reasons he gives for his choice.

Disk 2, Track 15

Now listen to part of a lecture on this topic in a sociology class.

Not surprisingly, women report more conflict between work and family roles. Women who work outside the home actually put in more hours of work at home. Women do more of the childcare and housework than their husbands do, whether the woman works full–time or not. Women are much more likely to leave the workforce entirely when their children are young. They're also more likely to stay home with a sick child or to be the one to rearrange their work schedule to go to a meeting at the child's school. They're more likely to feel overworked and stressed–out.

For most men, including men who are highly successful in their careers, family is far more important than work for their overall life satisfaction. The roles of husband and father are central to a man's mental and physical health. So it's not surprising that men carry emotional distress from the family into the workplace, even though they don't experience the same degree of role conflict or overload as women do. In one study of working men and women, men more often than women reported that an argument at home was followed by higher rates of argument with coworkers or supervisors at work the next day.

The same study reported that when the man came home overly tired from work, the wives did more of the work at home. The reverse pattern occurred less often: the husband did not do more of the work at home after his wife had had an especially hard day at work.

Explain how women and men experience conflict between their work and family roles.

Disk 2, Track 16

Now listen to part of a conversation between two students.

W: Hey, you doing anything special for spring break?
M: I might go to the beach. My sister and her husband want me to go to their beach house with them. My brother will be there too. I'd really like to go because I just want to relax and have some fun. But I'm torn between doing that and going on this biology trip, you know, the one in the rainforest?
W: Biology trip? You mean the one that your professor is leading?
M: Yeah, it's a study of the rainforest ecosystem. It costs money, but I know I'd learn a lot. I'd get some experience doing field research.
W: Oh, wow. That's a hard decision. The beach sounds great, but so does the rainforest. That seems like an opportunity you shouldn't pass up.
M: My family will be disappointed if I don't go to the beach. I haven't seen them in a long time, and the beach is a special place for us.
W: But you can go to the beach with your family anytime. You might not get another chance to go to the rainforest. You should talk to your family, explain that you have a great opportunity to do some research. You might not get another opportunity like this.
M: Hmm. Maybe not.
W: You need to think about your future. An experience like this might help you later, I mean, when you look for a job after graduation. You should stress that you did field research. That would look good in your record.

Describe the man's problem and the suggestions the woman makes about what he should do. What do you think the man should do, and why?

Disk 2, Track 17

Now listen to part of a lecture in an anthropology class.

Human culture could not have developed without the human hand. Chimpanzees and gorillas walk on their hands, and orangutans use their hands primarily for holding branches, but the human hand is both tool and toolmaker, as well as an extension of the brain. Next to the brain, the hand is probably our greatest possession. Other animals may run faster than us, or have better senses, but no other animal comes close to matching our manual skills.

The power of the human hand comes from the way the brain controls it. The brain coordinates the hand's actions with signals from the eyes, directing the hand by feeding it complex instructions at an almost automatic level. The human hand is capable of both brute strength and delicate tasks. The hand can perform hard physical labor, yet it's also sensitive to slight changes in form and texture—so much so, in fact, that the hand is a substitute eye to people who are blind.

A key aspect of our manual skill is the ability to use our fingers independently rather than having to use them all together. The human hand has two characteristics that make us different from any other animal: the opposable thumb and the double grip. The first of these, the opposable thumb, has the ability to oppose—to face—the other fingers, so it can touch every part of every other finger on the same hand. The second characteristic is the double grip. This means that one hand can hold two billiard balls separately, for example. We can grip one ball between our last two fingers and our palm, and hold the second ball between our forefinger and thumb. Having strength and delicacy combined like this makes the human hand more skilled than any limb on any other animal. The opposable thumb and the double grip put us in the top class for tool making and for doing whatever else our brain tells our hands to do.

Using points and examples from the lecture, explain why the human hand is a valuable possession.

Disk 2, Track 18

WRITING SECTION DIRECTIONS (*p. 112*)

The Writing section measures your ability to use writing to communicate in an academic environment. There are two writing questions.

Question 1 is an integrated writing task. You will read a passage, listen to a lecture, and then answer a question based on what you have read and heard. You have 20 minutes to plan and write your response.

Question 2 is an independent writing task. You will answer a question based on your own knowledge and experience. You have 30 minutes to plan and write your response.

Disk 2, Track 19

Now listen to part of a lecture on this topic in an ecology class.

The advantages of hydropower are well known, but there are also some serious disadvantages that should cause us to rethink its overall benefit.

First, hydropower facilities are not always convenient for everyone involved. When a dam is built on a river, water floods the land behind the dam. This forces the people who live in the flooded area to move. Forcing people to move is often bitter and controversial, especially if a community has maintained a particular way of life on the same land for several generations.

Second, utility companies often emphasize that hydroelectricity is environmentally friendly, "clean and green," but they fail to mention the long–term environmental hazards. Dams hold back silt and other debris, which collect behind the dam on the river bottom. This causes an accumulation of toxic heavy metals and other polluting substances, showing us that hydropower does indeed produce toxic waste. The buildup of silt means that future generations will have an expensive and dangerous mess to clean up.

Third, the huge dams built for hydroelectricity change a river's natural functions. By diverting water for power, dams remove water needed for healthy river ecosystems. The section of river below a dam often dries up, and birds that migrate there no longer have enough insects to feed on when the water level drops. Also, fish such as salmon depend on a steady flow of cool, fresh water. Native fish populations may decrease or disappear because of the warmer and slower–moving water caused by dams. The environmental changes caused by hydropower may not be obvious right away. Most people will notice air pollution around a coal–burning power plant, but they won't notice a smaller bird population near a hydropower plant.

While it's true that hydropower is a renewable energy source, it often carries a heavy environmental cost. Furthermore, even though water is a naturally recurring product, the water supply is subject to natural conditions, such as changing weather patterns and regional drought, so water as a source of fuel may not be reliable in the long run.

Summarize the points made in the lecture you just heard, explaining how they contrast with points made in the reading.

TEST 3

Disk 3, Track 1

LISTENING SECTION DIRECTIONS (*p. 138*)

The Listening section measures your ability to understand conversations and lectures in English. You will hear each conversation and lecture only one time. After each conversation or lecture, you will hear some questions about it. Answer the questions based on what the speakers state or imply.

You may take notes while you listen. You may use your notes to help you answer the questions.

In some questions, you will see this icon: 🎧. This means that you will hear, but not see, part of the question.

Some questions have special directions, which appear in a gray box. Most questions are worth one point. If a question is worth more than one point, the directions will indicate how many points you can receive.

You will now begin the first part of the Listening section.

Disk 3, Track 2

Questions 1 through 5. Listen to a conversation between a student and his academic adviser.

M: Hi! Are you busy right now?
W: Oh, hi, Sean. There's a meeting at two–thirty, but I have a few minutes. What can I do for you?
M: Well, I wanted to talk with you before I went to register for next semester. That'll be my last term here 'cause I hope to transfer to the university next year.
W: Great! Have you applied to the university yet?
M: Not yet. The deadline's not till March 1.
W: Right.
M: But I was, uh, I wanted to check with you to see if there are any other courses I still need before I transfer. I think I've filled all the requirements, but I, uh, just wanted to make sure before I register.
W: All right. Let me pull up your record. Let's see now … Sean Howard. Here we are. Hmm. All right, it looks like you've got all of your English and math credits, so you're OK there, as well as your humanities and, uh, social sciences. But for natural science … hmm … you took biology in your first year, but I don't see anything after that. You're required to have at least one more natural science course before you can transfer.
M: Oh, really? I thought I needed only one science course.
W: No, sorry, you need at least eight credits in natural science, and that means two courses.
M: I didn't know that. OK. Then I wonder which course I should take. What do you recommend?
W: Next semester … let's see … it looks like astronomy, botany, and ecology are all being offered. There's also a course in meteorology for non–science majors.
M: Meteorology? Do you mean, like, the weather?
W: That's right.
M: Hey, that might be kind of interesting. I always wanted to know how they forecast the weather.

W: Then that's the right course for you. Oh, and, Sean, it looks like you also need two credits in physical education.

M: Phys. ed!

W: Right. You're required to have four credits, and you've only got two so far.

M: Oh, boy. Well, OK, that shouldn't be too hard. Maybe I should take golf—that is offered in the spring, right?

W: Golf? Uh … yes, it is. Do you play?

M: Not very well, no. I've only played a couple of times, but I need to do better than that. My boss plays golf and he's always talking about it. It would be nice to know what he's talking about!

W: Then you'd better take golf. You've got to play golf with your boss!

M: OK, OK, you talked me into it! Hey, thanks for your time. I appreciate your help, and I'll get out of your way now.

W: Glad to help, Sean. Good luck with registration!

1. Why does the student go to see his adviser?
2. Why does the adviser say this:
"There's a meeting at two–thirty, but I have a few minutes."
3. What does the student want to do next year?
4. In which subject areas must the student take courses next semester?
5. What does the student imply about golf?

Disk 3, Track 3

Questions 6 through 11. Listen to part of a lecture in a biology class.

M: One type of immune response has to do with bees—actually any insect of that class, including hornets and fire ants. If you've ever been stung or bitten, you know how painful it is. But stings and bites usually aren't dangerous, unless you have lots of them at the same time, or unless you have an allergic reaction to the venom. A massive allergic reaction to a sting is known as anaphylaxis. The term anaphylaxis is Greek for "a lack of protection." But the name is sort of inaccurate. Anaphylaxis is actually a disease, a severe form of allergic, um, over–response by the immune system when it's suddenly faced with a foreign substance. That foreign substance is the bee's venom, or in some cases it's certain foods, like nuts, eggs, and shellfish … or drugs, especially antibiotics like penicillin. Anaphylaxis—or anaphylactic shock—is one of those true emergencies where minutes can make the difference between life and death. It can start within seconds, although sometimes it has a delay of thirty minutes or more.

W: Excuse me, Professor Watson, but how do you recognize it? I mean, there's a difference between a few seconds and thirty minutes. So how do you … like, how do you know when a person's in anaphylactic shock?

M: Sometimes it's hard to identify the real reason why someone is in trouble. Unfortunately, that's what happened last year to a little girl who ate a peanut cookie at a birthday party. No one who was with her at the time knew she was allergic to peanuts, so they didn't know why she suddenly went into respiratory distress. The reason, of course, was anaphylaxis. But by the time the medics got there, it was too late, and the girl died.
So, how do we identify anaphylactic shock? The first sign is the victim becomes very weak and feels sick. There may be an itchy rash near the site of the sting, if it's a bee sting, or a tingling in the mouth, if it's a food allergy. The tissues of the face and throat may swell up. The chest feels tight, and the person has trouble breathing—this is when every minute, every second matters. The blood pressure drops dangerously low. Finally, the person may lose consciousness and stop breathing. When this happens, the person's life is in danger. Anaphylactic shock, as you can see, can be life threatening in some cases.
What happens to the immune system? First, it has to be exposed previously to the offending substance—the bee venom, the peanuts, or whatever. People don't get anaphylaxis from their first bee sting. The immune cells that produce antibodies … they … uh … they have to be sensitized to the offending substance at least once before they overreact to it the second or third time. We don't understand why some unlucky immune systems go crazy the next time they encounter the same substance. But some immune systems do sort of go crazy. The cells pour out far more antibody than they need. This sets off a whole series of reactions involving the release of histamine into the bloodstream. Histamine makes the blood vessels dilate and get "leaky," and the liquid part of the blood leaks out into the tissues. This is what causes the skin rash, the potentially fatal swelling, the narrowing of the airways, and the drop in blood pressure. The worst part is all of this happens within minutes.

W: Because this can happen so fast—I mean, going into shock—how do we prevent—I mean, is there a way we can stop somebody from dying of this?

M: With anaphylaxis, a few minutes can make the difference between life and death, so the keys to survival are being prepared and acting quickly. The most important tool to have is called an epi–pen—basically an automatic syringe that lets you self–administer the drug epinephrine into your body, a drug that helps combat the effects of anaphylaxis.

6. What is the lecture mainly about?
7. According to the professor, what can initiate anaphylaxis?
8. Why does the professor tell a story about a little girl at a birthday party?
9. Listen again to part of the lecture. Then answer the question.
"People don't get anaphylaxis from their first bee sting. The immune cells that produce antibodies … they … uh … they have to be sensitized to the offending substance at least once before they overreact to it the second or third time. We don't understand why some unlucky immune systems go crazy the next time they encounter the same substance."
Why does the professor say this:
"We don't understand why some unlucky immune systems go crazy the next time they encounter the same substance."

10. The professor describes what happens during anaphylactic shock. Indicate whether each sentence below is a step in the process.
11. What can be inferred about surviving anaphylaxis?

Disk 3, Track 4

Questions 12 through 17. Listen to part of a talk in a United States history class.

In the early years of the twentieth century, 60 percent of the American population was rural, and half of the nation's towns and cities had fewer than ten thousand people. Up until that time, life on the farm was lonely, and farm families felt that they weren't keeping up with the urban population, which had electric lights, telephones, and access to the latest goods in department stores. Farm families were isolated, often with limited funds, and few could afford the time or the expense of shopping in the city. But all of this changed with the introduction of the mail–order catalog.

In 1872, a Chicago merchant named Montgomery Ward began sending copies of a catalog to thousands of farmers in the Midwest. The catalog was 280 pages long and offered farm families the opportunity to order any of the goods listed in it by mail. This is how Montgomery Ward and Company became the nation's first mail–order company. Ward had discovered something entirely new and profitable, a new method of conducting business. After that, the terms "mail–order house" and "mail–order catalog" were added to our vocabulary.

The most successful mail–order house was Sears and Roebuck, which entered the mail–order business in 1895. Just as Montgomery Ward had done with his catalog, Richard Sears advertised his products in catalogs that were sent to farm families. The Sears catalog sold food, clothing, machinery, tools, stoves—anything and everything a farm family might need.

The mail–order business spread rapidly, largely because of improvements in postal services. The post office established Rural Free Delivery in 1902 and Parcel Post in 1913. These new services meant that catalogs and goods would be delivered directly to the farm, so farmers didn't have to drive several miles into town to pick up packages. These new services greatly contributed to the success of mail–order houses.

Rural Free Delivery also had great benefit for farm families. Families that had previously been isolated could now receive newspapers, magazines, and mail–order catalogs in their mailboxes. This contact with the outside world broke their isolation and changed the outlook of rural America. Thanks to the mail–order houses of Montgomery Ward and Sears and Roebuck, no farm was too isolated to be aware of the latest clothing, furniture, farm equipment, music, and literature.

The wide distribution of the Sears catalog had another interesting effect. The Sears catalog had a lot to do with the similarity of goods available nationwide. Of course, this was also due to the mass–production of goods. Mass–production techniques made it possible to create reasonable copies of, for example, high–priced clothing. The two factors working together—mass production and nationwide distribution—tended to minimize regional differences in clothing styles. This is why there was a general lack of class and regional distinction in American clothing. People believed that if clothing of the same design and brand was widely worn by many people, then this was a sign of its value.

By 1910, both men and women could buy every article of clothing, ready–made, from mail–order catalogs like Sears. Sears didn't pretend to be a leader in fashion, but it did try to provide what average Americans wanted. Women wanted to dress more fashionably and they welcomed new styles. For farm women, the pictures of the smiling women on the pages of the Sears catalog were as close as they came to outside contacts during the long winter months. And for immigrants who wanted to become Americans, the Sears catalog was a textbook. Here they learned how to dress, how to furnish their homes, and—some catalogs even had recipes and menus for holiday dinners—how to cook American food.

12. What is the talk mainly about?
13. How did the mail–order business begin?
14. Why does the professor mention Rural Free Delivery and Parcel Post?
15. According to the professor, what two factors led to the similarity of goods available nationwide?
16. What does the professor mean when she says this: "And for immigrants who wanted to become Americans, the Sears catalog was a textbook."
17. Based on the information in the talk, would the professor most likely agree or disagree with each statement below?

Disk 3, Track 5

Questions 18 through 22. Listen to part of a conversation between a student and her tutor.

W: There's something I've always wondered about. OK. A glass of water is crystal clear. A bathtub full of water looks faintly blue. And the water in a swimming pool is light blue at the shallow end and a darker color blue at the deep end. Does water have a color? I mean, its own true color?

M: Believe it or not, it does.

W: OK. Then what is it?

M: It's blue, like a piece of blue glass. And like glass or any other relatively transparent substance, the thicker it is, the deeper the color. That's why a swimming pool is a darker blue at the deep end.

W: OK. Then what I learned as a kid was wrong. In grade school I was taught that water doesn't have a color, that it's clear, and clear isn't a color. But my own eyes tell me otherwise. So, why is this? I mean, why is water blue, like blue glass?

M: It's because water transmits light of every color, but it's clearest for colors with shorter wavelengths. That's why its peak transparency is in the blue–green part of the light spectrum.

W: That explains why most of the time it looks blue or green.

M: Well, there are actually lots of factors that affect the color of water.

W: Such as … what, like how deep the water is?

M: Right. And it's easy to see why. It's because light from water comes from three places: the top, the middle, and the bottom of the water.

W: I'm not sure I understand.

M: Think of it like this. Together, all three parts of the water—top, middle, and bottom—make up the blend of light that we see. Under certain circumstances, one may dominate the others. For example, in shallow water, light from the bottom is most important. In deep water, very little light comes from below, so reflections from the surface are the brightest.

W: So, that means, in a shallow puddle, the bottom is well lit, so it sort of contributes more to the scene. I mean, it affects the overall color more than … say uh … the invisible bottom of the ocean?

M: Uh … that's right. Because a shallow puddle is relatively transparent, the water adds virtually no blue light of its own.

W: And muddy water looks brown because…?

M: Because the light is scattered, primarily from the suspended sediments near the surface. That's another factor that affects the color of water—sediments. Even the cleanest, purest mountain lake contains a lot of tiny particles that scatter light.

W: That's because mountain lakes have a lot of silt from the glaciers, right?

M: That's right. Lakes fed by glaciers get their colors from the fine, suspended silt in the water, and also from the reflected light of the sky. Glacier–fed streams are usually sort of a milky blue, and hot springs are sometimes yellow because of the sulfur suspended in the water. Some water is green and some is brown, depending on the mineral content.

W: This is really interesting. I'm glad I asked you about this.

18. What is the main subject of the conversation?
19. What does the student mean when she says this:
"In grade school I was taught that water doesn't have a color, that it's clear, and clear isn't a color. But my own eyes tell me otherwise."
20. Listen again to part of the conversation. Then answer the question.
"Together, all three parts of the water—top, middle, and bottom—make up the blend of light that we see. Under certain circumstances, one may dominate the others. For example, in shallow water, light from the bottom is most important. In deep water, very little light comes from below, so reflections from the surface are the brightest."
"So, that means, in a shallow puddle, the bottom is well lit, so it sort of contributes more to the scene. I mean, it affects the overall color more than … say uh … the invisible bottom of the ocean?"
Why does the student say this:
"So, that means, in a shallow puddle, the bottom is well lit, so it sort of contributes more to the scene. I mean, it affects the overall color more than … say uh … the invisible bottom of the ocean?"
21. According to the conversation, what factors influence the color of water?
22. What can be inferred about a lake with brown water?

Disk 3, Track 6

Questions 23 through 28. Listen to part of a lecture in a communications class.

Throughout most of human history, a society's culture was defined and communicated primarily through the family. Early cultures communicated their values and beliefs to their children by oral tradition—word of mouth. Parents and grandparents had the job of passing on the culture's history and traditions. The older members of the family were storytellers and historians—our "cultural narrators."

The cultural narrator was valued for his or her wisdom and experience. The cultural narrator helped to sustain the society through the preservation of vital cultural information. Until the mid–twentieth century, the family was the medium by which culture was passed along.

Since the 1950s, however, the role of the cultural narrator has been taken over by television. What I mean is, the family storytellers have been replaced by television shows that tell us who we are, what we need, how we should speak, and what we should believe in.

In the sixties and seventies, as television became more a part of North American life, several writers and philosophers began to study what was going on. One of the most creative minds to explore this issue was Marshall McLuhan.

McLuhan studied English literature in his native Canada and in England, and then taught at several universities in the United States. As a Canadian scholar teaching in the U. S., McLuhan realized that he didn't understand his American students. He couldn't figure out their interests and values, why they spoke and acted and felt the way they did. So, he set out to learn more about the values of his students by studying their popular culture: the movies, television shows, music, pastimes—all the things that young Americans pursued in their leisure time.

McLuhan became convinced that electronic media played a significant role and that the media were responsible for the attitudes and values of his students. In fact, he went beyond his immediate interest in his own students to theorize that the media had prompted most of the social changes in Western culture. McLuhan's ideas soon made him the leading cultural critic and media theorist of his time.

McLuhan's ideas gained attention worldwide. He wrote several books about the effect of media on human development, including this one, *The Medium is the Message*, which is the book you'll be reading next in this course.

The Medium is the Message is McLuhan's most influential book. Although it was first published more than thirty years ago, it remains an important classic in the field of communications. It's a book—and an idea—that you'll come back to over and over again, and reading it will probably change your view of how we communicate.

Why is it such an important book? Well, you've probably heard the expression, "The medium is the message" because it's entered our vocabulary. What McLuhan meant by this statement was that how people learn—the medium—is more important than what they learn—the message. In other words, the method of communicating information has more influence on the public than the information itself. Communication is culture, and culture is communication.

McLuhan didn't consider himself a critic of the media in the sense of condemning it. He wasn't interested in deciding whether television was good or bad. He just wanted people to understand how it affected them so they could make their own informed decisions about it. We're just beginning to understand the ways that the media have affected our culture. Sociologists, psychologists, media ecologists—people in a multitude of fields are trying to explain the relationships among media, values, and behavior.

Is television good or bad for us? Does television cause human behavior, or merely record it? This question is of particular interest to researchers who study the effects of television—especially television violence—on children's behavior. And now that television is starting to merge with other electronic media, like the Internet, there are a growing number of issues and new questions calling for informed thinking about the relationship of the media to human development.

23. According to the professor, how did children acquire their culture throughout most of history?
24. What does the professor mean by the term "cultural narrator"?
25. According to the professor, why did Marshall McLuhan study popular culture?
26. What is the professor's opinion of *The Medium is the Message*?
27. Listen again to part of the lecture. Then answer the question.
"Well, you've probably heard the expression, 'The medium is the message' because it's entered our vocabulary. What McLuhan meant by this statement was that how people learn—the medium—is more important than what they learn—the message. In other words, the method of communicating information has more influence on the public than the information itself."
Why does the professor say this:
"In other words, the method of communicating information has more influence on the public than the information itself."
28. Listen again to part of the lecture. Then answer the question.
"Is television good or bad for us? Does television cause human behavior, or merely record it? This question is of particular interest to researchers who study the effects of television—especially television violence—on children's behavior. And now that television is starting to merge with other electronic media, like the Internet, there are a growing number of issues and new questions calling for informed thinking about the relationship of the media to human development."
What does the professor imply about the effects of the media on society?

Disk 3, Track 7

Questions 29 through 34. Listen to part of a talk in an agriculture class.

In the field of agriculture, marketing is sort of a complex system. Marketing is supplying people with goods and services—what people want, in the form they want it, and when they want it. In agriculture, marketing involves moving a wide range of products—food crops, animal products, fiber crops, flowers, wood, and so on.

Marketing links the producer with the consumer. All of the processes and infrastructure involved—harvesting equipment, storage and transportation facilities—all of these processes and infrastructure come under the broad heading of "agricultural marketing technology." The focus of agricultural marketing technology is on meeting consumer demand.

A lot has to be done before farm products are ready for the consumer. The typical North American consumer can't deal with live chickens or cattle, unshelled wheat, or raw logs. Typical North American consumers want their food ready to cook, their clothes ready to wear, their wood products in sizes ready to use, and so on.

Consumers also want certain products at certain times of the year. They expect to have roses at Valentine's Day and poinsettias at Christmas. So, producers and marketing specialists have to make these special products available when consumers want them.

Getting products to consumers involves several processes—we call them marketing functions. These functions convert the product from its original form into the form that consumers want, and then transport it to the consumers. Functions such as harvesting, assembling, grading, transporting—these are just some of the important functions of agricultural marketing.

The first function, harvesting—this begins on the farm or ranch. Harvesting methods vary for different types of products. Some products are harvested by machine, while others have to be harvested by hand. Harvesting includes a wide variety of activities—for example, picking apples, picking cotton, digging potatoes, cutting wheat, cutting roses, cutting timber, shearing sheep, milking cows, and so on.

A very important function that comes after harvesting is assembling. Assembling is the delivery of a product to a central location, like a packing shed, grain elevator, cotton gin, or processing plant. Assembling is gathering large quantities together to make marketing more efficient. Marketing professionals want to deal with large volumes, and some farms don't have large enough volumes, so they have to combine their product with the product of other farms.

Another function is grading, which means sorting products for uniformity. Grading can take place during or after assembling. Grading involves dividing up the product on the basis of several factors—for example, size, color, variety, or the presence of defects. When people buy eggs, they kind of want a uniform size, not a mixture of small, medium, and large eggs. Various standards are used in grading products. Sometimes the government sets the standards. Sometimes the standards are set by an association of producers, or even by the processing plant or supermarket.

A very important marketing function is transporting, moving the product from one place to another. Milk is moved from the dairy farm to a processing plant. Freshly picked tomatoes are moved to the packing shed or cannery. Wheat is moved to the grain elevator. Logs are moved to the sawmill. Agricultural products are transported in various kinds of vehicles: wagons, trucks, barges, airplanes, and railroad cars.

In order to market products, certain facilities must be available—what we call marketing infrastructure—the vehicles, roads, railroads, assembling and processing plants, storage facilities, and so on. All of these facilities are necessary infrastructure for marketing agricultural goods.

29. What does the professor mainly discuss?
30. Why does the professor say this:
"The typical North American consumer can't deal with live chickens or cattle, unshelled wheat, or raw logs. Typical North American consumers want their food ready to cook, their clothes ready to wear, their wood products in sizes ready to use, and so on."
31. Which of the following are examples of the marketing function of harvesting?
32. According to the professor, why is assembling an important function in agricultural marketing?
33. What is the purpose of grading agricultural products?
34. Why does the professor say this:
"Milk is moved from the dairy farm to a processing plant. Freshly picked tomatoes are moved to the packing shed or cannery. Wheat is moved to the grain elevator. Logs are moved to the sawmill."

Disk 3, Track 8

SPEAKING SECTION DIRECTIONS (p. 151)

The Speaking section measures your ability to speak in English about a variety of topics. There are six questions in this section.

Questions 1 and 2 are independent tasks in which you will speak about familiar topics. Your responses will be scored on your ability to speak clearly and coherently about the topics.

Questions 3 and 4 are integrated speaking tasks. You will read a passage, listen to a conversation or lecture, and then speak in response to a question about what you have read and heard. You will need to combine relevant information from the two sources to answer the question completely. Your responses will be scored on your ability to speak clearly and coherently and on your ability to accurately convey information about what you read and heard.

Questions 5 and 6 are integrated speaking tasks. You will listen to part of a conversation or lecture, and then speak in response to a question about what you have heard. Your responses will be scored on your ability to speak clearly and coherently and on your ability to accurately convey information about what you heard.

You will hear each conversation and lecture only one time. You may take notes while you listen. You may use your notes to help you answer the questions.

Disk 3, Track 9

What is your favorite place to study? Describe it and explain why you like studying there. Include details and examples in your explanation.

Disk 3, Track 10

Some people like humorous stories that make them laugh. Others prefer stories that are more serious and make them think. Which type of story do you prefer and why? Include details and examples in your explanation.

Disk 3, Track 11

Now listen to two students as they discuss the announcement.

M: Did you read the announcement from the dean?
W: You mean the one about the new credit requirements?
M: Yeah. It's kind of strict, don't you think? I mean, why should we have to take another mathematics course if we're not a math major?
W: The dean thinks we need more math and writing, and he knows what he's talking about. I guess the idea is that everyone needs stronger skills. Math is important in business. I know it's true in my mother's business. She's always telling me about how her employees make accounting errors that really hurt the business.
M: Well, yeah, I agree with you that math is important in business.
W: Almost every kind of job needs either math or writing, or both. I can see why graduate schools want good writers because grad students have to do so much writing, like, you know, they have to write a thesis or a dissertation.
M: Yeah. I want to go to graduate school in psychology.
W: Businesses need good writers, too. It's important for the company's reputation. For example, it looks bad if there are a lot of mistakes in written reports and company e–mail.

The woman expresses her opinion about the new credit requirements. State her opinion and explain the reasons she gives for holding that opinion.

Disk 3, Track 12

Now listen to part of a talk in a biology class.

The cat has several specialized nerve endings, or sensory receptors, throughout its skin that respond to various sensations. The hair follicles of the cat are richly supplied with several types of touch receptors. These are responsive to the slightest movement, and so they provide a close–range detection system. As with most meat–eaters, this system is highly developed in the stiff, coarse whiskers on the cat's face.

The cat's whiskers are long, stiff, highly touch–sensitive hairs. Cats generally have about twelve whiskers in rows on each upper lip, a few on each cheek, and a few bristles on the chin. The long sensory whiskers are more than twice as thick as the rest of the hairs in the cat's coat, and extend three times deeper into the skin. The whiskers have a rich supply of blood vessels and a dense network of nerves. The slightest whisker movement stimulates the nerve endings and provides the brain with information on the cat's immediate surroundings. Whiskers can even detect very slight motion such as air currents.

The whiskers are important in sensing and investigating close objects. Cats rely heavily on their whiskers in dim light, when their eyes cannot focus well on very close objects. The whiskers are sensitive to air currents deflected by objects. This is why the cat can feel its way in the dark without actually making contact with objects. Loss of the whiskers will hinder a cat's ability to get around in the dark.

Describe the whiskers of a cat, and explain how the whiskers function as sensory receptors.

Disk 3, Track 13

Now listen to part of a conversation between two students.

M: Hey, did you hear about the special event tonight?
W: Special event? No. What about it?
M: It's a panel discussion about politics. There'll be guest speakers, I think about three … or maybe four people, journalists and politicians, tonight in the lecture hall. It's going to be on television, so it should be good. You should definitely come to this!
W: I'd love to! Oh, no … tonight I have plans. I'll be meeting with my tutor. She's helping me study for a test.
M: That's too bad. Can't you cancel the meeting with your tutor? I mean, try to meet her at a different time or something.
W: I don't know. That might be hard. She's busy, too, and it's kind of hard to find a time that works for the both of us. My test is coming up, and I really need the extra time to study.
M: Why don't you ask her anyway? You never know unless you ask.
W: You think so? It's kind of short notice.

M: You can't miss the panel discussion!
W: Well, I don't know. I'd like to go. I love hearing about politics.
M: Another thing you could do is … this event will be on television, so you could record it and watch it later. I mean, it won't be as much fun as being there in person, but at least you'd get to see what they talk about. Do you have a VCR?
W: No, I don't.
M: I don't either. Otherwise I'd tape it for you. You must know someone who could record it!

Describe the woman's problem and the two suggestions the man makes about how to solve it. What do you think the woman should do, and why?

Disk 3, Track 14

Now listen to part of a lecture in a psychology class.

Some people have certain abnormalities in the brain that make it hard for them to process and absorb information. These problems, which can make learning to read and write difficult, are usually noticed first in school. A child with a learning disability may have trouble keeping up with his classmates, difficulty remembering, or difficulty concentrating.

One type of learning disability is dyslexia. A child with dyslexia has normal vision and intelligence, but has difficulty reading because he perceives the letters in words differently. He may see letters backwards, upside down, or sideways. This problem, this inability to process written information, makes it difficult for a child to learn to read and write.

Another type of learning disability causes some children to have trouble translating their thoughts into writing. They can usually communicate well by speaking, but when they try to write, they become completely blocked and can't write at all, or they can only write very slowly. Their handwriting may look like that of a much younger child, or they may have trouble with spelling.

A third type of learning disability is the inability to focus on a task for a long period of time. This problem, called attention deficit disorder, is caused by differences in brain activity that affect the ability to concentrate. The disorder is usually accompanied by hyperactivity—extreme overactivity. Children with attention deficit disorder have trouble sitting still, paying attention, and controlling impulses, and this interferes with schoolwork, friendships, and family life.

Fortunately, we now understand that learning disabilities can be treated. If left untreated, they can lead to a variety of problems for children later on, such as difficulty with reading and writing, or problems with math skills.

Using points and examples from the lecture, describe three types of learning disabilities, and explain how they can affect a child's ability to learn.

Disk 3, Track 15

WRITING SECTION DIRECTIONS (p. 157)

The Writing section measures your ability to use writing to communicate in an academic environment. There are two writing questions.

Question 1 is an integrated writing task. You will read a passage, listen to a lecture, and then answer a question based on what you have read and heard. You have 20 minutes to plan and write your response.

Question 2 is an independent writing task. You will answer a question based on your own knowledge and experience. You have 30 minutes to plan and write your response.

Disk 3, Track 16

Now listen to part of a lecture in a music theory class.

Music is made of the same medium as speech: the sound sequence. Just as language is made up of separate, ordered parts, music is made up of notes, chords, measures, phrases, tunes, and so on. Because both language and music have structure, our ability to understand and learn them comes naturally.

Just as we are able to separate the sounds in spoken language, we can distinguish the individual sounds that musical instruments make. When we hear someone speak a foreign language, we notice how continuous the speech seems, but we cannot distinguish single words. The experience of hearing a foreign music is sort of the same. We aren't sure what counts as a note, or where one note ends and another begins.

The sound system of a musical language defines musical sounds. This is why we are able to distinguish one sound from another, to recognize the difference between A and A–sharp. And, just as spoken languages limit their sounds to a small number of all of the sounds that the human voice can make, so do musical languages limit the pitches to a small number within the octave.

Like spoken language, music has syntax. Musical syntax refers to the relationships such as the hold between notes and chords and phrases. The primary purpose of musical syntax is to control and order the flow of information streaming to the ears. Musical syntax reduces the randomness of sound. It produces patterns of melody and harmony, thus allowing us to process a phrase and to understand it.

Music, like language, evolves over time. An example of a sound change in a musical language could be the introduction of a new instrument or the slow advance of a particular vocal technique—things that change the color of the sound.

When two musical communities come together and compete, musical influences are at the heart of this contact. One of the most dramatic results of competition in music is American jazz. Two very distinct musical languages, the African and European, had existed side by side in American society, so the ground was fertile for the evolution of jazz, a new musical language containing elements of both African and European music.

Summarize the points made in the lecture, explaining how they are similar to points made in the reading.

TEST 4

Disk 4, Track 1

LISTENING SECTION DIRECTIONS (*p. 174*)

The Listening section measures your ability to understand conversations and lectures in English. You will hear each conversation and lecture only one time. After each conversation or lecture, you will hear some questions about it. Answer the questions based on what the speakers state or imply.

You may take notes while you listen. You may use your notes to help you answer the questions.

In some questions, you will see this icon: . This means that you will hear, but not see, part of the question.

Some questions have special directions, which appear in a gray box. Most questions are worth one point. If a question is worth more than one point, the directions will indicate how many points you can receive.

You will now begin the first part of the Listening section.

Disk 4, Track 2

Questions 1 through 5. Listen to part of a conversation between two students.

W: How do you like your classes this semester?

M: Not bad, I guess. Thermodynamics is the hardest. It takes a long time for me to do the problems, and then I don't have enough time to do the reading for English and history. There just aren't enough hours in a day.

W: I hear you.

M: How are your classes?

W: Pretty good, actually. All of my professors are great, and I really like my discussion class in Russian history.

M: Oh, yeah? How come?

W: Well, it's really useful to get a chance to talk about what Dr. Finley says in the lecture, and also hear what other people have to say. We have two really cool TAs who lead the discussions.

M: Oh, yeah?

W: One guy is working on his doctorate in Russian studies, and he spent a year in Russia learning the language. He has this amazing ability to tie Dr. Finley's lectures to things that he's actually seen and experienced in Russia. He's a great storyteller. The other TA—Anna—her family is from Russia, and she also has great stories, but mostly I like her way of drawing everyone into the discussion.

M: That sounds great for you. But personally, I've never cared for discussion classes. I prefer the lecture format. I'd rather listen to my professor than to my classmates.

W: Really? I like the discussions because we can go beyond the lecture and the reading. Not that the lectures are boring or anything—I'm not saying that—what I mean is, I get a lot out of the discussions. I think I learn more, you know, when I get a chance to talk about Russian history. I certainly remember more of the details. And that sure helped me on the first test.

M: Well, that's good. I'm glad you like your class. So, are you still working in the pizza restaurant?

W: No. Not enough time. I need a job, but the restaurant was getting to be too much time. Somebody was always asking me to take their shift, and I'd end up working 25 hours a week. I never had enough time to study.

M: Hey, I know just the job for you! I saw—there's a notice on the job board in the Student Center—I just saw it today. There's a job opening for host of the graduate student lounge.

W: Oh, really? What does the host of the graduate student lounge do?

M: Oh, I don't know … make coffee and talk to people, stuff like that. But maybe you'd get a chance to do some reading during the quiet times.

W: You know, I think that might be just the kind of job I could handle right now.

1. What are the students discussing?
2. Listen again to part of the conversation. Then answer the question.
   "Not bad, I guess. Thermodynamics is the hardest. It takes a long time for me to do the problems, and then I don't have enough time to do the reading for English and history. There just aren't enough hours in a day."
   "I hear you."
   Why does the woman say this:
   "I hear you."
3. Why does the woman like her Russian history class?
4. What is the man's attitude toward discussion classes?
5. What does the man suggest the woman do?

Disk 4, Track 3

Questions 6 through 11. Listen to part of a lecture in a botany class.

W: Several of the processes related to growth and aging in plants involve the effects of hormones. Today I'll talk about two aging processes—the ripening of fruit and the falling of leaves in autumn. These processes involve a hormone called ethylene. What is ethylene? It's a chemical, a gas produced by plants as a hormone. Ethylene is unique among plant hormones because it's the only hormone that's a gas. The gaseous state is important because it enables ethylene to move through the plant. Like all other hormones, ethylene triggers certain responses in the plant. Ethylene is associated with a variety of aging processes. One example of the aging process is the ripening of fruit. The ripening of fruit involves several changes in structure and metabolism. Some of these changes are aging processes. One change is the weakening of cell walls, which softens the fruit. Another is the decrease in chlorophyll content, which causes the fruit to lose its greenness. Ethylene initiates or hastens both of these changes and also causes some ripened fruit to drop from the plant. A chain reaction occurs during ripening, as ethylene triggers aging. The aging cells then release more ethylene. Because ethylene is a gas, the signal to ripen spreads from fruit to fruit. You've heard the expression "One bad apple spoils the whole lot." Well, it really is true! Yes, Randy?

M: So, when we buy fruit, like peaches that are still kind of green, and we store them in a plastic bag, and the peaches ripen faster—is this because of ethylene? I mean, I think I get it. The bag traps the ethylene gas, and this speeds up the ripening.

W: Right. That's exactly what happens. Ethylene accumulates inside the plastic bag, and this starts a chain reaction. The signal to ripen spreads from one peach to another, and this causes all of the peaches to ripen faster.
By the way, the role of ethylene was discovered in sort of an interesting way. A century ago, citrus growers used to ripen fruit by "curing" it in sheds that were heated by kerosene stoves. The growers thought it was the heat from the stoves that ripened the fruit. However, they later discovered that the fruit didn't ripen after they started using newer, cleaner–burning stoves. Botanists figured out that the reason the fruit ripened in the sheds with kerosene stoves was because of ethylene—not heat—because, as it turns out, ethylene is a by–product of kerosene combustion. Nowadays, a lot of fruit is ripened in huge storage containers that have ethylene gas piped in. It's a new variation on the old curing shed. But in other cases, storage facilities have to slow down the ripening caused by natural ethylene. For example, apples are stored in bins that are flushed with carbon dioxide. Circulating the air with carbon dioxide prevents ethylene from accumulating, and carbon dioxide slows down the action of whatever ethylene isn't flushed away. This is how apples can be stored for several months before they're shipped to supermarkets.
Another aging process in plants where ethylene plays a role is the falling of leaves in autumn. When a leaf falls from a tree, the breaking point is a layer near the base of the leaf's stalk. A change in the balance of two hormones—ethylene and auxin—controls the falling of leaves. An aging leaf produces less and less auxin, a hormone that stimulates cell growth. The drop in auxin makes the cells of the breaking layer more sensitive to ethylene. As the influence of ethylene becomes stronger, the cells start producing enzymes that weaken the cell walls of the breaking layer. Finally, with the help of wind or rain, the leaf breaks away at that layer and falls from the tree

6. What is the lecture mainly about?
7. According to the professor, how is ethylene unique?
8. According to the lecture, what are two effects of ethylene?
9. Listen again to part of the lecture. Then answer the question.
"A chain reaction occurs during ripening, as ethylene triggers aging. The aging cells then release more ethylene. Because ethylene is a gas, the signal to ripen spreads from fruit to fruit. You've heard the expression 'One bad apple spoils the whole lot.' Well, it really is true!"
Why does the professor say this:
"One bad apple spoils the whole lot."
10. Based on the information in the lecture, indicate whether each process below is related to the hormone ethylene.
11. Listen again to part of the lecture. Then answer the question.
"An aging leaf produces less and less auxin, a hormone that stimulates cell growth. The drop in auxin makes the cells of the breaking layer more sensitive to ethylene. As the influence of ethylene becomes stronger, the cells start producing enzymes that weaken the cell walls of the breaking layer. Finally, with the help of wind or rain, the leaf breaks away at that layer and falls from the tree."
What does the professor imply about the falling of leaves?

Disk 4, Track 4

Questions 12 through 17. Listen to part of a discussion in a business class.

M1: Managers must manage. It's a simple statement, but let's think about what it means for a minute. Let's ask ourselves, what makes a manager? Tammy?

W: A manager is someone who supervises other people … and plans and carries out projects.

M1: That's right. A manager has the ability to set goals, and then to accomplish what he or she sets out to do. Business managers shoot for results. This means that once you set your business plan and budget for the year, you have to achieve the sales, the market share, the earnings—whatever you set out to do. Yes, Doug?

M2: But even the best managers can't achieve every goal. A lot can go wrong that's beyond your control. Say, for example, the whole economy goes into recession—that would interfere with your goals, like your sales, for example. Sometimes things go wrong, no matter what you do.

M1: You could say that about life in general. We're always being hit with things that are beyond our control. But good managers have to adjust to changing circumstances. They … they have to … but let me share a story I tell all my students. It's about two promising young people of equal intelligence and ability. Both are college students, and both want to go on to a top graduate school of business.
The first student, May, hands in all of her assignments and does exactly what's expected of her. She receives good grades—mostly As with a few Bs—during her first couple of years in college. But then one year she gets the flu before final exams, and she performs poorly on her exams. As a result, her grade point average slips to just above a C. May tells herself that it wasn't her fault, it was because she wasn't able to study when she was sick, and she vows to do better next year. But something always happens to wreck May's plans. Next year she misunderstands a question on the final and gets a C. May graduates with a B–minus average.
The second student, Kay, also wants to go to a top school, so she sets out to get an A average. She studies four hours every night. Her diligence and hard work pay off, and she gets all As her first three years. Then, in her senior year, she runs into trouble with one of her courses, advanced accounting. She works hard, but the material is difficult, and she has a hard time solving some of the problems. At midterm she's struggling for a B. She works harder, does some outside reading. She asks her professor for help, but the professor doesn't have much time for students. What does Kay do? After trying several different

approaches—studying harder, reading more, asking for help—what she ends up doing is finding a graduate student to tutor her. She works long and thinks hard. And, of course, you know the end of the story: Kay gets her A.
Now, what kind of manager is each student?

W: Kay is certainly a more successful student because she got all As.

M2: The first student, May, probably won't get into a top business school because the top schools require you have to have a high grade point average, and she didn't have that. So the other student, Kay, has a better chance of getting a top–notch business education.

M1: What you both said is true. But who's the better manager: May or Kay?

W: In my opinion, May wouldn't be a strong manager. She just drifted along. When she got the flu and blew it on her exams, she never really caught up. Kay is clearly the better manager.

M2: I agree with Tammy. I think Kay will be a better manager. She graduated with an A average, so that shows how hard she worked, but she also knew what to do when she was having trouble in her accounting course.

M1: Kay was a manager before she even reached business school. She had grasped the essentials of good business management—not because she worked so hard, but because when one action failed, she tried another, and another, until she achieved her goal. That is what managers do.

12. According to the discussion, what are the characteristics of a good manager?
13. Why does the professor tell a story about May and Kay?
14. What does the professor imply about the student named May?
15. In the story, what point does Kay illustrate?
16. Listen again to part of the discussion. Then answer the question.
"Now, what kind of manager is each student?"
"Kay is certainly a more successful student because she got all As."
"The first student, May, probably won't get into a top business school because the top schools require you have to have a high grade point average, and she didn't have that. So the other student, Kay, has a better chance of getting a top–notch business education."
"What you both said is true. But who's the better manager: May or Kay?"
Why does the professor ask this:
"But who's the better manager: May or Kay?"
17. What does the professor mean by this statement:
"Kay was a manager before she even reached business school."

Disk 4, Track 5

Questions 18 through 22. Listen to a conversation between a student and a professor.

M: Excuse me, Dr. Phillips.

W: Hello, Patrick. I got your message. You said something about a project you're working on.

M: Yeah, that's right. I'm … uh … we're, I mean, Student Activities is trying to find out what students think about the different events we sponsor. So I'm designing a study for them, and I was wondering if I could get your advice.

W: Sure. So, what can I do for you?

M: Well, like I said, we want to find out what students like and don't like about our events—like the concerts we have, the masquerade ball, the spring picnic, and so on. I know there's lots of ways we could get information like this—information from students—but I'm not sure which way is best. I'd like to get as much feedback as possible, from as many people as possible, but—like I said—I'm not sure about the best way to do it. Interviewing students might be a good way, but I think, uh, interviews would take a lot of time.

W: You're right about that. Face–to–face interviews are very time–consuming. Two other methods you could use are the survey and the poll. A survey can be highly structured and doesn't require a face–to–face situation, so that's an advantage. You could do a survey in the form of a printed questionnaire, or you could also do it over the telephone. Telephone surveys take more time.

M: I see what you mean. For our purpose, a printed survey might be best. But you also mentioned a poll. How's that different from a survey?

W: A survey is usually fairly structured, while a poll is much simpler in design. A poll is simply a headcount. The respondents are presented with a limited number of options. Are you for or against a masquerade ball? Do you prefer events like A, B, or C?

M: I see. So a poll probably wouldn't give us a lot to go on, but we could probably reach more people that way.

W: That's right. You know there's an excellent book that explains the pluses and minuses of each of these methods. It's called *How to Measure Attitudes*, and it's in our library … and probably the bookstore as well because it's used in some of our graduate courses. It shows you how to word questions to get the information you want, and there are lots of good samples of surveys.

M: I'd better write this down. *How to Measure Attitudes*.

W: I'd lend you my copy, but one of my assistants is using it.

M: Oh, that's all right. I'm sure I can get a hold of it. If we do, uh, if we decide to go with a printed survey, could you, uh, would you be willing to look at my draft first?

W: Of course. You could just slip it into my mailbox, or stop by anytime during my office hours.

M: OK. That would be great. I'll put the draft in your mailbox. Thanks. I really appreciate your time. Now I'd better get going and see if I can find that book.

W: OK, Patrick. Good luck.

18. Why does the student speak to the professor?
19. What kind of information does the student want to obtain?
20. According to the professor, what is one advantage of a survey?
21. Listen again to part of the conversation. Then answer the question.
"A survey is usually fairly structured, while a poll is much simpler in design. A poll is simply a headcount. The respondents are presented with a limited number of options. Are you for or against a masquerade ball? Do you prefer events like A, B, or C?"
Why does the professor ask this:
"Are you for or against a masquerade ball? Do you prefer events like A, B, or C?"
22. How does the professor help the student?

Disk 4, Track 6

Questions 23 through 28. Listen to part of a lecture in a psychology class. The professor is talking about adulthood.

M: We all change over the course of our adulthood. Some changes we go through are biological and are a natural part of aging. Some are cultural experiences, such as the changes related to our family life. A lot of the changes in adulthood involve social relationships and responsibilities. And then, there are some changes that are more internal and personal. Question?

W: Yes. Um, is what you're talking about—I mean these changes we experience—are they part of our biological clock?

M: I'm glad you brought up the biological clock. The term "biological clock" refers to the biological and chemical changes that occur with aging, as if a clock were ticking away in the background. Some changes in adults are biological. These changes are often easy to observe, like my hair turning gray. Some biological changes aren't directly visible, such as the … uh … the reduced efficiency of the neural connections in our brain. But some of the changes we go through have more to do with sociology than biology. There's also a "social clock" that defines the sequence of normal life experiences, such as … uh … the timing of education, career, marriage, and so on. Virtually all societies are organized into age strata, periods in life with norms for—that is, typical … uh … expectations, demands, social roles and responsibilities. People have different expectations of—and different attitudes toward—20–year–olds, 40–year–olds, and 70–year–olds. We generally expect a 20–year–old to act in a certain way, but we expect different behavior from someone who's 40 or 70. Our attitudes towards each age group form what we consider to be the age norms for that group.

W: Excuse me, Dr. Butler. Wouldn't these age norms be different in different cultures? I mean, in some cultures someone who's 40 is considered old, but in other cultures 40 is still kind of young.

M: Various cultures might define "old" and "young" differently, but every culture has a set of attitudes—age norms—for old people and a different set of attitudes for young people. For example, an older adult might be seen as having more—or less—status than a young adult—no matter how the culture defines what age is "old."

Early adulthood is the period from age 18 to 40. Early adulthood is when more new social roles are acquired than at any other time of life. The first new role is often independent adulthood, as the young person leaves home. Another new role is worker, as the young adult begin a career. Young adults also acquire the role of spouse, as most first marriages occur during early adulthood. A major new role is that of parent. Over 80 percent of adults in North America will eventually become parents, normally in their twenties or thirties.

The second stage of adulthood, middle adulthood, is roughly from age 40 to 65. In middle adulthood, the same social roles are still present—spouse, parent, worker—but they become less demanding and less confining than they were during early adulthood. A few new roles are added, like grandparent, or maybe caregiver to our own aging parents. This is the "sandwich generation," because people in middle adulthood are sandwiched between the needs of their children and the needs of their aging parents.

Late adulthood begins at age 65. Late adulthood is normally marked by a decline in the number of social roles. The role of worker is shed at retirement. The older adult is still a parent, but that role now has fewer duties. For many people, the role of spouse is given up to widowhood. Yes?

W: So far, you've been talking about people who have children. What about people who don't have children?

M: Adults who don't have children don't experience the role changes that accompany a child's development, yet their experiences do not otherwise differ in any substantial way. They follow the basic pattern of adulthood. By this I mean, they add new roles in early adulthood, change roles in middle adulthood, and shed roles in late adulthood.

23. What aspect of adulthood does the professor mainly discuss?
24. Why does the professor discuss the "biological clock"?
25. Why does the professor say this:
"People have different expectations of—and different attitudes toward—20–year–olds, 40–year–olds, and 70–year–olds. We generally expect a 20–year–old to act in a certain way, but we expect different behavior from someone who's 40 or 70."
26. Listen again to part of the lecture. Then answer the question.
"Various cultures might define 'old' and 'young' differently, but every culture has a set of attitudes—age norms—for old people and a different set of attitudes for young people. For example, an older adult might be seen as having more—or less—status than a young adult—no matter how the culture defines what age is 'old.'"
What does the professor imply about age norms?
27. Based on the information in the lecture, indicate whether each sentence below characterizes early adulthood, middle adulthood, or late adulthood.
28. What does the professor say about people who do not have children?

Disk 4, Track 7

Questions 29 through 34. Listen to part of a lecture in a music history class. The professor is talking about Baroque music.

W: The term "Baroque" refers to a style and a culture rather than a precise period in history. Architecture, painting, and music each have a style called Baroque. One of the most striking features of the Baroque style is its expressiveness. Baroque music is a vigorous style combining imagination with great feeling. There's great use of dissonance to express extremes of emotion, especially in vocal music. And compared to Renaissance music, Baroque music has more ornament. Trills and grace notes—little twists on notes—all find their way into musical notation. Baroque music is known for its virtuoso instrumental music. Instrumental music had been gaining in importance and came into its own around 1600. Music was freed from the necessity of words, and it now moved to dance rhythms rather than speech rhythms. The new style demanded new musical forms. It was in the Baroque era that some of the forms we know today began to take shape: the opera, the sonata, and the concerto.
The person generally given credit for inaugurating the Baroque style was Claudio Monteverdi. Monteverdi's career took place at the same time as other developments, like the rise of solo singing and, um, experiments to re-create Greek music and drama. These experiments led to a new form called opera. Monteverdi was the first of the great Italian opera composers, and he was also the first to explore the tone colors of the orchestra. Monteverdi was a revolutionary. He took musical risks, like doing exciting things with rhythms, and using dissonance to make the music more expressive. The golden age of Baroque instrumental music began with orchestral combinations like the one Monteverdi used in his opera *Orfeo*. The orchestra for *Orfeo* consisted of two harpsichords, two contrabasses, twelve members of the violin family, a double harp, two pipe organs, four trombones, two cornets, a small flute, three muted trumpets, and an assortment of other instruments. With these instruments, Monteverdi told the Greek legend of Orpheus. The instruments dramatized the story's characters and plot. For example, the high flute and a small violin accompanied the shepherd, brasses and organ music suggested the underworld, and so forth. *Orfeo* was full of expressive devices, and demanded masterful playing from strings and brass, as well as virtuoso singing.

M: Excuse me, Professor Stevens. Could you explain exactly what "virtuoso" means?

W: Sure. "Virtuoso" is an Italian word. It means highly skilled or … worthy. A virtuoso piece of music requires a highly skilled vocalist or a masterful player.

M: But a person can be a virtuoso, right? I mean, we can say, for example, "He's a real virtuoso."

W: Yes, that's right. A virtuoso is a musician who plays with great skill and technique, or who has an extraordinary individual style. It was the, um, violin virtuosos who perfected new forms of instrumental music in the Baroque period. All of the great violinmakers of the time were concentrated in Italy.
The terms "concerto" and "sonata" also come from Italian. The concerto and the sonata developed as vehicles for virtuoso musicians to show off their skills. The concerto became the dominant instrumental form of the Baroque period. Concertos feature solo instruments—usually violins—and orchestra, or they can feature groups of instruments and orchestra. The music is characterized by its dazzling virtuosity and ornamentation. Baroque concertos required a lot of technical skill—in both the composing and the performing.
The most famous of all Baroque concertos were for solo violin and orchestra. Vivaldi's *Four Seasons* are probably the best known examples. *The Four Seasons* are four related concertos—one for each season. They are pure, quintessential Baroque music—descriptive, expressive, elaborate—and with virtuoso violin playing. Before I go on, let's pause here so we can listen to the first of *The Four Seasons*. Here is "Concerto Number 1, Spring."

29. How does the professor develop the topic of Baroque music?
30. What characterizes Baroque music?
31. Why does the professor say this:
"Instrumental music had been gaining in importance and came into its own around 1600. Music was freed from the necessity of words, and it now moved to dance rhythms rather than speech rhythms. The new style demanded new musical forms. It was in the Baroque era that some of the forms we know today began to take shape: the opera, the sonata, and the concerto."
32. Why does the professor discuss the instruments of the orchestra for Monteverdi's opera *Orfeo*?
33. What does the professor mean when she says this:
"The concerto and the sonata developed as vehicles for virtuoso musicians to show off their skills."
34. What is the professor's opinion of the concertos called The Four Seasons?

Disk 4, Track 8

Questions 35 through 39. Listen to part of a conversation between a student and a professor.

W: Professor Beckman, do you have a minute?

M: Sure. What can I do for you, Amelia?

W: Well, I've decided to apply to the teacher certification program, and I wondered—I'd like it if you would, um, recommend me for the program.

M: Oh, so you want to be a teacher! Good, good, glad to hear it. What level do you want to teach?

W: Actually, grades six to eight interest me the most. I loved school—especially science—when I was that age.

M: Good, glad to hear it. I have a strong sense that you'll be a dedicated teacher. Now, you say you need a letter from me.

W: Yes. Would you be able to do that?

M: Of course, I'd be happy to. But tell me more about your decision to teach, and … uh … why you think you'll be good at it.

W: All right. Well, let's see, um, I guess I've known for a long time that I wanted to be a teacher, ever since I was in sixth grade myself. I loved science when I was a kid—still love science—and … I guess I, um, want to share my love of science with kids. I've worked with kids before—as a camp counselor for two summers—teaching nature classes and leading nature hikes and stuff like that—and I just had so much fun with the kids! I think I'm a pretty good counselor, and I love being in the woods myself.

M: Now remind me 'cause I tend to forget these things … you were in my Human Development course? Is that right?

W: Yes, and also General Psychology in my freshman year.

M: Right, right. Good. I'm trying to get a handle on this. I recall that your presentation in Human Development was very well thought of by your classmates. You did a study of adolescence—is that right?

W: Yes. I talked about identity and role confusion, and I looked at two groups of kids, one eleven and the other fifteen years old.

M: Right. You showed slides of the children's artwork.

W: That's right. They did self–portraits. It was interesting, too, because in a lot of ways the younger kids were more expressive … and more positive in their image of themselves. The older kids' art was more sophisticated technically, but in a lot of ways it was darker, even in the colors they used.

M: Hmm. Yes, I recall. Your report was very well done. I remember it well, and I'll mention it in my letter. So, when is it that you need this?

W: My entire application is due on March 15. There's a form for you to use … here. You send it directly to the Dean of the School of Education.

M: Right, right. I know these forms. You can just leave it with me. I'll fill it out and see that it gets there on time.

W: Thanks! I really appreciate your help.

M: And I'm happy to help.

35. What is the main purpose of the conversation?
36. Why does the student want to be a teacher?
37. Why does the student talk about being a camp counselor?
38. Listen again to part of the conversation. Then answer the question.
    "Now remind me 'cause I tend to forget these things … you were in my Human Development course? Is that right?"
    "Yes, and also General Psychology in my freshman year."
    "Right, right. Good. I'm trying to get a handle on this."
    Why does the professor say this:
    "I'm trying to get a handle on this."
39. What will the professor probably include in the form that he fills out?

Disk 4, Track 9

Questions 40 through 45. Listen to part of a lecture in an ecology class.

Several hundred million years ago, a large body of water covered Manitoba. This ancient ocean was home to brachiopods, trilobites, and corals. As these organisms died, they settled in layers on the ocean floor, where they became compressed and cemented together, and over millions of years, turned into limestone.

Wherever you find limestone, you also find crevices, tunnels and caves. A network of caves is formed when acidic rainwater seeps into the layers of limestone through cracks at the surface and dissolves some of the limestone. The limestone weakens and collapses near the surface and further below, creating sinkholes, or large pits in the limestone.

The limestone pits in Manitoba's Interlake region are like nothing else in the world. What makes these particular pits so unique? Well, for one thing, huge numbers of snakes migrate to these holes in the ground. If you go anywhere near the pits in the spring or fall, you'll find the region alive with thousands of red–sided garter snakes.

This is the world's largest concentration of snakes. Tens of thousands of these snakes congregate at the surface of their winter dens each year. They emerge in the spring after spending the winter hibernating in what are known as the "snake pits." In the fall, the snakes return to the pits to prepare for winter.

And why are snakes drawn to the limestone pits? Well, the availability of winter dens in the limestone bedrock makes this sort of an ideal home. Like all reptiles, snakes are ectotherms. This means they warm their bodies mainly by absorbing heat from their environment. The pits are the perfect location for the hibernating snakes because they shelter the snakes from winter temperatures that sometimes dip as low as minus 40 degrees Celsius.

Animals interact with their environment in a number of ways—for example, by responding behaviorally or physiologically, or by adapting over evolutionary time. The migration of garter snakes to the limestone pits is an example of a behavioral mechanism for dealing with seasonal variations in temperature. Moving to a new location is an animal's quickest response to an unfavorable change in the environment. By gathering in a mass below the frost line, the snakes are able to survive the harsh prairie winter.

Garter snakes have an optimal temperature for physiological function. They can, however, actually survive freezing temperatures for a short time—a few hours only—and at temperatures like minus–1 or minus–2 Celsius. They obviously can't stay frozen all winter long, but to survive in cold climates, they've adapted to situations like being exposed to freezing temperatures outside their dens on cold nights in the spring or fall. This ability to endure short freezes will get them through till morning.

The beginning of freezing in their bodies is a physiological response that serves as a signal to the snakes. Freezing tells them to alter their behavior, to move and find a warmer place. This physiological–behavioral response might also be helpful in their winter dens because, if the den temperature falls too low and some snakes begin to freeze, it could be a signal for all the snakes to move to deeper, warmer parts of the den.

These response mechanisms are only marginal abilities that allow the snakes to cope with short term freezes. About ten years ago, thousands of snakes died when they were trapped in shallower dens when the frost line fell during an extended period of freezing temperatures. They were apparently not able to get to lower depths in time.

40. What is the main purpose of the lecture?
41. What natural features of Manitoba does the professor discuss?
42. Why does the professor say this:
    "Well, the availability of winter dens in the limestone bedrock makes this sort of an ideal home."
43. How do the garter snakes deal with seasonal variations in temperature?

44. Listen again to part of the lecture. Then answer the question.
"They obviously can't stay frozen all winter long, but to survive in cold climates, they've adapted to situations like being exposed to freezing temperatures outside their dens on cold nights in the spring or fall. This ability to endure short freezes will get them through till morning."
What does the professor mean when he says this:
"This ability to endure short freezes will get them through till morning."
45. Listen again to part of the lecture. Then answer the question.
"The beginning of freezing in their bodies is a physiological response that serves as a signal to the snakes. Freezing tells them to alter their behavior, to move and find a warmer place. This physiological–behavioral response might also be helpful in their winter dens because, if the den temperature falls too low and some snakes begin to freeze, it could be a signal for all the snakes to move to deeper, warmer parts of the den."
What does the professor imply about the behavior of the snakes?

Disk 4, Track 10

Questions 46 through 51. Listen to part of a lecture in an architecture class. The professor is talking about the arch.

W: An arch is the spanning of a wall opening by means of separate units, such as bricks or blocks, which are assembled into an upward curve. The invention of the arch made it possible to span wide openings without large timbers. Before the arch, large window and door openings required a large wooden timber, and a supply of large trees. The arch was very important in regions where there were few large trees. The Babylonians, Egyptians, and Etruscans all used the arch, and it was later adopted by the Romans. The arch became a basic principle in the Roman system of construction in brick and concrete. The Romans contributed a lot to the development of architecture, especially its engineering aspects. They perfected a system of arch and vault construction. As a result, a larger variety of buildings appeared, each with a form suited to its function. The Roman approach to the building arts was always practical. The Romans undertook huge public work projects, including a network of bridges and aqueducts, all of which utilized the arch. To supply their vast public baths and fill the water needs of their citizens, they needed water in large amounts for their cities. Using their considerable engineering skills, the Romans built aqueducts so sturdy that many are still standing.
The Roman semi–circular arch is the most common and most elementary type of arch. It was made by taking wedge–shaped blocks—large bricks with angled sides—and placing them side by side, forming an upward curving, semi–circular opening. The block at the highest point—the center of the arch—is called the keystone. The keystone is the most important block because it holds the other blocks in place. The keystone locks the other stones together. The round arch is extremely strong and stable. It's primarily the wedge shape of the blocks that gives the arch its stability. The wedge–shaped blocks are locked together tightly, transferring their weight downward on either side. The arch is very sturdy and can support a heavy load. The arch is supported only from the sides. This is because of lateral thrust. The downward pressure is transformed into lateral thrust through the piers, the two vertical structures on either side of the opening. What I mean is, the … um … the weight of the arch and its load is converted from downward pressure into sideways—lateral—pressure. The massive piers that frame each side of the opening receive the pressure and therefore support the arch. Until the nineteenth century, arches were still widely used in public buildings in North America. However, the invention of steel beams in the nineteenth century—yes, did you have a question?

M: Yes. I was wondering … um … what you said implies that we don't see arches in public buildings anymore, I mean, in newer buildings. But what about the arches in our administration building, here on campus? It has lots of arches, and I'm pretty sure the building is fairly new.

W: I'm glad you mentioned our administration building because that's a perfect illustration of the decorative arch. You see, behind all that beautiful brickwork is a system of steel beams. The beams are doing the real work of holding up the building. The brick arches are just for show. Steel beams for wide spans have reduced the arch to a mostly decorative function. And, as you can see in our administration building, decorative arches remain popular today.

46. According to the professor, why was the arch an important development in architecture?
47. Listen again to part of the lecture. Then answer the question.
"The Romans undertook huge public work projects, including a network of bridges and aqueducts, all of which utilized the arch. To supply their vast public baths and fill the water needs of their citizens, they needed water in large amounts for their cities. Using their considerable engineering skills, the Romans built aqueducts so sturdy that many are still standing."
What does the professor imply about the public works projects of the Romans?
48. Identify the keystone in the drawing of the arch.
49. What reason is given for the stability of the arch?
50. Listen again to part of the lecture. Then answer the question.
"The downward pressure is transformed into lateral thrust through the piers, the two vertical structures on either side of the opening. What I mean is, the … um … the weight of the arch and its load is converted from downward pressure into sideways—lateral—pressure."
Why does the professor say this:
"What I mean is, the … um … the weight of the arch and its load is converted from downward pressure into sideways—lateral—pressure."
51. According to the professor, why are arches that are built today mostly decorative in function?

Disk 4, Track 11

SPEAKING SECTION DIRECTIONS (*p. 193*)

The Speaking section measures your ability to speak in English about a variety of topics. There are six questions in this section.

Questions 1 and 2 are independent tasks in which you will speak about familiar topics. Your responses will be scored on your ability to speak clearly and coherently about the topics.

Questions 3 and 4 are integrated speaking tasks. You will read a passage, listen to a conversation or lecture, and then speak in response to a question about what you have read and heard. You will need to combine relevant information from the two sources to answer the question completely. Your responses will be scored on your ability to speak clearly and coherently and on your ability to accurately convey information about what you read and heard.

Questions 5 and 6 are integrated speaking tasks. You will listen to part of a conversation or lecture, and then speak in response to a question about what you have heard. Your responses will be scored on your ability to speak clearly and coherently and on your ability to accurately convey information about what you heard.

You will hear each conversation and lecture only one time. You may take notes while you listen. You may use your notes to help you answer the questions.

Disk 4, Track 12

What is your most valuable possession? Describe it and explain why it is important to you. Include details and examples to support your explanation.

Disk 4, Track 13

Some universities focus on having excellent libraries, laboratories, and other facilities. Others focus more on hiring the most successful and qualified professors. Which system do you think benefits students more, and why? Include details and examples in your explanation.

Disk 4, Track 14

Now listen to two students as they discuss the job of resident assistant.

M: I think I'll apply for resident assistant. The cost of campus housing is going up again. I'd sure like to live on campus for free—and in a private room.

W: Are you sure about that? It may not be what it seems.

M: A private room with no rent? How could you go wrong with that?

W: I only know what my friend told me. She was an RA last year, and she said it took up a lot more of her time than she thought it would. It's that part about "managing routine problems of residents." She said there were people knocking on her door all hours of the day, with all kinds of problems—feeling homesick, complaining about their roommates—things like that. It was impossible for her to study in her room because there were so many interruptions.

M: No kidding. It was really like that?

W: That's what my friend said. The stress of being RA really affected her schoolwork too. She even had to drop a course because she couldn't keep up.

M: Wow.

W: And I'm suspicious about the job description, you know, the part where it says that RAs have "other related duties." You never know what that means. It could mean almost anything. I mean, what will they make you do for free rent?

The woman expresses her opinion about being a resident assistant. State her opinion and explain the reasons she gives for holding that opinion.

Disk 4, Track 15

Now listen to part of a lecture on this topic in a geology class.

By studying patterns of glaciation, we've known for a long time that climate change has happened in regular cycles. But more recent research tells us that climate change is not always gradual. Ice cores drilled from glaciers in Greenland challenge the theories about long, gradual cycles of climate change. The ice cores are evidence of a sort of "flickering climate"—sudden swings from warm to cold, and back again. The fact that these changes took place so quickly tells us that our climate is not as stable as we used to think.

The layers in the ice tell the history of climate change. They show us a period of global warming about 11,000 years ago. This warming took several decades, but was also marked by several sudden jumps in warming that each took less than five years. About half of the warming was concentrated in a single period of less than 15 years. This is very rapid climate change.

Researchers studying the ice cores have concluded that during our latest ice age the climate might have fluctuated wildly. Average annual temperatures may have risen several degrees in only a few years—only to slide back into sort of a deep chill again, an ice age that lasted thousands of years. Furthermore, the change from the latest ice age to the present warm period might have taken less than a human lifetime—not the thousands of years of gradual warming that most scientists once believed.

The professor discusses studies of the ice in Greenland. Explain how this research has advanced our understanding of past climate change.

Disk 4, Track 16

Now listen to a conversation between two students.

W: Hey, Michael, how's it going?

M: OK, I guess, but I just found out the bus company is changing their schedule, and they're canceling the bus that goes to my neighborhood. That means I won't be able to take the bus to campus anymore.

W: Oh, that's too bad. What are you going to do?

M: I don't know yet. I need to figure out some way to get to school after the end of the month. I don't have a car, and I live too far away to walk.

W: What about carpooling with another student? There must be someone who lives near you that drives to school. Have you checked the ride board?

M: No. What ride board?

W: There's a big bulletin board in the Student Center, you know, outside the cafeteria. It has a big map of the city, and there are places where people who drive can advertise for riders, and where people who need rides can look for people to carpool with. You should check it out. You could put your name up in the place where it lists people looking for rides. Maybe you'll find someone.
M: Oh, yeah? I wonder.
W: Or another thing, uh, have you ever thought about moving closer to campus? I mean, I share an apartment with roommates that's just five blocks away. It's great 'cause I can walk to campus.
M: Hmmm. I don't know. I like where I live now, and moving is a lot of trouble.
W: Yeah. Well, I hope you can figure out something. Good luck.
M: Thanks.

The students discuss two possible solutions to the man's problem. Describe the problem. Then state which of the two solutions you prefer and explain why.

Disk 4, Track 17

Now listen to an instructor talk about two methods of food preservation.

All foods will eventually spoil if they're not preserved. Food preservation is the process of preventing or slowing the natural decay of edible plants and animals, spoilage that results from microorganisms—bacteria, molds, and yeasts—that are present in the food.

The most natural method of preserving food is drying. Nature preserves the seeds for next year's crop by drying the outer layers of fruits and vegetables that are exposed to the sun and air. We copy nature's effects by exposing food to warm air, a method that removes all the water that would otherwise lead to spoilage. Microorganisms need moisture to grow, so removing the water will stop the microorganisms from growing.

Drying is a very ancient form of food preservation. Prehistoric people dried grains, fruits, and nuts in the sun. When fire was discovered, they learned to smoke meat and fish by the fireside. Native Americans dried and chopped meat, then mixed it with fat. The lack of moisture in the meat kept it from spoiling. Modern industrial science has perfected the techniques of drying and applied them to the mass production of a variety of foods, such as powdered eggs and milk, peas, mushrooms, coffee, soups, and salad dressings.

Another method of food preservation is curing. Curing is done by adding ingredients, such as salt, sugar, spices, or lemon juice. Curing is one of the oldest methods of food preservation and is still used in the production of many meats and fish. The ingredients used in curing have unique reactions with the food they're added to. For example, salt slows the growth of microorganisms and removes some of the water from the food. Sugar counteracts the hardening that's sometimes caused by salt. Lemon or lime juice added to raw fish will preserve the fish for a short time without removing all the moisture.

Using points and examples from the talk, explain how the two methods of food preservation keep food from spoiling.

Disk 4, Track 18

WRITING SECTION DIRECTIONS (*p. 198*)

The Writing section measures your ability to use writing to communicate in an academic environment. There are two writing questions.

Question 1 is an integrated writing task. You will read a passage, listen to a lecture, and then answer a question based on what you have read and heard. You have 20 minutes to plan and write your response.

Question 2 is an independent writing task. You will answer a question based on your own knowledge and experience. You have 30 minutes to plan and write your response.

Disk 4, Track 19

Now listen to part of a lecture on this topic in a philosophy class.

The philosophy of realism praises reason and logic, but ignores passion, emotion, and feeling. Critics of realism argue that if we want to really understand human beings in the world, we have to consider the total—the whole of human experience. But with all its emphasis on facts and reason and scientific methods, the philosophy of realism ignores the total human.

An important belief of realism is that anything that exists can be measured scientifically. But is that true? Can we measure our passions and feelings scientifically? Can the methods of science really solve big human problems like poverty? Critics of realism say no, because the underlying psychological causes of poverty are very complex and cannot be reduced to mathematics.

Bertrand Russell thought we could use the methods of science to achieve excellence in education. However, Russell also believed that students had to be measured against some objective, "real" criteria. Because of this view, students are compared to fixed standards, such as national examinations. So realism has led to an educational system that's based on standardized tests, like college entrance examinations and national tests for teachers. Many of our leaders praise the testing movement as "scientific" and "fact-based"—that is, based on realist philosophy. But critics of realism like to point out that the effects on students are negative. Standardized tests dehumanize people because they don't respect passion, emotion, and feeling, which are important parts of the total person.

Today, the realist ideal of our technological society shows little respect for the unity of knowledge. Think about how scientists often work on one small part of a large project without understanding the whole. Someone who works only on one small part may not understand how the whole project affects humanity, and this might be dangerous to humanity. For example, it's possible for scientists to work on a project that is antihuman, against life … a project like biological weapons. They might work on one small part of a weapon system without even knowing it.

Summarize the points made in the lecture, explaining how they contradict points made in the reading.

TEST 5

Disk 5, Track 1

LISTENING SECTION DIRECTIONS (*p. 224*)

The Listening section measures your ability to understand conversations and lectures in English. You will hear each conversation and lecture only one time. After each conversation or lecture, you will hear some questions about it. Answer the questions based on what the speakers state or imply.

You may take notes while you listen. You may use your notes to help you answer the questions.

In some questions, you will see this icon: 🎧. This means that you will hear, but not see, part of the question.

Some questions have special directions, which appear in a gray box. Most questions are worth one point. If a question is worth more than one point, the directions will indicate how many points you can receive.

You will now begin the first part of the Listening section.

Disk 5, Track 2

Questions 1 through 5. Listen to a conversation in the office of a campus newspaper.

W: Excuse me. Do you work for *The Hilltop Journal*?
M: Yes. I'm Dan MacGregor, the managing editor.
W: Nice to meet you. My name is Rhonda Davis—
M: Hello, Rhonda.
W: —and I'm interested in writing for the campus paper.
M: Are you in the journalism program?
W: No, but I'm an English major with an interest in the performing arts. I'm interested—I'd like to write arts reviews, stories about … uh … concerts and films and events in the arts. I've already done a lot of this kind of writing.
M: Hmm. We've already got a couple of journalism students who write reviews.
W: Do you have to be a journalism major to write for *The Journal*?
M: Strictly speaking, no. But it helps to be endorsed by a professor in the journalism department. It's like this. You see, we're not a big paper to start out with, and the administration just cut our funding, and there are lots of students who want to write for us, so I'm afraid it's pretty competitive.
W: Really? I guess I didn't know the full situation.
M: Yeah. We all wish it were different, actually, but you could still try. I mean, you could talk to one of the journalism professors, and show them some of your writing. If they endorse it, you could come back here. I just couldn't guarantee anything at present. Like I said, our budget was cut, and we had to reduce the size of our paper.
W: Well … OK, I thought I'd try. Thanks.
M: Wait. Before you go, here's something else you could try. If you really want to write reviews, you should send something to *The Clarion*.
W: The city newspaper?
M: Yeah, that's right. They sometimes print reviews by students. And if they print a few of your stories, they might end up offering you a regular column. It happened before to students from this college.
W: Really? *The Clarion*. Well, that's good to know. What would I do, just send something, like, to the editor?
M: Send it to the features editor. That's the person who edits the Living section, where they print the reviews.
W: Thanks! I really appreciate the information.
M: Do book reviews interest you? Because I think they were looking for a person to review books by local authors. They might have found somebody already for that, but anyway, you could ask about it.
W: Actually, I would be very interested in writing book reviews. As an English major, I've got a lot of experience with that!
M: I can imagine.
W: Thank you so much. You've been very helpful.
M: No problem. I wish you luck.

1. Why does the woman go to the campus newspaper office?
2. Why does the man say this:
"Hmm. We've already got a couple of journalism students who write reviews."
3. Listen again to part of the conversation. Then answer the question.
"…you could talk to one of the journalism professors, and show them some of your writing. If they endorse it, you could come back here. I just couldn't guarantee anything at present. Like I said, our budget was cut, and we had to reduce the size of our paper."
What does the man mean when he says this:
"I just couldn't guarantee anything at present."
4. What does the man say about the city newspaper?
5. What will the woman probably do?

Disk 5, Track 3

Questions 6 through 11. Listen to part of a lecture in an astronomy class. The professor is talking about the auroras.

W: For centuries, people have told stories to explain the moving lights in the night sky—the curtains of greenish–white light with pink fringe. People described these lights as the breath of the Earth, powerful spirits, or angel light. An early twentieth–century explorer wrote about the "bloody red" and "ghostly green" lights. These lights, of course, are the aurora borealis—the northern lights—and, in the south, the aurora australis. Most of the time they're greenish–yellow, but sometimes they take colors from violet to red. The auroras can be seen at any time of the year, with the right atmospheric conditions. They're most often seen near the North and South Poles, during times of maximum solar activity. The closer to the North or South Pole you are, the better you can see the lights.
The auroras occur in the ionosphere. The ionosphere is the layer of the upper atmosphere where high energy solar radiation strips electrons from oxygen and nitrogen atoms, and leaves them as positively charged ions. The auroras are the result of a complex interaction between the solar wind and the Earth's magnetic field. Here's what happens. The sun's heat charges the particles in the solar wind, a stream of electrically charged subatomic particles that continually emanates from the sun. As the solar wind approaches Earth, it's deflected by Earth's magnetic field and diverted north and south toward the magnetic poles. The interaction between the solar wind and the magnetosphere generates beams of

electrons. These electrons collide with atoms and molecules within the ionosphere near Earth's magnetic poles. The collisions rip apart molecules and excite atoms. Thus, oxygen and nitrogen atoms in the ionosphere become "excited," or ionized. The auroras happen when these ionized atoms return to their normal state from their excited, energized states. The ions combine with free electrons—as they do so, they emit radiation. Part of this radiation is visible light: the aurora borealis and aurora australis. Yes, Simon?

M: Uh … it sounds kind of like electricity.

W: Yes, that's right. The auroras are an electrical phenomenon. As you know, an electrical generator has two components: a conductor and a magnetic field. To generate electricity, the conductor has to move across the field to produce a force. With the auroras, the conductor is the solar wind carrying a stream of charged particles.

M: So, what happens is, when, uh, when the charged particles reach Earth's magnetic field, they, uh, move along in the field towards the north and south magnetic poles.

W: Exactly. And then the particles collide with gases in the atmosphere—oxygen and nitrogen—and the oxygen and nitrogen atoms get excited. And then, when the particles get de–excited and return to their normal state, they emit the auroras by releasing energy in the form of light. Oxygen releases either dark red or ghostly green. Nitrogen emits rosy pink or magenta. The activity of the auroras varies with the sun's activity. When the sun is quiet, the auroras can be seen only in a small area. When the sun is active, however, the aurora borealis can be seen across southern Canada and the northern United States.

6. What aspect of the auroras does the professor mainly discuss?
7. What colors are commonly seen in the auroras?
8. Listen again to part of the lecture. Then answer the question.
"The auroras can be seen at any time of the year, with the right atmospheric conditions. They're most often seen near the North and South Poles, during times of maximum solar activity. The closer to the North or South Pole you are, the better you can see the lights."
Why does the professor say this:
"The closer to the North or South Pole you are, the better you can see the lights."
9. Why does the professor say this:
"As you know, an electrical generator has two components: a conductor and a magnetic field. To generate electricity, the conductor has to move across the field to produce a force. With the auroras, the conductor is the solar wind carrying a stream of charged particles."
10. The professor briefly explains how the auroras are formed. Indicate whether each sentence below is a part of the process.
11. Listen again to part of the lecture. Then answer the question.
"And then the particles collide with gases in the atmosphere—oxygen and nitrogen—and the oxygen and nitrogen atoms get excited. And then, when the particles get de–excited and return to their normal state, they emit the auroras by releasing energy in the form of light. Oxygen releases either dark red or ghostly green. Nitrogen emits rosy pink or magenta."
What can be inferred about the auroras?

Disk 5, Track 4

Questions 12 through 17. Listen to part of a lecture in a political science class. The professor is discussing political parties.

M: At the heart of the system of government called "democracy" is the institution of elections. The electoral system is the basic machinery by which popular government is exercised. And at the heart of the electoral system are political parties that organize voters and compete for support on issues. Participating in democratic politics means joining or supporting a political party. It means taking sides on central political issues. Political parties are the mechanism for selecting candidates and gaining support at the polls. Parties vary significantly in different countries, but all parties have certain common features. Political parties are voluntary organizations, generally national in scope, made up of people who agree to some degree on public policies. In the United States and Canada, political parties are stable, and each party tends to embrace a wide range of views and interests. The democratic institutions of these countries operate essentially on a two–party system. Why a two–party system? Or, should I say why has the two–party system prevailed in so many democratic states? For one thing, the essence of politics is debate; there must be someone to debate with. A one–party system means one party monopolizes power and talks only to itself. A one–party system can only be totalitarian, and therefore quite distinct from democracy. Yes, Sandra?

W: Isn't it true that another reason we have two parties is because, uh, because liberal and conservative attitudes are basic human—uh, I mean they're a basic part of our nature. In fact, almost everything that we think or do seems to come down to having—to there being two different ways of seeing the world.

M: That's an interesting idea. We even have the saying, "There are two sides to every coin." In every democratic society, there are generally two dominant parties—one for each side of the coin. In the United States, it's the Democrats and the Republicans. In Canada, it's the Liberals and the Conservatives. In both countries, the two parties are balanced enough so the minority party can become the majority by gaining an additional small share of the votes. The two parties have lasted so long because they have the ability to adjust to changes in events and in public opinion. But in addition to the two major parties, there are also several smaller parties on the margins of political power. There are lots of political factions that sometimes compete at elections. Parties are closely associated with various pressure groups, interest groups, lobbies, occupational organizations, and other groups that want to influence the decisions of the state. The purpose of each major party is to capture the legislative and executive organs of the state in order to get the party's policies accepted. The aim of parties is to win elections. However, winning an election isn't the same thing as capturing the power of the state. What really happens is, the state captures the winning party. Why is this? Well, for one thing, the experience of government tends to soften the contrasts of political debate. Government is a responsible business, while politics is a game with teams competing for victory.

W: Excuse me, Dr. Reed, but isn't it—I mean, then what you're really saying is, government and politics aren't the same thing. You said that government is a serious business, but politics is like a game.

M: Right! Politics is a game. In politics, teams and individuals take risks, and there are winners and losers. Competition is the essence of politics. But with government, collaboration and compromise are necessary because the job has got to get done.
So, why do we need political parties? We need parties because, for one reason, the process of policy formation takes place there. Parties maintain research offices and establish connections with press and citizens groups. This is how political parties develop information and thinking on major issues. The major parties retain enough differences so they can appeal to different groups of voters, and so they can offer alternatives to the independent voters who don't vote purely on the basis of party loyalty. However, the party platforms tend to balance each other in the types of issues they take up. For example, when one party introduces a plan for education reform, the other party generally takes up education as well.

12. How does the professor develop the topic of political parties?
13. Listen again to part of the lecture. Then answer the question.
"Why a two–party system? Or, should I say why has the two–party system prevailed in so many democratic states? For one thing, the essence of politics is debate; there must be someone to debate with. A one–party system means one party monopolizes power and talks only to itself. A one–party system can only be totalitarian, and therefore quite distinct from democracy."
Why does the professor say this:
"Why a two–party system? Or, should I say why has the two–party system prevailed in so many democratic states?"
14. Listen again to part of the lecture. Then answer the question.
"There are lots of political factions that sometimes compete at elections. Parties are closely associated with various pressure groups, interest groups, lobbies, occupational organizations, and other groups that want to influence the decisions of the state."
What does the professor imply about political parties?
15. Based on the information in the lecture, indicate whether each statement below describes political parties.
16. What does the professor mean when he says this:
"In politics, teams and individuals take risks, and there are winners and losers. Competition is the essence of politics. But with government, collaboration and compromise are necessary because the job has got to get done."
17. Why does the professor say this:
"However, the party platforms tend to balance each other in the types of issues they take up. For example, when one party introduces a plan for education reform, the other party generally takes up education as well."

Disk 5, Track 5

Questions 18 through 22. Listen to part of a conversation between two students.

W: My linguistics class is really getting good. Today the lecture was about the social aspects of language, like slang and accents, and stuff. But the thing that really intrigues me is something called a lingua franca.

M: Lingua franca?

W: Yeah. A lingua franca is sort of common language used by people who speak different languages. There are a lot of places in the world where everybody's first language is different, and the people need to communicate with other groups, so everybody starts using one language for social or commercial relationships. That language that connects them all is a lingua franca.

M: That makes sense—kind of a universal business language. Where did the name "lingua franca" come from?

W: From the name of one of the first languages like that. It was like, in the Middle Ages, countries with ports on the Mediterranean needed a common trade language. So a new language sort of evolved. It was basically Italian, mixed with French, Spanish, and other languages. It was called Lingua Franca, which meant "Frankish language." After that, "lingua franca" came to mean all languages used that way. So, any language can be a lingua franca if it connects lots of people who speak different languages. Most of the time lingua francas have been trade languages.

M: That means English is a lingua franca because English is an international business language.

W: Yeah. You're right about that. English is definitely a lingua franca. In East Africa, Swahili is a lingua franca that's understood in every marketplace. It's because there are hundreds of tribes in East Africa, and each tribe speaks a different language. So most of the people there learn at least some Swahili as a second language.

M: Interesting. And … uh … isn't there some other language like that … I think it's called something like "pigeon" … you know, like the birds, like the pigeons that carry messages.

W: It's not "pigeon" like the birds! It's a different word—here, let me show you—it has the same pronunciation, but a different spelling. A "pidgin" is a type of language. It's a simplified language that's a mixture of two or more languages. It has words from both languages.

M: Oh, yeah. Now I remember. We studied pidgins in anthropology.

W: My professor said there are lots of different pidgins based on English that developed in different parts of the world. It was because people from English–speaking countries had to communicate with the local people. Pidgins have a simple grammar and vocabulary, so they're easy to learn.

M: That's cool. Your class sounds interesting.

W: Yeah, we're learning some pretty amazing stuff.

18. What are the students mainly discussing?
19. What is the woman's attitude toward her linguistics class?
20. According to the conversation, which languages are lingua francas?

21. Why does the woman say this:
"It's not 'pigeon' like the birds! It's a different word—here, let me show you—it has the same pronunciation, but a different spelling."
22. Based on the conversation, indicate whether each sentence below describes a lingua franca or a pidgin.

Disk 5, Track 6

Questions 23 through 28. Listen to part of a talk in a biology class.

The bird's bill is composed of a horny sheath over a bony core. The entire structure has evolved in numerous ways to the specialized needs of its owner. The bird's bill is highly modified for a variety of activities—such as cutting and crushing seeds, probing tree crevices for insects, drinking nectar from flowers, catching fish, and so on. There's a large variety in the diets of birds throughout the world. Different birds have evolved different bill types to assist in their feeding. What I mean is, the shape of the bird's bill is specially adapted to specific foods.

A large number of birds are primarily seed eaters. These birds typically have stout, cone–shaped bills and strong jaw muscles for crushing seeds. The edible kernel of a seed is protected by a husk, or shell, which must be removed before the seed can be digested. The smaller finches, sparrows, and grosbeaks use their heavy conical bills to process seeds by removing the outer covering before swallowing them. Larger birds, such as pigeons and pheasants, swallow seeds whole and rely on grit in the gizzard to remove the husks and crush the seeds.

A wide variety of birds are nectar drinkers. These birds prefer the sweet liquid nectar of flowering plants. The co–evolution of birds and flowers has led to specialization, in which the bird's bill is adapted for the collection of nectar. The bill evolved so that it could reach the nectar at the bottom of a flower's long tubular corolla. Birds who drink nectar have long, narrow bills and tongues with finely divided tips that form a brush. The tongues are very long, and the edges roll inwards to make a narrow scoop, so the bird can sort of lap up nectar, taking several licks every second. The tongue holds the nectar by capillary action—a physical force that causes fluids to rise in narrow tubes. The tongue moves in and out rapidly, carrying nectar up tiny grooves in the tongue, all the way to the mouth.

Hummingbirds can stick their long tongues out far beyond the tips of their bills. This enables them to reach the nectar at the base of flowers. But along with drinking nectar, hummingbirds will also grab any insect they meet. As they flit from flower to flower, they consume the flower's nectar as well as insects and spiders that provide them with protein.

Birds that eat insects collect their food in a number of ways. The warblers have short, slender, tweezer–like bills, that they sort of use like tweezers to pick small insects off leaves and twigs. Plovers pluck insects from the soil with their short bills. Starlings have longer bills, which they push into the earth and force open to make a hole, and then look down the hole for insects.

The insect eater's tongue—like the bill—is specialized to the bird's diet. The tongue of some woodpeckers is long, sticky, and barbed, which makes it easier for the bird to catch its insect prey. Several species of woodpeckers use their bills as wedges to pry the bark off trees to reach the insects underneath and then lap them up with their long, sticky tongues.

23. What is the main idea of the talk?
24. Select the bird that is most likely a seed eater.
25. Listen again to part of the talk. Then answer the question.
"A wide variety of birds are nectar drinkers. These birds prefer the sweet liquid nectar of flowering plants. The co–evolution of birds and flowers has led to specialization, in which the bird's bill is adapted for the collection of nectar."
Why does the professor say this:
The co–evolution of birds and flowers has led to specialization, in which the bird's bill is adapted for the collection of nectar."
26. Select the bird that is most likely a nectar drinker.
27. Listen again to part of the talk. Then answer the question.
"But along with drinking nectar, hummingbirds will also grab any insect they meet. As they flit from flower to flower, they consume the flower's nectar as well as insects and spiders that provide them with protein."
What does the professor imply about hummingbirds?
28. What physical features are characteristic of birds that eat insects?

Disk 5, Track 7

Questions 29 through 34. Listen to part of a talk in a chemistry class.

Chemistry is sometimes called the central science. This isn't surprising, since most of the processes going on around us involve chemical changes. Here are just a few of them:

A plant grows by changing simple substances into more complex substances.
The steel in a car rusts.
Eggs, sugar, flour, and baking powder are mixed and baked into a cake.
Emissions from a power plant cause the formation of acid rain.

Chemistry is the science that deals with the materials of the universe and the changes these materials go through. Chemistry is at the heart of our efforts to create new materials to make our lives better—for example, to produce new sources of energy. Chemists work on a lot of different things. Some examine the fundamental particles of matter. Others are looking for molecules in space. Still others are looking for ways to control the diseases that threaten our food supply or us.

But whatever the work, all chemists need certain skills. When my former students come back to visit me, they all say the same thing. They say that what's essential in their success is an understanding of the fundamentals, the ability to solve problems, and the ability to communicate.

Some people think education is just storing information in the brain. A lot of students just want to memorize lists of facts and then sort of spit it all out on tests. Of course, storing facts in the brain is important. The language of chemistry is unfamiliar at first, and you do have to memorize a lot of terms and definitions. You have to learn the vocabulary before you can communicate. Memorizing facts is important, but it's just the beginning of education. Don't stop there. Don't be afraid to do some thinking of your own, and don't be afraid to trust yourself to figure things out. Analytical thinking is the center of education.

Chemistry courses have a reputation for being difficult. This isn't surprising, since chemical systems are, well, complicated. Don't expect to understand everything right away. Just remember that even experienced chemists don't understand everything at first. It's not a disaster to make a mistake, but it could be, if you don't learn from your mistake.

To solve a typical chemistry problem, you have to go through the given information and decide what information is really important. If you can't do one of the homework problems, don't just look up the answer in the back of the book. That's not how you learn. You'll learn more if you go back and review the relevant material, and then try the problem again. Don't be afraid to struggle with it. If you do struggle with the problems, then find a classmate to work with, and struggle together. Actually, this is kind of a good way to learn about how scientists work together, trying one thing and then another until they come up with a solution.

It takes time to learn chemistry. You might not understand everything at first, and you might not be able to do the problems the first time you try. You might feel frustrated when you make a mistake. Just keep working—and learning from your mistakes—and you'll make steady progress.

29. What is the main purpose of the talk?
30. According to the professor, why is chemistry sometimes called the central science?
31. Listen again to part of the talk. Then answer the question. "But whatever the work, all chemists need certain skills. When my former students come back to visit me, they all say the same thing. They say that what's essential in their success is an understanding of the fundamentals, the ability to solve problems, and the ability to communicate." Why does the professor mention her former students?
32. What does the professor imply about memorizing information?
33. Listen again to part of the talk. Then answer the question. "You'll learn more if you go back and review the relevant material, and then try the problem again. Don't be afraid to struggle with it. If you do struggle with the problems, then find a classmate to work with, and struggle together. Actually, this is kind of a good way to learn about how scientists work together, trying one thing and then another until they come up with a solution." Why does the professor say this: "Actually, this is kind of a good way to learn about how scientists work together, trying one thing and then another until they come up with a solution."
34. What does the professor imply about making mistakes?

Disk 5, Track 8

SPEAKING SECTION DIRECTIONS (*p. 237*)

The Speaking section measures your ability to speak in English about a variety of topics. There are six questions in this section.

Questions 1 and 2 are independent tasks in which you will speak about familiar topics. Your responses will be scored on your ability to speak clearly and coherently about the topics.

Questions 3 and 4 are integrated speaking tasks. You will read a passage, listen to a conversation or lecture, and then speak in response to a question about what you have read and heard. You will need to combine relevant information from the two sources to answer the question completely. Your responses will be scored on your ability to speak clearly and coherently and on your ability to accurately convey information about what you read and heard.

Questions 5 and 6 are integrated speaking tasks. You will listen to part of a conversation or lecture, and then speak in response to a question about what you have heard. Your responses will be scored on your ability to speak clearly and coherently and on your ability to accurately convey information about what you heard.

You will hear each conversation and lecture only one time. You may take notes while you listen. You may use your notes to help you answer the questions.

Disk 5, Track 9

Describe an object, plant, or animal that represents your native country and explain its significance. Include details and examples to support your explanation.

Disk 5, Track 10

Some universities are very large and have several thousand students. Others are small and have only a few thousand students. Which size of university do you think is better for students, and why? Include details and examples in your explanation.

Disk 5, Track 11

Now listen to two students as they discuss the science seminar.

M: I'm going to enroll in the science seminar.
W: Why? You're not a science major.
M: You don't have to be a science major, but you can earn credits that count toward the science requirement.
W: I didn't know that.
M: I need science credits, and the seminar looks like a good way to get them. I used to like science when I was a kid, and I read a lot of books about nature. Then later I lost interest because most science classes are boring. I didn't like the one science class I took here, but it seems like this seminar will be different, and probably more interesting. I like the idea of studying with advanced students.
W: That doesn't bother you? I mean, they're students, not teachers.

M: That doesn't bother me at all. I see it as a good opportunity. Maybe advanced students will make science more exciting and real. Maybe I'll start to like science again. The only thing I don't like is the part about writing reports.
W: Oh, but you'll have all those advanced students to help you.
M: Yeah!

The man expresses his opinion about the science seminar. State his opinion and explain the reasons he gives for holding that opinion.

Disk 5, Track 12

Now listen to part of a talk on this topic given by a dance instructor.

By imagery, I mean visualization, using your mind's eye. For example, if you visualize your shoulders as you practice a turn, what happens if you imagine your shoulders to be very heavy, or light as air? If you focus on a part of your body—let's say, your neck—while you perform a dance step, and then perform exactly the same sequence by focusing on your back, or your feet, what happens? The change in focus will change how you perform the step.

There are certain basic images that will help you develop an awareness that will fill your whole body. I want you to identify with each image as much as possible. For example, the image of a leaf—don't just think about all the different things a leaf can do. Identify with the leaf, find out what a leaf would do from the point of view of a leaf. Become a leaf swept up by the wind. Let the wind play with you. Let the image control your expression.

Water is a powerful image. Imagine yourself slicing through water. Whatever body surface leads the movement is the bow of a ship cutting through the water. Or think of your feet and hands splashing through water. Or imagine you're completely under water. Move underwater like a fish. Using different images of water will give you a wider range of techniques for expressing yourself. The images will increase your sense of mental clarity. Some of my students have even reported having fewer muscle aches after using the water imagery.

The instructor describes the use of imagery in dance. Explain how specific imagery can affect a dancer's experience and performance.

Disk 5, Track 13

Now listen to a conversation between two students.

W: I don't know about you, but I'm going crazy this semester!
M: Why? What's going on?
W: I'm just so busy! Some of my classes are really difficult. I'm stressed out because I have a big test and a paper due next week. I'm worried about my grades, especially geology—I'm afraid I might fail that course. Ugh! I just wish I had more time to study!
M: Wow. I know what you mean. There aren't enough hours in the day.
W: The Student Service Club keeps me busy too. We have meetings every week. I'm the club president, which means I have a lot to do, much more than I can deal with right now.
M: Well, your coursework is more important than being president of the club. Couldn't you just quit the club? I mean, if you're concerned about failing a course…
W: Quit the club? That would disappoint a lot of people. I can't just walk out—I'm the president. But … I don't have the time to do everything I'm supposed to. I mean, I've really been neglecting my duties.
M: Then isn't there someone else who can help you with your duties? I mean, you'd better ask for help, get other people to chip in and do more of the work. You're the president, but you're not the only one in the club, right? Ask other people to cover for you, at least until you get your grades up again.

The students discuss two possible solutions to the woman's problem. Describe the problem. Then state which of the two solutions you prefer and explain why.

Disk 5, Track 14

Now listen to part of a lecture in a history class.

The trend in the early twentieth century was to systemize the home, to make it a rational, well–organized system. Americans were redesigning their living spaces according to function. The kitchen was divided into separate areas for food preparation, cleanup, and storage. A new creation, the living room, replaced the parlor and library of earlier periods. The living room dominated the main floor and filled several distinct functions. It held bookcases and a fireplace, and families gathered here for everyday activities and entertaining guests. The dining room had built–in cabinets for storing the fine china. A hallway joined the kitchen, living room, and dining room, organizing the flow of traffic. The second floor contained bedrooms and a bath, with built–in closets and shelves.

Another sign of the home systemizing movement was the establishment of domestic science and home economics courses at technical colleges. College kitchens, dining rooms, and laundries served as laboratories where students studied and experimented in housekeeping science. Domestic science became an established field of study, composed of separate disciplines, with annual conferences for professionals.

The philosophy of home economics was that the home required systemization as much as the factory did. The home, especially the kitchen, became a factory where American women served as production experts. Their goals were increased efficiency and the reduction of boring labor. New technology helped women reduce housekeeping to a science. Electric machinery, especially the washing machine and the vacuum cleaner, enhanced human performance in the home. By the 1920s, the electric washing machine and vacuum cleaner had become standard equipment in middle class homes.

Using points and details from the lecture, explain the movement toward systemizing the home in the period described by the professor.

Disk 5, Track 15

WRITING SECTION DIRECTIONS (*p. 243*)

The Writing section measures your ability to use writing to communicate in an academic environment. There are two writing questions.

Question 1 is an integrated writing task. You will read a passage, listen to a lecture, and then answer a question based on what you have read and heard. You have 20 minutes to plan and write your response.

Question 2 is an independent writing task. You will answer a question based on your own knowledge and experience. You have 30 minutes to plan and write your response.

Disk 5, Track 16

Now listen to part of a lecture on this topic in a psychology class.

Today, most psychologists think intelligence tests are limited in what they can measure and what they can be used for. Intelligence tests can't be used to predict success in life. Even some of the people who first developed the tests started to see this. For example, as early as 1947, Lewis Terman and his colleagues realized that IQ alone couldn't always predict a person's achievement in life. Terman designed a long–term study of children who scored in the highest range—the top one percent—of the Stanford–Binet Test. This means the children all had an IQ of 140 or higher. The purpose of the study was to see whether a high IQ would predict genius and great achievement in adulthood. The researchers found that this high–IQ group of people did become more academically and professionally successful than their peers of average intelligence. However, none of them achieved true genius. On the contrary, some of the subjects didn't fulfill their potential or make much of themselves. What these results point out is that intelligence tests alone can't predict greatness or achievement in life.

A major problem with intelligence tests is that there's a lot of disagreement on just how to define intelligence. Many psychologists now think that most intelligence tests are really just testing a child's ability to do well in school—what we might call "school–house intelligence." The concept of IQ is useful in identifying school–house intelligence, but IQ can't explain the source of original ideas and beautiful creations.

In the past thirty years, psychologists have been coming up with new definitions and theories of intelligence. One of the most prominent theories is that a person's motivation and creativity are more important than a high IQ in predicting achievement. Creativity is the ability to think about something in new ways and come up with unique solutions to problems. Psychologists believe that most intelligent people are motivated people. They have high energy and drive and are interested in many things. They know how to use their skills to find creative solutions to real–life problems.

Summarize the points made in the lecture you just heard, explaining how they cast doubt on points made in the reading.

TEST 6

Disk 6, Track 1

LISTENING SECTION DIRECTIONS (*p. 260*)

The Listening section measures your ability to understand conversations and lectures in English. You will hear each conversation and lecture only one time. After each conversation or lecture, you will hear some questions about it. Answer the questions based on what the speakers state or imply.

You may take notes while you listen. You may use your notes to help you answer the questions.

In some questions, you will see this icon: . This means that you will hear, but not see, part of the question.

Some questions have special directions, which appear in a gray box. Most questions are worth one point. If a question is worth more than one point, the directions will indicate how many points you can receive.

You will now begin the first part of the Listening section.

Disk 6, Track 2

Questions 1 through 5. Listen to a conversation in a university library.

W: Excuse me. Could you please tell me if there are any study rooms here in the library?

M: Yes, um, most of the rooms have already been reserved, but I think we have a few left.

W: Do you mean I have to reserve it ahead of time?

M: Oh yes, and the sooner the better. The rooms on the third floor are already completely booked for the quarter.

W: Oh. Um … how does it work then—I mean how can I—do I just sign up here for the times I want?

M: Yeah. Usually people want an hour or two at a time. You're limited to ten hours a week—that's if it's available. Like I said, we're fairly booked up. You really need to come in early in the quarter, or before the quarter starts would be even better.

W: Wow! I didn't realize space was so tight.

M: Yeah, it's true. Enrollment is up 12 percent over last year, and it really makes a difference. So, um, what would you like to do?

W: Well, actually it's for me and two of my classmates. We're working on a presentation together, and we need a quiet space to meet and talk.

M: What time of day do you want—morning, afternoon, or evening? There are more rooms open in the evening.

W: One of my classmates is a commuter—she carpools from Spring Valley and has to leave campus at six o'clock. So evenings wouldn't work. Actually, um, I think afternoons are best for all of us. Is there anything available … like, after three o'clock?

M: Let me check. That's always a busy time.

W: Oh …

M: Wait a minute. I just thought of something. Does it matter if it's in the Communications Building? They have some rooms over there.

W: Well, sort of. We, um, we were hoping to be here in the library.

M: The Communications Building is the one just behind us. You can even get there from the ground floor of this building.

W: Oh, really? I didn't know that. Well then, maybe we could try that. Did you say they had rooms available?

M: Yes. They have rooms … it looks like from one to five every day of the week.

W: Great! Can we reserve one of those, um, from three to five o'clock … on Tuesday, Wednesday and Thursday? Starting tomorrow?

M: Sure, I can do that. I just need to see your student I.D.

W: No problem.

1. What is the purpose of the conversation?
2. Listen again to part of the conversation. Then answer the question.
"Yes, um, most of the rooms have already been reserved, but I think we have a few left."
"Do you mean I have to reserve it ahead of time?"
"Oh yes, and the sooner the better. The rooms on the third floor are already completely booked for the quarter."
Why does the man say this:
"Oh yes, and the sooner the better."
3. According to the man, why are so few study rooms available?
4. Why does the woman need a study room?
5. Why does the man say this:
"The Communications Building is the one just behind us. You can even get there from the ground floor of this building."

Disk 6, Track 3

Questions 6 through 11. Listen to part of a talk in a meteorology class.

W: I'm glad to see everyone made it to school safely this morning. I wish I could say the same for myself, but I had a rather close call when I was getting on the expressway. I was on the on–ramp, and my car suddenly skidded and turned completely around, so I ended up with my car facing backward. Luckily, there was no one right behind me. I was able to turn my car around and slowly drive on. You see, what had happened was, I ran into a patch of black ice. And the nature of black ice is that you just don't see it coming because it's practically invisible. Generally, the formation of ice requires two conditions: the presence of water and temperatures below freezing. However, black ice can form on the highway when the air temperature is slightly above freezing but the ground temperature is below freezing. That's how it was at seven o'clock this morning when I was driving to campus. The air temperature was 34 degrees Fahrenheit; however, the overnight low had been in the low twenties, so the ground temperature was below freezing. The black ice formed when evaporation on the wet surface of the pavement—it was mist, actually, water vapor—when the mist was exposed to above–freezing air temperatures. The evaporation lowered the surface temperature to below freezing, and this then froze the very thin layer of mist on the surface of the pavement.

M: Excuse me, Dr. West. I'm not sure I heard you correctly. Are you saying it's possible for ice to form, even when it's not freezing outside?

W: Yes, and black ice is a good example of this. The air temperature can be above freezing, but the temperature of a wet surface like pavement can be lower. The same thing happens when wet laundry is left hanging outside and it freezes solid at an air temperature of 35 degrees. Water evaporates from the wet clothes, which are colder than the air, and the vapor rising from the laundry freezes. So your clothes are then covered with a thin film of ice. One of the reasons black ice takes us so much by surprise is that we don't expect to find ice when the thermometer says it's above freezing—the air temperature, that is. But air temperature can be deceiving, and we have to be careful, especially on mornings like today.
We usually think of ice formation as the freezing of liquid water, but ice can also form by the process of sublimation. Sublimation is when water changes state from a gas directly to a solid—or from a solid to a gas—without first becoming a liquid. Ice formed in this way—by sublimation—forms directly from water vapor, or mist, which is a gas.

M: So, what you're saying is, black ice is formed by sublimation?

W: Yes. Black ice is formed by sublimation—directly from water vapor on the surface of the road. Black ice is a form of frost. Some other forms of frost are ground frost and the frost you see on windows on cold winter nights. It can look like delicate feathery patterns of crystals on your windowpane, or it can be fernlike crystals several centimeters long on the twigs and branches of trees. Water vapor forms as frost on the surface of an object if the temperature of the surface falls below both the freezing point and the point at which water vapor condenses to a liquid. In the case of window frost, the temperature of the window glass has to be below freezing. The window is chilled because it's losing heat to the colder air outside. By the way, the beautiful patterns of window frost are due to its slightly curved crystals, because of organic impurities on the glass—dust and dirt—that interfere with crystal growth.

6. What is the talk mainly about?
7. Why does the professor talk about her drive to school this morning?
8. The professor briefly explains how black ice forms. Indicate whether each sentence below is part of the process.
9. Listen again to part of the discussion. Then answer the question.
"Excuse me, Dr. West. I'm not sure I heard you correctly. Are you saying it's possible for ice to form, even when it's not freezing outside?"
"Yes, and black ice is a good example of this. The air temperature can be above freezing, but the temperature of a wet surface like pavement can be lower. The same thing happens when wet laundry is left hanging outside and it freezes solid at an air temperature of 35 degrees."
Why does the professor say this:
"The same thing happens when wet laundry is left hanging outside and it freezes solid at an air temperature of 35 degrees."
10. Which of the following sentences illustrates sublimation?

11. What factors cause frost to form in beautiful patterns on window glass?

Disk 6, Track 4

Questions 12 through 17. Listen to part of a lecture in a psychology class.

Every culture has some set of rituals associated with death. These rituals serve an important function, and are a way for societies to control the grief caused by death. Death rituals give the bereaved family and friends specific roles to play. The roles differ from one culture to another; however, in every culture the roles sort of give shape to the days and weeks following the death of a loved one. Death rituals prescribe what the family should wear, who should be called, what behavior should be shown, and so on.

Depending on the family's religion, they may need to gather friends and family for a wake, arrange to sit shiva, or arrange a memorial service. There are different cultural expectations for how the bereaved persons should act. They may be expected to show little emotion, or they may be expected to scream and tear their hair.

The rituals also have roles for friends, who often act as support givers. For example, friends may bring food to the home of the bereaved family, or drop in to offer help, or send flowers or sympathy cards. Whatever the social rules are, everyone has a role to fill.

Death rituals can strengthen family connections. Funerals bring family members together, just like weddings do. Rituals can also give meaning to the death by emphasizing the life of the person who died. A funeral or memorial service usually includes some sort of biography or personal memories of the person. Most people feel that it's extremely important to review the deceased person's life. Reviewing the life and accomplishments of the loved one—sharing stories and memories with family and friends—this makes the death easier for the survivors to accept.

But when the funeral or memorial service is over, what happens then? How do the survivors cope with the loss of a spouse, a parent, a child, a friend, or a lover? Once past the rituals, the grieving person moves through a complex grief process.

One theory states that there are four stages of grieving: numbness, yearning, despair, and reorganization. In the first stage, the bereaved person feels numbness—a lack of feeling. Or he or she feels shock, disbelief, confusion, a sense of unreality—normally lasting a few days after the death. In the second stage—yearning—the bereaved person yearns for and may actively search for the lost one. This is a time of anxiety and guilt, fear and anger. The third stage is when the person feels great despair, exhaustion, depression, or withdrawal. He or she may feel disorganized and unable to do normal activities. Finally, in the fourth stage—reorganization—the person takes control of his or her life again. This is a time of healing. The person feels energy again, takes up normal activities again, and finds new relationships.

The four stages of grieving—numbness, yearning, despair, and reorganization—are not the same for everyone, nor does everyone necessarily go through every stage. The stage theory is just one of many models that psychologists use to help people manage the loss of a loved one.

12. What topics does the professor discuss?
13. According to the professor, what important function do death rituals serve?
14. Why does the professor say this:
"Depending on the family's religion, they may need to gather friends and family for a wake, arrange to sit shiva, or arrange a memorial service. There are different cultural expectations for how the bereaved persons should act. They may be expected to show little emotion, or they may be expected to scream and tear their hair."
15. According to the professor, why do death rituals include roles for friends?
16. What does the professor imply about funerals and memorial services?
17. The professor talks about the process of grieving the loss of a loved one. Indicate whether each sentence below describes a stage in the process.

Disk 6, Track 5

Questions 18 through 22. Listen to part of a conversation between two students. They are both taking a music theory class.

W: Well, I don't know about you, but I'm totally confused about today's lecture, especially the part about music and noise.

M: It's not so bad, really. I think I got 'most everything in my notes.

W: So then … what is the difference between music and noise? Professor King said noise is a random sound, but then he said the sounds of a cymbal and a drumbeat were examples of noise. I'd say they're examples of music—since they're sounds made by musical instruments! What do you think he meant?

M: OK. Do you remember how he said that noise is a random sound?

W: Uh–huh.

M: Well, it's a random sound that has irregular sound waves.

W: But how's a sound that's noise different from a sound that's music?

M: Well, if you could take a picture of a musical note, you'd see that it has regular waves that repeat themselves. That's because music is a sound that's in a pattern we can hear or discern. Noise is different from music because it doesn't have a pattern.

W: But why is the sound of a drumbeat noise instead of music? Isn't a drumbeat a note? And then … so … doesn't it have a regular pattern of waves?

M: Maybe you're taking what he said too literally. Maybe he meant a drumbeat is as close as a musical instrument can get to making just noise.

W: Maybe a single drumbeat is like a word spoken out of context. A single word with no context is just noise!

M: Now there's a thought!

W: The other thing I didn't get was what he said about antinoise. First noise, then antinoise? What do you think he meant?

M: Think of it as the opposite of noise. It's like—wait, let me back up. Sound has waves, right?

W: Right.

M: Well, we can describe these waves as "in phase" or "out of phase" with each other. "Out of phase" means reversed.

W: Uh–huh.

M: If you add two out–of–phase waves together at the same frequency, the result is antinoise—silence.
W: Antinoise is silence?
M: Right! And there's a computer program that proves this. A microphone picks up the sound and sends it back to the computer, and then the computer reads the waves and makes sort of a mirror image, or a reverse copy of the wave. Then you can play it back against the original sound, and when the two waves meet, they sort of overlap each other … exactly at the high and low peaks. This eliminates the sound, creating zero sound—antinoise.
W: How do you know all this? Professor King didn't talk about this.
M: It's all in our book. Didn't you do the reading?
W: No, I didn't have time. I guess I'd better do that now.
M: Yeah, you should. But it's better to do the reading before the lectures 'cause then you'll have a better idea of what he's talking about.
W: Yeah, you're right. I guess I have some catching up to do.

18. What are the students mainly discussing?
19. According to the conversation, what is noise?
20. Listen again to part of the conversation. Then answer the question.
"Well, if you could take a picture of a musical note, you'd see that it has regular waves that repeat themselves. That's because music is a sound that's in a pattern we can hear or discern. Noise is different from music because it doesn't have a pattern."
"But why is the sound of a drumbeat noise instead of music? Isn't a drumbeat a note? And then … so … doesn't it have a regular pattern of waves?"
Select the sentence that best expresses how the woman probably feels.
21. How does the man help the woman understand the meaning of "antinoise"?
22. What will the woman probably do?

Disk 6, Track 6

Questions 23 through 28. Listen to part of a discussion in an art class. The class is talking about murals.

W1: I know you're all excited about our class project. But before we get started on the design of our mural, let's review some of the technical requirements for murals. What factors do we need to keep in mind? Yes, Lydia?
W2: The mural has to be permanent. It has to last as long as the building. And it has to be sturdy enough to put up with conditions like the walls being washed.
W1: Good points. Yes, David?
M: It should have a flat finish so you can look at it from all angles without seeing any glare. And the design should be laid out so you can see it while you're walking rather than standing still.
W1: Yes, those are all things we need to bear in mind. We want people to take in our mural—all of it—from a moving position, since they'll be observing it as they walk through the lobby to the elevators. And let's not forget that our mural is more than just a large–scale work of art done on a wall instead of a canvas. The term "mural" implies a distinct feeling or nature, a quality that's appropriate to the architecture and the function of the room. A mural is an integral part of the building. If it's painted in an existing building, like ours will be, it should be planned to fit into the architectural design, instead of giving the impression that it's a surface decoration. Now, what are some of the technical requirements for our wall?
M: Obviously, the wall shouldn't move. It shouldn't shrink or settle because that could cause cracks in the paint or plaster.
W1: Yes, it's vital that our wall be perfectly immovable. And for murals like ours—remember, our mural will be on the interior side of an exterior wall—another important requirement is that dampness should be excluded. Dampness can result from water seeping through porous materials or through joints, corners, or flaws in the building construction. When water leaks through a wall, it may dissolve the salts that are in the building materials. When the moisture dries, the salts are deposited in the form of white, moldy–looking film on the surface of the plaster. This greatly weakens the plaster, which can crumble or crack, and, of course, it's disastrous to the mural.
W2: Can moisture make the paint peel off?
W1: Yes, it can. When moisture penetrates a wall coated with paint, it causes the plaster to expand and the paint to peel off—either in small flakes or in big pieces. And we don't want that happening to our work, so we'll need to take measures to prevent it. Our goal will be to reduce expansion of the plaster and to lessen the condensation of moisture on the surface. So our first rule is to exclude dampness as much as possible.
M: Don't we also need to guard the plaster from extreme changes in temperature?
W1: Yes. So, how are we going to do this?
M: We could create an air space between the outer wall of the building and the plaster. We could do this by building a screen or, um, like a false wall just inside the exterior wall, and then we put the plaster for the mural on this false wall. There'd be like an inch of air space between the false wall and the exterior wall. The air space would have an insulating effect. What I mean is, it would slow down any temperature changes on the plaster.
W1: Yes, you're correct about the insulating effect of an air space. Now, to do this—it's called "furring" the wall—what we do is, we attach thin strips of wood to the exterior wall, and then we build another wall on top of this. The furring of the wall creates an air space of one–half to one inch between the outer and inner walls. That's enough to protect our mural from moisture and temperature changes, as well as the mechanical strains and stresses of the wall itself.

23. Why is the class discussing the technical requirements of murals?
24. According to the discussion, what factors should be considered in planning a mural?
25. What does the instructor mean when she says this:
"The term 'mural' implies a distinct feeling or nature, a quality that's appropriate to the architecture and the function of the room. A mural is an integral part of the building."
26. The instructor briefly explains how moisture damages a mural. Indicate whether each sentence below is a part of the process.

27. What is the purpose of having an air space between the outer wall and the plaster?
28. Why does the instructor say this:
"Now, to do this—it's called "furring" the wall—what we do is, we attach thin strips of wood to the exterior wall, and then we build another wall on top of this."

Disk 6, Track 7

Questions 29 through 34. Listen to part of a lecture in a botany class. The professor is talking about seeds.

Our study of the life cycle of a plant usually starts with the germination of a seed. The seed contains the hereditary information the plant needs to grow. It also contains enough food to nourish itself during germination.

Heredity—the genes inherited from the parent plant—decides several things about the life of the plant. Heredity determines what the plant will look like, how it will grow, and what kind of seeds it will bear. Inside the seed is all the genetic information the plant needs to grow to maturity. An individual plant's survival depends partly on its hereditary characteristics. But a plant depends on more than just heredity. It needs the outside world to supply its daily needs: sunlight, carbon dioxide, nutrients, and water.

Some seeds germinate as soon as they're in a suitable environment. Other seeds remain dormant and won't germinate until a specific environmental cue causes them to "wake up" and come out of dormancy. Seeds of desert plants germinate only after a heavy rainfall. If they germinated after a slight rain, the soil might soon be too dry to support the seedlings. Seed dormancy increases the chances that germination will take place at a time and place that are best for the seedling.

Germination begins when water penetrates the seed's outer coating and reaches inside to the live embryo. Water is a basic requirement, and no seed will germinate unless it absorbs water. This is because the embryo inside the seed is dehydrated, and cells need water for active metabolism. Water is the substance in which most of the chemical reactions of the plant take place.

For a seed to sprout and grow, it needs a great deal of energy. Seeds get this energy by converting the energy of their stored fuel molecules, and this requires oxygen. Germination also requires a certain combination of temperature and light, which, in North America, is triggered by the start of spring. Some seeds respond early in the season, others much later. Each plant species has an ideal temperature at which the largest number of seeds will germinate.

When the embryo takes in water, it often swells to several times its original size. It gets this first burst of energy by tapping its own food stores. Eventually, the seed expands enough to rupture its coating and burst through the seed case.

The first organ to emerge from the germinating seed is the embryonic root. The root pushes outward into the soil and anchors the seedling. Now the seedling begins to gather up water and nutrients through thousands of tiny hair–like roots. After a certain period, the seedling sprouts upward. The tip of the shoot has to break through the soil surface. Light is the environmental cue that tells the seedling when it's broken ground. Only when the seedling senses light will it straighten up and begin to grow taller. As it straightens up and grows, it unfolds its solar collectors, its first leaves. Once the seedling has its main leaves, it doesn't need its embryonic food stores anymore because now it draws most of its growth energy directly from the sun.

The germination of a seed is a critical stage in the plant's life cycle. The tough seed becomes a fragile seedling, and only a small fraction of seedlings survive long enough to become parent plants. Because the chances of a seedling's survival are so low, plants make up for this by producing enormous numbers of seeds.

29. What aspect of seeds does the professor mainly discuss?
30. What role does heredity play in the life of a plant?
31. Listen again to part of the talk. Then answer the question.
"Some seeds germinate as soon as they're in a suitable environment. Other seeds remain dormant and won't germinate until a specific environmental cue causes them to "wake up" and come out of dormancy. Seeds of desert plants germinate only after a heavy rainfall. If they germinated after a slight rain, the soil might soon be too dry to support the seedlings."
Why does the professor say this:
"Seeds of desert plants germinate only after a heavy rainfall."
32. What environmental factors are required for a seed to germinate?
33. How does a seed obtain the energy it needs for germination?
34. The professor explains how a seed becomes a young plant. Summarize the process by putting the events in order.

Disk 6, Track 8

Questions 35 through 39. Listen to a conversation between a student and a professor.

M: Hi, Professor Barker.
W: Hello, Sam. How are you?
M: OK, I guess. Um, did you get a chance to read the draft of my term paper yet?
W: Yes, I've looked at it. It's is about organizational redesign, right?
M: Yeah, that's right.
W: Let's see … here it is. All right. OK. You … uh … you start out by defining organizational redesign.
M: Right. It's changing the goals, responsibilities, and relationships within an organization.
W: Right. That's a good way to begin. All right, then … let's see … you talk about how inappropriate organizational designs can create severe problems. The introduction is OK. Everything you say is clearly relevant. The body of your paper is where you start to stray a bit. Basically, you're trying to do too much. You introduce a lot of threads … and then don't develop all your ideas.
M: Oh. Could you, uh, maybe be more specific?
W: Sure. Uh, for example, here you summarize Peterson's four steps for managers to follow in organizational redesign. And then you list Roswell's plan, and then you also describe Jordan and his six–point plan. What you end up with is lots of ideas, some of them overlapping and duplicating each other. What you need to do is narrow this down to the three or four … or five steps that you believe are necessary for redesigning an organization. Do you see what I mean?
M: Uh, I think so.
W: It would also be good to illustrate your points with examples from a real organization, for example, a case study of a company that's successfully

redesigned itself. You need to make this real.

M: Mm–hmm. I see what you mean. I need to show how redesign actually works in the real world. I actually thought of an example, but I don't know if it's right for this paper. It's a nursery business—you know, they grow plants and flowering shrubs and things. It's a business I actually know. My uncle is the superintendent there.

W: And the nursery has a performance problem that needs attention?

M: Sort of. My uncle was telling me about some changes he'd like to see in the business. I don't know … it's just an idea … maybe it would work here.

W: It sounds like it might be an idea worth pursuing.

M: OK.

W: So, to recap what we said. You need to focus on three or four essential steps for organizational redesign and then illustrate them with a real–world example of what a real business could do, or has done, along these lines. Does that make sense?

M: Yes, it does. This helps me a lot. Thanks for your time.

W: You're welcome.

35. Why does the student go to see the professor?
36. According to the student, what is organizational redesign?
37. Listen again to part of the conversation. Then answer the question.
"Sure. Uh, for example, here you summarize Peterson's four steps for managers to follow in organizational redesign. And then you list Roswell's plan, and then you also describe Jordan and his six–point plan. What you end up with is lots of ideas, some of them overlapping and duplicating each other. What you need to do is narrow this down to the three or four … or five steps that you believe are necessary for redesigning an organization."
What does the professor imply about the student's paper?
38. What suggestions does the professor make for the student's paper?
39. Why does the student mention the nursery business where his uncle works?

Disk 6, Track 9

Questions 40 through 45. Listen to part of a lecture in a geography class. The professor is talking about the Northwest Passage.

It was the promise of wealth that first drew European powers to look for a westward route to Asia. It was wealth rather than the idea of a New World that drove Columbus and other Europeans to search for a western route to China and Japan. However, they soon realized that the North American continent was a barrier to progress. So, they began to search for a way around the northern edge of the continent, a Northwest Passage that would link the Atlantic to the Pacific. For the next 500 years, they nudged their ships through the Arctic waters, looking for the Northwest Passage.

In the sixteenth century, the Spanish, Portuguese, French, and English all sent expeditions to the northern shores of North America. They were all driven back by the ice. The Englishman Martin Frobisher spent several years exploring what is now Canada and searching for wealth in the Arctic. He made three voyages in search of the Northwest Passage, and he did reach the mouth of the passage, but stopped when he found what he thought was gold. This "gold" turned out to be iron ore. In 1607, Henry Hudson began his exploration of the Canadian Arctic. He discovered the bay that later became Hudson Bay, but the voyage ended in tragedy when the crew rebelled. The Northwest Passage wasn't crossed until almost 300 years later, when a Norwegian explorer completed the trip in three years.

The Northwest Passage is actually a number of possible routes through a deadly maze of sea ice, narrow straits, and oddly shaped islands. Today, icebreakers can follow the passage with ease, but to attempt it without this technology still requires a great deal of courage. Depending on ice conditions, one route might be open while another is blocked. The passage changes from year to year, and even from week to week.

In the summer of 2000, a Canadian Mountie took a large patrol boat into the heart of the Northwest Passage. He expected to encounter ice, but to his surprise, there were no bergs, no growlers, and no pancake ice. In fact, he found no ice at all. For the past few summers now, vast stretches of the Northwest Passage have been free of ice. The departure of the ice is the result of natural, long–term atmospheric patterns that have warmed the Arctic in recent decades and also of the heating of the planet by greenhouse gases.

In the Arctic, temperatures have risen 3 to 4 degrees. That small difference has changed the landscape for thousands of miles. The ice has disappeared at a rate of about 3 percent each decade since the 1970s, and ice sheets that used to be ten feet thick are now less than six feet from top to bottom. Climate experts now predict that, in 50 years or less, the passage will be free of ice throughout the summer. Canadian officials say it's only a matter of time before all kinds of ships—everything from supertankers to sailboats—will start crossing these once impassable waters.

There are potential consequences to shipping in the passage. Ships could disrupt the polar bears and bowhead whales that live there. There could be an increase in the smuggling of polar bear hides and walrus tusks. An increase in the number of tourists could mean an increase in the amount of trash they leave behind. The biggest concern, however, is the threat of an oil spill from a supertanker. An oil spill would damage this pristine region and be extremely difficult to clean up.

40. How does the professor organize the information that she presents?
41. According to the professor, why did European powers start looking for the Northwest Passage?
42. Why does the professor talk about Martin Frobisher and Henry Hudson?
43. Listen again to part of the lecture. Then answer the question.
"The Northwest Passage is actually a number of possible routes through a deadly maze of sea ice, narrow straits, and oddly shaped islands. Today, icebreakers can follow the passage with ease, but to attempt it without this technology still requires a great deal of courage. Depending on ice conditions, one route might be open while another is blocked. The passage changes from year to year, and even from week to week."
What can be inferred about the Northwest Passage?
44. Why does the professor say this:
"The ice has disappeared at a rate of about 3 percent each decade since the 1970s, and ice sheets that used to be ten feet thick are now less than six feet from top to bottom."
45. According to the professor, what are the possible consequences of an increase in shipping in the Northwest Passage?

Disk 6, Track 10

Questions 46 through 51. A historian has been invited to speak to an architecture class. The class has been studying the history of domestic architecture. Listen to part of the talk.

In New England today, around eighty houses that were built in the seventeenth century are still standing. Many of these houses—and the documents relating to them—have been thoroughly studied, and some of the houses have been carefully restored to their original condition. These early houses of New England are the greatest single source of knowledge about domestic architecture of the seventeenth century, particularly about details of plan and construction.

All seventeenth–century houses were not alike. There was some variety in their floor plans, with each house being shaped by the circumstances of the family and the characteristics of the site. Nevertheless, it's possible to identify the three most common plan types, which were the one–room plan, the two–room plan, and the added lean–to plan. We can even figure out the order in which they probably evolved.

The one–room plan was the simplest and the earliest design. It was used in the early cottages at Plymouth and Salem, dating back to the 1620s, and it remained common in smaller and poorer dwellings throughout the century. In the one–room plan, the front door opened into a small entry room, which was then called the "porch." In the porch, there was a steep staircase built up against a massive chimney. The large main room was a combination living–dining–cooking room called the "hall." In this room, there was a huge fireplace set into the chimney mass. The staircase in the porch led to one large sleeping room upstairs.

The second house design was the two–room plan, which was simply the one–room plan with a parlor added at the other side of the chimney and porch. The result was a house with two fireplaces, one in the hall and one in the parlor, that were set back–to–back in the central chimney structure. In several earlier examples of this design, the parlor was actually built onto an older one–room house, enlarging the smaller house. But more common in later examples, both rooms were built at the same time when families could afford it. Upstairs, there were two sleeping rooms, called the "hall chamber" and the "parlor chamber," after the room below each.

The third design, the added lean- to plan, was the result of an addition at the back of the house, making this the largest of the three plans. The lean–to addition had roof rafters leaning against the second–story wall of the main house. The added space was used as a kitchen. The cooking was done in a fireplace added to the back of the central chimney structure. There were two more rooms built on either side of the kitchen. On the cold side of the kitchen, there was a pantry for food storage, and on the warm side, facing the sun on the south, there was a bedroom. Above the kitchen, under the lean- to roof, there was attic space for storage or more sleeping rooms, which you reached by a staircase leading up from the kitchen.

These three house plans form a logical evolutionary sequence. The one–room plan was the earliest design. Then the two–room plan was most common up until around 1650. By the year 1700, the lean–to plan was dominant. However, it's important to note that the one–room plan—although it came earliest—continued to be built throughout the seventeenth century. So, it's best not to try to determine the age of a colonial house strictly by its plan type, which is not a perfect indicator of the house's age.

46. According to the speaker, why are seventeenth–century houses significant to architectural historians?
47. Where was the main staircase located in a seventeenth–century house?
48. Why does the speaker say this:
"In several earlier examples of this design, the parlor was actually built onto an older one–room house, enlarging the smaller house. But more common in later examples, both rooms were built at the same time when families could afford it."
49. Identify the kitchen in the floor diagram of the added lean- to plan.
50. Based on the information in the talk, indicate whether each sentence below characterizes the one–room plan, the two–room plan or the added lean–to plan.
51. Why does the speaker say this:
"However, it's important to note that the one–room plan—although it came earliest—continued to be built throughout the seventeenth century. So, it's best not to try to determine the age of a colonial house strictly by its plan type, which is not a perfect indicator of the house's age."

Disk 6, Track 11

SPEAKING SECTION DIRECTIONS (*p. 280*)

The Speaking section measures your ability to speak in English about a variety of topics. There are six questions in this section.

Questions 1 and 2 are independent tasks in which you will speak about familiar topics. Your responses will be scored on your ability to speak clearly and coherently about the topics.

Questions 3 and 4 are integrated speaking tasks. You will read a passage, listen to a conversation or lecture, and then speak in response to a question about what you have read and heard. You will need to combine relevant information from the two sources to answer the question completely. Your responses will be scored on your ability to speak clearly and coherently and on your ability to accurately convey information about what you read and heard.

Questions 5 and 6 are integrated speaking tasks. You will listen to part of a conversation or lecture, and then speak in response to a question about what you have heard. Your responses will be scored on your ability to speak clearly and coherently and on your ability to accurately convey information about what you heard.

You will hear each conversation and lecture only one time. You may take notes while you listen. You may use your notes to help you answer the questions.

Disk 6, Track 12

What is your idea of the perfect vacation? Describe it and explain why it would be the ideal vacation for you. Include details and examples in your explanation.

Disk 6, Track 13

Some students attend lecture classes in which only the teacher speaks. Other students have discussion classes in which everyone speaks. Which type of class do you think is better for students, and why? Include details and examples in your explanation.

Disk 6, Track 14

Now listen to two students as they discuss the notice.

M: Oh no, the college is announcing a 10 percent fee increase. Why do they think they can do that? Our fees are already too high!
W: This is the first time they've raised the fees since I've been a student here. It's only 10 percent—that's not too bad. And you don't live on campus, so the rent increase doesn't even affect you.
M: You live on campus, don't you? Do you want to pay a higher rent next year?
W: Well, I think a new gymnasium is a fantastic idea, so it's all for a good cause. And the new gym is something that will benefit everyone, even you, because students who live off campus can use the facilities. The old gym is really small, and it's always crowded when I'm there. The showers are kind of old and kind of disgusting, and there are no saunas.
M: Yeah, I know what you mean.
W: I was actually thinking of joining a health club in town, but the membership fee is really expensive there. So, for me, it's great news having a nice new gym on campus. The fee increase will come to less than I'd have to pay to join a club in town. So, who am I to complain?

The woman expresses her opinion about the fee increase. State her opinion and explain the reasons she gives for holding that opinion.

Disk 6, Track 15

Now listen to part of a lecture on this topic in a history class.

Speaking of the uniformity of goods, let me say something about the clothing industry—men's clothing in particular. The greatest factor in the formation of the industry was the Civil War, which created a huge demand for uniforms for the soldiers. The need to outfit an army prompted the government to specify measurements to the manufacturers, and this led to the standardization of sizes. Then, after the war, there was a great demand for civilian clothing for all the returning soldiers. Manufacturers increased production—with the help of standardized sizes and new and better sewing machines—and were able to produce clothing to fit most of the male population. By the year 1900, most American men were completely clothed in mass–produced, ready–to–wear garments. They could buy suits, shirts, hats, and shoes with well–established brand names.

Women, on the other hand, continued to sew much of their own clothing long after men were buying all theirs ready–made. But this eventually changed, and by 1910 even women could buy every article of clothing ready–made, either from mail–order catalogs or from department stores. One of the earliest mass–produced garments for women was the shirtwaist, which today we call the blouse. The shirtwaist or blouse was very popular because it was suitable for every occasion. The shirtwaist was produced in standard sizes in a variety of fabrics, making it convenient and affordable for women of all social classes.

The professor discusses the history of the clothing industry. Explain how this industry contributed to the uniformity of goods.

Disk 6, Track 16

Now listen to a conversation between a student and a professor.

W: Hi, Professor Benson.
M: Hello, Katherine. How are you?
W: Fine. I'm looking forward to graduation at the end of the year.
M: That's great! So, what will you do after that?
W: I haven't decided yet. It's either look for a job or go to graduate school. My parents want me to apply to graduate school. I want to go to graduate school someday, but right now I'm tired of studying. I'd like to take a break from school, get a job and earn some money, but my parents and my friends think I should go to grad school now rather than later. I just don't know!
M: Hmmm. It's always a tough choice. If you want to go to graduate school, you'll need to apply early. That means you should start now. You should research graduate programs and find out about their admissions requirements, like whether you have to take an entrance examination.
W: Yeah, I know. You have to turn in your application early, like months in advance.
M: Sometimes it really is better to do something else for a while. It's not a bad idea to take a year off and work. If you decide to look for a job, you need to write a résumé, you know, summary of all your qualifications and work experience. The Career Center here gives workshops on résumé writing, and I would recommend doing that.

Describe the woman's problem and the two suggestions the professor makes about how to deal with it. What do you think the woman should do, and why?

Disk 6, Track 17

Now listen to part of a talk in a psychology class. The professor is discussing sleep and problem solving.

Our brains are always working, even when we sleep. Studies on sleep show that while we're sleeping, our brains continue to work on problems that confused us during the day. We also know that sometimes the right answer to a problem might come to us more easily after eight hours of sleep.

Creativity and problem solving seem to be directly linked to getting enough sleep. In one study, two groups of college students were given a simple mathematics test. One group had just had eight hours of sleep, and the other group had seven hours of sleep or less. The students who had eight hours of sleep were three times more likely than the sleep–deprived students to figure out the correct answer in the math test.

The results of that study support research on the brain that indicates what happens to our memories during sleep. We think that our memories are reorganized and restructured during sleep before they are put into long–term storage in our brains. Our memories start in one area in the brain and are later pushed out to another part of the brain, where they can join up with other memories. This process, this transfer and restructuring of memories happens while we sleep. It seems to help our creativity in a way that makes it easier to solve a mathematical problem. The changes that improve our problem–solving ability happen during "slow wave" or deep sleep, which usually occurs in the first four hours of the sleep cycle.

This study has important results for students and workers who are overtired. It should remind us that sleep is often the best medicine. Too many people don't get enough sleep, and this contributes to accidents, health problems and—for students—lower test scores.

Using points and details from the talk, explain how sleep and problem solving are connected.

Disk 6, Track 18

WRITING SECTION DIRECTIONS (*p. 286*)

The Writing section measures your ability to use writing to communicate in an academic environment. There are two writing questions.

Question 1 is an integrated writing task. You will read a passage, listen to a lecture, and then answer a question based on what you have read and heard. You have 20 minutes to plan and write your response.

Question 2 is an independent writing task. You will answer a question based on your own knowledge and experience. You have 30 minutes to plan and write your response.

Disk 6, Track 19

Now listen to part of a lecture on this topic in a biology class.

We've learned a lot about the effects of early influences on the physical characteristics of both animals and humans. One thing we know is that almost any kind of stimulation—either positive or negative—any stimulation of the young shortly after birth will affect their rate of growth as well as their resistance to stress. Daily handling—such as touching, hugging, and massaging—can promote healthy growth and boost the immune system. Exposure to cold, on the other hand, can have negative effects and leave the young animal more vulnerable to disease.

Another thing we know is that malnutrition early in life can have lifelong consequences. If the food intake of the young is limited, this will decrease the rate of growth and the body size of the adult. Animal studies show some interesting results. For example, deer born during a period of food scarcity, or in a crowded population, will remain relatively small in size, even if their adult diet is adequate or the density of the population decreases. The effect of poor nutrition on deer can also extend to the following generation, as the offspring of small deer will also be small.

The eating habits acquired early in life tend to last throughout life, affecting eating behaviors. For example, rats that are used to eating a low–protein diet will continue eating it by choice, even if a more protein–rich diet is available to them later.

With humans, low protein intake or almost any other form of nutritional deficiency during early childhood will result in a slowing of growth, smaller body size, physical deformation, or tendency to get sick—characteristics that can last a lifetime.

Moreover, poor nutrition affects the mental development of children. Children who don't eat well don't learn well in school. They may have difficulty paying attention and may not be able to remember information. As a result, these children may develop negative attitudes toward school. Several behavioral problems in school children have been linked to poor eating habits.

Summarize the points made in the lecture you just heard, explaining how they support points made in the reading.

HOW TO SCORE SPEAKING

<table>
<tr><th colspan="2">INDEPENDENT SPEAKING
Score Levels for Speaking Questions 1 and 2</th></tr>
<tr><td>4</td><td>A response at this level
• effectively addresses the task and is generally well developed and coherent; and
• demonstrates effective use of grammar and vocabulary, but may contain minor language errors that do not interfere with meaning; and
• demonstrates clear, fluid speech with high overall intelligibility, but may contain minor problems with pronunciation or intonation.</td></tr>
<tr><td>3</td><td>A response at this level
• conveys ideas and information relevant to the task, but overall development is somewhat limited, and connections among ideas are sometimes unclear; and
• demonstrates somewhat effective use of grammar and vocabulary, but may contain language errors that do not seriously interfere with meaning; and
• demonstrates generally clear, somewhat fluid speech, but may contain minor problems with pronunciation, intonation, or pacing and may occasionally require some listener effort.</td></tr>
<tr><td>2</td><td>A response at this level
• is related to the task, although the development of ideas is limited, and connections among ideas are unclear; or
• demonstrates a limited range and control of grammar and vocabulary; or
• demonstrates some clear speech, but contains problems with pronunciation, intonation, or pacing and may require significant listener effort.</td></tr>
<tr><td>1</td><td>A response at this level
• fails to provide much relevant content because ideas that are expressed are inaccurate, limited, or vague; or
• demonstrates a limited control of grammar and vocabulary that severely limits expression of ideas and connections among ideas; or
• demonstrates fragmented speech with frequent pauses and consistent problems with pronunciation and intonation that obscure meaning and require great listener effort.</td></tr>
<tr><td>0</td><td>A response at this level
• is not related to the topic; or
• is absent.</td></tr>
</table>

INTEGRATED SPEAKING Score Levels for Speaking Questions 3–6	
4	**A response at this level** effectively addresses the task by conveying relevant information and appropriate details from the listening and reading texts; and demonstrates a coherent expression of ideas, with appropriate grammar and vocabulary, but may contain some minor language errors; and demonstrates clear, fluid speech with high overall intelligibility, but may contain minor problems with pronunciation or intonation.
3	**A response at this level** conveys information relevant to the task, but shows some incompleteness, inaccuracy, or lack of detail; and demonstrates a fairly coherent expression of ideas, but may contain some errors in grammar or vocabulary that do not seriously interfere with meaning; and demonstrates generally clear, somewhat fluid speech, but may contain minor problems with pronunciation, intonation, or pacing and may occasionally require some listener effort.
2	**A response at this level** conveys some relevant information but omits key ideas, shows limited development, or shows misunderstanding of key ideas; or demonstrates a limited expression of ideas, inaccurate or unclear connections among ideas, or limited or inaccurate grammar and vocabulary; or demonstrates some clear speech, but contains problems with pronunciation, intonation, or pacing and may require significant listener effort.
1	**A response at this level** fails to provide much relevant content because ideas that are expressed are inaccurate, limited, or vague; or demonstrates a limited control of grammar and vocabulary that severely limits expression of ideas and connections among ideas; or demonstrates fragmented speech with frequent pauses and consistent problems with pronunciation and intonation that obscure meaning and require great listener effort.
0	**A response at this level** is not related to the topic; or is absent.

HOW TO SCORE WRITING

INTEGRATED WRITING Score Levels for Writing Question 1	
5	**A response at this level** - effectively addresses the task by conveying relevant information from the lecture; and - accurately relates key information from the lecture to information in the reading; and - is well organized and coherent; and - contains appropriate grammar and vocabulary, with only occasional minor language errors.
4	**A response at this level** - generally conveys relevant information from the lecture, but may have minor omissions; and - is generally good in relating information from the lecture to information in the reading, but may have minor inaccuracies or vagueness of some content or connections among ideas; and - is generally well organized; and - contains appropriate grammar and vocabulary, but may have noticeable minor language errors or occasional lack of clarity.
3	**A response at this level** - contains some relevant information from the lecture, but may omit one key point; or - conveys some connections between the lecture and the reading, but some content or connections among ideas may be incomplete, inaccurate, or vague; or - contains errors in grammar or usage that result in vagueness of some content or connections among ideas.
2	**A response at this level** - contains some relevant information from the lecture, but may have significant omissions or inaccuracies of key points; or - omits or largely misrepresents the connections between the lecture and the reading; or - contains language errors that obscure meaning of key ideas or connections among ideas.
1	**A response at this level** - contains little or no relevant content from the lecture; or - fails to connect points from the lecture and reading; or - contains language errors that greatly obscure meaning, or - is too brief to allow evaluation of writing proficiency.
0	**A response at this level** - only copies sentences from the reading; or - is not related to the given topic; or - is written in a language other than English; or - is blank.

INDEPENDENT WRITING Score Levels for Writing Question 2	
5	**An essay at this level** ➳ effectively addresses the task by clearly stating an opinion; and ➳ is well organized and well developed with appropriate examples, reasons, or details; and ➳ displays unity and coherence; and ➳ uses language effectively, with sentence variety and appropriate word choice and only occasional minor language errors.
4	**An essay at this level** ➳ addresses the task well, but some points may not be fully supported; and ➳ is generally well organized and sufficiently developed with examples, reasons, or details; and ➳ displays unity and coherence, but may have some redundancy or lack of clarity; and ➳ contains sentence variety and a range of vocabulary, but may have noticeable minor language errors that do not interfere with meaning.
3	**An essay at this level** ➳ addresses the task with some development and some appropriate supporting details; or ➳ displays unity and coherence, but connections among ideas may be occasionally unclear; or ➳ is inconsistent in using language effectively, with errors in grammar and vocabulary that occasionally obscure meaning; or ➳ contains an accurate but limited range of sentence structures and vocabulary.
2	**An essay at this level** ➳ displays limited development in response to the task, with inappropriate or insufficient supporting details; or ➳ contains inadequate organization or connections among ideas; or ➳ contains an accumulation of errors in grammar and usage.
1	**An essay at this level** ➳ is flawed by serious disorganization or underdevelopment; or ➳ contains little or no detail, or details that are irrelevant to the task; or ➳ contains serious and frequent errors in grammar and usage.
0	**An essay at this level** ➳ is not related to the given topic; or ➳ is written in a language other than English; or ➳ is blank.

PROGRESS CHARTS

Record your scores for Test 1 through Test 6 on the following pages. Use the charts to check your achievement and set goals for future practice.

- Use Progress Charts 1 through 4 to record your section scores.
- Use the Score Conversion Tables to find your approximate TOEFL score for each section.
- Use Progress Chart 5 to record your approximate TOEFL scores.

Example of Progress Chart 2 – Listening

% Correct	Test 1	Test 2	Test 3	Test 4	Test 5	Test 6
100%	34	52	34	52	34	52
		51		51		51
	33	50	33	50	33	50
	32	49	32	49	32	49
		48		48		48
90%	31	47	31	47	31	47
	30	46	30	46	30	46
		45		45		45
	29	44	29	44	29	44
	28	43	28	43	28	43
80%		42		42		42
	27	41	27	41	27	41
	26	40	26	40	26	40
		39		39		39
	25	38	25	38	25	38
	24	37	24	37	24	37
70%		36		36		36
	23	35	23	35	23	35
	22	34	22	34	22	34

Example of Progress Chart 5 – TOEFL® Scores

Section	Test 1	Test 2	Test 3	Test 4	Test 5	Test 6
Reading	18	20	19	21	20	20
Listening	17	16	18	18	18	18
Speaking	18	19	19	20	20	20
Writing	20	20	22	20	22	22
Total Test	73	75	78	79	80	80

PROGRESS CHART 1 – READING

Circle the points earned for each test. Draw a line to connect the circles.

% Correct	Test 1	Test 2	Test 3	Test 4	Test 5	Test 6
100%	70	44	70	44	70	44
	69		69		69	
	68	43	68	43	68	43
	67	42	67	42	67	42
	66		66		66	
	65	41	65	41	65	41
	64	40	64	40	64	40
90%	63		63		63	
	62	39	62	39	62	39
	61		61		61	
	60	38	60	38	60	38
	59	37	59	37	59	37
	58		58		58	
	57	36	57	36	57	36
80%	56		56		56	
	55	35	55	35	55	35
	54	34	54	34	54	34
	53		53		53	
	52	33	52	33	52	33
	51	32	51	32	51	32
	50		50		50	
70%	49	31	49	31	49	31
	48		48		48	
	47	30	47	30	47	30
	46	29	46	29	46	29
	45		45		45	
	44	28	44	28	44	28
	43		43		43	
60%	42	27	42	27	42	27
	41	26	41	26	41	26
	40		40		40	
	39	25	39	25	39	25
	38	24	38	24	38	24
	37		37		37	
	36	23	36	23	36	23
50%	35		35		35	
	34	22	34	22	34	22
	33	21	33	21	33	21
	32		32		32	
	31	20	31	20	31	20
	30		30		30	
	29	19	29	19	29	19
40%	28	18	28	18	28	18

PROGRESS CHART 2 – LISTENING

Circle the points earned for each test. Draw a line to connect the circles.

% Correct	Test 1	Test 2	Test 3	Test 4	Test 5	Test 6
100%	34	52	34	52	34	52
		51		51		51
	33	50	33	50	33	50
	32	49	32	49	32	49
		48		48		48
90%	31	47	31	47	31	47
	30	46	30	46	30	46
		45		45		45
	29	44	29	44	29	44
	28	43	28	43	28	43
80%		42		42		42
	27	41	27	41	27	41
	26	40	26	40	26	40
		39		39		39
	25	38	25	38	25	38
70%	24	37	24	37	24	37
		36		36		36
	23	35	23	35	23	35
		34		34		34
	22	33	22	33	22	33
	21	32	21	32	21	32
60%		31		31		31
	20	30	20	30	20	30
	19	29	19	29	19	29
		28		28		28
	18	27	18	27	18	27
50%	17	26	17	26	17	26
		25		25		25
	16	24	16	24	16	24
	15	23	15	23	15	23
		22		22		22
40%	14	21	14	21	14	21

CHARTS

PROGRESS CHART 3 – SPEAKING

Circle the points earned for each test. Draw a line to connect the circles.

% Correct	Test 1	Test 2	Test 3	Test 4	Test 5	Test 6
100%	24	24	24	24	24	24
	23	23	23	23	23	23
90%	22	22	22	22	22	22
	21	21	21	21	21	21
	20	20	20	20	20	20
80%	19	19	19	19	19	19
	18	18	18	18	18	18
70%	17	17	17	17	17	17
	16	16	16	16	16	16
	15	15	15	15	15	15
60%	14	14	14	14	14	14
	13	13	13	13	13	13
50%	12	12	12	12	12	12
	11	11	11	11	11	11
40%	10	10	10	10	10	10
	9	9	9	9	9	9
	8	8	8	8	8	8
30%	7	7	7	7	7	7
	6	6	6	6	6	6
20%	5	5	5	5	5	5

PROGRESS CHART 4 – WRITING

Circle the points earned for each test. Draw a line to connect the circles.

% Correct	Test 1	Test 2	Test 3	Test 4	Test 5	Test 6
100%	10	10	10	10	10	10
90%	9	9	9	9	9	9
80%	8	8	8	8	8	8
70%	7	7	7	7	7	7
60%	6	6	6	6	6	6
50%	5	5	5	5	5	5
40%	4	4	4	4	4	4
30%	3	3	3	3	3	3
20%	2	2	2	2	2	2

PROGRESS CHART 5 – TOEFL® SCORES

Use the Score Conversion Tables on pages 384–385 to find your approximate TOEFL score for each section. Write each section score below in the correct box for each test. To calculate the total test score, add the section scores for that test.

Section	Test 1	Test 2	Test 3	Test 4	Test 5	Test 6
Reading						
Listening						
Speaking						
Writing						
Total Test						

Example

Test 1	Points Earned	TOEFL Section Score
Reading	44	18
Listening	24	17
Speaking	14	18
Writing	6	20

Total Test: 18 + 17 + 18 + 20 = 73

CHARTS

SCORE CONVERSION TABLES

To find your approximate TOEFL scores for Test 1 through Test 6, use the tables below. Make sure to look in the correct column: Tests 1, 3, 5, or Tests 2, 4, 6. Go down the column and find the number of points you earned. You will find your TOEFL section score on the same line, in the right column.

READING

Points Earned		TOEFL® Section Score
Tests 1, 3, 5	**Tests 2, 4, 6**	
69–70	43–44	30
67–68	42	29
65–66	41	28
62–64	39–40	27
60–61	38	26
58–59	37	25
56–57	35–36	24
54–55	34	23
53	33	22
50–52	32	21
46–49	29–31	20
45	28	19
42–44	27	18
40–41	25–26	17
38–39	24	16
37	23	15
35–36	22	14
32–34	20–21	13
30–31	19	12
29	–	11
27–28	17–18	10
26	16	9
25	–	8
24	15	7
21–23	13–14	6
20	12	5
19	–	4
16–18	10–11	3
14–15	9	2
13	8	1

LISTENING

Points Earned		TOEFL® Section Score
Tests 1, 3, 5	**Tests 2, 4, 6**	
34	52	30
33	51	29
–	50	28
32	49	27
31	47–48	26
30	46	25
–	45	24
29	44	23
28	43	22
27	42	21
–	41	20
26	40	19
25	38–39	18
24	37	17
–	36	16
23	35	15
21–22	33–34	14
–	32	13
20	31	12
19	29–30	11
18	28	10
17	26–27	9
15–16	23–25	8
14	21–22	7
13	20	6
12	18–19	5
10–11	15–17	4
9	14	3
7–8	11–13	2
5–6	8–10	1

SPEAKING

Points Earned Tests 1–6	TOEFL® Section Score
24	30
23	29
22	28
21	27
20	26
19	24
18	23
17	22
16	20
15	19
14	18
13	17
12	15
11	14
10	13
9	11
8	10
7	9
6	8
5	6
4	5
3	4
2	3
1	1

WRITING

Points Earned Tests 1–6	TOEFL® Section Score
10	30
9	28
8	25
7	22
6	20
5	17
4	14
3	11
2	8
1	5

NOTES